Wealth and Power

Is political equality viable when a capitalist economy unequally distributes private property? This book examines the nexus between wealth and politics and asks how institutions and citizens should respond to it.

Theories of democracy and property have often ignored the ways in which the rich attempt to convert their wealth into political power, implicitly assuming that politics is isolated from economic forces. This book brings the moral and political links between wealth and power into clear focus. The chapters are divided into three thematic sections. Part I analyses wealth and politics from the perspective of various political traditions, such as liberalism, republicanism, anarchism, and Marxism. Part II addresses the economic sphere, and looks at the political influence of corporations, philanthropists, and commons-based organisations. Finally, Part III turns to the political sphere and looks at the role of political parties and constitutions, and phenomena such as corruption and lobbying.

Wealth and Power: Philosophical Perspectives will be of interest to scholars and advanced students working in political philosophy, political science, economics, and law.

Michael Bennett is a Lecturer at Nottingham Trent University, working in the interdisciplinary tradition of politics, philosophy, and economics. His research focuses on the relationship between capitalism and democracy and has been published by journals including the *Journal of Politics*, the *Journal of Business Ethics*, and the *Critical Review of International Social and Political Philosophy*. He completed his PhD at the University of York in 2017 on epistemic democracy and capitalism. He has since been a postdoctoral researcher at Utrecht University and a visiting researcher at the University of Arizona and the London School of Economics.

Huub Brouwer is Assistant Professor of Ethics and Political Philosophy at Tilburg University, where he works at the intersection of economics and political philosophy, in particular on the morality of markets and the design of just systems of taxation. Huub was the editor of the *Erasmus Journal of Philosophy and Economics* in 2018-2019. He obtained his PhD, in which he argues for a comeback of desert in debates about distributive justice, from Tilburg University in January 2020, and has published in journals such as the *Journal of Moral Philosophy*, *Philosophical Studies*, and *Proceedings of the Aristotelian Society*. He was a postdoctoral researcher at Utrecht University as part of the research project 'Private Property & Political Power in Liberal-Democratic Societies.' Huub has been a visiting researcher at Gothenburg University, Oxford University, Pompeu Fabra University, and Yale University.

Rutger Claassen is Professor of Political Philosophy and Economic Ethics at the Department of Philosophy and Religious Studies of Utrecht University. He was the principal investigator of the research project 'Private Property & Political Power in Liberal-Democratic Societies' (2017–2022) and currently is the principal investigator of the project 'The Business Corporation as a Political Actor', funded by the European Research Council (ERC-Consolidator Grant, 2020-2025). He has published extensively on the moral value of economic institutions such as markets, property, and corporations in journals such as *Economics & Philosophy*, *Law & Philosophy*, and *Politics, Philosophy & Economics*. Rutger is the author of *Capabilities in a Just Society: A Theory of Navigational Agency* (CUP, 2018). He is the founding Program Director of the BA-program in Philosophy, Politics & Economics (PPE) at Utrecht University.

Routledge Studies in Contemporary Philosophy

Epistemic Injustice and the Philosophy of Recognition
Edited by Paul Giladi and Nicola McMillan

Evolutionary Debunking Arguments
Ethics, Philosophy of Religion, Philosophy of Mathematics, Metaphysics, and Epistemology
Edited by Diego E. Machuca

The Theory and Practice of Recognition
Edited by Onni Hirvonen and Heikki J. Koskinen

The Philosophy of Exemplarity
Singularity, Particularity, and Self-Reference
Jakub Mácha

Wealth and Power
Philosophical Perspectives
Michael Bennett, Huub Brouwer, and Rutger Claassen

Philosophical Perspectives on Memory and Imagination
Anja Berninger and Íngrid Vendrell Ferran

Unconscious Networks
Philosophy, Psychoanalysis, and Artificial Intelligence
Luca M. Possati

Updating the Interpretive Turn
New Arguments in Hermeneutics
Edited by Michiel Meijer

For more information about this series, please visit: https://www.routledge.com/Routledge-Studies-in-Contemporary-Philosophy/book-series/SE0720

Wealth and Power
Philosophical Perspectives

Edited by Michael Bennett,
Huub Brouwer, and Rutger Claassen

NEW YORK AND LONDON

First published 2023
by Routledge
605 Third Avenue, New York, NY 10158

and by Routledge
4 Park Square, Milton Park, Abingdon, Oxon, OX14 4RN

Routledge is an imprint of the Taylor & Francis Group, an informa business

© 2023 Michael Bennett, Huub Brouwer, and Rutger Claassen

The right of Michael Bennett, Huub Brouwer, Rutger Claassen to be identified as the authors of the editorial material, and of the authors for their individual chapters, has been asserted in accordance with sections 77 and 78 of the Copyright, Designs and Patents Act 1988.

The Open Access version of this book, available at www.taylorfrancis.com, has been made available under a Creative Commons Attribution-Non Commercial-No Derivatives 4.0 license.

Trademark notice: Product or corporate names may be trademarks or registered trademarks, and are used only for identification and explanation without intent to infringe.

ISBN: 978-1-032-00319-1 (hbk)
ISBN: 978-1-032-00320-7 (pbk)
ISBN: 978-1-003-17363-2 (ebk)

DOI: 10.4324/9781003173632

Typeset in Sabon
by KnowledgeWorks Global Ltd.

Contents

Author Biographies viii
Preface xi

1 Introduction: The Wealth-Power Nexus 1
MICHAEL BENNETT, HUUB BROUWER, AND RUTGER CLAASSEN

PART I
Theoretical Orientations 23

2 What about Ethos? Republican Institutions, Oligarchic Democracy, and Norms of Political Equality 25
JESSICA KIMPELL JOHNSON

3 Two Liberal Egalitarian Perspectives on Wealth and Power 47
RICHARD ARNESON

4 Public Choice and Political Equality 67
BRIAN KOGELMANN

5 Private Wealth and Political Domination: A Marxian Approach 85
IGOR SHOIKHEDBROD

6 Anarchism and Redistribution 104
JESSICA FLANIGAN

PART II
Power in the Economic Sphere — 125

7 Why Does Worker Participation Matter? Three Considerations in Favour of Worker Participation in Corporate Governance — 127
THOMAS CHRISTIANO

8 Taming the Corporate Leviathan: How to Properly Politicise Corporate Purpose? — 145
MICHAEL BENNETT AND RUTGER CLAASSEN

9 The Power of Big Tech Corporations as Modern Bigness and a Vocabulary for Shaping Competition Law as Counter-Power — 166
ANNA GERBRANDY AND PAULINE PHOA

10 Economic Power and Democratic Forbearance: The Case of Corporate Social Responsibility and Philanthropy — 186
EMMA SAUNDERS-HASTINGS

11 Independence in the Commons: How Group Ownership Realises Basic Non-Domination — 206
YARA AL SALMAN

PART III
Wealth and Democratic Institutions — 227

12 Hidden in Plain Sight: How Lobby Organisations Undermine Democracy — 229
PHIL PARVIN

13 No Money, No Party: The Role of Political Parties in Electoral Campaigns — 252
CHIARA DESTRI

14 Constitutions against Oligarchy — 274
ELLIOT BULMER AND STUART WHITE

15 Automation, Desert, and the Case for Capital Grants   295
   HUUB BROUWER

16 The Power of Private Creditors and the Need for
   Reform of the International Financial Architecture   314
   ANAHÍ WIEDENBRÜG AND PATRICIO LÓPEZ TURCONI

Index   337

Author Biographies

Yara Al Salman is an Assistant Professor of political philosophy working at Utrecht University. Yara obtained her PhD degree in political philosophy from Utrecht University in 2022 for her dissertation on group ownership.

Richard Arneson is a Distinguished Professor at the University of California, San Diego, where he holds the Valtz Family Chair in Philosophy. His short book *Prioritarianism* has recently been published (Cambridge). He writes mainly on social justice issues, consequentialism in moral theory, and applied ethics.

William Elliot Bulmer is a Senior Programme Officer (Constitution Building) at the International Institute for Democracy and Electoral Assistance, where he supports democratic constitutional change processes around the world. As well as specialising in comparative constitutionalism and the politics of constitutional change, he has a long-standing interest in the economic dimensions of political power.

Thomas Christiano is a Professor and Head of Philosophy at the University of Arizona. He wrote *The Constitution of Equality* (Oxford, 2008) and *The Rule of the Many* (Routledge, 1996). He is Co-Editor in Chief of *Politics Philosophy and Economics*. His research is on democracy, distributive justice, international law, and economic justice.

Chiara Destri is a Postdoctoral Researcher at Goethe University Frankfurt. She has been Marie Curie Fellow at Sciences Po, Postdoctoral Fellow at Justitia Amplificata, and Max Weber Fellow at the European University Institute. Her work has been published in *Critical Review of International Social and Political Philosophy*, *Res Publica*, and *Ethical Theory and Moral Practice*.

Jessica Flanigan is the Richard L. Morrill Chair of Ethics and Democratic Values and an associate professor of Leadership Studies and Philosophy, Politics, Economics, and Law (PPEL) at the University of Richmond.

Author Biographies

Anna Gerbrandy is a Professor of Competition Law at Utrecht University School of Law. She holds multiple positions of trust within the University and in societal organisations. Anna is a research director of the School of Law and Crown–appointed member of the Social and Economic Council of the Netherlands.

Jessica Kimpell Johnson (DPhil Oxford) is the Director of Research for the Karsh Institute of Democracy at the University of Virginia. She is also a lecturer in political theory and manager of the Nau Lab on the History & Principles of Democracy at the University of Virginia.

Brian Kogelmann is an Assistant Professor in the John Chambers College of Business and Economics at West Virginia University, College Park. He works at the intersection of philosophy, politics, and economics.

Patricio López Turconi is a lawyer with research interests in the fields of international law, international organisations, and human rights. He holds a law degree from Universidad Torcuato Di Tella and an LL.M. from Georgetown University Law Center. Patricio has worked extensively on state obligations under international law, serving as a consultant for the Ministry of Economy of the Argentine Republic and the O'Neill Institute at Georgetown Law.

Phil Parvin is a Reader in Politics and Head of International Relations, Politics, and History at Loughborough University, UK. He is the author of two books: *Karl Popper* (2013, Bloomsbury) and *Political Philosophy: A Complete Introduction* (2013, Hodder, with Clare Chambers). He has published numerous articles on a range of topics in contemporary political philosophy, including democratic participation, localism, deliberative democracy, migration, political ignorance, representation, and inequality. He is currently writing a monograph on the role of lobby groups in the theory and practice of democracy.

Pauline Phoa is an Assistant Professor of European Law at Utrecht University School of Law and a post-doctoral researcher at the ERC-funded 'Modern Bigness' project headed by Anna Gerbrandy.

Yara Al Salman is an Assistant Professor of political philosophy working at Utrecht University. Yara obtained her PhD degree in political philosophy from Utrecht University in 2022 for her dissertation on group ownership.

Emma Saunders-Hastings is an Assistant Professor of Political Science at the Ohio State University. She is the author of *Private Virtues, Public Vices: Philanthropy and Democratic Equality* (University of Chicago Press, 2022). Her research has also appeared in journals including the *American Political Science Review* and the *Journal of Politics*.

Igor Shoikhedbrod is an Assistant Professor with a joint appointment in Political Science and Law, Justice, and Society at Dalhousie University. He is also the author of *Revisiting Marx's Critique of Liberalism: Rethinking Justice, Legality and Rights* (2019) with Palgrave Macmillan.

Stuart White is a Fellow in Politics at Jesus College, Oxford, and lecturer in the Department of Politics and International Relations, Oxford University. He is the author of *The Civic Minimum* (2003) and *Equality* (2006), and co-editor, with Bruno Leipold and Karma Nabulsi, of *Radical Republicanism: Recovering the Tradition's Popular Heritage* (2020). He is currently interested in applying republican ideas to discussion of the UK's constitutional future and he is writing a book on republican political economy, *The Wealth of Freedom*.

Anahí Wiedenbrüg is a researcher working at the intersections of political theory and political economy. Her work focuses on drawing out the normative implications and socio-political impact of developments in the international financial architecture since the breakdown of the post-war system. Outside of academia, Wiedenbrüg has extensive experience in working in multilateral fora.

Preface

The chapters in this book have been commissioned in the context of the research project 'Private Property and Political Power in Liberal-Democratic Societies (2017–2022),' funded by the Dutch Research Council (NWO). The project investigated various manifestations of the nexus between private wealth and the political power it wields. Providing a political-philosophical lens to look at this issue, it inquired which normative frameworks help us to adequately evaluate such boundary-crossings. We would like to thank the Dutch Research Council for its financial support.

In this context, we invited leading experts to shed light on these issues from multiple perspectives. Drafts of these chapters were presented at a workshop in June 2021. COVID intervened so that we could not hold the event in person but had to convene online for three days. We thank all authors for their cooperation and for bearing the long, but still very lively, online sessions.

Over the last two years, Abeba Collee, Noa Harmsen, and Sam Langelaan provided invaluable editorial assistance for which we are profoundly grateful. We would also like to thank all the anonymous referees, who did wonderful work suggesting improvement of the chapters. Finally, we thank the editors of Routledge for their smooth and supportive collaboration in publishing this work.

Michael dedicates his contribution to his parents Kathy and Paul, and thanks his wife Mary for her continued support and encouragement. Huub dedicates his contribution to his grandparents Cor and Martha, and thanks his partner Pierre for his love, support, and sense of humour. Rutger thanks his wife Carine and his children, for providing a continuous source of joy, support, and welcome distraction at home.

Michael Bennett, Huub Brouwer, and Rutger Claassen
April 2022

1 Introduction

The Wealth-Power Nexus

Michael Bennett, Huub Brouwer, and Rutger Claassen

As candidate, one of Donald Trump's most striking claims was that his personal wealth made him more trustworthy than rivals who had to rely on rich corporate backers. It's hard to deny that accelerating inequality is a major driver of our turbulent politics today. This is starkest in the ways the rich attempt to convert their wealth into political power.

As an example, consider the world's largest company: Walmart (Fortune 500). Walmart is active in 26 countries and has 11,400 stores and 2.3 million employees (Walmart Annual Report 2021). In 2020, Walmart's CEO was paid a salary of $23 million, which is 1,078 times more than the median worker at Walmart (Institute for Policy Studies 2021). Walmart is active in US politics, spending between $6 and $8 million on lobbying annually during the past decade (Open Secrets 2022). The company has lobbied against the rise of the federal minimum wage in the United States and in favour of a federal programme that provides poor Americans with food stamps. The reason is that Walmart receives about $13 billion in revenue from food stamps spent at Walmart, to a significant degree by its own employees.[1] Walmart employs various strategies to avoid paying taxes, including accelerated depreciation of its assets and concentration of profits in a set of 22 shell companies in tax shelter Luxembourg (Americans for Tax Fairness 2015).

Walmart was founded in 1962 by Sam Walton. His heirs still own just under 50% of the shares of the company, making the Walton family the wealthiest family in the United States, with a net worth of $238 billion. Like many wealthy individuals in the United States, the Walton family has its own charitable foundation: the Walton Family Foundation. The Walton heirs, however, have only contributed $58.5 million to the foundation, which amounts to about 0.04% of their net worth (O'Connor 2014). The foundation has mainly been funded through tax-avoiding trusts established by the first generation.

But it's not fair to pick on Walmart only. We could have chosen any famous company, and there's a good chance we would discover they were paying massively unequal salaries, donating money to politicians,

DOI: 10.4324/9781003173632-1

using a business model that takes advantage of government regulations, and moving around the world to avoid taxes.

This kind of nexus between wealth and power forms the background against which the chapters of this volume are framed. At its heart lies the question of whether political equality is viable given the unequal private property holdings characteristic of a capitalist economy. This question is becoming increasingly obtrusive in an age of accelerating economic inequality. The volume approaches the relationship between private property and political power from two angles. First, wealth can influence politics, for example through campaign finance and lobbying. Second, power can arise in the supposedly voluntary private sphere, for example through the power of companies over their workers and the unaccountable power of philanthropists and corporate social responsibility (CSR). Our contributors also discuss mechanisms and institutions that have attracted less attention from political theorists and philosophers, such as sovereign debt, competition law, and common property regimes (CPRs). The volume moves from broad theoretical perspectives in Part One ('Theoretical Orientations') through to detailed analysis of economic and political policy areas an institutions in Parts Two ('Power in the Economic Sphere') and Three ('Wealth and Democratic Institutions'). Our ambition is to connect concrete and topical issues with fundamental debates in political theory and philosophy, engaging with and drawing on other disciplines such as political science, economics, and law in the process.

The remainder of this chapter situates our work in the context of the history of political thought and recent work in the social sciences and political philosophy. It then develops a basic conceptual framework to organise the breadth of work on the topic, followed by brief introductions to the chapters in each part of the volume.

1 Background and Contemporary Research

1.1 Historical Background

In the premodern world, it was commonplace that wealth and power would go together. This was equally clear to monarchs as it was to republicans. An interesting example of how the rules of property could be adapted for political purposes comes from the Byzantine empire in the tenth century (McGeer 2000). After a series of bad winters, the emperor passed new land laws, forbidding poor peasants from selling their land to wealthy nobles. The emperor described his laws as an attempt to protect the poor from being exploited by the nobles. However, it's likely that his true motive was to prevent land falling into the hands of aristocrats who might challenge his own power. The emperor was manifesting the common premodern assumption that wealth and political power would unavoidably combine one way or another. The city republics of ancient Greece and Rome and medieval Italy faced the same issue, and it was widely assumed that the dispersal of political power was only sustainable so long as economic resources were also dispersed along roughly similar lines. Sometimes, cities attempted to deliberately engineer this kind of economic equality through agrarian laws which redistributed land or restricted its transfer. However, most thinkers (including Aristotle and Machiavelli) were relatively pessimistic about the prospects for this kind of deliberate engineering. Instead, there was a tendency to think that cities lucky enough to have the socioeconomic preconditions for constitutional government could enjoy constitutional government, and cities which did not would be governed by other kinds of regimes.

European liberal modernity claimed to cut this ancient connection between wealth and power. The historian Rafe Blaufarb (2019) has described the French Revolution and its global influence as effecting a 'great demarcation' between property and power, private and public spheres. Modern democracies would far outstrip the ambitions of ancient republics in the scale and diversity of the populations they would seek to govern. The liberal ideal is one in which the public realm of the creation and administration of law would proceed in perfect independence from the inequalities of private life. Of course, this was accompanied by a great deal of worrying that the poor would fail to appreciate the merits of this ideal and would expropriate the rich, justifying, somewhat ironically, the restriction of political rights according to property holdings. As it happened, the later, twentieth-century erosion of property qualifications did not lead to widespread expropriation. However, the triumph of the great demarcation was almost from the beginning accompanied by a socialist critique. For Karl Marx, the separation of political and economic realms was a contradiction which a better society of the future would supersede by subordinating the economy fully to democracy.

After the Second World War, the potential contradiction between capitalism and democracy was attenuated by an era of high marginal tax rates on income and relative economic equality in the wealthy nations. The topic fell low on the agenda of political theorists and philosophers. However, after 40 years of renewed growth of inequality in many countries, the old problem is raising its head again.

1.2 Contemporary Social Science

Over the last decade, increasing economic inequality has been pushed to prominence in economics and in public debate by Thomas Piketty (2014) and his associates (Atkinson, Piketty, and Saez 2011; Atkinson 2015; Alstadsæter, Johannesen, and Zucman 2018). In particular, they popularised the concept of the U-shaped pattern in inequality in the twentieth century, with the income and wealth share of the richest falling in the first half of the century and then rising again since the 1970s. Since then, further studies have confirmed a picture in which inequality is currently on the rise in most countries in the world (Chancel et al. 2021).[2] Wealth inequality may be judged from a variety of perspectives (such as its intrinsic unfairness, or its detrimental economic effects on growth). Here, it forms the background for the political question whether democracy is subverted by economic inequality. Political scientists have long been interested in this question and come to various conclusions (Schattschneider 1960; Lindblom 1977; Dahl 2005; Schlozman, Verba, and Brady 2012). However, the topic is inherently difficult to study. Studies of campaign finance in the United States have found it notably difficult to establish a link between campaign donations and electoral success, or of legislators advancing donor's interests (Levitt 1994; Ansolabehere, de Figueiredo, and Snyder 2003). This runs contrary not only to folk wisdom in general but also to the folk wisdom of politicians themselves, who certainly act as though campaign donations were crucial to their success.

A recently prominent approach has attempted to cut the Gordian knot of figuring out the mechanisms by instead looking directly at overall outcomes and asking how far they reflect the preferences of the wealthy versus the rest. In a famous paper, Martin Gilens and Benjamin Page used a dataset of 1779 instances in which the public had been surveyed on policy questions appearing before the US Congress (Gilens and Page 2014; see also Bartels 2010; Gilens 2014). They found that the preferences of business interest groups and citizens at the 90th percentile of income had predictive power for what Congress would do. For example, when fewer than one in five members of the wealthy group supported a policy change, it occurred around 18% of the time. But when four in five supported a change, the change had a 45% chance of happening. By contrast, the preferences of citizens at the median level of income had no statistically significant impact on what Congress did. The vast majority of research of this kind focuses on the United States. However, some studies have purported to find similar effects in other countries, such as the Netherlands (Schakel 2021).

Other social scientists have tended to approach the topic through a less quantitative route, focusing on the transformation of the party system in European countries, particularly social democratic parties. Peter Mair (2013) wrote about the 'hollowing out' of mass parties, leading to a state of what Colin Crouch (2004; 2011) called 'post-democracy': politics without any clear ideological alternative to neoliberalism. Wolfgang Streeck (2017) has pursued a similar line, laying the blame on globalisation for pushing countries towards a race to the bottom in competition for investment capital and trade competitiveness.

1.3 Contemporary Political Philosophy

The relationship between wealth and power has not been a major topic in recent political philosophy, and it is part of the ambition for this volume to change that. While some of the particular issue areas covered in this volume have been addressed, work on these issues has largely proceeded in isolation from one another. Nonetheless, three particular debates are worth mentioning.

First, money in politics has played an important role in interpretations of John Rawls' (1999; 2001) idea of a property-owning democracy. For Rawls, the first principle of justice requires equal political liberties, and moreover that these rights be given their *fair value* – equal in substance and not merely in form. Given that this is lexically prior to considerations of distributive justice, it is potentially highly significant for the design of economic as well as political institutions. For Rawls, it is the fair value of political liberties, which requires us to move from a capitalist welfare state to the more robustly redistributive property-owning democracy or liberal socialism. These ideas are explored in detail in a volume edited by Martin O'Neill and Thad Williamson (2014). William Edmundson (2017) has argued that the corruption of political equality cannot be prevented so long as the means of production are privately owned, and that Rawls's theory of justice should therefore properly be understood as endorsing a form of liberal socialism. Others, such as Alan Thomas (2016) have defended the idea that the fair value of political liberties might be realised by property owning democracy. Richard Arneson weighs in on the debate in this volume.

The theoretical debate on property-owning democracy has fed through to more applied discussions about campaign finance. This topic (addressed here by Chiara Destri) is the subject of a relatively sizeable literature in political philosophy, albeit one that tends to be rather dominated by the context of US constitutional law (see among others Beitz 1990; J. Cohen 2001; Christiano 2012; Pevnick 2016; Bennett 2020).

The second major debate in political theory in which wealth and power has played an important role is the debate within neo-republicanism, addressed in this volume by Jessica Kimpell Johnson. The version of republicanism revived by Phillip Pettit (1999) focused on the principle of non-domination. John McCormick (2011) charged Pettit with advancing an aristocratic version of republicanism, and argued for a plebeian alternative drawing on Machiavelli. This has led to an interesting debate on republicanism's attitude to democracy and oligarchy and the extent to which capitalism's influence on democracy is a source of domination (White 2011; Gourevitch 2014; Vergara 2020). McCormick also put on the agenda the idea of class-specific political institutions inspired by the Roman Tribunate, which aristocrats were banned from participating in, an idea which has intrigued many thinkers concerned with problems of oligarchy, including Stuart White and Elliot Bulmer in this volume.

The third debate worth mentioning is a collection of discussions around the nature and power of corporations. Corporate power has been a locus of broader discontents with the world of growing inequality and the entanglement of wealth and power. Part of the discussion has been about what the corporation *is*, normatively speaking, with David Ciepley (2013) making an influential argument for viewing corporations as franchises of government rather than the result of the exercise of individual economic liberties. This discussion connects to a somewhat separate line of debate about democracy in the workplace, addressed here by Thomas Christiano (see, among others, McMahon 1994; Ferreras 2017; Singer 2019). Others have raised questions about the political implications of practices of CSR, addressed here by Emma Saunders-Hastings (Scherer and Palazzo 2007; Hussain and Moriarty 2014). Finally, concerns about corporate power have also manifested in a new movement within the world of competition and antitrust law to look at firms' political impacts beyond their impact on economic welfare, a topic which Gerbrandy and Phoa address here.

While some of the chapters in this volume contribute to these debates, others treat topics which have barely registered in political theory and philosophy, such as lobbying (Phil Parvin), CPRs (Yara Al Salman), public choice theory (Brian Kogelmann), and sovereign debt (Anahí Wiedenbrüg and Patricio López Turconi). Our ambition is to bring together these disparate strands in order to get a broader perspective on the general phenomenon of wealth's relationship to power. To do this, it is useful to have a minimal orienting framework.

2 Conceptual Framework

In this section, we set out a general conceptual framework for thinking about the relationship between wealth and power. The framework is intended to be a means through which the various contributions to the volume can be located in relation to one another. It has three elements: first, the idea of liberalism's public/private divide: a division between a power-wielding state from which wealth should be absent, and a market economy from which power should be absent; second, the two ways the division can be transgressed by the power of the wealthy: by the wealthy subverting the power of the state, and by directly exercising power within the economy; and third, the four different approaches to responding to the transgression, either aiming to reassert the public/private divide or to move beyond it.

2.1 Liberalism's Public/Private Divide

A core feature of liberalism is the division of social life into two distinct spheres, each with its own norms and characteristics (Walzer 1984; Ciepley 2013). Liberalism's public/private distinction is complex topic with important applications to various subjects, particularly religion, gender, and the family. Here, we focus only on public/private in political economy.

In this context, we can loosely think of the public sphere as consisting of the government, politicians and political parties, and the activists and media organisations, who make up the 'informal' public sphere. By contrast, the private sphere consists of workers, investors, and consumers transacting on the market and organised into firms. The underlying distinction, however, is not between types of organisations but between norms. In their private capacities, people are legitimately oriented towards their private interests. They are free to pursue their own projects in life, dispose of their property as they wish, and contract and co-operate with whomever they want. By contrast, in their public capacities, people should be oriented towards the public interest. Realising normative ideals of justice is the responsibility of the public sphere. A significant part of the public interest consists in the proper ordering and regulation of the private sphere.

Liberalism is defined (at least in part) by the sharp distinction it seeks to enforce between these spheres. This entails a view about the legitimate distribution of power. Public institutions need to have political power in order to promote the public interest, especially when this requires regulating the private sphere. Political power is coercive and inescapable for citizens: it sets general rules that all citizens have to obey. Minimally, this implies rule-of-law norms about public authorities treating citizens equally. But it is usually also taken to imply a demand for democratic accountability and political equality: an equal opportunity to determine the laws. Conversely, the private sphere is supposed to be a realm in which (political) power is absent. Were power to be found in the private sphere, it would be subject to the same demand for democratic accountability and would have to become part of the public sphere in order to satisfy this demand.

2.2 Transgressing the Public/Private Divide

This book concentrates on the potential of private wealth to generate power, a transgression of the private/public divide. It is useful to distinguish two different ways in which this happens. Both of them lead to the exercise of 'power' by 'wealth' (i.e., wealthy individuals or organisations).

We refer to the first kind of transgression as *wealth in the state*. This exercise of power is mediated: wealth crosses into the state and captures public policies for private interests. Recall that according to the standard liberal public/private distinction, the public sphere is charged with regulating the private sphere to promote the public interest. This is represented by the downward arrow in Figure 1, showing the exercise of power or influence from the state over the private sphere. This creates an

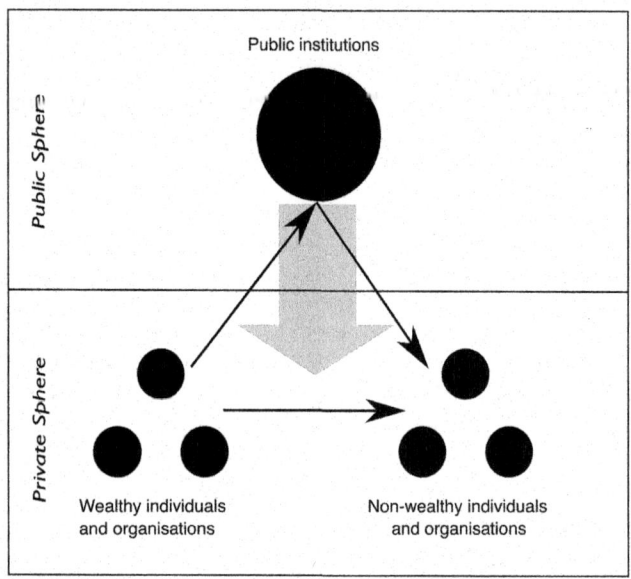

Figure 1 Types of transgressions of the private/public divide.

opportunity for wealthy private agents to hijack the state's power. This is represented by the arrows from the wealthy to the non-wealthy via public institutions.

The means by which this can occur are various. Sometimes people seek to directly and intentionally use their economic resources to influence state policy. This encompasses a spectrum of motivations, from economic agents engaging instrumentally in politics to further their economic goals (for example, a company lobbying for subsidies), to people using their economic resources to further unrelated political goals (such as a billionaire donating to abortion campaigners). These topics are the subject of the chapters by Phil Parvin and Chiara Destri. Beyond this, there are emergent influences, which arise when economic forces influence political outcomes without anyone directly intending that they do so. This includes the following (non-exhaustively): capital flight (the threat of disinvestment prompting revisions in government policy); sovereign debt financing (on which see the chapter by Anahí Wiedenbrüg and Patricio López-Cantero); and citizens' differential participation in politics according to socioeconomic class.

We turn now to the second type of transgression of the liberal public/private distinction, which we call *power in the economy*. This involves wealthy individuals or organisations directly exercising power over less wealthy individuals or organisations within the economy (without the mediation of the state). This is represented in Figure 1 by the arrow connecting the wealthy with the non-wealthy. The scope of this transgression depends on how exactly one understands power in the economy and its badness, which is a controversial topic. To illustrate, consider three views we can label 'the libertarian,' 'the economic,' and 'the radical.' On a libertarian view, the absence of power from the economy means that in markets, transactions must be consented to, whereas in politics, minorities are coerced into compliance. On this view, power exercised directly in the economy means force or fraud which renders exchanges involuntary (such a view obviously raises questions about the legitimacy of property rights, on which see Chapter 6 by Jessica Flanigan's). The economic view is encapsulated in models of perfect competition in which no individual has any power to determine prices. Power in the economy on this view is what economists call 'market power': the ability of a market agent to influence prices. Other sources of market failures, particularly externalities and information asymmetries, might also count as instances of power on this view; they certainly depart from the ideal of perfect competition. Finally, a radical view would hold that property itself is a kind of power such that inequality in private property holdings entails inequality of power, and a market economy can only claim to be free from unequal power insofar as property holdings are equalised.

The two ways of transgressing of the private/public divide (wealth in the state and power in the economy) can coexist in a vicious feedback loop. For example, a company might lobby the government for unfair advantages, which it uses to increase its market power, which it uses to further lobby the government. Walmart's use of the food stamp programme in the United States, with which this introduction started, is an example of this dynamic.

2.3 Approaches to Transgressions

This brings us to the key question of responses to transgressions of the liberal public/private divide. We propose a taxonomy of four ideal-type approaches: insulation, market failure regulation, redistribution, and economic democracy strategies (for an overview, see Figure 2). These each bear a different relation to the private/public distinction, and the two types of transgressions mentioned above.

A first distinction is between strategies which attempt to protect the public sphere from economic influences, and all other strategies, which try, one way or the other, to reduce power concentrations in the economy.

Strategies of *insulation* aim to better police the boundary between the public sphere and the private to reduce the influence of the economy over politics. In particular, they try to prevent economic inequality spilling over into political inequality. Insulation is the best understood approach and the traditional centrepiece of discussions about wealth and power. Insulation strategies can be seen most clearly in attempts to

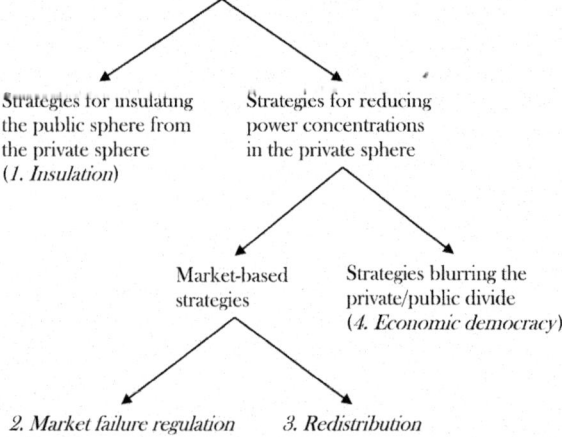

Figure 2 Ways of responding to transgressions of the private/public divide.

curb intentional influences such as bribery or unequally funded political speech: anti-corruption laws, political finance laws and policies for the funding of speech in the broader public sphere (see the chapters by Parvin and by Destri). On a more fundamental level, the design of the constitution influences the extent to which public institutions can function without problematic forms of interference (on which see Brian Kogelmann's chapter). Stretching the metaphor of insulation somewhat, this can extend to constitutional measures intended not merely to frustrate the disproportionate influence of the wealthy but to actively counterbalance it by increasing the political power of the non-wealthy (see the chapter by Stuart White and Elliot Bulmer). These policies and procedures are supplemented by informal social norms around corruption and the use of wealth for political purposes (addressed by Kimpell Johnson and by Richard Arneson). By definition, insulation strategies only address the problem of wealth in the state, and do not attempt to deal with the problem of power in the economy.

The other, non-insulation strategies envisage reforms of the private sphere itself to prevent the emergence of concentrated power within the economy. By definition, such strategies directly address the problem of power in the economy. However, they can also indirectly address the problem of wealth in the state by making the private sphere more compatible with the public sphere; rather than reducing economic influences on politics, they reform the private sphere such that the influence of the economy over politics is more benign. Within this set of strategies, we can make a distinction between those strategies which accept the economic domain as a private sphere dominated by markets, and those strategies which import public norms of democracy into the 'private' economic realm.

Let's first discuss the market-based strategies. These engineer the economy such that the self-seeking norms of the private sphere remain viable. The goal is to realise the ideal of the market as a sphere free from power.[3] The key distinction within this category is between strategies of *market failure regulation* and strategies of *redistribution*. This distinction tracks the distinction made in the previous section between libertarian, economic, and radical interpretations of the ideal of the power-free market.

Strategies for regulating market failures ensure the integrity of the market on the libertarian and economic interpretations. On the libertarian view sketched in the previous section, the prevention of force or fraud is all that is required. On the economic view, the possibilities are much more extensive. Of particular interest is competition/antitrust policy, working to curb market power in the strict sense (on which see Anna Gerbrandy and Pauline Phoa's chapter). More generally, regulations to keep competition fair by correcting market failures fall into this category.

Strategies of redistribution counter power on the more radical interpretation of power in the economy.[4] The classical form of this strategy refers to the welfare state, with its social insurance and benefit programmes. More ambitious redistributive agendas aim to realise what James Meade (1964) and Rawls called 'property-owning democracy' (O'Neill and Williamson 2014). In practice, this would likely require some kind of heavily progressive taxation funding a universal entitlement, either as a lump-sum grant when people reach adulthood ('basic capital') or as an ongoing stream ('basic income'). Some advocates of basic income explicitly make the connection with allowing people to escape relations of power in the economy (Zwolinski 2012; Widerquist 2013), and Huub Brouwer in his chapter discusses redistributive schemes in the context of automation.

Finally, the approach of *economic democracy* is to deal with the direct exercise of power in the economy by importing norms and associated institutions for dealing with power from the public sphere. Whereas the market-based approaches respond to power in the economy with a demand for independence in the market, the economic democracy approach responds to power in the economy with a demand for democratic accountability. Policies which might form part of an economic democracy approach include worker participation (discussed by Igor Shoikhedbrod and Thomas Christiano in this volume), CPRs (examined by Yara Al Salman), and reforms to increase democratic input in corporate governance (analysed in the chapter by Michael Bennett and Rutger Claassen). Private parties who engage in CSR and philanthropy are often criticised on the basis that these activities *should* be subject to greater democratic accountability, a topic addressed by Emma Saunders-Hastings's chapter. What these have in common is that they blur the public/private divide by creating hybrid institutional forms in the economy which are governed by a complex mixture of public and private norms.

When it comes to both the regulation of market failures, redistribution and economic democracy, these strategies may be prized not only for their contributions to keeping power out of the economy, but also, as a consequence, for keeping wealth out of the state. Traditionally, the idea of making the private sphere more compatible with the public sphere (regulating the economy in the interests of democracy) has been understood solely in terms of (re)distribution (Beitz 1990; Machin 2012). However, our framework makes it clear that strategies of regulating market failures and strategies of economic democracy can also make a contribution in this regard.

These four strategies are unlikely to be simple substitutes for one another, delivering the same results via different routes. At the limit, total success in one approach might render the others redundant: if we were solely concerned with keeping power out of the state, and if we could totally insulate politics from the economy, attempting to use the other strategies to render economic influences on politics more benign would be unnecessary. However, if we take a broader view of our goals (a direct concern for power in the economy beyond its influence on the problem of wealth in the state), and/or a more realistic view of any strategy's prospects of success, the four approaches are more likely to be complementary. Which strategies we should endorse or put emphasis on will depend on considerations of cost and efficacy as well as normative ideals.

3 Overview of the Contributions

3.1 Theoretical Orientations

Part One of the volume addresses the general topic of money and power through five different theoretical lenses. Each of the major theoretical traditions of European political thought has a distinctive view of the topic, and their views of this topic are part of what distinguishes them. Each chapter in this first part of the volume looks at money and politics from a different theoretical tradition: republican, egalitarian liberal, classical liberal, Marxist, and anarchist.

We start with the oldest of these traditions, and one which has always foregrounded the problem of wealth and power: republicanism. Starting with the contemporary debate, Jessica Kimpell Johnson (Chapter 2) argues the predominant character of republican responses to wealth and power in the last decade has been constitutional and institutional in nature. Kimpell Johnson traces this institutionalist approach historically from the work of James Harrington, culminating with the Federalists and informing the contributions of John McCormick and Phillip Pettit today. She argues that this approach neglects key elements of the classical republican concern about norms, which warns that the functioning of institutions is dependent on systems of norms and the character of political culture. Developing a supportive civic culture of political equality among citizens must be integral to the contemporary programme for republican freedom – as laws and institutions alone, even if they aim at political equality, will neither be stable nor sufficient. The chapter ends by briefly engaging with how Tocqueville's ideal of the free citizen could be coupled with 'localism' to suggest practices for developing norms of equal access and influence.

The next two chapters represent different sides of the dominant political tradition today, liberalism. Richard Arneson (Chapter 3) examines the egalitarian incarnation of liberalism which has flourished in the wake of John Rawls. Taking equality as the central value, he constructs a conceptual map of how egalitarianism relates to the question of capitalism and democracy. Starting from fundamental issues in moral philosophy, Arneson distinguishes between two types of egalitarian view. Welfarist egalitarians evaluate social arrangements according to their influence on the distribution of well-being. Relational egalitarians, on the other hand, prioritise the elimination of social hierarchy. Welfarist egalitarians are likely to object to the political inequality on instrumental grounds, whereas relational egalitarians are directly committed to a principle of equality of opportunity for political influence. Arneson stretches the two views to their limits using a series of examples, and shows how they can produce divergent assessments of the influence of money in politics under different circumstances. One interesting upshot is that relational egalitarians are not as categorically opposed to the influence of economic inequality in politics as they might initially appear: wealth is just only one potential threat to political equality, and conceptually it could counteract as well as exacerbate other potential threats.

While Arneson addresses a literature connecting liberalism with moral philosophy, Brian Kogelmann (Chapter 4) looks instead at a body of work which connects liberalism with political economy. His subject is public choice theory, the pre-eminent contemporary expression of classical liberal ideas about money and politics. Public choice theory analyses political institutions using the tools and methods of economics. Kogelmann asks what public choice theory can teach us about political equality as a normative ideal, by focusing on the relationship between rent seeking and political inequality. One important lesson from public choice theory is that political inequality is sometimes driven by unequal wealth, but is sometimes driven by other, more subtle factors. Thus, even if we lived in a society where wealth was distributed in a perfectly equal manner, political inequality would still be a significant problem. Kogelmann canvasses some of the novel proposals public choice theorists have made for addressing the problem of rent-seeking. He concludes by asking whether democracy is doomed to descend into crony capitalism as some public choice theorists have suggested. Hope on this score is not necessarily foolhardy, but it does require relaxing some of public choice theory's assumptions about human selfishness.

Having put two different accounts of liberalism on the table, the next chapter (Chapter 5) proceeds to their classic antagonist. The relationship between economic and political power plays centre stage in the critique of liberalism advanced by Karl Marx and his successors. Igor Shoikhedbrod takes us on a journey from Marx's own earliest attempts to grapple with the subject through to contemporary democratic socialists. Shoikhedbrod argues that Marx's approach was shaped in his very first journalistic work, which reported on how wealthy forest owners were able to get the customary practice of gathering fallen forest wood criminalised by the Prussian state as an instance of property theft. Shoikhedbrod proceeds to elaborate a Marxian account of political domination and contrast it favourably with liberal egalitarian and neo-republican attempts to address the problem. Finally, he surveys contemporary proposals for democratising the economy, including worker-owned and managed cooperatives, as well as democratic control over investment. In the terms set out above, Shoikhedbrod's Marxian perspective is that the influence of economic structures on political equality is so fundamental and intransigent that attempts at insulation will necessarily fail. Instead, an economic democracy strategy is required which ultimately abolishes capital as a social relation in order to make true democracy possible.

Jessica Flanigan (Chapter 6) closes Part One by providing an even more radical perspective, from the anarchist tradition. She concentrates on individualist or rights-based anarchists who focus on the wrongness of coercion. These thinkers do not share the concern to purify political power from economic influences which can be traced in the other political traditions, because they hold that our goal should instead be the eradication of power altogether. Flanigan asks how this ideal can be approximated so long as states still exist. She argues that unjust enforcement of many public policies has meaningfully determined the status quo distribution of property. In light of this, a 'smaller' (more laissez-faire) state is not necessarily a better state because it entrenches a distributive pattern that has been determined by injustice. Instead, increasing redistribution or social programmes in some ways may reduce the burdens of being subject to unjust law enforcement and compensate people for the imposition of a property system without their consent. In particular, Flanigan argues in favour of a basic income to achieve these goals.

3.2 Power in the Economic Sphere

The chapters in Part Two of the volume turn to concrete constellations of power in the economic sphere, critically discussing them with reference to normative standards of democracy and legitimacy. The first three chapters in this part focus on corporations, the fourth compares corporations and philanthropy, while the final chapter in this part turns to the commons as an alternative venue.

Thomas Christiano's contribution (Chapter 7) focuses on worker participation in firms. Workplaces are taken by many philosophers as quintessential sites of power, where employers routinely dominate the working conditions, actions, and ultimately lives of their employees. Christiano takes a broad view of worker participation, including co-determination, works councils, union bargaining, and worker cooperatives. He argues that on several important values, a case can be made for worker participation, whatever its precise form. First, worker participation is economically efficient: firms subject to co-determination do not perform worse than firms in other jurisdictions, and worker cooperatives are no less efficient than their capitalist counterparts. Second, worker participation scores well on the value of equality, understood as equality of power between workers and owners of firms. It helps redress the power imbalances in labour markets. Third, worker participation also leads to greater and better political participation, since it helps those at the lower scale of the income ladder to be more informed participations in politics. Finally, worker participation sensitises firms to the wider concerns of society with respect to widespread negative externalities (like environmental pollution). Importantly, for Christiano, these conclusions hold while accepting the context of a market-based economy. To redress the power balance is compatible with free markets as the main site of economic cooperation.

Michael Bennett and Rutger Claassen (Chapter 8) turn to positive action by corporations. Corporations are increasingly asked to pursue a substantive 'purpose,' instead of simply acting for the market-induced aim of profit maximisation. They compare this emerging 'purpose regime' not just to the regime of profit-maximisation, but also to the early nineteenth-century regime of 'special incorporation.' At that time, corporations still had to be chartered by governments, for a substantive public purpose (operating a bridge, digging a canal, etc.). The historical public purpose regime relied less on market discipline and more on democratic accountability for its legitimacy. In a way, today's call for 'purpose' resembles this earlier practice. Bennett and Claassen argue that the politicisation of corporate purpose is welcome, but that this earlier episode shows how politicisation can go wrong. Arbitrariness and corruption marked the relations between business and governments during the special incorporation regime, which partly explains its demise. To avoid such problems, they propose three desiderata for 'proper politicisation,' and finish with a discussion of various proposals for corporate reform which may realise these desiderata.

In their chapter, Anna Gerbrandy and Pauline Phoa (Chapter 9) take issue with the way markets are constructed through the provisions of competition (antitrust) law. Their focus is on the large tech companies structuring the platform economy. Gerbrandy and Phoa argue that we should see the tech companies as examples of 'modern bigness.' This phenomenon emerges when a company is able to project different types of power (they note the 'instrumental,' 'discursive,' and 'structural' forms of power) across different domains in society (they note the personal, social, economic, and political domains). This poses problems for competition law's ability to be a 'counter power,' for the latter is traditionally conceived only to provide a solution to firms' market power. Modern bigness, however, threatens notions of the personal autonomy and agency of market agents, as well as the integrity of the political domain. All of these were assumptions for treating market power as a distinct problem. Gerbrandy and Phoa argue that competition law may have to expand its scope, although in the end, this is a political question, which also depends on the availability of alternative regulatory mechanisms, with which competition law has to work in tandem.

Emma Saunders-Hastings' chapter (Chapter 10) also discusses the use of economic power for seemingly positive purposes. Her aim is to compare the democratic credentials of two related yet distinct practices: CSR initiatives by corporations, and philanthropy by wealthy donors. Both CSR and philanthropy are exercises of economic power for the benefit of third parties. As such, they may conflict with public goals set by the democratic procedures of states and other public bodies. To evaluate such initiatives, Saunders-Hastings argues in favour of a forbearance approach. While they are not themselves democratic practices, it is sufficient if CSR and philanthropy are not undemocratic, i.e., are not interfering with democratic processes, nor undermining the pursuit of democratically adopted projects. Measured against this standard, Saunders-Hastings argues that CSR practices are often less worrisome than philanthropy. CSR initiatives often are publicly visible and aim to create good will, as when companies like Disney donate to the Make-a-Wish Foundation. They follow the standards of morality set by the public, instead of trying to subvert them. By contrast, philanthropic initiatives are more likely to work outside of the spotlight to influence policy makers' and others who make public policy. For example, philanthropic gifts in the area of education or pension plans are often conditional on education policy being sensitive to donors' rather than citizens' preferences. Through such philanthropic initiatives, influence is exercised that avoids public scrutiny, thus undermining democratic legitimacy.

Yara Al Salman's contribution (Chapter 11) discusses the power-related effects of ownership institutions. She adopts a republican conception of non-domination, which leads her to identify two criteria for legitimate ownership institutions. These institutions have to be able to help people exercise their basic capabilities, and do so in a way that gives them control over the resources needed to do so. Al Salman applies these criteria to compare individual and group ownership, arguing that group ownership performs much better than commonly thought. In particular, a conception of group ownership she calls 'sharing in common,' can help people collectively control their resources, reducing arbitrary dependence on others. This conception is inspired by CPRs for agricultural purposes, studied empirically by Elinor Ostrom and others. However, 'sharing in common' is a more demanding idea than what occurs in most CPRs because it requires democratic relations of equal power. Al Salman illustrates her argument with a discussion of newly emerging knowledge commons such as Wikipedia. In such arrangements, power is shared equally, and consensus is required for decision-making. These demands do not (*pace* many economic arguments) disable an efficient use of resources, as the success and survival of such knowledge commons attests. Commons structures are thus an avenue for economic power under democratic control which is different from, but complementary to, the forms of corporate accountability discussed in the preceding chapters.

3.3 Wealth and Democratic Institutions

The chapters in Part Three discuss how inequalities in wealth can undermine the functioning of democratic institutions.

In his chapter, Phil Parvin (Chapter 12) points out that there has been an explosion in the number and influence of lobby groups in the United Kingdom, United States, and Europe. This prompts him to ask what role (if any) lobbyists should play in a democracy. Parvin argues that lobbyists can potentially play a central and positive role in democratic decision-making, but that ensuring fairness and equality of access would require a fundamental re-ordering of democratic practice as it exists in the world. Lobbying is in theory a benefit to democracy: not only is it protected by widely endorsed commitments to rights to free speech and assembly, but it is also instrumental in supporting democratic functioning and representation. However, Parvin considers two common objections to lobbying: the egalitarian and the libertarian objection. The egalitarian objection holds that lobbying skews democratic decision-making by allowing elites to influence democratic decision-making to their advantage. The libertarian objection takes lobbying to be problematic because it distorts the functioning of free markets by enabling 'crony capitalism' and allowing interest groups to enlarge the state. Parvin ends the chapter by pointing out that avoiding the harmful aspects of lobbying is difficult because lobby groups representing elite interests have engaged in norm capture: interests contrary to those of elites have come to be regarded as infeasible, inadmissible, and dangerous.

In Chapter 13, Chiara Destri discusses the role of money in politics by focusing on campaign finance and political parties. She argues that philosophical debates about campaign finance have typically overlooked the importance of political parties. To make her case, Destri starts out by claiming that parties are ideally suited to organise political campaigns in accordance with the democratic ideal of collective self-rule because they can perform epistemic, justificatory, and motivational functions. After outlining the normative debate on campaign finance, she goes on to argue that campaign regulations affect parties' capacity to discharge these three functions, as well as their internal structure. Destri ends the chapter by arguing that campaign finance regulation should be designed in a way that harnesses internal democracy in parties. This could be done by a two-staged voucher system that gives citizens two vouchers: one to fund their party of choice and one to support internal candidates at party primaries and their local branch delegates that are sent to the party conference.

In the next chapter, Elliot Bulmer and Stuart White (Chapter 14) ask how constitutionalism can be used to address the dangers of oligarchy. They start by drawing a distinction between oligarchical *capture* of the state and oligarchical *distortion* of public policy. By oligarchical capture, they refer to the undue opportunity for political influence that the wealthy and/or business corporations can come to hold. By oligarchical distortion, they refer to the impact of oligarchic power on public policy, to the way this can skew policy away from the interests of the wider community. They then consider how provisions within a codified and entrenched constitution can serve to limit oligarchical distortion and oligarchic capture.

In Chapter 15, Huub Brouwer looks at two prominent proposals for responding to growing wealth inequality: a basic income and a capital grant. He examines the choice between a basic income and a capital grant from the perspective of automation. Automation, Brouwer points out, can lead to technological unemployment if machines carry out similar work at much lower costs than humans. He defends two main claims. First, he argues that a universal and a conditional basic income do not provide a good solution to the problem of technological unemployment. Second, he defends the claim that technological unemployment strengthens the case for a capital grant, supplemented with a generous system of contribution benefits, which is to replace the unemployment benefit scheme.

Many of the chapters in the edited volume discuss the wealth-power nexus by focusing on a single country, and most contributors focus on the United States, the United Kingdom, and Europe. In Chapter 16, Anahí Wiedenbrüg and Patricio López Cantero take a different perspective. They focus on the power that private creditors have when dealing with low- and middle-income countries as sovereign debtors. Wiedenbrüg and López Cantero argue that private creditors hold relational and structural power over low- and middle-income countries and describe how this power is exercised in problematic ways at the time of lending, restructuring and pushing for, or inhibiting, reforms to the international financial architecture. The chapter ends by defending the claim that a quasi-legal, soft-law approach is the best way to address harmful power asymmetries between creditors and debtors. The authors briefly discuss a list of desiderata for the establishment of such multilateral, soft-law regime.

4 Conclusion

This volume brings together a wide range of topics that are all aspects of the wealth-power nexus. We hope that the volume will stimulate debate on these matters in political theory and adjacent fields. Although the volume does cover a wide range of topics, it is also limited in one important respect. As mentioned at various places in this introduction, the social science literature on wealth and democracy is overwhelmingly based on research in Western countries, particularly the United States, and our political philosophy tradition (from ancient debates on oligarchy to modern ones on property-owning democracy) is Western as well. At the same time, the question about wealth and its relation to power and political influence is universal. Anthropologists have worked to draw on both Western and non-Western societies to gain more generalised lessons about hierarchy and egalitarianism, but such anthropological work remains disconnected from the political economy themes of this volume (Boehm 2001; Anderson 2017). Most of the chapters in this volume assume a background of advanced capitalism and established democracy, and some adjustments will need to be made to apply these analyses to developing economies and less established democracies. The contributors to this volume were mainly based in the United States, the Netherlands, and the United Kingdom, with others based in Argentina, Canada, and France. While we hope that our insights can be valuable for thinking about capitalism and democracy in general, we wish to acknowledge our geographical biases and limitations.

Notes

1 In 2015, the American Coalition for Tax Fairness estimated that Walmart receives $6.2 billion worth of subsidies each year (Americans for Tax Fairness 2015).
2 Blanchet, Saez, and Zucman recently launched a website called 'realtime inequality,' which tracks income and wealth inequality in the United States every quarter. They have data available from January 1979 onward.
3 Such strategies are basically equivalent to Taylor's idea of 'market-anti-power' (Taylor 2013).
4 Libertarians may object that redistribution fundamentally violates the ideal of the market (and of freedom from power). We take no stance on this question here.

References

Alstadsæter, Annette, Niels Johannesen, and Gabriel Zucman. 2018. 'Who Owns the Wealth in Tax Havens? Macro Evidence and Implications for Global Inequality'. *Journal of Public Economics* 162 (June): 89–100. https://doi.org/10/gdzcvg.

Americans for Tax Fairness. 2015. 'Walmart on Tax Day: How Taxpayers Subsidize America's Biggest Employer and Richest Family.' Retrieved on 22 February 2022 from https://americansfortaxfairness.org/files/Walmart-on-Tax-Day-Americans-for-Tax-Fairness-1.pdf.

Anderson, Elizabeth. 2017. 'The Problem of Equality from a Political Economy Perspective: The Long View of History'. In *Oxford Studies in Political Philosophy, Volume 3*. Oxford: Oxford University Press. https://doi.org/10.1093/oso/9780198801221.003.0003.

Ansolabehere, Stephen, John M. de Figueiredo, and James M. Snyder. 2003. 'Why Is There so Little Money in U.S. Politics?'. *The Journal of Economic Perspectives* 17 (1): 105–30.

Atkinson, Anthony B. 2015. *Inequality: What Can Be Done?* Cambridge, MA: Harvard University Press.

Atkinson, Anthony B., Thomas Piketty, and Emmanuel Saez. 2011. 'Top Incomes in the Long Run of History'. *Journal of Economic Literature* 49 (1): 3–71. https://doi.org/10.1257/jel.49.1.3.

Bartels, Larry M. 2010. *Unequal Democracy: The Political Economy of the New Gilded Age*. New York, NY/Princeton, NJ: Princeton University Press.

Beitz, Charles R. 1990. *Political Equality: An Essay in Democratic Theory*. Princeton, NJ: Princeton University Press.

Bennett, Michael. 2020. 'An Epistemic Argument for an Egalitarian Public Sphere'. *Episteme*. https://doi.org/10.1017/epi.2020.42.

Blaufarb, Rafe. 2019. *The Great Demarcation: The French Revolution and the Invention of Modern Property*. Oxford/New York, NY: Oxford University Press.

Boehm, Christopher. 2001. *Hierarchy in the Forest: The Evolution of Egalitarian Behavior*. Revised edition. Cambridge, MA: Harvard University Press.

Chancel, Lucas, Thomas Piketty, Emmanuel Saez, and Gabriel Zucman. 2021. 'World Inequality Report 2022'. World Inequality Lab. https://wir2022.wid.world/www-site/uploads/2021/12/WorldInequalityReport2022_Full_Report.pdf.

Christiano, Thomas. 2012. 'Money in Politics'. In *The Oxford Handbook of Political Philosophy*, edited by David Estlund, 241–58. Oxford: Oxford University Press.

Ciepley, David. 2013. 'Beyond Public and Private: Toward a Political Theory of the Corporation'. *American Political Science Review* 107 (01): 139–58. https://doi.org/10.1017/S0003055412000536.

Cohen, Joshua. 2001. 'Money, Politics and Political Equality'. In *Fact and Value: Essays on Ethics and Metaphysics for Judith Jarvis Thomson*, edited by Alex Byrne, Robert C. Stalnaker and Ralph Wedgwood, 47–80. Cambridge, MA: MIT Press.

Crouch, Colin. 2004. *Post-Democracy*. Malden, MA: Polity.

——. 2011. *The Strange Non-Death of Neo-Liberalism*. Cambridge: Polity Press.

Dahl, Robert A. 2005. *Who Governs?: Democracy and Power in the American City*. Second Revised edition. New Haven, CT: Yale University Press.

Edmundson, William A. 2017. *John Rawls: Reticent Socialist*. Cambridge/New York, NY: Cambridge University Press.
Ferreras, Isabelle. 2017. *Firms as Political Entities: Saving Democracy through Economic Bicameralism*. Cambridge: Cambridge University Press.
Gilens, Martin. 2014. *Affluence and Influence: Economic Inequality and Political Power in America*. Princeton, NJ: Princeton University Press.
Gilens, Martin, and Benjamin I. Page. 2014. 'Testing Theories of American Politics: Elites, Interest Groups, and Average Citizens'. *Perspectives on Politics* 12 (03): 564–81. https://doi.org/10.1017/S1537592714001595.
Gourevitch, Alex. 2014. *From Slavery to the Cooperative Commonwealth: Labor and Republican Liberty in the Nineteenth Century*. New York, NY: Cambridge University Press.
Hussain, Waheed, and Jeffrey Moriarty. 2014. 'Corporations, the Democratic Deficit, and Voting'. *Georgetown Journal of Law & Public Policy* 12: 429.
Institute for Policy Studies. 2021. 'Annual Excess Report.' Retrieved on 22 February 2022 from https://ips-dc.org/wp-content/uploads/2021/05/report-executive-excess-2021-PDF.pdf.
Levitt, Steven D. 1994. 'Using Repeat Challengers to Estimate the Effect of Campaign Spending on Election Outcomes in the U.S. House'. *Journal of Political Economy* 102 (4): 777–98. https://doi.org/10/djwxh2.
Lindblom, Charles. 1977. *Politics and Markets: The World's Political Economic Systems*. New York, NY: Basic Books.
Machin, Dean J. 2012. 'Political Inequality and the "Super-Rich": Their Money or (Some of) Their Political Rights'. *Res Publica* 19 (2): 121–39. https://doi.org/10.1007/s11158-012-9200-8.
Mair, Peter. 2013. *Ruling the Void: The Hollowing of Western Democracy*. London: Verso.
McCormick, John P. 2011. *Machiavellian Democracy*. Cambridge/New York, NY: Cambridge University Press.
McGeer, Eric. 2000. *The Land Legislation of the Macedonian Emperors*. Toronto, ON: Pontifical Institute of Mediaeval Studies.
McMahon, Christopher. 1994. *Authority and Democracy: A General Theory of Government and Management*. Princeton, NJ: Princeton University Press.
Meade, J. E. 1964. *Efficiency, Equality and the Ownership of Property*. London: Allen & Unwin.
O'Connor, Clare. 2014. 'Report: Walmart's Billionaire Waltons Give Almost None of Own Cash to Foundation.' *Forbes*. Retrieved on 21 February 2022 from https://www.forbes.com/sites/clareoconnor/2014/06/03/report-walmarts-billionaire-waltons-give-almost-none-of-own-cash-to-family-foundation/?sh=18ad596f7d52.
O'Neill, Martin, and Thad Williamson, eds. 2014. *Property-Owning Democracy: Rawls and Beyond*. Chichester: Wiley-Blackwell.
Open Secrets. 2022. 'Walmart.inc.' Retrieved on 21 February 2022 from https://www.opensecrets.org/Lobby/clientsum.php?id=D000000367&year=2020.
Pettit, Philip. 1999. *Republicanism: A Theory of Freedom and Government*. Oxford/New York, NY: Oxford University Press.
Pevnick, Ryan. 2016. 'Does the Egalitarian Rationale for Campaign Finance Reform Succeed?' *Philosophy & Public Affairs* 44 (1): 46–76. https://doi.org/10.1111/papa.12064.

Piketty, Thomas. 2014. *Capital in the Twenty-First Century*. Translated by Arthur Goldhammer. Cambridge, MA: Harvard University Press.
Rawls, John. 1999. *A Theory of Justice*. Revised edition. Cambridge, MA: Belknap Press.
———. 2001. *Justice as Fairness: A Restatement*. Edited by Erin Kelly. Cambridge, MA: Belknap Press.
Schakel, Wouter. 2021. 'Unequal Policy Responsiveness in the Netherlands'. *Socio-Economic Review* 19 (1): 37–57. https://doi.org/10/gf7q62.
Schattschneider, E. E. 1960. *The Semisovereign People: A Realist's View of Democracy in America*. New York, NY: Holt, Rinehart and Winston.
Scherer, Andreas Georg, and Guido Palazzo. 2007. 'Toward a Political Conception of Corporate Responsibility: Business and Society Seen from a Habermasian Perspective'. *The Academy of Management Review* 32 (4): 1096–120. https://doi.org/10.2307/20159358.
Schlozman, Kay Lehman, Sidney Verba, and Henry E. Brady. 2012. *The Unheavenly Chorus: Unequal Political Voice and the Broken Promise of American Democracy*. Princeton, NJ: Princeton University Press.
Singer, Abraham. 2019. *The Form of the Firm: A Normative Political Theory of the Corporation*. Oxford/New York, NY: Oxford University Press.
Streeck, Wolfgang. 2017. *Buying Time: The Delayed Crisis of Democratic Capitalism*. Second edition. London: Verso.
Taylor, Robert S. 2013. 'Market Freedom as Antipower'. *The American Political Science Review* 107 (3): 593–602. https://doi.org/10/gg5fsp.
Thomas, Alan. 2016. *Republic of Equals: Predistribution and Property-Owning Democracy*. New York, NY: Oxford University Press.
Vergara, Camila. 2020. *Systemic Corruption: Constitutional Ideas for an Anti-Oligarchic Republic*. Princeton, NJ: Princeton University Press.
Walmart. 2021. 'Annual Report.' Retrieved on 21 February 2022 from https://corporate.walmart.com/media-library/document/2021-annual-report/_proxyDocument?id=00000178-f54f-db6f-adfe-fdcf018d0000.
Walzer, Michael. 1984. 'Liberalism and the Art of Separation'. *Political Theory* 12 (3): 315–30.
White, Stuart. 2011. 'The Republican Critique of Capitalism'. *Critical Review of International Social and Political Philosophy* 14 (5): 561–79.
Widerquist, K. 2013. *Independence, Propertylessness, and Basic Income: A Theory of Freedom as the Power to Say No*. New York, NY: Palgrave Macmillan.
Zwolinski, Matt. 2012. 'Classical Liberalism and the Basic Income'. *Basic Income Studies* 6 (2): 1–14.

PART I
Theoretical Orientations

2 What about Ethos?

Republican Institutions, Oligarchic Democracy, and Norms of Political Equality

Jessica Kimpell Johnson

In response to months of pro-democracy protests in Hong Kong, former U.S. President Donald J. Trump said in the fall of 2019, 'I stand with freedom,' adding 'but we are also in the process of making the largest trade deal in history [with China]' (Lynch 2019). The comment came as the president suggested that to secure better trading terms with China, he might veto unanimously passed legislation by the U.S. Congress aimed at protecting the rights of the democracy protestors. The tension between democracy and capitalism was apparent, as one end seemingly needed to bend to the other. Since the 2008 global financial crisis, this relationship has come under increasing scrutiny, with concerns that capitalism is deepening and entrenching steep inequality sharpened by widespread recognition that Western democracies are oligarchic. In the United States, this concern was reinforced by the coronavirus pandemic that laid bare longstanding structural inequalities and inequities. Those already most vulnerable were hit hardest by the pandemic-related economic contraction, while the wealthy benefited the most from the recovery (Federal Reserve 2021). Months before the pandemic, the Pew Research Center found that economic inequality in the United States, whether measured by income or wealth, 'continues to widen.' Income growth was most rapid for the top 5% of families, the wealth gap between upper-income and middle-and lower-income families was widening, and the richest families were 'getting richer faster,' also being the only group to have gained wealth since the Great Recession (2020). While these and other examples in this chapter draw from the United States, the trends they embody are likely to have wider relevance and resonance.

In this chapter, I examine the tension between democratic political equality and wealth inequality in capitalist societies from the republican perspective. The republican tradition has a long lineage of connecting citizens' material conditions with their capacity for the exercise of political power and their security against subjection to the arbitrary will of another. Thus, it is fitting that contemporary thinkers interested in securing freedom as non-domination – understood

DOI: 10.4324/9781003173632-3

as freedom from arbitrary interference (Pettit 1997, 2012) – are increasingly focused on the interconnection between the political and economic spheres and the ways in which socioeconomic inequality enables political inequality.[1]

Many republican thinkers, old and new, consider steep inequality in resources as a threat to freedom. If socioeconomic elites disproportionately influence and direct laws in their favour, they undermine the republican ideal of equal access and influence (Pettit 2012), and thereby subject others to the exercise of arbitrary power. The predominant character of the republican response in the last few decades[2] to the problem of the influence of wealth, however, is largely constitutional and institutional in nature. Most proposals by contemporary republicans use institutions and laws as tools to counteract the lopsided influence of the wealthy. This can take the form of proposals to curb extremes through pre-distribution or redistribution or to establish and structure institutions to create 'plebeian' channels or veto points, with the goal of producing laws that reflect the views of the socioeconomic many not just the few (see Bulmer and White 2022, for discussion).

This constitutional-institutional thrust of the literature is in keeping with the compromises that modern republicanism made when confronted with the problem of how to secure freedom from arbitrary political power amid the inequality and self-interested motivations of commercial society. Setting aside whether this combination is ultimately reconcilable, the moderns' solution was to make institutions do the work of resolving the conflicting interests and motivations of democratic commercial societies. If institutions could be designed to manage and facilitate clashes between groups, the output would be, as Madison said, justice and liberty (2008).

The modern solution of relying on institutions to secure freedom amid commercialism and inequality is increasingly in doubt. Institutions often reflect rather than manage or correct for asymmetries in power that resource inequality has produced. Moreover, this framework – the origins of which are identifiable in Harrington's work, culminate with the Federalists and inform John McCormick's and Philip Pettit's contributions – neglects crucial features of the classical republican concern about norms. That perspective warns that the functioning of institutions is dependent on systems of norms and the character of political culture. Developing a supportive civic culture of political equality among citizens must be integral to the contemporary programme for republican freedom – as laws and institutions alone, even if aimed at political equality, will neither be stable nor sufficient. On that theme, the chapter ends by briefly engaging with the possibility that Tocqueville's ideal of the free citizen coupled with 'localism' could suggest grounds for developing norms of equal access and influence.

1 Oligarchical Democracy and the Constitutional-Institutional Correctives

Republicans today argue that freedom requires equal political access and influence. If one were to measure political power concretely in terms of access to decision makers and influence over policy outcomes, again the COVID-19 pandemic illustrates the disproportionate power possessed by those with wealth from access to testing, protective equipment, medical treatments, and vaccinations to the shaping of government responses and actions of political leaders. During the early phase of the pandemic in March 2020, President Trump boasted of fielding phone calls from corporate executives and celebrities; in one anecdote, it seems a call from celebrity chef Wolfgang Puck about the financial suffering of his restaurant business during the public health crisis prompted Trump to instruct the Treasury and Labor secretaries to look into restoring the tax deductibility of meals and entertainment costs for corporations, 'something the hospitality industry's lobbyists have pursued for years' (Hohmann 2020). About ten months later, the U.S. government's $900 billion pandemic relief package included tax breaks for corporate meal expenses – derisively known as the 'three-martini lunch' – estimated to cost $6 billion in lost tax revenue (Editorial Board 2020).

The republican tradition presents two broad options to the political problem of inequality: either reduce the power that wealth brings to bear in politics by (1) reducing inequality among citizens – thereby overtly tending not only to the political but also the economic sphere – or by (2) insulating the political process through institutional design and other measures from the imbalance such discrepancies in resources could bring to bear. In the contemporary literature, the first approach is reflected in proposals arguing that non-domination requires political and economic reform, from supporting basic income, establishing democratic forms of economic governance, dismantling central features of a capitalist economy, and instantiating 'socialist republicanism' (White 2011; Gourevitch 2013; Casassas and De Wispelaere 2016; Muldoon 2019). In keeping with the second approach, socioeconomic inequality produced by capitalist societies could be consistent with securing freedom insofar as class-based institutions and mechanisms 'empower' the many (McCormick 2011; Hamilton 2014; Vergara 2020) or sufficient protections 'safeguard' citizens' political power in light of discrepancies in wealth (Pettit 2012). Two exemplars of this second approach are John McCormick and Philip Pettit. I focus on their work because it has significantly influenced the character of contemporary republican thought and, in particular, the related literature from both approaches described above on resource inequality and freedom.

The concern about the threat to freedom by inequality in resources is central to McCormick's work. 'Economic inequality is perhaps the greatest threat to the civic liberty that republics ... promise to their citizens.' While freedom depends on political equality, as 'every citizen ought to influence law- and policy-making in a relatively equal way' and 'government ought to be responsive and accountable to all citizens on a fairly equal basis,' elites routinely 'bring their resources to bear on politics' at the expense of the many (2018, 45). This threat posed by elites to freedom, which McCormick argues was a preoccupation of pre-eighteenth-century republics, has not received sufficient attention in democratic thought despite today's democracies being no less vulnerable 'to corruption, subversion and usurpation by the wealthy,' and electoral institutions – their 'institutional centerpiece' – failing to keep public officials accountable to the many (2011, 1–2).

The disproportionate influence of socioeconomic elites could be lessened in McCormick's account by establishing class-based institutions and other mechanisms that reduce their influence by empowering the many to deliberate and decide on policy, from establishing assemblies with veto or legislative authority that exclude the wealthiest citizens from eligibility to appointment procedures that combine lotteries and elections. The fact that the socioeconomic few dominate the many, McCormick argues, reflects a 'failure to provide the people with the proper *institutional channels* through which they can challenge the elite's power and privilege' (emphasis added, 2011, 17). McCormick draws ideas for elite constraining institutions from Machiavelli, whom McCormick argues was deeply concerned about the corrupting influence of economic inequality. Accordingly, one can derive from Machiavelli's work 'ways of securing greater political equality among citizens in decidedly inequitable circumstances' (14).[3]

The problem of securing freedom amid socioeconomic inequality is also present in Pettit's work because the role of democratic institutional and constitutional design is to facilitate 'equally shared control' by citizens of their government (2012, 169). To ensure the state acts in a non-arbitrary manner towards citizens, the state 'should deliver policy under a system of control to which we each have equal access,' involving 'equal ease' of access (25, 169). This kind of control could be incompatible with extremes in wealth insofar as they could 'jeopardize the freedom as non-domination of the less well off' (85). Therefore, the ideal of freedom 'imposes severe constraints on how large or pervasive' material inequalities can be (90). If citizens' 'basic liberties' are properly resourced and entrenched, however, allowing them equal influence and ease of access to contestatory channels over the making, administering, and adjudicating of law, background inequality in private wealth is permittable. When each citizen enjoys a 'threshold of free undominated choice' and public protections are sufficient to serve as a 'bulwark against the advantages on which the rich can draw,' that is 'consistent with some people having such private sources of power and wealth that they enjoy free undominated choice in a yet greater range and with yet greater security' (128, 88).

This chapter focuses on the constitutional-institutional dimensions in the works of Pettit and McCormick, and the meaning of these terms draws entirely on Pettit's and McCormick's usage and examples, referring narrowly to fundamental legislative, executive and judicial arrangements, and their associated channels (assemblies, courts) and processes (election, sortition, appeals, etc.). These elements are central in their accounts for securing freedom amid resource inequality and to their own self-understanding of their projects. McCormick frames his account as addressing the failure to provide the people (or the many) institutional channels to counteract the elite, and he considers his own account as 'plebeian' or 'democratic' and Pettit's as 'aristocratic' along institutional lines. (Are there assemblies or other mechanisms in the political order reserved specifically for the socioeconomic many or not? Are institutions designed to facilitate control over the few or to constrain the majority?) One might argue that placing Pettit and McCormick in the same category of approach collapses the elite/aristocratic versus plebeian/democratic distinction between them. Yet, shifting the focus to their constitutional-institutional approach exposes a shared problem that otherwise might not be revealed.

Institutional design remains at the forefront of republican literature in part because McCormick's critique of Pettit focuses on his constitutional and institutional proposals, and McCormick's reading of Machiavelli likewise focuses on his institutions for curbing elite influence amid inequality. While Pettit also draws on Machiavelli as a standard bearer for freedom as non-domination and an inspiration, among others, for his 'contestatory' institutions, McCormick's critique is that Pettit does not appeal to the elite constraining institutions Machiavelli thought necessary for securing freedom. McCormick argues that the institutions Pettit endorses – such as judiciaries, tribunals, commissions, ombudsmen, and local boards, through which 'the citizenry might contest, review, or amend decisions made by elected elites' – are limited and often reinforce elite influence (2011, 149). For example, McCormick critiques Pettit's ombudsmen by comparing them to the Roman tribunate, arguing that Pettit's ombudsmen are neither group-specific – not exclusively serving the many in resistance to elite influence – nor have any formal power (150). To resist the elites, McCormick argues that one must re-institutionalise class conflict, noting that Machiavelli 'recommends that republics build class division and class conflict into their constitutions' (11).

Those addressing the problem of socioeconomic inequality and freedom also interpret and respond to Pettit's and McCormick's works along constitutional-institutional lines (see Hamilton 2014; Vergara 2020). Even accounts that take the first approach described earlier, arguing that political reform must be accompanied by significant intervention in the economic sphere, still largely follow this institutionalist track. For example, David Casassas and Jurgen De Wispelaere argue that a republican political economy of democracy requires a 'constellation of political and economic institutions,' establishing an economic floor and ceiling and extending democratic control to economic governance (2016, 284). This institutional-constitutional character is also reflected more broadly in the republican literature – in interpretations of Pettit's work and in the debates on the relationship of republicanism to (liberal) constitutionalism, judicial review, and supranational institutions.[4] Pettit's republicanism is characterised as having an institutional and 'juridical' cast (Aitchison 2016) and as placing 'juridical and institutional relationships at its core' such that one can understand oneself to be free insofar as one can access 'instituted anti-powers' (Hoye 2017). Exceptions exist, in particular among those who respond to Pettit (Coffee 2015; Simpson 2017). But the thrust of the literature, especially pertaining to contemporary discussions of socioeconomic inequality and republican freedom, has focused on institutions. While Pettit's own work deals extensively with norms, I show in the last section how it fails to adequately address a crucial dimension of the classical republican concern with norms, and this reveals problems for institutionalist-constitutional accounts.

2 Modern Republicanism and Constitutional-Institutional Solutions to Inequality

Despite their differences, McCormick and Pettit remain within the framework of late eighteenth-century modern republicanism, which embodies the argument that proper constitutional and institutional design can curb the exercise of arbitrary power even amid socioeconomic conditions of inequality. This section turns to Harrington to show the early character of this institutionalist-constitutionalist republicanism that culminates with the Federalists and informs the works of McCormick and Pettit. Whereas Pettit sees Harrington as unproblematically aligned with neo-Roman republicanism, McCormick associates Harrington with aristocratic republicanism, classifying him as a thinker as 'ochlophobic' as Cicero (2018, 141). Harrington's thinking is more nuanced than either interpretation. This section argues that Harrington sees resource inequality as a political problem for republican freedom. With the Roman Republic as his example and Machiavelli also as his source, Harrington considers the elite's propensity for predation as a source of corruption and designs institutions to thwart their efforts to consolidate property. Despite inheriting much from Machiavelli, Harrington departs from him[5] with relevant implications: Harrington's concern about the threat of the elites prompts him to reject the very solutions McCormick draws from Machiavelli.

Harrington relies on 'orders' to solve what he sees as the two main sources of corruption in a commonwealth: the rule of private interest and an imbalance in property in relation to the form of political rule. In so doing, he sheds the classical republican reliance on norms and civic virtue. He instead relies on constitutional-institutional solutions for securing freedom, thereby laying the foundation for modern institutionalist republicanism. Indicative of this departure is that his commonwealth of Oceana sits outside the understanding of corruption shared by classical republicans.

The classical tradition is obsessed with corruption and the fragility of the republic. Its anxiety about the constant threat of political instability results fundamentally from the unstable combination of two elements: the ideal of rule in the common good and the natural inclination of human beings towards private interest. Because the human material of the republic is considered naturally self-interested, thinkers identify a range of conditions, institutional, cultural, and socioeconomic, that encourage cooperation and stave off factions and rising individualism. Naturalist metaphors are used by classical republican thinkers because they consider the republic as depending ultimately on a biological substance – its human material, a substance subject to hubris and graspingness, and ultimately to nature. Accordingly, corruption is expressed by the tradition's use of biological tropes to describe political change. Drawn from ideas of ancient Greek historians, the state is analogous to the individual, as both undergo a life cycle of birth, maturation, decline, and death. Because of this analogy there is a sense of the inevitability of decline. It is precisely the human material of the republic that makes it so: 'The body politic, like the human body, begins to die from the very moment of its birth and carries within itself the causes of its destruction,' Rousseau said (2011, 214). Harrington's Oceana, however, is an 'immortal commonwealth.' What explains this extraordinary departure on the matter of, as Pocock said, 'the republic's existence in time' (2003, vii)?

Harrington remains vexed by the republican problem of securing the rule of law when those who 'resolve be but men' (2008, 21). The problem remains 'unless you can show such orders of a government' that 'shall be able to constrain this or that creature.' He identifies the principle on which 'such orders may be established' that would 'give the upper hand in all cases unto common right or interest.' To illustrate, he draws from a 'common practice,' grounded in 'dividing and choosing' (22). Two girls must divide a cake, and although he refers to them as 'silly girls,' each acts rationally to support the principle he advances: if one were to both divide and choose, the outcome would be unjust according to the interests of at least one of the rational agents; whereas, if division and selection were divided, with each protecting her own private interest, the outcome would be fair – each receives an equal part. Harrington applies this principle to political order: if a senatorial body has the power to divide and choose, 'a commonwealth can never be equal.' The few will continuously cut larger pieces of property for themselves, as exemplified in Rome, if not simply 'keeping the whole cake' (24). This principle of dividing and choosing underpins separate political functions – the senate divides (or debates) and the assembly of the people chooses (or resolves), and such an order is thought to constrain all, especially the few.

This division of function is crucially situated in a political order undergirded by widespread and relatively equal property distribution. Framed by Harrington's 'doctrine of balance,' Oceana is an 'equal commonwealth' because it is 'equal both in the balance or foundation and in the superstructures, that is to say in her agrarian law [limiting and redistributing landed property] and in her rotation' (33). These superstructures preserve the foundational equal distribution of property and thus the distribution of political power, protecting against what Harrington sees as the elite's predisposition to consolidate property. The orders resting on equal property distribution allow the common interest of citizens in secure property to rule; yet, as in the cake example, individuals' private motivations to protect their own property work to block the capacity of others to gain disproportionately.[6] Grasping elites are constrained by Harrington's orders from making partiality towards themselves, to increase their holdings, into the rule that governs. Harrington even anticipates that those in power – in the senate *and* the assembly – might collude to undermine the agrarian law. He attempts to block this form of interest 'of the ruler or rulers' with his other superstructure provision, namely rotation in office, which ensures those in power cannot develop or act on a set of interests distinct from those who are ruled.

The 'orders' that secure freedom and prevent the consolidation of property do not depend on civic spiritedness or widespread habits or norms of civic virtue. Despite retaining the ideal of the citizen-soldier-farmer and the notion of property as the material basis for civic personality, these are but vestiges of classical republicanism. While their emergence is important to Harrington's larger theory of political change from the Gothic balance to the commonwealth, the disposition of actors to place the common good ahead of private interest is not integral to the internal stability of the commonwealth. Corruption and political stability have a structural rather than individual character. Rule 'not according unto the balance [of property is] violent,' and consolidation of property in the hands of a few would corrupt the commonwealth just as a 'building swaying from the foundation must fall' (12, 16). Trust not in men, but in orders, he said (64). Because Harrington's commonwealth does not ultimately rest on, in Machiavelli's terms, 'good customs' and 'good citizens,' it can be 'immortal' (71). Oceana is freed from the biological metaphor of inevitable decline; it is a commonwealth 'without flaw' (32).

This reliance on institutions rather than civic character echoes in the modern constitutional and institutional design of the eighteenth century.

Hume argues that one could make an individual, 'notwithstanding his insatiable avarice and ambition, co-operate to the public good' by configuring institutions with 'checks and controls' and a 'skillful division of power,' whereby separate interests 'concur with public [good]' (1987, 42–43). The Federalists address the concern about the exercise of arbitrary political power by factions through 'the extent and proper structure of the Union' (Madison 2008, 55). They proposed that institutions incorporate selfishness and sectionalism as part of the system of checks and balances. In casting the republic over a large territory that accommodated commercial society, they did not counter the political sociology of the small state anti-commercial republican thesis; they did not claim that the American republic could reproduce the political culture of such republics. Given the variety of interests of large territorial and commercial societies, marked by 'different and unequal faculties of acquiring property,' their clash-of-interests model of republican government considered '[t]he regulation of these various and interfering interests forms the principal task of modern legislation and involves the spirit of party and faction in the necessary and ordinary operations of government' (50). The extended, federal, commercial republic meant that 'society itself will be broken into so many parts, interests and classes of citizens,' and the 'great variety of interests, parties, and sects' would serve as checks on each other such that 'a coalition of a majority of the whole society could seldom take place on any other principles than those of justice and the general good' (259–260). Constitutional and institutional design facilitated the clash of factions so as to prevent a majority faction, in particular, from ruling in its interest amid socioeconomic inequality: '[e]very shilling with which they overburden the inferior number is a shilling saved to their own pockets' (51).

McCormick is critical of modern republican constitutionalism because it lacks a plebeian magistracy, yet he remains in its framework as his account focuses on institutions as solutions to securing political equality amid socioeconomic inequality. Despite the Federalists' 'disembodiment of government' from social class – with no plebeians *and* no nobility (Manin 1994, 33), McCormick is correct that the 'people' as a homogenous entity obscures differences between the elites and the many. His proposal, however, to institutionally facilitate a class-based clash of interests is consistent with the Federalists' model that prioritises institutional solutions in the name of facilitating clashes of interests (see also Hamilton 2014). Similarly, Camila Vergara incorporates 'plebeian power' into the constitutional-institutional framework to counter oligarchic domination, but like McCormick's account, this re-institutionalisation of class conflict – despite appealing to pre-modern constitutionalism – retains the sole institutionalist focus of modern republicanism (2020).

Moreover, although McCormick aligns with Harrington's focus on institutions as solutions, McCormick preserves a feature Harrington rejects, namely that the clash between the many and the few is an essential feature of the republic and necessary for liberty. For Harrington, inequality was a foundational source of corruption: the Roman Republic was 'crooked in her birth' because founder Romulus had 'planted the commonwealth upon two contrary interests or roots,' causing 'a perpetual feud and enmity between the senate and the people, even to the death' (2008, 160, 155). Harrington argues that the Roman tribunate failed to protect the people against the elites, so the very institution praised by McCormick was unable to thwart the increasing consolidation of property by the few to stave off domination and the collapse of the republic. In Harrington's view, when Rome's agrarian law became 'obsolete,' the few 'came to eat up the people,' and 'battening themselves in luxury' brought 'so mighty a commonwealth, so huge a glory, unto so deplorable an end' (162).

Harrington departs from Machiavelli not because he lacks concern about the elites, but because the solution – the tribunate – did not work. Harrington's commitment to an agrarian law also shows how far he is from McCormick's other aristocratic republican, Cicero, who viewed the Gracchi brothers' attempts to (re)introduce an agrarian law as deeply unjust and ignominious. McCormick acknowledges that the tribunate 'was a necessary, but ultimately insufficient institutional means of protecting Rome's liberty.' Yet, in corrupt conditions marked by a concentration of wealth, he argues for implementing class-based institutions that take inspiration from the tribunate, which even Machiavelli indicates 'could not definitively solve the problem of economic inequality' (2018, 66).

The Federalists, McCormick and Pettit inherit Harrington's emphasis on constitutional and institutional design as solutions for securing freedom without adopting Harrington's redistributive components. Harrington's account would support the contemporary approach that requires substantial resource pre-distribution and/or redistribution rather than managing the effects of inequality through institutionalising class conflict or through political and juridical channels of contestation.[7] At the same time, however, Harrington's work does not transmit the lesson from the tradition also passed on to him by Machiavelli: fundamentally, norms shape and sustain (or subvert) institutions, providing the context in which they function (or not).

3 Freedom's Norms, Political Equality, and the Free Citizen

Concern about the decline of democracy pervaded the first decades of the twenty-first century,[8] and the central tenet of classical republicanism became familiar to many. norms are essential supports for laws and institutions, and their erosion is destabilising. In the United States, democratic norms that constrain the transfer of power were violated, as lawmakers weakened the powers of a gubernatorial office after their party's member was not re-elected (Associated Press 2018), and those who lost fair elections in 2020 used rhetoric and futile lawsuits to undermine belief in the legitimacy of elections. The importance of norms for political stability, in particular for constraining elite behaviour, is captured by Levitsky and Ziblatt: 'Without robust norms, constitutional checks and balances do not serve as the bulwarks of democracy we imagine them to be' (2018, 7).

Political culture, composed of attitudes, beliefs, and values, helps form the ethos of a political community. The sources in republican thought from which the 'mixed constitution' tradition derives, from Aristotle and Polybius to Montesquieu, all offer accounts of institutions whose functioning and stability is intertwined with norms. The same is true of Cicero, Machiavelli, and Rousseau as representatives of aristocratic, democratic, and communitarian lines in the republican tradition identified by contemporary thinkers. These 'laws' of 'mores, customs, especially of opinion' are such that the 'success' of all else depends on them, Rousseau argues, adding: they are 'the true constitution of the state' (2011, III.1.191).[9]

McCormick provides an institutionalist reading of Machiavelli, yet Machiavelli's description of Roman institutions demonstrates that they were enmeshed in norms. Machiavelli attends to the emergence and role of the tribunate in the Roman Republic and a number of other institutions that channelled conflicts, from formal means to indict political figures to prosecuting calumnies (2003, I.7–8). But he shares a sense among classical republican thinkers of the limited power of institutions compared to political culture, arguing that 'free institutions' are unstable when imposed on a 'servile' people, and un-free institutions could not be long-imposed on a 'free people' (I.16–18; I.49).

Machiavelli warns that the functioning of institutions, including those McCormick highlights, depends on civic norms – and that institutions do not work in the ways intended in the absence of the right political culture. In praising the conflict between the few and the many as critical to securing freedom, Machiavelli argues that 'when the material is not corrupt, tumults and other troubles do no harm, but, when it is corrupt, good legislation is of no avail ... until such time as the material has become good' (I.17.159). He explains that while Roman institutions and procedures – such as the appointment of consular and other high-level offices or practice of citizen-initiated law – remained constant, as the moral and political culture changed, they no longer functioned as they had in the past or as intended. 'Institutions and laws made in the early days of a republic when men were good,' Machiavelli argues, 'no longer serve their purpose when men have become bad.' In a state of corruption, those who had more 'power' offered themselves for appointment whereas 'virtuous citizens' refrained. Similarly, rather than 'a tribune or any other citizen' proposing laws because of a desire 'to serve the public' – in time, 'only the powerful proposed laws, and this for the sake, not of their common liberties, but to augment their own power.' He observes, 'This institution was good so long as the citizens were good' (I.18.161–2). Likewise, the Roman censorship, he notes, functioned only when norms were already 'healthy' (I.49.230). Finally, Machiavelli's example of Cincinnatus demonstrates that the dictatorship in the Roman Republic depended on prevailing Roman attitudes and values (I.4.114; III.25.475–6). Rousseau likewise explains that in the 'beginning days of the republic,' frequent use was made of the dictatorship: 'there was no fear either that a dictator would abuse his authority or that he would try to hold on to it beyond his term of office.' It was 'toward the end of the republic,' when marked by moral decay that the same institution was occupied by Sulla and Caesar (2011, IV.6.240).

The few contemporary accounts that propose institutions to address the problem of freedom and economic inequality *and* appeal to norms routinely gesture towards the norms needed but fail to explain how they develop. Muldoon's socialist republicanism proposes a participatory democratic vision of a decentralised state with parliamentary institutions, worker-controlled workplaces, community-directed investment, and 'a political culture of solidarity and public-spiritedness' (2019, 49). He recognises that the 'problem could not be addressed by simply establishing new political and economic institutions,' and the solution requires 'a corresponding shift in the political culture of its citizens.' Yet, no explanation is provided for how to go from a political culture of 'egoism, individualism and competition' towards 'solidarity, public spiritedness and self-discipline,' or how to get 'social instincts in the place of egotistical ones.' He acknowledges that he does not outline a 'political strategy' on how this could be achieved (64–65). But the problem is deeper. There is scarce attention in this body of institutional-constitutional republican thought to transitions, including addressing how such institutions would function in the corrupt conditions they are meant to ameliorate.[10]

This transition problem glossed over by contemporary thinkers is related precisely to the tight interdependence in the republican tradition between institutions and norms for securing freedom as non-domination.[11] Rousseau speaks to the conundrum this creates: to establish the right laws and institutions, 'the effect would have to become the cause.' The 'social spirit' that is the 'work of the constitution would have to preside over the writing of the constitution itself. And men would be, prior to the advent of laws, what they ought to become by means of the laws' (2011, II.7.182). Contemporary accounts that do appeal to norms tend to propose laws and institutions that presuppose commitments and behaviours that those laws and institutions are supposed to create. The problem of this approach is captured powerfully by W.E.B. Du Bois' sense that a main failure of the Freedmen's Bureau was that it presupposed the 'good-will' it needed to foster (1994, 22).

Pettit's account inherits the interconnection between institutions and norms, as he argues that 'civic virtue' and 'civility' must support laws and institutions, otherwise they will be 'dead, mechanical devices.' He surmises: '[I]f the laws of the state are to be truly effective, those laws will have to work in synergy with norms' (1997, 241). Recently McCormick has attended to Machiavelli's description of the decay of 'mores, customs, and morality' in the decline of the Roman Republic. But McCormick argues that Machiavelli views its collapse as due less to the decay in civic norms and more 'to deeper structural causes,' namely 'socioeconomic causes' (2018, 46–47; see also, Maher 2016). Competing interpretations of Machiavelli's position exist, including that norms had to have been corrupted for certain socioeconomic factors to be at play such that elites could act through political means to, as McCormick says, 'amass ever greater wealth' (2018, 47). Nevertheless, even accepting McCormick's account, one cannot avoid the centrality of norms. On this Machiavelli is clear, Pettit says: 'there is no hope of enforcing a republic of laws in a society that is not already characterized by [good customs].' Pettit cites Machiavelli's advice that 'good morals' need laws and laws need 'good morals' (1997, 242; 2012, 84).

For Pettit, freedom requires both the establishment of an institutionalised system of influence and control ('contestatory' sites) and the presence of a 'contestatory citizenry' (2012, 260–261; 225–226). Such a citizenry is shaped and constrained by norms, which 'are regularities of behaviour in a society' and that 'as a matter of shared awareness most members conform to them, most expect others to approve of conformity or disapprove of non-conformity, and most are reinforced in this pattern of behaviour by that expectation' (128). In his account, citizens must be 'willing to live on equal terms with others' and committed to the value of equal access and influence (280, see also 242). These commitments help constitute the 'contestatory culture' that underpins Pettit's institutions (225). But how do these fundamental commitments on the part of citizens arise? What generates norms of equal access and influence that shape and constrain their political behaviour, including the behaviour of those who could dominate because of their resources?

On the one hand, Pettit says that contestatory institutions will themselves generate norms among the citizenry of 'equally accessible influence' or 'equal respect in collective decision-making.' There are 'norms we might expect to develop,' he argues, in a society *with a system of popular influence* that is designed to be individualised, unconditioned and efficacious' (emphasis added, 2012, 262, 264). Such norms will 'emerge and crystalize at each site where contestation is brought or heard, answered or adjudicated,' with 'sites of opposition and contestation envisaged in the system of influence,' being 'electoral campaigns and debates, judicial and cognate hearings, parliamentary discussions, exchanges between branches of government, public justifications of policy ' (261). It is not obvious, however, that Pettit's contestatory institutions will generate the necessary norms. His account largely tracks liberal constitutionalism (Bellamy 2007; Celikates 2013), and liberal constitutionalist institutions have not generated norms grounded on a widespread commitment to equality of access and influence.

On the other hand, Pettit's institutions require that certain norms and commitments exist prior to the institutions designed to foster them. For the institutions and laws associated with his conception of republican democracy and social justice to be implemented in a non-arbitrary manner, one must assume that the commitment to equal access and influence is already widespread. Citizens must see the implementation of these institutions as consistent with a commitment they already collectively share. In some cases, it seems citizens' commitment to equal access and influence gives rise to those very institutions: 'A dispensation for ensuring a suitable degree of popular influence has to assume institutional form at some point,' and as such institutions 'emerge and stabilize, they are bound to gain acceptance and to license associated norms of argument' (2012, 263).

Additionally, for Pettit's contestatory channels to function as intended – to facilitate the equal democratic control necessary for freedom – contestation itself must already be marked by the right kind of character. Citizens must have already internalised a commitment to equal access and influence; for as they engage, they must give reasons that appeal to the shared value of living on equal terms and justify their contestation by reference to the shared value of equal access and influence, expecting that others will do likewise (2012, 262). A 'contestatory culture' is marked by 'a civic vigilance' that 'appeals to a public standard like the idea of equal influence' (225, 227). That 'contestatory spirit' he says, 'counts as a form of civic virtue' and 'consists in a willingness to challenge public proposals and policies' when they do not treat 'all members as equals' (228). Such commitment must be assumed by Pettit's contestatory institutions because mere contestation – in the absence of a shift in norms and attitudes towards equal access and influence – is unlikely to generate those very norms and regularities of behaviour to facilitate the equal control necessary for non-arbitrary law. Despite trying to distance his conception from the classical notion of a virtuous citizen, Pettit's contestatory citizen must be disposed to appeal to shared values in political deliberation and action and be committed to 'a regime of equally shared influence' (262). McCormick argues that Pettit's institutional design aligns with the Federalists' (2011), and yet Pettit's conception of contestation is more demanding than the behaviour assumed in their clash-of-interests model.

This argument – that the functioning of Pettit's contestatory institutions requires the pre-existence of norms that constrain citizens' engagement – shares commonalities with Bagg's criticism of Vergara's plebeian assemblies. Bagg argues that for plebeian institutions to function as oligarchical constraints, they must presume a shared class-based identity or solidarity that does not yet exist. 'Class-based solidarity and mass-elite tension must be created rather than presumed' (2022, 11). McCormick suggests that once in place, class-based institutions would 'raise the class consciousness of common citizens' to reinforce those institutions (2011, 16). It is unclear in the absence of existing or explicit class-based identity or conflict, however, what constituency implements class-based constitutional change, or if implemented, that plebeian institutions would function as intended in the absence of the identity and ideology they are meant to eventually create.[12] Similarly, Lawrence Hamilton says, 'given the right climate – the political will, ideology, and institutional configuration,' political representatives could regulate the economy, exercising 'control' over economic policy and its implementation (2014, 190–191). But, how is this 'right climate' generated?

Those using a republican notion of freedom to restructure political and economic institutions must engage with features of political culture, including the extent to which contrary norms exist encouraging the socioeconomic inequality their proposals are meant to address. For example, as Phil Parvin (2022) argues, the power of lobbyists, who largely reflect elite interests, resides in their 'capture' of institutions *and* 'background norms and ideas implicit in the political culture' of today's democracies. In short, the problem of ensuring non-domination amid inequality is also cultural (e.g., Thatcherism), not merely that 'existing political institutions have allowed the shift towards oligarchy' (White 2019, 257). This harks to a long-standing tension in the republican tradition between virtue and commerce (Hont and Ignatieff 1983), understood as representing competing sets of values, attitudes, motivations, and incentives. Our contemporary context is marked by a key tension: republican democracy requires political power be distributed equally, while a capitalist economy distributes property and income unequally. This context is also one of contrasting cultures of capitalism and political equality: an ethos of competition, profit, and maximisation of self-interest versus an ethos of cooperation, public goods, and a shared commitment to equal access and influence.

Thinkers cannot simply assume the norms that their proposed institutions need to function or downplay (or ignore) whether such institutions would be insulated from continued or new forms of elite capture. Socioeconomic elites neither act as if they are constrained by a commitment to equal influence nor are penalised for it. There are norms that exist that prevent people from jumping a queue, but no norms of political equality that discouraged a billionaire in 2020 from running for the

U.S. presidency by spending $57 million of his personal money in his campaign's first weeks and nearly $1 billion in just over three months. Moreover, a basic commitment to ensure equality of access and influence through voting does not exist. U.S. lawmakers from the Republican Party have enacted or proposed hundreds of new election restrictions, 'potentially amount[ing] to the most sweeping contraction of ballot access in the United States since the end of Reconstruction' (Gardner 2021). This decay is not solely attributable to inequality between elites and the many, but to elite infighting and partisanship. Yet, it impacts the viability of non-domination inspired institutional proposals.

Elite accountability is a core issue for democratic governance, and proposals offering political and economic institutions aimed at reducing the power differentials associated with inequalities in income and wealth are merited. The argument in this chapter is analogous to Casassas and De Wispelaere's that 'an economic floor really only promotes republican freedom in conjunction with a wider set of public policies' (2016, 289): namely, such policies and institutions really only promote republican freedom and reduce the imbalance in power in conjunction with a wider civic culture that embraces the ideas and values motivating those policies and institutions.

Republican thought might be well-served in thinking about norm generation by engaging with political sociology, cultural studies, and anthropology to identify practices conducive for building egalitarian political norms. Moreover, as the republican literature has taken a constitutional-institutional turn, it has focused on the application of non-domination to the nation-state, supra-national institutions and the global order. Work remains to be done below nation-states and supra-national institutions, even when these do not fully reflect freedom. As Melvin Rogers (2020) has shown, African American thinkers in the nineteenth century advocated for a civic virtue of racial solidarity in the absence of constitutional protections to secure freedom. They viewed freedom as requiring not only reform of law and institutions but also a transformation in public sentiment and the system of cultural value. To help produce a civic culture involving norms of equal access and influence, engaging with the grounded practices of citizens – which dovetails with Tocqueville's thought – could be fruitful.

Tocqueville argues that institutions have limitations and that freedom depends on the development of certain civic habits and norms: 'What is more powerless than institutions, when ideas and mores do not nourish them all!' (2002, 340). In *Democracy in America*, he explains, 'One must seek the causes of the mildness of government in circumstances and mores rather than in the laws' (2000, 242). Alexander Jech argues that 'the great aim of democratic statecraft' for Tocqueville was to provide conditions that would allow citizens to practice what Tocqueville calls, 'the art of being free' (2017, 10). States undermine the conditions necessary for developing a 'democratic character' when 'the most important affairs' do not belong to them, being 'brought under the authority of some specially appointed group within society' (18). By contrast, a 'democratic spirit' is fostered by entrusting citizens with matters of importance and through combined action, they come to regard themselves as responsible for such action (29). Jech's account underscores critiques of the participatory freedom deficit in Pettit's account (Urbinati 2012). Pettit is not sensitive to 'the importance of the objects lying within the citizen's domain,' Jech argues. 'It is not enough to expand the range of choices available to someone, if the most important matters remain up to someone else, even if these matters are decided upon in a non-dominating fashion' (2017, 32).

Republican thought ought to embrace a form of localism that embodies Tocqueville's ideal of the free citizen – conceiving, initiating and joining in combined action on important rather than residual affairs. The local is not Tocqueville's quaint New England town or merely a political ward of a larger state. 'For generations, the locus and nature of power seemed settled, reflecting the vertical lines of political authority,' as Bruce Katz and Jeremy Nowak explain, '[n]ational and state government sat at the apex, writing laws, promulgating rules, distributing resources, and running the country,' whereas localities 'resided at the bottom, acting as administrative arms of higher levels of government more than as agents in charge of their own future.' This picture no longer exists, they argue, as the 'location of power is shifting as a result of profound demographic, economic and social forces' (2017, 1). Localities are 'generators and recipients of an unprecedented flow of goods, people, capital and ideas across national and continental borders, all facilitated by new ubiquitous technologies' (40). Localism is not reducible to local government but refers to networks of civic, private, and public actors. The nature of this power is horizontal rather than vertical, appealing to the ways citizens co-govern themselves (224). Community wealth building and 'new localism' involve 'reimagining power' in these ways; relatedly, Yara Al Salman's (2022) notion of 'group ownership,' developing common property regimes with democratic control, suggests how the organisation of property could allow for combined action while affirming equal access and influence.

These approaches offer more frequent and deeper opportunities for participation in problem-solving, decision-making, and coordinated action than 'vigilant' moments of contestation. The stakes in dealing with economic, social, and environmental challenges are no less than in national politics, but in localities, the barriers to entry are lower and opportunities for economic inclusion and regular engagement of diverse constituencies are higher. Given this, Vergara's local plebeian institutions are more compelling for possibly generating norms of equal access and influence among citizens than others that focus on large-scale institutions. Yet, the opportunities for meaningful participation remain infrequent, narrowly political, and are part of an institutionalised structure of vertical power – the concerns and energies of the many are channelled up to the nation-state to express a popular will, not necessarily into the immediacy of those communities. The sketch of republican localism in this section connects with White's notion of 'prefigurative republican politics as political action itself that embodies republican democratic values in its internal practices.' Yet it would cast the effort involving 'networked horizontalism' not just as a means to exert pressure towards institutional and constitutional change but also as a set of practices that are norm generating (2019, 253).

The local presents opportunities for practices that could foster commitments to political equality out of the lived experience of citizens. In Charlottesville, Virginia, the home of Thomas Jefferson's university and of white supremacist violence in 2017, local actors and community stakeholders are challenging Lost Cause mythology, reclaiming built environments and democratising memory and public spaces. In so doing, they are creating and affirming an inclusive civic identity. In this case, the local is the site of challenge to norms of inequality and the development of a culture of equal access and influence. Institutions are neither the only reason for nor the only solution to discrepancies in political power due to socioeconomic inequality. Proposals for institutional and constitutional reform to remediate the imbalance cannot robustly do so without a political culture that also demands it.

Notes

1 Bryan (2021) argues that economic crises endemic to capitalism suggest its incompatibility with non-domination.
2 In the 1990s and early 2000s republican contributions regularly invoked civic virtue, see Viroli (2002), Maynor (2003), Pettit (1997), and Skinner (1993). See Kimpell (2015) for a critique of these approaches to political order, freedom, and virtue.
3 See Balot and Trochimchuk (2012) for a critique of McCormick's interpretation of the 'democratic' nature and sanguine reading of the people in Machiavelli's thought.
4 See Nadeau (2012), Aitchison (2016), Hoye (2017), Daily (2019), Watkins (2015), Lazar (2019), Celikates (2013), Bellamy (2007, 2019), and Vergara (2020).
5 See Campos Boralevi (2011).
6 Pocock calls this 'Harrington's method of mechanizing virtue.' Harrington draws on Venice for this insight: 'men [were] fed into processes which made their behavior ... distinterested whether they so intended it or not' (2003, 393–394).
7 Another division between class-based versus non-class-based accounts is possible, in which Harrington would align with Rousseau. Neither McCormick (2018) nor Pettit, however, find Rousseau helpful to their projects.
8 See Freedom House (2021).

9 See also Dahl (1956, 143).
10 An exception is White (2019, 248).
11 See also Kimpell (2009).
12 Maher claims Machiavelli argues that civic virtue emerges from social conflict facilitated by class-based institutions. But the argument rests on an unusual notion of civic virtue, namely, 'self-interested' motives can underpin virtuous political activity (2016, 1011), insofar as self- or class-interest is expressed through political procedures rather than patronage systems. It is unclear how the account differs from the Federalists' clash-of-interests model and relatedly why a 'class-based form of social discord' develops virtue, whereas other self-interested or factional discord, likewise expressed through political procedures, would not.

References

Aitchison, Guy. 2016. "Three Models of Republican Rights, Juridical, Parliamentary and Populist." *Political Studies* 65(2): 339–355.
Al Salman, Yara. 2022. "Independence in the Commons: How Group Ownership Realises Basic Non-Domination." In *Wealth and Power: Philosophical Perspectives*, edited by Michael Bennett, Huub Brouwer, and Rutger Claassen. London: Routledge.
Associated Press. 2018. "Wisconsin Republicans Approve Bill to Weaken Incoming Democratic Governor." *The Guardian*, December 5, 2018.
Bagg, Samuel. 2022. "Do We Need an Anti-oligarchic Constitution?" *European Journal of Political Theory* 21(2): 399–411.
Balot, Ryan, and Stephen Trochimchuk. 2012. "The Many and the Few: On Machiavelli's 'Democratic Moment.'" *The Review of Politics* 74: 559–588.
Bellamy, Richard. 2007. *Political Constitutionalism: A Republican Defense of the Constitutionality of Democracy*. Cambridge: Cambridge University Press.
———. 2019. *A Republican Europe of States*. Cambridge: Cambridge University Press.
Bryan, Alexander. 2021. "The Dominating Effects of Economic Crisis." *Critical Review of International Social and Political Philosophy* 24(6): 884–908.
Bulmer, Elliot, and Stuart White. 2022. "Constitutions Against Oligarchy." In *Wealth and Power: Philosophical Perspectives*, edited by Michael Bennett, Huub Brouwer, and Rutger Claassen. London: Routledge.
Campos Boralevi, Lea. 2011. "James Harrington's 'Machiavellian' anti-Machiavellism." *History of European Ideas* 37(2): 113–119.
Casassas, David, and Jurgen De Wispelaere. 2016. "Republicanism and the Political Economy of Democracy." *European Journal of Social Theory* 19(2): 283–300.
Celikates, Robin. 2013. "Freedom as Non-Arbitrariness or as Democratic Self-Rule? A Critique of Contemporary Republicanism." In *To Be Unfree: Republicanism and Unfreedom in History, Literature, and Philosophy*, edited by Christian Dahl and Tue Anderson Nexo, 37–54. Bielefeld: Transcript Verlag.
Coffee, Alan M.S.J. 2015. "Two Spheres of Domination: Republican Theory, Social Norms and the Insufficiency of Negative Freedom." *Contemporary Political Theory* 14: 45–62.
Dahl, Robert. 1956. *Preface to Democratic Theory*. Chicago, IL: University of Chicago Press.

Daily, Eoin. 2019. "Republicanising Rights? Proportionality, Justification and Non-domination." In *Constitutionalism Justified, Rainer Frost in Discourse*, edited by Ester Herlin-Karnell and Mattias Klatt, 198–216. Oxford: Oxford University Press.
Du Bois, W.E.B. 1994. *The Souls of Black Folk*. New York, NY: Dover Publications.
Editorial Board. December 2020. "The Martini Lunch Tax Code." *The Wall Street Journal*, December 21, 2020. https://www.wsj.com/articles/the-martini-lunch-tax-code-11608594584.
Federal Reserve. 2021. "Distribution of Household Wealth in the U.S. since 1989." https://www.federalreserve.gov/releases/z1/dataviz/dfa/distribute/chart/#range:2005.3,2020.3;quarter:124;series:Corporate%20equities%20and%20mutual%20fund%20shares;demographic:networth;population:1,3;units:levels.
Freedom House. 2021. "Freedom in the World 2021: Democracy Under Siege." https://freedomhouse.org/report/freedom-world/2021/democracy-under-siege.
Gardner, Amy, et al. 2021 "How GOP-backed Voting Measures Could Create Hurdles for Tens of Millions of Voters." *The Washington Post*, March 11, 2021. https://www.washingtonpost.com/politics/interactive/2021/voting-restrictions-republicans-states/?utm_campaign=wp_main&utm_source=twitter&utm_medium=social.
Gourevitch, Alex. 2013. "Labor Republicanism and the Transformation of Work." *Political Theory* 41(4): 591–617.
Hamilton, Lawrence. 2014. *Freedom Is Power: Liberty Through Political Representation*. Cambridge: Cambridge University Press.
Harrington, James. 2008. *The Commonwealth of Oceana and a System of Politics*, edited by J.G.A. Pocock. Cambridge: Cambridge University Press.
Hohmann, James. 2020. "A Phone Call with Trump." *The Washington Post*, March 31, 2020. https://www.washingtonpost.com/news/powerpost/paloma/daily-202/2020/03/31/daily-202-a-phone-call-with-trump-can-open-doors-for-executives-celebrities-and-others-with-coronavirus-asks/5e82c11988e0fa101a7566f3/.
Hont, Istvan, and Michael Ignatieff, eds. 1983. *Wealth and Virtue: The Shaping of Political Economy in the Scottish Enlightenment*. Cambridge: Cambridge University Press.
Hoye, J. Matthew. 2017. "Neo-Republicanism, Old Imperialism, and Migration Ethics." *Constellations* 24(2): 154–166.
Hume, David. 1987. "Of the Independency of Parliament." In *Essays Moral, Political and Literary*, edited by Eugene Miller, 42–46. Indianapolis, IN: Liberty Fund.
Jech, Alexander. 2017. "What Has Athens to Do with Rome? Tocqueville and the New Republicanism." *American Political Thought* 6(4): 550–573.
Katz, Bruce, and Jeremy Nowak. 2017. *The New Localism: How Cities Can Thrive in the Age of Populism*. Washington, DC: Brookings Press.
Kimpell, Jessica. 2009. "Neo-Republicanism: Machiavelli's Solutions for Tocqueville's Republic." *European Political Science Review* 1(3): 375–400.
———. 2015. "Republican Civic Virtue, Enlightened Self-Interest and Tocqueville." *European Journal of Political Theory* 14(3): 345–367.
Lazar, Orlando. 2019. "A Republic of Rules: Procedural Arbitrariness and Total Institutions." *Critical Review of International Social and Political Philosophy* 22(6): 681–702.
Levitsky, Steven, and Daniel Ziblatt. 2018. *How Democracies Die*. New York, NY: Crown.

Lynch, David. 2019. "Trump Says He Might Veto Legislation." *The Washington Post*, November 22, 2019. https://www.washingtonpost.com/business/2019/11/22/trump-says-he-might-veto-legislation-that-aims-protect-human-rights-hong-kong-because-bill-would-impact-china-trade-talks/.

Machiavelli. 2003. *The Discourses*, edited by B. Crick. London: Penguin.

Madison, Hamilton, and John Jay. 2008. *The Federalist Papers*, edited by Lawrence Goldman. Oxford: Oxford University Press.

Maher, Amanda. 2016. "What Skinner Misses about Machiavelli's Freedom: Inequality, Corruption, and the Institutional Origins of Civic Virtue." *Journal of Politics* 78(4): 1003–1015.

Manin, Bernard. 1994. "Checks, Balances and Boundaries: The Separation of Powers in the Constitutional Debate of 1787." *The Invention of the Modern Republic*, edited by Biancamaria Fontana, 27–62. Cambridge: Cambridge University Press.

Maynor, John. 2003. *Republicanism in the Modern World*. Cambridge: Polity Press.

McCormick, John. 2011. *Machiavellian Democracy*. Cambridge: Cambridge University Press.

———. 2018. *Reading Machiavelli: Scandalous Books, Suspect Engagements, and the Virtue of Populist Politics*. Princeton, NJ: Princeton University Press.

Muldoon, James. 2019. "A Socialist Republican Theory of Freedom and Government." *European Journal of Political Theory* (May 2019).

Nadeau, Christian. 2012. "Republicanism." In *Routledge Companion to Social and Political Philosophy*, 254–265. New York, NY: Routledge.

Parvin, Phil. 2022. "Hidden in Plain Sight: How Lobby Organisations Undermine Democracy." In *Wealth and Power: Philosophical Perspectives*, edited by Michael Bennett, Huub Brouwer, and Rutger Claassen. London: Routledge.

Pettit, Philip. 1997. *Republicanism: A Theory of Freedom and Government*. Oxford: Oxford University Press.

Pettit, Philip. 2012. *On the People's Terms: A Republican Theory and Model of Democracy*. Cambridge: Cambridge University Press.

Pew Research Center. January 2020. Report: "Trends in U.S. Income and Wealth." https://www.pewresearch.org/social-trends/2020/01/09/trends-in-income-and-wealth-inequality/.

Pocock, J.G.A. 2003. *The Machiavellian Moment: Florentine Political Thought and the Atlantic Republican Tradition*. Princeton, NJ: Princeton University Press.

Rogers, Melvin. 2020. "Race, Domination, and Republicanism." In *Difference without Domination*, edited by Danielle Allen and Rohini Somanathan, 59–92. Chicago, IL: University of Chicago Press.

Rousseau. 2011. "On the Social Contract." In *The Basic Political Writings*, edited by Donald A. Cress. Indianapolis, IN: Hackett Publishing.

Simpson, Thomas W. 2017. "The Impossibility of Republican Freedom." *Philosophy & Public Affairs* 45(1): 27–53.

Skinner, Quentin. 1993. "The Republican Ideal of Political Liberty." *Machiavelli and Republicanism*, edited by Gisela Bock, Quentin Skinner and Maurizio Viroli, 293–309. Cambridge: Cambridge University Press.

Tocqueville. 2000. *Democracy in America*, edited by H. C. Mansfield and Delba Winthrop. Chicago, IL: University of Chicago Press.

———. 2002. "To Beaumont, on Liberty and Despotism." *The Tocqueville Reader: A Life in Letters and Politics*, edited by Olivier Zunz and Alan S. Kahan, 339–341. Oxford: Wiley-Blackwell.

Urbinati, Nadia. 2012. "Competing for Liberty: The Republican Critique of Democracy." *American Political Science Review* 106(3): 607–621.

Vergara, Camila. 2020. *Systemic Corruption: Constitutional Ideas for an Anti-Oligarchic Republic*. Princeton, NJ: Princeton University Press.

Viroli, Maurizio. 2002. *Republicanism*. New York, NY: Hill and Wang.

Watkins, David. 2015. "Institutionalizing Freedom as Nondomination: Democracy and the Role of the State." *Polity* 47(4): 508–534.

White, Stuart. 2011. "The Republican Critique of Capitalism." *Critical Review of International Social and Political Philosophy* 14(5): 561–579.

———. 2019. "Horizontalism, Public Assembly, and Republican Politics." In *Republicanism and the Future of Democracy*, edited by Yiftah Elazar and Genevieve Rousseliere, 247–263. Cambridge: Cambridge University Press.

3 Two Liberal Egalitarian Perspectives on Wealth and Power

Richard Arneson

In the first quarter of 2021, the top 1% of households in the United States had 32.1% of the nation's wealth, while the bottom 50% held 2.0%. Is this a problem? An increasing chorus of social scientists finds that the affluent have more influence on choice of laws and public policies than the nonaffluent, and especially that the extremely rich have greatly disproportionate impact on the content of the laws and public policies we all are coerced to obey (Gilens 2012; Gilens and Page 2014; Bartels 2016). The United States is in the vanguard of this tendency, but the same trend is discernible across contemporary wealthy democracies.

This chapter sketches how liberal egalitarian doctrines of social justice respond to this issue. Let's say this is the problem of wealth and power. I begin by dividing liberal egalitarianism into two schools, welfarist and relational. Section 2 gives the welfarist egalitarian perspective, while Section 3 provides the relational egalitarian perspective. The latter is somewhat more complicated, and Section 4 analyses a crucial notion in this approach: equal opportunity for political influence (EOPI). Section 5 contrasts the implications of the two approaches.

1 Background

1.1 Liberal Egalitarianism

The division that structures the discussion in this chapter is between what we can label for convenience as *relational egalitarians* and *welfarist egalitarians*. Relational egalitarianism (sometimes called 'democratic egalitarianism') is here understood as an approach that takes protecting the equal basic liberties to be the fundamental liberal principle that takes priority over other justice values. It includes the right to an equal democratic say among these basic liberties. Welfarist egalitarianism refers to an approach that takes equally meeting the needs of all members of society (or in other words increasing and equalising individual welfare (well-being)) to be what matters morally for its own sake. It upholds the basic liberties including the right to an equal democratic

DOI: 10.4324/9781003173632-4

say as instrumentally necessary to promoting well-being fairly (equally) distributed.

For the welfarist egalitarian, what in itself makes a society more or less just is entirely the degree to which its arrangements bring about good quality lives for its members and spread out that good evenly across persons. For the relational egalitarian, these facts about individual welfare are not in themselves even a part of what makes a society just or unjust. From this perspective, achieving justice consists in building a democratic society controlled equally by all its citizens, a society of free persons cooperating together without hierarchy, without excessive inequalities in political and economic power and social status, on a footing of equal basic liberty. In other words, what matters for justice is establishing institutions and practices that induce people to relate as equals, as equally functioning members of democratic society. Equal liberty for all is the rock-bottom value, and it is understood as incompatible with social hierarchy. The welfarist egalitarian is not opposed to hierarchy per se, rather to bad hierarchy, understood as the kind that results in avoidably bad lives for people and maldistribution of what good there is.

From each of these two versions of liberal egalitarianism there arises a sharp critique of current wealth inequality's impact on the functioning of democracy. The critiques differ. This chapter explores the differences between these approaches to what each of them will identify as a big problem. Besides clarifying and contrasting the welfarist egalitarian and relational egalitarian reasons for opposing the dominating influence of wealth on democratic politics, this essay uses the contrast to comment on the plausibility of these two versions of liberal egalitarianism. On this issue I lean towards welfarist egalitarianism, but the main task is to highlight where they stand, and to glean from both what insights they can deliver regarding the stance we ought to take towards the wealth and power issue. The question is how strongly we ought to be committed to building and sustaining a democratic political order, and to what sort of democratic political order we should be committed.

1.2 Democratic Decision-Making

Political decisions might be reached in ways that are more or less democratic, and it may be helpful here to give a partial characterisation of democracy. The more these features obtain, the more democratic the process. Each feature can vary by degree. (1) All adult members of society have a vote that counts the same as all others in majority rule elections that determine the content of laws and other public policies. (2) Elections take place against a backdrop of freedom of speech and freedom of political association. (3) When the majority will of voters changes, the majority can immediately bring about a corresponding shift in law or public policy. (Imagine a regime in which if and only if the will of the majority on some issue stays constant for 50 years, or 100, the will of the majority is then instituted. This regime would not be a democracy.) (4) There are no political constraints on the types or character of issues that are within the scope of majority will decision-making. (5) All adult members of society have EOPI.

These five features are not a full characterisation of democracy. That would also specify rules for agenda setting appropriate for democracy and specify what groups of people should constitute a single society within which the majority rules (Goodin 2007).

Also, not all features of this partial characterisation are of equal importance, if democracy is to be prized for its place in a non-hierarchy ethic, as the relational egalitarian affirms. From that standpoint, (1), (2), and (5) are the central planks.

1.3 The Problem of Wealth and Power, and Two Remedies

Inequalities in citizens' wealth holdings are thought to bring about inequalities in citizens' opportunity to influence their government's political decision-making. This might come about in several ways.

Inequality of wealth can bring about greater political influence for the rich. This can occur via several mechanisms, described at length in some of the other chapters in this volume. (1) Campaigns for elected public office as now structured require candidates to raise large sums of money, and large contributors to political campaigns can engage in implicit quid pro quo bargaining. As is said, who pays the piper calls the tune (Destri 2022). (2) Public officials including legislators who cater to wealthy special interests while in office find the door open to lucrative careers working for those special interest enterprises after their term of office ends (Kogelmann 2022; Parvin 2022). (3) The wealthy may belong to social networks more likely to include elected officials and other politically influential agents compared to the networks of the less wealthy, and informal interaction among those in one's social network may provide opportunities for influence (Parvin 2022). (4) When issues are debated in a legislature, interested parties may lobby the elected officials urging that any policy changes enacted be congenial to their special interests, and the wealthy can use their wealth to organise these lobbying efforts (Kogelmann 2022; Parvin 2022). (5) The wealthy can use their wealth to sponsor public discourse that favours their policy views. In this way they help shape the background public opinion that in turn affects the calculations of legislators about what laws and policies to support (Kimpell Johnson 2022; Parvin 2022). (6) An indirect influence occurs when it is believed that wealthy owners of productive resources will withdraw these resources from jurisdictions that accord them unfavourable treatment. For example, an increase in taxes on corporations may spur some corporations to relocate to a place where corporate tax rates are lower

(Shoikedbrod 2022).[1] (7) Wealth can help wealthy individuals who seek to be politically well informed succeed in this aim more than the non-wealthy with similar aims; plausibly, being informed enhances one's opportunity for political influence (Kogelmann 2022).

If morality requires us to reduce or extinguish unequal opportunity for political influence, there are two broad strategies available: *insulate* and *eliminate*. The insulation strategy tolerates inequality of wealth but pursues ways of keeping possession of greater than average wealth from conferring above-average opportunity for political influence. A well-known example is campaign finance reform (Ackerman and Ayres 2002). The elimination strategy pursues ways of reducing power concentrations in the private sphere (Bennett, Brouwer, and Claassen 2022). The most obvious way of doing this is to compress the distribution of wealth across individual citizens through redistribution. Insulation and elimination might be pursued in tandem, or only one might be embraced.

2 The Welfarist Egalitarian Perspective on Wealth and Power

The welfarist egalitarian holds that justice requires boosting the well-being of all persons who shall ever live, while giving some priority to achieving gains for those who would otherwise be very badly off, or worse off than others. There's an intramural disagreement here. Prioritarians hold that it is morally more valuable to achieve a welfare gain for a person the worse-off in absolute terms she would otherwise be over the course of her life, regardless of how her condition compares to that of others (Parfit 1995; Adler 2012). Egalitarians by contrast hold that how well off one person is compared to others matters for its own sake, and that justice requires increasing the total of people's well-being and also equalising people's well-being (Temkin 1993; Otsuka and Voorhoeve 2018). The intramural dispute between upholding equality or priority is nontrivial (Adler and Holtug 2019), but the two views share enough in common so that grouping them together makes sense for purposes of clarifying welfarist and relational egalitarianism.

Welfarist egalitarianism could be upheld as one among several social justice values. Here we interpret this doctrine as the sole fundamental justice value, or at least as ruling the roost, taking priority over any other such values there might be. On such a view, political and social arrangements should be set so that over the long run they bring about the greatest reachable equality/priority-adjusted total sum of individual well-being.

The alert reader might well surmise that the implications of welfarist egalitarianism regarding wealth and power will be hopelessly indeterminate in the absence of some understanding of what individual welfare really is. The issue can be restated: what in itself makes a person's life go better for her rather than worse? Or in still other words, what is it a person seeks for its own sake, insofar as she is being rationally prudent?

A first response is that it is not really the case that welfarist egalitarianism has no implications for wealth and power public policy without specifying some particular conception of welfare. In some circumstances, on any non-crazy conception of welfare, steps to prevent wealth inequality from having an impact on the political process, whether by an insulation or an elimination strategy, will clearly be required by welfarist egalitarian justice. In other circumstances, the reverse will be clearly be true.

What rises and falls with the conception of well-being that completes the welfarist ideal? Perhaps the crucial divide is between the idea that welfare consists in gaining objectively valuable goods and the view that it is subjective, bottoming out in people's desires. For the purposes of the wealth and power issue, one consideration is that on the former view, beyond some modest point, wealth increases are as likely to distract one from making welfare enhancing choices as boost one's prospects. With a small income, Arneson drinks beer and lives well, and with a large income, he uses cocaine and lives less well, or comes vastly to overvalue the improvement in his welfare that a fancy yacht will afford him, compared to a canoe. This amplifies the tilt of welfarist egalitarianism towards channelling wealth towards those who have little. And this dampens the likelihood that more political power in the hands of the rich will bring about justice gains. The contrast here is with desire fulfilment views.

Abstracting from the contrasts between egalitarianism and prioritarianism and between objective list and desire-fulfilment accounts of welfare, we can set out the basic response of welfarist egalitarianism to the wealth and power issue. This social justice doctrine seeks to reduce the impact of unequal wealth holdings on political decision-making when, only when, and to the degree that doing so is part of the best strategy for maximising equality-weighted welfare summed across persons over the long run. Social justice is here conceived mainly as the standard for assessing institutions and social practices as they combine to affect people's welfare prospects.

The causal linkages that determine what welfarist egalitarianism implies for wealth and power in given circumstances are complex. Reducing the impact of wealth inequality on the political process might enhance its democratic character, and thereby the good functioning of democracy, and thereby generate greater well-being more fairly distributed. But the opposite might be the case in some circumstances: wealth inequality can be a countervailing force against majority tyranny, the ability of elected officials to entrench their power and subvert democracy, or the entrenched power of officials in state bureaucracies to manipulate the political process against democratically elected officials and the will of the majority (see Kogelmann 2022). And when the impact of wealth on political power enhances democracy, the upshot might be good or bad from the welfarist egalitarian perspective. The will of the democratic majority might be to redistribute advantages from worse-off citizens to a majority coalition of better offs. The will of the democratic majority might be to enact policies that are good for growth and prosperity in the short term but prosperity-dampening in the long run, in a complex world of climate change and conflicts over access to water, food, and habitable shelter (Cowen 2018). Alternatively, the will of the majority might over the long haul tend towards prosperity and sensible policies that tame and complement prosperity, boosting the actual quality of people's lives and tilting towards improving the lives of those who would otherwise be badly-off and worse-off.

While the relationship between welfarist egalitarianism and wealth and power is ultimately contingent, three examples can help to further illustrate the likely tilt of welfare egalitarianism when it comes to wealth and power in contemporary liberal democracies.

1. Welfarist egalitarianism tends to favour egalitarian redistribution of wealth and income and related pro-poor policies, and insofar as the influence of the rich and even more the super-rich on politics puts the brakes on instituting such policies, welfarist egalitarianism stoutly supports squashing the (here) excessive political influence of the rich and super rich.
2. The more it is the case that a stable majority of voters in a democracy is disposed to solidarity with all members of society and is disinclined to see itself as 'us' versus a 'them' composed of other members of society whose welfare interests somehow count for less, welfarist egalitarianism favours measures that facilitate control of political decision-making by majority rule.
3. Unequal wealth's impact on the political process may extend beyond affecting the quality of political decision-making and of the laws and other public policies. The outsize influence of the wealthy on the political process can have indirect effects that register in a welfarist egalitarian accounting. These effects could be positive or negative. Beyond some point, the disproportionate control of political decision-making by the wealthy might discourage constructive engagement in the process by non-wealthy citizens, resulting in their missing opportunities to widen their outlook beyond their private concerns. Mill (1861, ch. 3) speculates the structure and operation of the political system likely has effects on citizen virtue. A widespread perception that politics is a rigged game might reach a tipping point past which social trust and cooperation between social groups in everyday interactions diminish.

3 Relational Egalitarianism and the Anti-Hierarchy Perspective on Wealth and Power

This section and the next explore the relational egalitarian ideal and its implications for the problem of wealth and power. This ideal can be variously interpreted, and some advocates see it as one component of a theory of justice, not its entirety (for discussion, see Lippert-Rasmussen 2018). The discussion in this chapter treats relational egalitarianism as a proposed complete theory of justice for assessing institutions and social practices. So viewed, it is a full-fledged rival to welfarist egalitarianism. In this treatment, the ideas of John Rawls loom large. Rawls's view is that justice requires, as a first priority, achieving political democracy in a form that liberates us from social hierarchy, the avoidance of which is the core of relating as equals. Relational egalitarianism thus yields a basis for a stringent and uncompromising rejection of significant inequality of wealth precisely for its adverse impact on political democracy. The upshot is stiff opposition to the impact of wealth on political decision-making, very different from the highly contingent opposition to inequality of wealth as undermining political democracy that welfarist egalitarianism delivers. In this perspective, relational egalitarianism is stalwart and firm in its stance against social hierarchy, whereas the stance of welfarist egalitarianism is wishy-washy. The issue of wealth and power shines a bright light on the contrast between these two versions of liberal egalitarianism.

That's the big picture. But the details turn out to be important, and they complicate the comparison. I shall try to show that depending on circumstances, the relational egalitarian view will retract its opposition to inequalities of wealth that in some respects undermine the degree to which the democratic ideal can be achieved, and the welfarist will condemn inequalities of wealth that undermine democracy in some circumstances in which the relational egalitarian will not. The two approaches can pull together, but sometimes one will zig where the other zags. So, becoming clear which approach if either should attract our allegiance will be an important factor in arriving at a reasonable view on the wealth and power issue.

3.1 Rawls

John Rawls, the most prominent political philosopher of the twentieth century, provides an account of social justice that gives content to the idea of relating as equals (Rawls 1996, 1999a, 2001). On this view, we live together on just terms when we cooperate with others to build and sustain institutions that protect equal basic liberties for all citizens, as a first priority. These protected civil rights establish a status of inviolability for all. We are morally bound to refrain from sacrificing the basic liberties of some, or even of everybody, to gain greater prosperity or greater opportunities for competitive success. None of these liberties may permissibly be curtailed except to protect the overall set of them for all over the long run. As a second priority, just institutions must be arranged to fulfil a strong equality of opportunity principle: all those with the same ambition and same native talent potential must have the same chances of success in competitions for social positions and roles that confer advantages and authority greater than others enjoy. This principle requires a fair provision of schooling and socialisation to all, entirely offsetting deficits in the ability and willingness of one's parents or guardians to provide one a fair start in life that develops one's potential to attain superior positions. Finally, as a third priority, institutions must combine in their effects so that any inequalities in basic resources across persons that obtain make those with least resources as well off as possible in resource holdings.

Not all freedoms to do what one wants qualify as basic liberties meriting special priority. Traffic laws massively restrict our freedom to drive vehicles and walk on public roads just as we like. But intuitively, it seems, sensible traffic laws that facilitate everyone's opportunity to travel wherever they want to go with reasonable speed and safety are not violating basic liberties. Rawls proposes that basic liberties are those that are especially needed for the development and exercise of our capacity to comply with fair terms of cooperation (play fair with others) and our capacity to choose and revise our life aims and pursue them. In other words, the basic liberties are those needed by free persons to develop and exercise their capacities (1) to behave morally and (2) to be rationally prudent by looking out for their own self-chosen interests.

Let's take stock. The Rawlsian account of justice has two striking features that differentiate it sharply from any welfarist egalitarianism. One is that within the constraint of respecting basic liberties, justice requires real freedom for all to pursue self-chosen aims, with fair shares of general-purpose resources, *not* maximal fair attainment of good quality life, individual fulfilment.[2] As Rawls puts it, in the justice as fairness doctrine he advances, the right is prior to the good.

The second striking feature comes into view only when we understand the stringency of Rawls's idea that the equal basic liberties have priority over the other justice values (and that within this lower-ranked set, attaining strong equal opportunity has strict priority over making the worst-off best off). Rawls writes, 'Each person possesses an inviolability founded on justice that even the welfare of society as a whole cannot override' (1999a, 3). And not only welfare. The inviolability to which Rawls here alludes comes to this: the three components of Rawls's principles are rank-ordered absolutely and exceptionlessly. The first-priority equal basic liberties must be fulfilled to the greatest extent we can attain, and no trade-offs at all are allowed that would countenance slightly lesser basic liberty in exchange for greater fulfilment of the lesser ranked equal opportunity and resource distribution norms.

Rawls specifies the equal basic liberties by a list: 'freedom of thought and liberty of conscience, the political liberties and freedom of association, as well as the freedoms specified by the liberty and integrity of the person; and finally, the rights and liberties covered by the rule of law' (Rawls 1996, 291). The political liberties centrally include the right to a democratic say – the right to an equal vote in majority rule elections that determine directly or indirectly the content of laws and public policies. Moreover, the right to a democratic say is fulfilled only when the right is more than formal: each person with the same political ambition and political talent has the same chance of being politically influential.

Rawls supposes the strict priority attached to the equal basic liberties is a nonbinding constraint, in that we will be able to fully protect the equal basic liberties as best we can and still have lots of resources and administrative capacity remaining to boost fulfilment of the lesser ranked principles. But he is assuming that his principles are a realistic utopia: in modern times, they can be implemented, and when implemented, people will become motivated fully to comply with them – enforcement is needed only to assure each person that others will be complying.

However, in actual circumstances of the modern world, this 'realistic utopia' is a utopia plain and simple. Short of genetic manipulation of human psychology that could not be guaranteed to work out well, human psychological nature brings it about that some of us will seek our own good at the expense of others, or fanatically oppress others in the service of oddball aims or worse. We tend to divide people into 'us' and 'them' and such moral inclinations as we have get harnessed to boosting the advantages of us over them. Rawls supposes the basic liberties can be secured in a fully adequate manner, but just consider police protection to uphold the rule of law. There is no upper limit to what resources we might devote to enforcement: even a police officer at everyone's elbow always would not suffice, unless the reliable compliance of police themselves with rule of law values could somehow be secured. Greater resources devoted to socialisation might keep paying off just a little in greater compliance, no matter what budget we have now. And given strict priority of basic liberties, the protection of even one individual's right, and even a small basic liberty right at that, takes strict priority over any gains we might achieve by deploying resources towards fulfilment of equality of opportunity and doing the best we can for the worst off.

Even if one were to figure out a way to relax this conclusion a bit, it will remain the case that Rawls's position comes close to the affirmation that each person's right to a democratic say (interpreted to require EOPI) must be upheld whatever the consequences. The only clear exception obtains when upholding the set of basic liberties in dire circumstances is best achieved by accepting lesser fulfilment of one or another liberty in the set. Then justice requires a trade-off between basic liberties. As one component of the equal basic liberties, the right to a democratic say might be subject to that sort of trade-off. The upshot is that there is very little room in the Rawls version of relational/democratic egalitarianism for compromising with the top priority justice requirement, that each member of society has a right to a democratic say.

3.2 Kolodny

As stated so far, the Rawlsian view of relational egalitarianism might seem insufficient to capture the social equality ideal of justice as non-hierarchy. We can imagine a society that fully protects the Rawlsian basic liberties yet is heavily larded with social hierarchy in many institutions and practices. Bosses might dominate employees, for example (Dahl 1985; Anderson 2017; Christiano 2022).

A natural starting point is the thought that inequalities of power and authority are opposed to relational equality. But as Samuel Scheffler (2003) has commented, inequalities of power and authority are ubiquitous in modern society, and not all seem intuitively, on their face, objectionable. So evidently, we need an account of objectionable hierarchy.

Niko Kolodny (2014) provides orientation. He proposes there are three prima facie problematic relations of inequality: (1) some have asymmetric power over others (without being firmly disposed to refrain from exercising it for the reason that doing so would wrong those others), (2) some have greater authority than others, in the sense of being able to issue commands that others obey (without being firmly disposed to refrain from exercising it for the reasons just given), and (3) some are esteemed and revered more than others for having traits that either morally ought to attract no such response or that are the traits that make one a person and should attract the same esteem and reverence for each and every person). A society that achieves the ideal of social equality lacks (1)–(3), except that (1) and (2) can be rendered unobjectionable, or at least very much less objectionable, to the degree that they are (a) continuously avoidable, on the part of those who are getting the short end of the stick, by taking acceptable available exit options, or alternatively (b) are regulated by a democratic government in which all have EOPI.

Apart from its capacity to take away the badness of hierarchy it regulates, the democratic state is a crucial component of a society of equals. The state massively coerces its citizens, and in most circumstances, for most people, exit from the state is unfeasible or at least very onerous. So, if a subgroup of citizens dominates the state, there exists a pervasive social hierarchy. (It does not follow that an authoritarian or monarchical state cannot in any circumstances be bringing about the greatest fulfilments of the society of equals ideal that can be achieved. Imagine a ruler with unchecked political power who sets in place rules and policies that bring about a flat non-hierarchical society whose members all relate only as equals – except that all are under the thumb of the unchecked ruler.

But this is an outlier possibility.) In expectable situations a non-hierarchical government would be a crucial component of the closest approximation to the non-hierarchical society that we can bring about.

Kolodny (2014) is discussing the justification of democracy, not presenting a theory of justice. But (here I follow Kolodny forthcoming) I submit that his ideas fit Rawls' theory of justice hand to glove. In particular, they explain how protecting the equal basic liberties eliminates objectionable social hierarchy in all institutions and social practices. When the Rawlsian equal basic liberties are fully secured, any social hierarchies such as boss-worker or doctor-patient are regulated by a democratic government in which all have EOPI. (Even if there is zero regulation in place, this is the level of regulation democratic government enacts.)

Kolodny social equality is also consistent with the existence of inequalities of power and authority that are continuously avoidable by those who are getting the short end of the stick. Having genuine exit options takes the sting of evil from inequalities of power and authority. Even if EOPI fails to fully obtain, genuine exit options make such non-political inequalities acceptable. Genuine exit options to a relation of inequality obtain only if one has viable alternatives. The project of sustaining viable alternatives centrally involves having adequate resources: if I can't meet my basic needs unless I continue to submit to lesser power and authority in employment and marriage, for example, I don't have the viable option of exiting these relations of inequality. This 'continuously avoidable' component of the ideal of social equality puts pressure on Rawls's strict priority for equal basic liberties over the lesser-ranked norms regulating inequalities in people's access to social and economic resources. After all, fulfilment of these norms is arguably just the ticket to ensure that relations of inequality are continuously avoidable, thus helping to ensure we are relating as equals, living in a society free from objectionable social hierarchy. So, let's drop the strict, absolute priority relations among the components of Rawls's theory of justice. Equal basic liberties are the jewel in the crown of this ideal, but this jewel, though very important, can be sacrificed sometimes to enhance other features of the crown. Henceforth in this essay we shall consider relational/democratic egalitarianism as plausibly exemplified in the amalgam Kolodny-Rawls theory of justice for institutions and social practices.

3.3 The Implications of Relational Egalitarianism for Wealth and Power

Inequality of wealth is inherently menacing to the goal of sustaining a society in which people relate as equals. The problem is that inequality of wealth threatens this fundamental condition of EOPI. Either wealth inequality must be squashed or it must somehow be insulated from the political process, so it does not deprive some citizens of EOPI.

This implication of relational egalitarian justice for the wealth and power problem is obvious, and obviously practically important, but should not be overstated. Complete fulfilment of relational egalitarian justice would obtain only if each member of society enjoys a right to a democratic say incorporating EOPI. But other social conditions besides the impact of wealth inequality can and do block the fulfilment of this right to a democratic say. More importantly, it can also happen that inequality of wealth, and wealth's influence on political decision-making, counteracts these other impediments to guaranteeing for all the right to a democratic say – or more specifically, its EOPI component. In possible and likely circumstances, when we are not able to achieve complete fulfilment of relational egalitarian justice no matter what we do, the closest we can come to achieving this ideal will involve tolerating unequal wealth and wealth's impact on politics because seeking to reduce them would exacerbate other conditions that are inimical to relational egalitarianism.

Here's one example illustrating this abstract possibility: suppose that attempts to reduce the political influence of the wealthy would strengthen the political power of a majority coalition of voters bent on pursuing their interest, so that this majority becomes rigidly stable over time and turns into majority tyranny (see Section 4 for elaboration).

Here's another example: compression of holdings of wealth beyond some point brings about increased opportunity to influence political outcomes accruing to the political class in society, comprising especially incumbents in office who can use winning office to gain electoral advantages for themselves and the network of advisors and collaborators they cultivate. At an extreme, a group of incumbents and their cronies might succeed in giving such electoral advantages to themselves that even though democratic elections continue to be held, in practice none but the de facto authoritarian rulers have any chance of being re-elected, and re-elected again, forming a dynasty that endures in the long-run (Levitsky and Way 2010). Or by this process even the forms of democracy might eventually be discarded.

Another possible scenario involves a party in power that espouses a social justice agenda in which equalising ownership of wealth looms large, firmly opposes the wealthy as enemies of social justice, but ends up tightening its grip on power independently of whether or not the wealth equalisation agenda is stably advanced (Corrales and Penfold 2015). Another scenario involves increased power accruing to an entrenched state bureaucracy. For example, imagine a regime in which the top military leaders have great leverage. Their implicit threat is: 'don't mess with us or there will be a coup.' Yet another example involves not the formation of a permanent stable majority that rules, but shifting majority coalitions, from which some voters regarded as pariahs by the rest are always excluded. The pariahs might be a despised racial or ethnic group or adherents of an unpopular religion.

4 Equal Opportunity for Political Influence

The idea of EOPI stands in need of clarification (see also Kogelmann 2022). Picture a democratic society in which a stable majority of voting citizens votes for its own interests and persistently wins. This problem case is often described as the problem of permanent minorities. Suppose wide freedom of speech and freedom of organisation prevails. Each adult citizen has an equal democratic say in the form of a vote that counts the same as anyone else's in free elections. But the same individuals form a majority coalition, over and over again. The voters who are not part of this coalition never have any chance of being part of a winning coalition that is able to enact laws to its liking. Given this characterisation of the circumstances, does equality of political influence prevail here?

Rawls formulates EOPI (which he refers to as the fair value of the political liberties) in ways that seem to identify it with equal chances to exert control over the content of political decisions among those equally ambitious to gain such control and equally politically talented. When the fair value of the political liberties obtains, 'citizens similarly gifted and motivated have roughly an equal chance of influencing the government's policy and of attaining positions of authority irrespective of their economic and social class' (Rawls 1996: 358; also Rawls 2001: 149).

But a gifted and motivated agent seeking to have political influence might have far less of it than others over the long run simply because her views are unpopular. Not having the same chance as others of getting one's way does not intuitively make it the case that one has unequal opportunity for influence. Kolodny accordingly interprets EOPI as requiring that the equally politically talented and ambitious would have had the same chances of being decisive in controlling political decisions if any pattern of political opinion among voters were as likely as any other. Or we might say that EOPI requires that one should have the same chance of making an impact on the choice of laws and policies as anyone else with comparable levels of political ambition and talent, and whose political views are (at the outset) exactly as popular among voters as one's own.

However, so formulated, EOPI could obtain even in the scenario in which a stable majority just votes its interests and exploits a stable convergence of interests to get its way. Consider again a stereotypical example of tyranny of the majority. A stable majority of voters recognises that they have common interests and uses the power of the ballot to promote their interests by winning elections over and over and over.

Oddly, Kolodny EOPI might be satisfied in this situation. There are two stylised possibilities. In one, no voters are open to being influenced by others, and everyone has the same opportunity for political influence: zero. In another possible situation, members of the stable majority might be open to influence from others in a degenerate sense: anyone who raises considerations as to where the self-interest of the majority lies will get a hearing from majority voters and will have an equal chance of swaying minds. Each is perfectly willing to entertain arguments from any voter as to how the stable majority's interests might best be understood and pursued. And members of the out-groups, the permanent minority, are open to persuasion by all others, as to how their interests might be best advanced. But we should not count these scenarios as fulfilling EOPI in any normatively attractive sense.

There is nothing mysterious or latently paradoxical in the idea that a democracy can be a tyranny. Having a vote that counts the same as everyone else's vote in political elections that will decide how society is to be governed is having a little bit of power over others. If many people pool their bits of political power, the result can become some just exercising naked power over others. The franchise can function as a club or gun. To reiterate, the problem is not merely that elections are resulting in some always winning and some always losing. And the fact that these scenarios sketched might be unlikely does not detract from their force as challenging the notions of EOPI currently on offer.

It seems the formulation of EOPI should incorporate a motivational component: in a true democracy, citizens seek to discern what policies would be fair, are disposed to consider anyone's arguments regarding what policies meet that standard and cast their ballots for whatever they end up believing after considering arguments. The rough idea is that each has equal opportunity for making a contribution to the discussion which others evaluate by their own lights.

The degree to which one's views resonate with others and affect their views, or not, does not diminish EOPI, but the degree to which other factors such as social status or one's ability to pay for billboards and TV ads affect one's impact on people's uptake of one's views does diminish EOPI. This suggestion is in the spirit of a comment by Jeremy Waldron to the effect that when citizens are committed to respecting people's rights and disagree about what rights people have, majority rule is the fair political procedure (Waldron 2006).

Nor would it be problematic if the society described fails to be an ideal deliberative democracy, in which all citizens are committed to voting on the basis of sustained deliberation and the deliberation is rationally conducted, with political proposals correctly assessed according to their merits. Perhaps few exercise their opportunities for influence and deliberation languishes. Perhaps deliberation is inept. Neither situation is tantamount to establishing a regime of social hierarchy. But EOPI (reasonably interpreted) requires that all must be disposed (a) to attend in an even-handed way, time permitting, to anyone who wants to offer moral arguments for policy choice, and (b) to evaluate by their own lights any arguments offered. Notice that such deliberation as occurs under EOPI need not be high quality rational deliberation. What is required is that those seeking to influence political decision-making make sincere appeals, according to their own beliefs about what ought to be done and why, and those addressed make sincere attempts to evaluate these arguments according to their own deliberative standards, and people vote according to their political opinions so formed.

If we accept this construal of EOPI, we will see this norm as multi-dimensional, as is the broader idea of a political decision process being democratic (recall Section 3 of this essay). Political decisions might be reached against a backdrop of more or less free speech and association, more or less unequal influence in the hands of the wealthy, the party in power or the entrenched state bureaucracy, with voters regarding their franchise more as a bit of power or more as a responsibility to promote fair policy choice by their lights, and so on. The influence of unequal wealth on the political process is one threat to true, social equality democracy among others.

5 Contrasting Implications

As just characterised, welfarist and relational egalitarianisms approach the problem of wealth and power in a very different spirit. For the welfarist, inequalities in power and authority are in themselves from the moral standpoint a 'don't care' – they matter not even a little, as tiebreakers between policies otherwise evenly balanced. Of course, these inequalities as we know are supremely important in instrumental terms, and the historical record of aristocracies, monarchies, dictatorships and tyrannies assessed by egalitarian welfarist standards is generally abominable. Since relationalists and welfarists will assess instrumental effects by different standards, the impact of these effects on policy recommendations will sometimes push the practical policy recommendations of these contrasting approaches further apart. Liberals of these different stripes may find themselves fighting on opposite sides of the barricades, the one opposing a political regime the other supports.

To illustrate the divergence, two stylised hypothetical examples will be considered. I believe the divergence will show up in real-world events, but showing that will not be attempted in this chapter. The upshot of the two examples is that the divergence between the two liberal egalitarian perspectives is far starker when we shift from focusing on what social justice requires within a single country and focus more broadly on justice across the globe. So, further reflection on global justice will help clarify which if either perspective should attract our allegiance. A further upshot is that if the shift to a global justice perspective is morally required and if we are concerned about the wealth and power issue, we had better pay less heed to wealth and power considered country by country and give more weight to global governance issues.

Picture an imaginary social democratic capitalist country, call it Norway*. Its institutions do not seek to equalise wealth, and any attempts to insulate wealth from power are perfunctory. Looking at their effects, the impacts of wealth on power are not detrimental in welfare terms. Norway*'s government collects a large fraction of citizens' earned incomes at not especially progressive rates, and expends these funds in ways that are pro-poor – compressing the distribution of post-tax income, eliminating poverty, providing health care, old-age pensions and unemployment compensation, etc. By measurable proxies for individual well-being such as longevity, good health over the life course, income, and schooling attainment, Norway*'s worse-off citizens score well compared to those of other economically developed and wealthy countries.

I submit that if we are evaluating the impact of Norway*'s policies on its citizens, these policies taken together qualify as tolerably just by welfarist egalitarian standards (Kenworthy 2020, forthcoming). This is unavoidably a vague judgment call, which others may contest.

Norway* is perhaps an ideal capitalist welfare state. But from a Rawls-Kolodny relational egalitarian perspective, this regime falls short. To be sure, Norway* as described protects several equal basic liberties. Its transfer policies that get basic resources in the hands of citizens in the lower deciles of the income distribution will register in relational egalitarian terms as increasing the extent to which citizens enjoy real and not merely formal freedom to pursue self-chosen aims. (One has real freedom, for example, to travel to Paris, if there is some course of action one can choose and execute that would bring it about that one actually gets to Paris.) More resources in the hands of impoverished and vulnerable citizens mean that they have greater continuous freedom to exit relations of inequality if they have a mind to do that. But it clearly fails to secure EOPI, and clearly more could be done to secure it. Nor is strong equal opportunity for competitive success (ranking just below equal basic liberties in priority for the relational egalitarian) as close to fulfilment as it could be.

But whether all things considered, relational and welfarist egalitarians should arrive at very different assessments of the justice of Norway* is a subtle matter. Greater EOPI fulfilment might directly or indirectly have a positive impact on the quality of life of the Norwegian* people, especially those worse off. The same goes for greater fulfilment of Rawlsian strong equal opportunity. Having increased freedom to exit from relations of inequality will register as valuable for its own sake in relational assessment and as instrumentally valuable in welfarist assessment. This might in a wide range of circumstances come out about a wash. And recall, Rawls-Kolodny social justice relaxes the stringent Rawlsian priority relations, so some large boosts to making the worst off better off can compensate for a slight restriction of freedom of speech.

In passing, I note that the welfarist will not attach great normative significance to the degree to which relations of inequality in social life are regulated by a democratic state over which all have equal opportunity for influence. Just suppose Norway* does as well as can be done in this respect. Suppose I am a worker under the thumb of a tyrannical mean boss or a woman stuck in a marriage to a man who is a dominating jerk. Suppose the laws are not useful in mitigating my plight, nor in prohibiting ways of domination that are especially worsening my life. Why does it ease and at an extreme extinguish the moral badness of the oppression I am enduring that these relations of inequality are regulated by a democratic state in which EOPI prevails? Suppose we could work either to enact social arrangements that free me from bad hierarchy or instead work to make the political decision-making process a bit closer to satisfying EOPI (without any helpful regulation actually being passed)? But the scenario depicted here might be empirically farfetched, so not likely to actually arise.

The second example contrasting the implications of welfarist and relational versions of egalitarianism involves global justice and assumes that relational egalitarian principles apply with force among people sharing dense social relations and in particular shared state membership. Suppose Norway* as so far described faces border control issues. It must decide whether to have loose or tight immigration restrictions, at the limit open borders for those seeking entry for purposes of settling permanently on its territory. It also faces issues concerning whether to allow temporary migrants from abroad who seek to be guest workers on its territory taking paid employment for periods of months or years.

Facing these issues, welfarist egalitarianism, counting at the same moral value the effects of its border control policies on all who might be affected, favours policies whose long-run impact do most to increase equality-weighted individual well-being. Suppose a candidate border control policy would have a negative welfare impact on current citizens but a positive impact on outsiders seeking admission. Adjusting for the welfare impact of these migrants on the welfare of people in the home countries they leave behind (and other indirectly affected people elsewhere) cosmopolitan welfarist egalitarianism, over the long run, judges the candidate policy favourably. If another candidate policy does even better in its overall impact on equality-weighted well-being levels, welfarist egalitarianism opts for this alternative, and so on. Welfarist egalitarianism takes the same line in evaluating the subset of possible border control policies that are politically feasible in the sense of being capable of gaining selection in democratic politics.

Let's stipulate a further stylised empirical fact. Suppose that the border control policies that might be enacted have differential effects on the wealthy and the non-wealthy in the economically developed country (here, Norway*). Negative impacts of policies more towards the open-borders end of the spectrum would fall entirely on the non-wealthy current citizens. This might be so due to various causal links. Non-wealthy voters facing border control issues might fear that admitting poor but ambitious outsiders will lessen the economic prospects of current non-wealthy citizens due to competition for employment. Or non-wealthy voters might have attachments to current cultural practices and folkways that they reasonably fear will undergo undesired shifts with a substantial influx of foreigners. Or the non-wealthy voters might fear that the social changes resulting from an increased immigrant population in the nation will erode political support for generous welfare state policies and in this way lower their own economic prospects.

In this hypothetical – or maybe not so hypothetical – scenario, a wealthy society fails to attain EOPI, and so to be just by relational egalitarian standards. However, it would be benign according to egalitarian welfarism, insofar as the wealthy have disproportionate influence and use it to enact more just border control policies, thereby doing better according to cosmopolitan welfarist egalitarian standards. The politically feasible set of policies is expanded to include more just policy options. This will be an instance of relational inequality bringing about greater justice by welfarist egalitarian lights.

Moreover, if relational egalitarianism requires no social inequality in each separate political society taken one by one, then inequality of wealth, prosperity and individual well-being between countries is no bar to fulfilment of social equality across the globe. As Rawls notes, the material requirements for democracy and even the genuine democracy that sustains EOPI are modest (Rawls 1999b: 105–111). Poor citizens can build and sustain democracy. Once a country is not disabled by extreme poverty from being able to sustain democracy and relations of equality across its members, further economic growth and prosperity are not required by justice. A qualification to this picture is that weak interactions between politically sovereign nations and their people must not be such as to amount to one nation dominating another and exercising power over its poorer and weaker neighbours. But Norway*'s simply having greater material wealth per capita than, say, Botswana* (and not sharing it) does not violate relational egalitarian justice.

So, from a global justice perspective, what sort of global governance do we need, and what steps now would be best to take, to make progress along this front? How does the wealth and power issue shed light on what sort of world we should be working to build? If the domination of poor countries by rich countries, and their holding fast to their far greater prosperity and hence flourishing, strike us as manifestly unjust, what principles of justice best explain and justify this conviction? Does liberal egalitarianism in some version offer sound guidance? These are good questions, so it seems anyway to me.

Notes

1 A related issue concerns the private financing of state debt, on which see Wiedenbrüg and López Turconi (2022) in this volume.
2 A large issue needs to be flagged here. Ronald Dworkin, a prominent liberal egalitarian, affirms both that treating people as equals centrally involves issues of fair distribution of resources, and denies that our justice standards for fair distribution of resources should register at all the well-being outcomes or opportunities that this distribution generates (Dworkin 2000, 2011). In his view personal responsibility issues drive us to this view. A full discussion of liberal egalitarianism must reckon with arguments advanced from the Dworkin family of views.

References

Ackerman, Bruce, and Ian Ayres. 2002. *Voting with Dollars: A New Paradigm for Campaign Finance*. New Haven, CT: Yale University Press.
Adler, Matthew. 2012. *Well-Being and Fair Distribution*. Oxford: Oxford University Press.
Adler, Matthew, and Nils Holtug. 2019. "Prioritarianism: A Response to Critics." *Politics, Philosophy, and Economics* 18, 101–144.
Anderson, Elizabeth. 2017. *Private Government: How Employers Rule Our Lives (and Why We Don't Talk about It)*. Princeton, NJ: Princeton University Press.
Bartels, Larry. 2016. *Unequal Democracy*. Princeton, NJ: Princeton University Press.
Bennett, Michael, Huub Brouwer, and Rutger Claassen. 2022. "Introduction: The Wealth-Power Nexus." In *Wealth and Power: Philosophical Perspectives*, edited by Michael Bennett, Huub Brouwer, and Rutger Claassen. London: Routledge.
Christiano, Thomas. 2022. "Why Does Worker Participation Matter? Three Considerations in Favor of Worker Participation in Corporate Governance." In *Wealth and Power: Philosophical Perspectives*, edited by Michael Bennett, Huub Brouwer, and Rutger Claassen. London: Routledge.
Corrales, Javier, and Michael Penfold. 2015. *Dragon in the Tropics: The Legacy of Hugo Chavez*, 2nd ed. Washington, DC: Brookings Institution Press.
Cowen, Tyler. 2018. *Stubborn Attachments: A Vision for a Society of Free, Prosperous, and Responsible Individuals*. San Francisco, CA: Stripe Press.
Dahl, Robert. 1985. *A Preface to Economic Democracy*. Berkeley and Los Angeles, CA: University of California Press.
Destri, Chiara. 2022. "No Money, No Party: The Role of Political Parties in Electoral Campaigns." In *Wealth and Power: Philosophical Perspectives*, edited by Michael Bennett, Huub Brouwer, and Rutger Claassen. London: Routledge.
Dworkin, Ronald. 2000. *Sovereign Virtue: The Theory and Practice of Equality*. Cambridge, MA: Harvard University Press.
Dworkin, Ronald. 2011. *Justice for Hedgehogs*. Cambridge, MA: Harvard University Press.
Gilens, Martin. 2012. *Affluence and Influence*. Princeton, NJ: Princeton University Press.
Gilens, Martin, and Benjamin Page. 2014. "Testing Theories of American Politics: Elites, Interest Groups, and Average Citizens." *Perspectives on Politics* 12 (3): 564–581.

Goodin, Robert. 2007. "Enfranchising All Affected Interests, and Its Alternatives." *Philosophy and Public Affairs* 35 (1) (Winter): 40–68.
Kenworthy, Lane. 2020. *Social Democratic Capitalism*. Oxford: Oxford University Press.
———. Forthcoming. *Would Socialism Be Better?* (June 2020 draft).
Kimpell Johnson, Jessica. 2022. "What About Ethos? Republican Institutions, Oligarchic Democracy and Norms of Political Equality." In *Wealth and Power: Philosophical Perspectives*, edited by Michael Bennett, Huub Brouwer, and Rutger Claassen. London: Routledge.
Kogelmann, Brian. 2022. "Public Choice and Political Equality." In *Wealth and Power: Philosophical Perspectives*, edited by Michael Bennett, Huub Brouwer, and Rutger Claassen. London: Routledge.
Kolodny, Niko. 2014. "Rule Over None II: Social Equality and the Justification of Democracy." *Philosophy and Public Affairs* 42 (4) (Fall): 287–336.
———. Forthcoming. *The Pecking Order: Social Hierarchy as a Philosophical Problem*. Cambridge, MA: Harvard University Press.
Levitsky, Steven, and Lucan Way. 2010. *Competitive Authoritarianism: Hybrid Regimes After the Cold War*. Cambridge: Cambridge University Press.
Lippert-Rasmussen, Kasper. 2018. *Relational Egalitarianism: Living as Equals*. Cambridge: Cambridge University Press.
Mill, John Stuart. 1861. *Considerations on Representative Government*. Edited by J. M. Robson. Toronto: University of Toronto Press. https://www.gutenberg.org/ebooks/5669.
Otsuka, Michael, and Alexander Voorhoeve. 2018. "Equality versus Priority." In *The Oxford Handbook of Distributive Justice*, edited by Serena Olsaretti, 65–85. Oxford: Oxford University Press.
Parfit, Derek. 1995. *Equality or Priority? The Lindley Lecture*. Lawrence: University of Kansas.
Parvin, Phil. 2022. "Hidden in Plain Sight: How Lobby Organisations Undermine Democracy." In *Wealth and Power: Philosophical Perspectives*, edited by Michael Bennett, Huub Brouwer, and Rutger Claassen. London: Routledge.
Rawls, John. 1996. *Political Liberalism*. New York, NY: Columbia Press.
———. 1999a. *A Theory of Justice*, Revised edition. Cambridge, MA: Harvard University Press.
———. 1999b. *The Law of Peoples*. Cambridge, MA: Harvard University Press.
———. 2001. *Justice as Fairness: A Restatement*, edited by Erin Kelly. Cambridge, MA: Harvard University Press.
Scheffler, Samuel. 2003. "What Is Egalitarianism?" *Philosophy and Public Affairs* 31(1): 5–39.
Shoikedbrod, Igor. 2022. "Private Wealth and Political Domination: A Marxian Approach." In *Wealth and Power: Philosophical Perspectives*, edited by Michael Bennett, Huub Brouwer, and Rutger Claassen. London: Routledge.
Temkin, Larry. 1993. *Inequality*. Oxford: Oxford University Press.
Waldron, Jeremy. 2006. "The Core of the Case against Judicial Review." *Yale Law Journal* 115 (6) (April), 1346–1406.
Wiedenbrüg, Anahí, and Patricio López Turconi. 2022. "The Power of Private Creditors and the Need for Reform of the International Financial Architecture." In *Wealth and Power: Philosophical Perspectives*, edited by Michael Bennett, Huub Brouwer, and Rutger Claassen. London: Routledge.

4 Public Choice and Political Equality

Brian Kogelmann

Public choice theory is a branch of economics that analyses political institutions using the tools and methods of economics. Before the public choice revolution (starting in the late 1950s with Anthony Downs' *An Economic Theory of Democracy* and Duncan Black's *The Theory of Committees and Elections*), most economists focused their attention on markets while largely ignoring politics. Much economic analysis consisted of identifying market failures – cases where markets fail to deliver optimal distributions of goods – and then proposing ways governments could remedy these failures. There was never much thought as to whether governments *could* or *would* follow the economist's advice. Public choice theory changed the conversation. By carefully applying the economic way of thinking to political institutions, public choice theorists recognised that just as markets fail, so too do governments. Governments might improve the functioning of markets, but they might also make them worse. As such, it is no surprise that libertarians and classical liberals have embraced public choice economics as an ineliminable tool in the analysis of public policy and politics more generally (Boettke and Piano 2019).

This chapter is about what public choice theory can teach us about political inequality.[1] Given that libertarians and classical liberals tend to embrace public choice economics, one might think that public choice has little to say about political inequality, a topic that is typically of concern to those on the political left. This is false. Fundamental to public choice analysis is the idea of *rent seeking*. While public choice theorists are often concerned about the negative economic consequences of rent seeking, rent seeking is also a major driver of political inequality as well, or at least so shall I argue.[2]

This relationship between rent seeking and political inequality is important, as it offers a fresh perspective on political inequality, one that political philosophers can learn much from. In particular, public choice theory teaches us that rent seeking is *sometimes* driven by inequalities in wealth, but is at other times driven by other, more subtle factors. Thus, *even if* we lived in a society where wealth was distributed in a perfectly

DOI: 10.4324/9781003173632-5

equal manner, political inequality would still be a significant problem. Beyond teaching us about some of the root causes of political inequality, public choice theorists have also offered novel proposals for how to remedy this problem. Thus, political philosophers can gain new insights about how to fight a pervasive problem confronting the body politic.

One important point to flag before beginning. This paper engages with much work from the social sciences. Most of the work discussed analyses the political institutions of the United States of America. There are two reasons for this. First, public choice theory was initially developed in the United States, so it is unsurprising that much of the analysis is parochial in this way. Second, I am a citizen of the United States, so it is the country I know best. Though the US-centric focus of this paper is, in some sense, limiting, public choice theory itself is by no means a parochial discipline. In fact, a core insight of public choice theory is that it is institutions, not people, that drive outcomes. Examining the diversity of political institutions that scatter the globe is essential, from a public choice perspective, to better understand how government can be improved so we can all live better together.

1 On Political Equality

The purpose of this chapter is to examine what public choice theory can teach us about some of the sources of and remedies for political inequality. But before beginning this investigation, we need an understanding of what political equality is. Many philosophers embrace political equality as a governing value that democratic societies ought to realise (e.g., Dahl 1989; Brighouse 1996; Christiano 1996; Knight and Johnson 1997; Dworkin 2000; Cohen 2001). Political equality is typically defined as an equal capacity or ability among citizens to influence political decisions. Political inequality, then, occurs when some have a greater capacity to influence political decisions than others.

This is not a good way of understanding what political equality is. The reason why is that not *every* instance of an unequal capacity to influence political decisions is normatively problematic, in the sense that not *every* instance of unequal capacity to influence political decisions runs afoul of our intuitions (Dworkin 2000, 364). For instance, those who have good arguments for their positions have a greater capacity to influence political decisions than those who have poor arguments; not only does this not seem problematic, but it also seems to be justified. Expert pundits, journalist, and political analysts have a greater capacity to influence political decisions than the average citizen who isn't on CNN every night. Once again, this is not terribly concerning.

For this reason, I do not think it is helpful to define political equality in terms of an equal capacity to influence political decisions. Very often, there will be an unequal capacity to influence political decisions.

Sometimes this is regrettable, other times it is desirable. Instead of focusing on an equal capacity to influence political decisions, we should define political equality in terms of the *kinds* of influence on political decisions that are normatively acceptable (in that they do not run afoul of our intuitions) and the kinds of influence that are normatively problematic (in that they *do* run afoul of our intuitions). Political equality is achieved when all sources of normatively problematic influence are absent from the democratic process. Political equality is consistent with an unequal capacity to influence political decisions *so long as* all this unequal influence is of the acceptable kind.

This is the approach David Estlund takes when he defines political equality. He defines political equality as 'the insulation of political influence from differential wealth or social rank' (Estlund 2000, 133). Here, Estlund highlights two sorts of unacceptable political influence. First, there is something wrong with Althea having more influence than Bertha if this unequal influence is grounded in Althea's superior wealth. Second, there is something wrong with Althea having more influence than Bertha if this unequal influence is grounded in Althea's superior social status. There is nothing wrong, according to Estlund's definition of political equality, with an unequal capacity to influence political decisions so long as the sources of this unequal influence are not differential wealth or differential social rank.

Estlund's definition is a good start, but it does not go far enough. For there are other examples of unequal political influence that do *not* result from differential wealth or social rank, that *also* strike us as normatively suspect. Consider an example: Cassidy and Dupree share the same representative in the legislature. Cassidy and Dupree have similar jobs, make a similar income, and occupy the same social rank in their society. Cassidy is childless and has a lot of time on her hands; she spends most of that time consuming political news. Dupree has two children and is a single parent; as such, he has no time to keep up with current events, so he is deeply uninformed about politics. Due to this information asymmetry, the representative is more likely to respond to Cassidy's interests than Dupree's. For, if the representative votes against Cassidy's interests, then Cassidy will know this and sanction her at the ballot box. But if the representative votes against Dupree's interests, then Dupree will likely never know and is thus unlikely to ever hold the representative accountable. This will strike many as an unacceptable case of unequal political influence, but one that stems from differences in political knowledge, not differences in wealth or social rank.

Of course, many times differences in political knowledge will arise from differences in wealth or social rank. Someone who works one job is better able to inform herself about politics than someone who must work two. Yet, it would be a mistake to claim that *all* instances of differential political knowledge are the result of differential wealth or social rank. As the case above illustrates, it is possible for there to be differences in political knowledge that result in unequal influence that are not grounded in differential wealth or social rank.

As another example, someone with a college degree might be better able to inform themselves about politics than someone who went to trade school, but the college-educated is not necessarily wealthier or of a higher social status than the tradesman (many of whom make considerable salaries and occupy important positions in their communities). If this differential knowledge translates into unequal influence, then once again we have what seems like a problematic case of unequal influence, but one that is not grounded in differential wealth or social rank.

With these brief remarks, let me now propose a definition of political equality (building on Estlund's) that accounts for the cases I have just run through.

> Political equality is achieved when political decisions are insulated from influence grounded in (*i*) differential wealth, (*ii*) differential social rank, and (*iii*) differential political knowledge.[3]

Adding clause (*iii*) to Estlund's definition allows us to account for the sorts of cases I just ran through. We now have a working definition of political equality. Our guiding questions now are: What does public choice theory teach us about the causes of political inequality? And, moreover, what does public choice theory teach us about how to eliminate political inequality? Before answering these questions, we need an overview of the public choice approach to economic inquiry, which I offer in the next section.

2 The Public Choice Paradigm

Public choice theory is most simply defined as application of the tools and methods of economics to the study of politics (Buchanan and Tullock 2004, xxi). By 'tools and methods of economics' I mean the rational choice paradigm that has embedded itself into the very heart of the economics discipline. Hence, public choice theory applies rational choice theory to the study of politics. This is typically done through the use of formal models. The pioneers of the field were John von Neumann and Oskar Morgenstern, Duncan Black, Kenneth J. Arrow, Anthony Downs, James M. Buchanan and Gordon Tullock, William H. Riker, and Mancur Olson (Amadae 2003, 11).[4] Though public choice theory relies heavily on formal models, there is also much work in the field that seeks to verify these models empirically (e.g., Mueller 2003, Part IV).

Public choice theory applies the rational choice paradigm to the study of politics. At its base, rational choice theory says that all persons have preferences, and, when confronted with options, choose the option most likely to satisfy their preferences. When formalised in a model, there are further refinements made. For instance, rational persons all have preferences possessing a certain structure. Preferences are reflexive (option *a* is always at least as good as itself), complete (either *a* is at least as good as *b* or *b* is at least as good as *a*), and transitive (if *a* is at least as good as *b* and *b* at least as good as *c*, then *a* is at least as good as *c*). Moreover, rational persons are presumed to choose not just an option that satisfies their goals, but rather the option that *best* satisfies their goals.

There is nothing about the rational choice paradigm *as such* that says persons are selfish. They just choose their most choice-worthy option, given their preferences. If one has preferences to help the poor, then choosing one's most choice-worthy option will often involve behaviour many deem altruistic. In order to generate substantive predictions, though, rational choice theorists must give content to persons' preferences. And when they model political actors – such as voters, politicians, bureaucrats – public choice theorists typically assume what many would deem (but are not necessarily) selfish preferences. For instance, Buchanan and Tullock write: 'we must assume that individuals will, on average, choose "more" rather than "less" when confronted with the opportunity for choice in a political process, with "more" and "less" being defined in terms of measurable economic position' (Buchanan and Tullock 2004, 28). In other words, political actors seek wealth.[5]

This has led to the characterisation that public choice theory is the study of 'politics without romance' (Buchanan 1999b). Overall, it has led to quite a pessimistic picture of government and politics. As mentioned in the introduction, before the public choice revolution, economists mostly focused on market failures, but after the revolution they began focusing on government failures. As Buchanan writes in a foundational paper, the goal of public choice is to show that 'any attempt to replace or to modify an existing market situation, admitted to be characterised by serious externalities, will produce solutions that embody externalities which are different, but precisely analogous, to those previously existing' (Buchanan 1999a: 63). To put it another way, remedying market failures through the state will often result in government failures, which in some (but not all) cases may be more serious than the market failures they were meant to resolve, in that the externality produced by government failure is larger than the one produced by the initial market failure.

Public choice theory has become a wide-ranging field of scholarly inquiry, examining electoral systems, voting rules, bureaucratic agencies and even non-democratic forms of government. One key aspect of public choice theory is the study of *rent seeking* (e.g., Tollison 1982; Tullock 2005; Lindsey and Teles 2019). Having nothing to do with landlords, the term 'rent' means payment to an owner of a resource over and above that which the resource could command in any alternative use. Those who seek rents are thus seeking extranormal returns on their productive resources.

Rent seeking is ubiquitous and all around us. Indeed, firms trying to maximise profits are, technically, seeking rents (Buchanan 1999c, 103).

Though rent-seeking behaviour is ubiquitous, public choice theorists note that it is especially pernicious in politics. This is so for a few reasons. First, it destroys resources (Tullock 2005, 103–121). To acquire rents from the government, one must typically lobby, which is expensive. Many persons or firms will lobby for rents (for instance, an exclusive government contract), but only one firm will get it. Everyone who does *not* acquire the rents has destroyed wealth for no gain. Indeed, rent seeking in politics is akin to an auction where all persons lose their bids regardless of whether their bid is the highest and they win the prize. In these cases, it is clear that the total sum of the bids will often be greater than the prize everyone was initially bidding for.

Beyond this, rent seeking is usually done to create special privileges in the marketplace, which leads to economic inefficiency. Markets work best when firms are constantly challenged by competitors, but firms often seek rents by asking the government to regulate away their competition. Those who braid hair for a living like licensing requirements; it means less competition for them. But, all things equal, the price of hair-braiding services would be reduced and the quality of the service higher if there was open market access and hence greater competition. Olson (1982) saw the economic inefficiency that follows from rent seeking as such a huge problem that he deemed it the major cause of the 'decline' of prosperous nations such as Great Britain and the United States.

Rent seeking is pervasive in democratic societies and causes significant economic harm. But is it a threat to political equality? That depends on the characteristics of those who successfully capture rents. If those who capture rents are the most meritorious, or have the most compelling arguments, then rent seeking is not a threat to political equality. Yet, if successful rent seekers are those with (*i*) differential wealth, (*ii*) differential social rank, or (*iii*) differential political knowledge, then rent seeking *is* a threat to political equality. In the next section I show that (*i*) and (*iii*) largely determine who is able to effectively seek rents.[6] Hence, rent seeking is a significant threat to political equality. To do this, I outline two central (but not the only) causes of rent seeking highlighted by public choice economists: campaign contributions and interest group monitoring.

3 Sources of Political Inequality

3.1 Campaign Contributions and Legislative Favours

At the heart of public choice economics is the idea that politics is just another way for persons to engage in exchange with one another (Buchanan 1999b, 50). How does exchange occur in politics? One way is logrolling in a legislature. Politician A might have a bill she likes, which politician B dislikes. Politician B has her own favoured bill, but politician A is not a fan. Here, politician A can vote for B's favoured bill and B can vote for A's favoured bill so both get something they want.[7]

Logrolling is not the only example of exchange in politics. Exchange can also occur between citizens and politicians. This is largely accomplished through campaign contributions (Munger and Denzau 1986; Hinich and Munger 1989; Buchanan and Tullock 2004, 273; Tullock 2005, 36; Holcombe 2018, ch. 4). More specifically, citizens donating to political campaigns is 'a straightforward *quid pro quo* of money for services: campaign contributions resemble bribes, although provision of services may be perfectly legal' (Morton and Cameron 1992, 88). The idea here is simple. Individuals and firms want rents from the government: tax breaks, favourable regulations, government contracts, and so on. To get these, they make donations to politicians' election or re-election campaigns. In return for the donation, politicians legislate favourably for their patrons.

Some are sceptical that campaign contributions really do effectively buy political influence. In particular, some empirical work suggests that there is little connection between campaign contributions and legislative outcomes (e.g., Ansolabehere *et al.* 2003; Dawood 2015, 340–342). Other empirical work points in the opposite direction (e.g., Stratmann 2005; Gilens 2012, 239; Gilens 2021). However, it is important to note how limited these studies are. They often look at whether donations effect how politicians vote on final bills. Yet, there are subtler ways influence can manifest that are not easily measured. Instead of purchasing votes on final bills, campaign contributions may purchase goods like: making sure that a bill one supports is prioritised on the agenda; making sure that a bill one opposes never reaches the floor for a vote; inserting an amendment or earmark; making sure that a bill one opposes but will inevitably be passed is a bit more palatable and so on.

Assuming that campaign contributions do buy influence, we must now ask: is this a case of normatively problematic political inequality? Recall, the ideal of political equality demands that political influence be insulated from (*i*) differential wealth, (*ii*) differential social rank, and (*iii*) differential political knowledge. The ability to buy political influence through campaign contributions is clearly only available to the wealthy. Indeed, it should be no surprise that donations to political campaigns are highly stratified by income bracket (Schlozman *et al.* 2018, 212–214). So, rent seeking via campaign contributions violates political equality. It is a way of exerting unequal political influence that is fundamentally grounded in differential wealth, which is prohibited by our definition of political equality.

3.2 Asymmetric Information and Interest Groups

Contributing to political campaigns is not the only way one can seek rents. Also relevant are *interest groups*. Although interest groups sometimes make contributions to political candidates, that is not the main way they exert influence. Rather, they engage in pressure campaigns in hopes of influencing legislators to vote a certain way. For instance, if a corn subsidy bill is up for vote, members of an interest group dedicated to corn farmers will call and email their legislators in hopes of pressuring them to support the bill, so they can obtain the subsidy. This is sometimes called grassroots lobbying (Schlozman et al. 2012, 404; Schlozman et al. 2018, 171–172).[8] This method of rent seeking is not obviously at odds with the ideal of political equality, so I will walk through it a bit slower.

First, let us look at how interest groups exert influence on politicians through pressure campaigns. Susanne Lohmann (1998) builds an instructive model. To begin, we know that it is costly to acquire political information and, moreover, persons often have an incentive to *not* acquire political information and thus be rationally ignorant (Downs 1957). Interest groups acquire costly political information and then disperse this information for their members to consume. Since members of the interest group are more informed than the public at large on a specific legislative issue, representatives have an incentive to vote on that issue according to the wishes of the interest group, even if doing so is at the expense of the larger public. In short: 'Because special interests are better able to monitor the quality of their political representation, incumbents have electoral incentives to bias policy towards special interests' (Lohmann 1998, 812).

As an example of this, an interest group for corn farmers acquires information about legislation pertaining to corn subsidies, and then provides this information to its members. On legislative issues that involve corn subsidies specifically, the corn farmers will be far better informed compared to members of the general public. When it comes time to vote for corn subsidies, it is no surprise that legislators do the bidding of corn farmers, even when subsidies harm the majority. If the legislator votes against the corn farmers, they are informed enough to hold her accountable at the ballot box; if the legislator votes against the general public, they will probably never know.

This is a violation of political equality. The corn farmers (who are in the minority) exert more influence on this particular issue than the general public (who are in the majority), and this is because the corn farmers are better informed (through their interest group) than the general public. Hence, clause (*iii*) of our definition of political equality is violated. This case could be avoided if the general public also had their own interest group that informed them about the relevant legislation. Then, both sides would be equally informed, so there would be no knowledge differential. Politics does not work out this way in practice, though, and it is worth spending some time to understand why.

Relevant here is Mancur Olson's book *The Logic of Collective Action* (1971). Olson begins by noting that it is a mystery why any interest groups form in the first place. Interest groups attain collective benefits for members of the relevant group. Returning to our example, an interest group for corn farmers seeks and acquires rents for all corn farmers. Since all corn farmers benefit from the interest group's activity, the rational action for any individual corn farmer is *not* join the group, but reap the benefits anyways. Given this logic, it is surprising there are any interest groups at all.

And yet, there *are* interest groups, so something must explain this. Olson argues that some groups form because they are better able to resolve this collective action problem when compared to others. There are several factors that determine whether a group of individuals will be able to successfully resolve this collective action problem. If a group is small, monitoring other members may be possible (Olson 1971, 43), individuals may feel a stronger sense of duty to contribute (Hardin 1982, 40) and the transaction as well as monetary costs associated with group formation will be lower (Olson 1971, 46). The key factor, though, is whether interest groups are able to offer selective benefits for their members (Olson 1971, 133). An interest group for corn farmers can offer selective benefits that, plausibly, all corn farmers want: crop insurance, reduced prices on combine equipment, special weather advisories, discounts at Cabela's and more. To attain these selective benefits, corn farmers must join the group. It is unlikely that an interest group opposed to corn subsidies will be able to do this. The group of persons opposed to corn subsidies is large and heterogeneous. There is not one package of selective benefits all such persons want.

The point here is that there are structural reasons why only *some* interest groups are capable of successfully forming. As such, we will never live in a world where all interests have a corresponding interest group that can monitor the legislative process for them and pass this information along to its members. Some groups – those who can offer selective benefits to their members – will always be more informed on certain issues than others, and thereby exert more influence. This, though, is a violation of political equality. Clause (*iii*) of our definition of political equality says that unequal influence may not stem from differential political knowledge, but interest groups allow for precisely that.

4 Eliminating Political Inequality

Rent seeking causes great economic harm. The last section showed that it is also a threat to political equality. Those who are able to successfully seek and acquire rents are the wealthy, and those who are more informed due to their capacity to form interest groups. This is fundamentally at odds with what political equality demands. How do we combat such threats? Public choice theorists have many answers, and in this section I survey some of them.

Public choice theory is first and foremost a methodological approach used in social science. It formulates predictions about, and offers explanations for, what we observe in the world around us. There is also a normative component to public choice – sometimes called *constitutional political economy* – that analyses the sorts of rules we can implement to achieve better outcomes (Buchanan 1999d).[9] Instead of offering normative imperatives for individuals to follow – 'don't seek rents!' – the public choice theorist maintains her pessimistic view of human nature and asks: what rules can we implement to achieve better outcomes? The normative component of public choice theory thus focuses on reforming the rules, not the players. In this sense, public choice theorists take seriously Rousseau's dictum that we take 'men as they are and laws as they might be' (Rousseau 1987, 17).[10] The paper by Elliot Bulmer and Stuart White (2022) in this volume is, I believe, a contribution to the field of constitutional political economy.

So, what institutional changes can be implemented to eliminate rent seeking and thus secure greater political equality? One of the most frequent proposals – and this is in line with the tight connection between public choice theory and libertarianism and classical liberalism that I noted in the paper's introduction – is to reduce the scope of government. Buchanan writes: 'So long as governmental action is restricted largely, if not entirely, to protecting individual rights, personal and property, and enforcing voluntarily negotiated private contracts, the market process dominates economic behaviour and ensures that any economic rents that appear will be dissipated by the forces of competitive entry' (Buchanan 1999c, 108).

The idea here is simple. Rent seekers compete for rents doled out by the government. Utility companies fight for government contracts, and firms fight for regulations that will be favourable to them. Thus, to eliminate rent seeking, we can eliminate government involvement in these sorts of activities. There might be a ban on the state contracting with private companies, and there might be a ban on state regulation of markets. This proposal eliminates rent seeking not by constraining the rent *seekers*, but by eliminating the *rents* themselves. Most will reject this proposal, as they believe government should play a large and extensive role in society. There are other proposals in the literature, however, that don't try to eliminate the rents themselves, but rather try to disincentivise persons from seeking rents.

One proposal is to force any rents acquired through rent seeking to be shared among all those in the relevant community, not just those who seek the rents. Buchanan proposes something along these lines when he writes, '... if government decides to restrict the production or sale of a commodity, thereby creating the opportunity for economic rents, each person in the community must be granted an *equal* share in the prospective rents' (Buchanan 1999c, 111). Let's consider an example of this. Suppose a firm makes x profits a year. They want to implement a regulation that will reduce competition. As a result of eliminating competition, they now make $x + k$ in profits a year. The proposal here is that the firm does not get sole ownership of k. Instead, k is taxed and distributed equally among everyone in the relevant community. This should disincentivise persons and firms from seeking rents: 'If this sharing is announced in advance and becomes generally known, it will not be rational for anyone to invest resources in trying to secure differential advantages' (Buchanan 1999c, 111).

This proposal is an enticing one, but hard to implement. The big issue is that the value of k is never clear. According to the proposal, the firm gets to keep its normal profits (value x) but must redistribute profits from rent seeking (value k). However, disentangling x and k is no easy task. One cannot simply say: the firm made x the year before the regulation and $x + m$ in the year after, therefore $m = k$. This is because we do not know what the firm would have made the year after the regulation were the regulation never implemented, as there are many considerations that could have influenced the firm's profits besides the introduction of a new regulation.

Another proposal is to hand out rents randomly. Buchanan writes: 'A more plausible means of assigning "rights" to [rents] would be for government to distribute such "rights" randomly in each situation. In this setting, all persons have equal expected values of rights, and they have little or no incentive to engage in rent seeking' (Buchanan 1999c, 111–112).[11] Consider an example of how this might work. Several firms are interested in acquiring a government contract to provide a public utility. Such a prize invites rent seeking. One way to combat this is to just give out the contract randomly. Of all the firms able to provide the service, one is chosen via sortition. If rents are allocated in this way, then there is no longer reason to seek them, as all the campaign contributions and interest group pressure in the world will not change the fundamental laws of probability.

There are issues with this proposal. First, by handing out contracts randomly, governments are no longer able to choose the best firm for the job. Not all firms will be able to provide the same quality of service at the same price, so selection by lottery may select a poor candidate. Beyond this, selecting for government contracts in this way *incentivises* firms providing the relevant service to do a poor job, as merit is totally eliminated from the selection criteria. And finally, not all rent seeking can be dealt with via sortition. Though government contracts can be handed out randomly, how do we randomly decide between competing health and safety regulations? How do we randomly decide between different financial regulations?

yet another proposal is to introduce some kind of generality constitutional amendment limiting the sorts of legislation that can be passed. F.A. Hayek, for instance, wrote that '[The First Amendment] ought to read, "Congress shall make no law authorising government to take any discriminatory measure of coercion"' (Buchanan and Congleton 2003, epigraph). The basic idea is to pass a new constitutional amendment specifying that laws may not provide differential benefits between persons or firms.

While a nice idea, it is hard to see how a generality amendment could actually be written and applied in practice. Buchanan and co-author Roger Congleton, for instance, write that applied to tax law 'persons may be treated in accord with the generality norm when their coerced exactions for sharing do not depart significantly from equality in the labour time required to meet these exactions. For example, a tax-sharing scheme satisfies the generality norm when the person who earns $120,000 annually is subjected to a tax of $10,000, whereas the person who earns $12,000 annually is taxed for $1,000' (Buchanan and Congleton 2003, 60). In both cases, each person is taxed one month's worth of work, so the law does not discriminate between persons. While the law does not discriminate in this sense, it does discriminate in another: the tax will be a greater burden on the poor person than the rich one. So maybe the law does not satisfy generality after all. Interpretive issues concerning what generality actually requires make this proposal difficult to implement.

My favoured proposal for reducing rent seeking is to introduce greater secrecy in the legislative process.[12] By secrecy, I mean this: when representatives vote on bills (either on the legislature floor or in committee), they do so by the secret ballot. Citizens will know which bills pass or fail, and they will know the total number of votes for and against each bill, but they will not know in which direction individual legislators cast their votes. To put it another way, I propose that voting in legislatures proceed in much the same way it does among citizens in democratic elections: results of the vote are made public, but how individuals cast their ballots remains secret.

This will eliminate much rent seeking for two reasons. Consider first campaign contributions as a cause of rent seeking. As a general rule, in order for persons to engage in non-contemporaneous exchange with one another (I give you apples today for your oranges in the future) they need some kind of *credible commitment* that the other party will live up to their end of the deal (North 1993). Exchanges between donors and politicians have this general problem: I give the politician a donation today, in exchange for legislative favours later on. This credible commitment problem is resolved through reputation effects (Snyder 1992). I observe the politician do me a favour, so I'm willing to contribute again next time. Forcing legislators to vote by the secret ballot eliminates this credible commitment. With no way to verify that the legislator will make good on her end of the bargain, it's unlikely that I would be willing to engage in the exchange in the first place. Consider: if you were going to pay someone to perform a service for you, but it was impossible for you to verify that they actually completed the service, would you still engage in the trade? Most would not.

Moreover, secrecy in the legislature levels down information, so interest group members now possess the same information as normal persons. Interest groups, we saw, effectively seek rents by acquiring costly political information and then dispersing it to their members. These groups write emails and newsletters saying: your representative voted to end corn subsidies, so you (the corn farmer) should vote her out. This pressures legislators to serve myopic interests rather than the general public. But, if representatives vote by secret ballot, then there is no way for the interest group to send those kinds of emails and newsletters to its members. Interest group members are now in the same epistemic position as the rest of us. Given this, there is no longer any reason for politicians to bias the preferences of informed interest group members over the preferences of the general public.[13]

5 Is Political Inequality Inevitable?

The last section overviewed different proposals to limit rent seeking. Such proposals might inspire optimism that political equality really is within our grasp. I would now like to end on a pessimistic note. Some public choice theorists believe that rent seeking (and hence political inequality) is inevitable, and that it will get worse over time. This thesis is advanced by Michael C. Munger and Mario Villarreal-Diaz (2019).[14]

The authors begin by defining *capitalism* and *crony capitalism*. Capitalism is 'a social system based upon the recognition of individual rights, including private property rights where all goods, both intermediate goods and final goods, are owned privately' (Munger and Villarreal-Diaz 2019, 332). In contrast there is crony capitalism, defined as 'a social system where the government intervenes aggressively into the economy, typically with political instruments that benefit large corporations and enterprises to the detriment of smaller businesses and private citizens' (332). The authors' thesis is that capitalism, when coupled with democratic politics, will inevitably morph into crony capitalism.

Why is this the case? Munger and Villarreal-Diaz distinguish between two ways of making profits. First, firms can make profits by 'engaging in productive activities that create value for others' (339). Call these *real profits*. Real profits are what we think of when we think of firms making profits, and it is exactly what we want from a market economy. The second way of making profits is by using 'the power of the state to extract resources from others or to protect those existing products from competition' (340). Call these *crony profits*. Crony profits derive from rent seeking, and they are precisely what we don't want.

Firms need to invest resources in order to make profits. They have a choice to invest resources into activities that will generate real profits, or into rent seeking activities that generate crony profits. By basic public choice assumptions – in particular, that persons are self-interested, narrowly defined in terms of wealth – it becomes clear that a rational, profit-maximising firm will invest resources strictly into productive activities if and only if the last dollar spent on acquiring real profits is more profitable than the first dollar spent on acquiring crony profits (340–341). While it is logically possible for this to be true, it is incredibly unlikely.

So far, Munger and Villarreal-Diaz (2019) have only argued that firms will often have incentive to pursue crony profits. However, can't we use some of the strategies discussed in the prior section to prevent rent seeking? The problem here is that politicians have little incentive to stop rent seeking, and thus little incentive to implement the reforms previously discussed. The reason why is that rent seeking is a lucrative business for most politicians: 'Encouraging corporate dependence on the state and collecting revenues from running artificial rent-seeking contests are primary money-making enterprises of successful politicians' (335). Thus, the problem is that private actors and firms often have reason to seek rents, and politicians often have reason to grant rents. All players in the game have strong reason to keep the game going, making it exceedingly difficult to change the game's rules. Under these circumstances, there is no reason to think that rent seeking and hence political inequality can be stopped.

I am not quite as pessimistic about the possibility of achieving political equality in our lifetime, for two reasons. First, Munger and Villarreal-Diaz do not distinguish between different *types* of democratic regimes. A democratic society might start off with rules that significantly limit rent seeking. For instance, many countries prohibit private citizens from making large contributions to political campaigns in the manner that is permitted in countries like the United States.

So, some countries might start out with the right kinds of political institutions, which may prevent a descent into crony capitalism. However, what about the countries whose political institutions permit extensive rent seeking from the start? Is their fate really sealed? I am still not so sure. The authors' argument consists of a rigid application of the basic public choice assumptions, that firms and politicians are narrowly self-interested. I do think that, very often, these assumptions are descriptively accurate. But they may not always be. It may be that, in some rare cases, firms and politicians are capable of reforming their political institutions for the greater good, in a manner contrary to their narrow material interests.

Note, some public choice theorists themselves believe this to be true. Geoffrey Brennan and James M. Buchanan (2000) discuss the possibility of constitutional reform. The authors admit that 'to hold out hope for reform in the basic rules describing the sociopolitical game, we must introduce elements that violate the self-interest postulate' (Brennan and Buchanan 2000, 162). In particular, for genuine constitutional reform to happen, 'persons must be alleged to place positive private value on "public good" for the whole community of persons, over and beyond the value placed on their own individualized or partitioned shares' (163). Public choice theory offers numerous insights into some of the sources of and remedies for political inequality. But it may be that to actually implement these remedies, we must go beyond the theory of public choice, and awaken the better angels of our nature.

Notes

1 There are other attempts in the literature to draw a close connection between democratic theory and public choice theory. Thrasher (2019), for instance, offers a reconstruction of Buchanan's normative theory of democracy.
2 This is not to say that *all* political inequality results from rent seeking. Rather, the claim is that rent seeking is the source of *some* of the political inequality we confront.
3 I do not mean to suggest that these are the *only* causes of unjustifiable unequal influence; there may be others. I add differential political knowledge to Estlund's list and stop there because I believe focusing on differential political knowledge in conjunction with the public choice literature highlights interesting insights that political philosophers have thus far neglected.
4 This does not mean these theorists all agreed with one another; in fact, they disagreed extensively. For instance, Buchanan saw little relevance in Arrow's acclaimed impossibility theorem. For more on this debate, see Kogelmann (2018a).
5 Why choose to model persons so pessimistically in the analysis politics? I analyse the main arguments in Kogelmann (2015).
6 This is not to say that (*ii*) differential social rank plays no role at all. Holcombe (2018) develops a theory of rent seeking where those able to successfully capture rents are non-political elites who have close relationships with political elites (thus lowering the transaction costs of rent seeking). This, in my view, is a story about how rent seeking is facilitated through differential social rank. For space constraints, however, I cannot examine this theory in detail.
7 For a normative defence of logrolling, see Thrasher (2016).
8 Note, this is not the only way of understanding lobbying. 'Lobbying' is an ambiguous term that can refer to many different activities. Sometimes it refers to grassroots lobbying of the kind I discuss in this section. Sometimes it refers to the exchange of campaign contributions for legislative services, as discussed in the prior section. For other accounts of what lobbying can mean in the public choice literature, see Hall and Deardorff (2006). For further analysis, see Phil Parvin's (2022) chapter in this volume.
9 The normative component of public choice theory is deeply intertwined with the social contract tradition. For an overview, see Kogelmann (2018b).
10 For criticism of this approach, see Jessica Kimpell Johnson's (2022) paper in this volume.
11 See also Lockard (2003).

12 I propose this in Kogelmann (2021b: ch. 2). For a more general discussion of secrecy and transparency as applied to questions in political philosophy, see Kogelmann (2021a).
13 There are several objections to this proposal: given membership in political parties, won't we be able to guess how representatives voted? Won't representatives declare how they voted? What about accountability? I address these objections in Kogelmann (2021b: ch. 2).
14 A similar position is also taken by public choice economist Holcombe (2018).

References

Amadae, S.M. 2003. *Rationalizing Capitalist Democracy*. Chicago, IL: University of Chicago Press.

Ansolabehere, Stephen, John M. Figueiredo, and James M. Snyder. 2003. "Why Is There so Little Money in U.S. Politics?" *Journal of Economic Perspectives* 17 (1): 105–130.

Boettke, Peter J. and Ennio E. Piano. 2019. "Public Choice and Libertarianism." In *Oxford Handbook of Public Choice, Vol. 1*, edited by Roger D. Congleton, Bernard Grofman, and Stefan Voigt, 814–830. Oxford: Oxford University Press.

Brennan, Geoffrey and James M. Buchanan. 2000. *The Reason of Rules*. Indianapolis, IN: Liberty Fund.

Brighouse, Harry. 1996. "Egalitarianism and Equal Availability of Political Influence." *Journal of Political Philosophy* 4 (2): 118–141.

Buchanan, James M. 1999a. "Politics, Policy, and the Pigovian Margins." In *The Collected Works of James M. Buchanan, Vol. 1*, 60–74. Indianapolis, IN: Liberty Fund.

———. 1999b. "Politics without Romance: A Sketch of Positive Public Choice Theory and Its Normative Implications." In *The Collected Works of James M. Buchanan, Vol. 1*, 45–59. Indianapolis, IN: Liberty Fund.

———. 1999c. "Rent Seeking and Profit Seeking." In *The Collected Works of James M. Buchanan, Vol. 1*, 103–115. Indianapolis, IN: Liberty Fund.

———. 1999d. "The Domain of Constitutional Economics." In *The Collected Works of James M. Buchanan, Vol. 1*, 377–395. Indianapolis, IN: Liberty Fund.

Buchanan, James M. and Roger D. Congleton. 2003. *Politics by Principle, Not by Interest*. Indianapolis, IN: Liberty Fund.

Buchanan, James M. and Gordon Tullock. 2004. *The Calculus of Consent*. Indianapolis, IN: Liberty Fund.

Bulmer, Elliot, and Stuart White. 2022. "Constitutions Against Oligarchy." In *Wealth and Power: Philosophical Perspectives*, edited by Michael Bennett, Huub Brouwer, and Rutger Claassen, 274–294. London: Routledge.

Christiano, Thomas. 1996. *The Rule of the Many*. Boulder, CO: Westview Press.

Cohen, Joshua. 2001. "Money, Politics, and Political Equality." In *Fact and Value*, edited by Alex Byrne, Robert Stalnaker, and Ralph Wedgwood, 47–80. Cambridge, MA: MIT Press.

Dahl, Robert A. 1989. *Democracy and Its Critics*. New Haven, CT: Yale University Press.

Dawood, Yasmin. 2015. "Campaign Finance and American Democracy." *Annual Review of Political Science* 18: 329–348.

Downs, Anthony. 1957. *An Economic Theory of Democracy*. New York, NY: Harper and Row.

Dworkin, Ronald. 2000. *Sovereign Virtue*. Cambridge, MA: Harvard University Press.

Estlund, David. 2000. "Political Quality." *Social Philosophy & Policy* 17 (1): 127–160.

Gilens, Martin. 2012. *Affluence and Influence*. Princeton, NJ: Princeton University Press.

———. 2021. "Campaign Finance Regulations and Public Policy." *American Political Science Review* 115 (3): 1074–1081.

Hall, Richard L. and Alan V. Deardorff. 2006. "Lobbying as Legislative Subsidy." *American Political Science Review* 100 (1): 69–84.

Hardin, Russell. 1982. *Collective Action*. Baltimore, MD: Johns Hopkins University Press.

Hinich, Melvin J. and Michael C. Munger. 1989. "Political Investment, Voter Perceptions, and Candidate Strategy: An Equilibrium Spatial Analysis." In *Models of Strategic Choice in Politics*, edited by Peter C. Ordeshook, 49–68. Ann Arbor, MI: University of Michigan Press.

Holcombe, Randall G. 2018. *Political Capitalism*. Cambridge: Cambridge University Press.

Lohmann, Susanne. 1998. "An Information Rationale for the Power of Special Interests." *American Political Science Review* 92 (4): 809–827.

Kimpell Johnson, Jessica. 2022. "What About Ethos? Constitutions, Oligarchic Democracy and Norms of Political Equality." In *Wealth and Power: Philosophical Perspectives*, edited by Michael Bennett, Huub Brouwer, and Rutger Claassen, 25–46. London: Routledge.

Knight, Jack and James Johnson. 1997. "What Sort of Political Equality Does Deliberative Democracy Require?" In *Deliberative Democracy*, edited by James Bohman and William Rehg, 279–320. Cambridge, MA: MIT Press.

Kogelmann, Brian. 2015. "Modeling the Individual for Constitutional Choice." *Constitutional Political Economy* 26: 455–474.

———. 2018a. "Buchanan and Arrow on Democracy, Impossibility, and Market." In *Exploring the Political Economy and Social Philosophy of James M. Buchanan*, edited by Paul Aligica, Christopher J. Coyne, and Stefanie Haeffele, 123–141. London: Rowman & Littlefield.

———. 2018b. "Rawls, Buchanan, and the Search for a Better Social Contract." In *Exploring the Political Economy and Social Philosophy of James M. Buchanan*, edited by Paul Aligica, Christopher J. Coyne, and Stefanie Haeffele, 17–38. London: Rowman & Littlefield.

———. 2021a. "Secrecy and Transparency in Political Philosophy." *Philosophy Compass* 16: e12733.

———. 2021b. *Secret Government: The Pathologies of Publicity*. Cambridge: Cambridge University Press.

Lindsey, Brink and Steven M. Teles. 2019. *The Captured Economy*. Oxford: Oxford University Press.

Lockard, Alan A. 2003. "Decision by Sortition: a Means to Reduce Rent-Seeking." *Public Choice* 116 (3/4): 435–451.

Morton, Rebecca and Charles Cameron. 1992. "Elections and the Theory of Campaign Contributions." *Economics and Politics* 4 (1): 79–108.

Mueller, Dennis C. 2003. *Public Choice III*. Cambridge: Cambridge University Press.

Munger, Michael C., and Arthur T. Denzau. 1986. "Legislators and Interest Groups: How Unorganized Interests Get Represented." *American Political Science Review* 80 (1): 89–106.

Munger, Michael C., and Mario Villarreal-Diaz. 2019. "The Road to Crony Capitalism." *The Independent Review* 23 (3): 331–334.

North, Douglass C. 1993. "Institutions and Credible Commitment." *Journal of Institutional and Theoretical Economics* 149 (1): 11–23.

Olson, Mancur. 1971. *The Logic of Collective Action*. Cambridge, MA: Harvard University Press.

———. 1982. *The Rise and Decline of Nations*. New Haven, CT: Yale University Press.

Parvin, Phil. 2022. "Hidden in Plain Sight: How Lobby Organizations Undermine Democracy." In *Wealth and Power: Philosophical Perspectives*, edited by Michael Bennett, Huub Brouwer, and Rutger Claassen, 229–251. London: Routledge.

Rousseau, Jean-Jacques. 1987. *On the Social Contract*. Indianapolis, IN: Hackett Publishing.

Schlozman, Kay Lehman, Henry E. Brady, and Sidney Verba. 2018. *Unequal and Unrepresented*. Princeton, NJ: Princeton University Press.

Schlozman, Kay Lehman, Sidney Verba, and Henry E. Brady. 2012. *The Unheavenly Chorus*. Princeton, NJ: Princeton University Press.

Snyder, James M. 1992. "Long-Term Investing in Politicians: Or, Give Early, Give Often." *Journal of Law & Economics* 35 (1): 15–43.

Stratmann, Thomas. 2005. "Some Talk: Money in Politics. A (Partial) Review of the Literature." *Public Choice* 124 (1/2): 135–156.

Thrasher, John. 2016. "The Ethics of Legislative Vote Trading." *Political Studies* 64 (3): 614–629.

———. 2019. "Democracy Unchained: Contractualism, Individualism, and Independence in Buchanan's Democratic Theory." *Homo Oeconomicus* 36: 25–40.

Tollison, Robert D. 1982. "Rent Seeking: A Survey." *Kyklos* 35 (4): 575–602.

Tullock, Gordon. 2005. *The Rent-Seeking Society*. Indianapolis, IN: Liberty Fund.

5 Private Wealth and Political Domination
A Marxian Approach

Igor Shoikhedbrod

This chapter elaborates a Marxian approach to grappling with the contradictory relationship between private wealth and political domination in contemporary capitalist societies. It begins by offering a theoretical diagnosis of the normative issues generated by the relationship between private wealth (a manifestation of private power) and political domination, and concludes by briefly outlining a range of preliminary proposals for democratically transforming this relationship.

The chapter opens by tracing Karl Marx's earliest engagement with issues of private wealth and political domination back to his early journalistic reflections concerning 'The Debates on the Law on Thefts of Wood.' In these journalistic reflections, Marx describes how a customary practice of gathering fallen forest wood was criminalised by the Prussian state as an instance of property theft. Marx demonstrates the extent to which wealthy landowners were able to bend the scales of justice to their pecuniary interests by transforming the state into the servant of private power. The consequence of such a transformation, according to Marx, is not only the perversion of state functions but the corruption of the law over and against the interests of the poor. I argue that Marx's formative essay sets the context for his subsequent writings on the tension between civil society and the state, which later paved the way for his analysis of capitalist accumulation, concentration, and domination.

The second section of the chapter considers the contradictions of capital and its resultant forms of domination by drawing on Marx's discussion of the contradiction between a socialised process of production and a distinctly private form of appropriation. This section seeks to draw out the political implications of Marx's insights, focusing on the ways in which capital, qua private wealth and power, limits the scope for democratic self-determination. The section also elaborates a specifically Marxian account of political domination in contrast to liberal egalitarian and neo-republican versions, and briefly looks at how Marx's insights have been reconstructed by a range of contemporary Marxian commentators.

DOI: 10.4324/9781003173632-6

The final section offers a range of preliminary proposals for democratically transforming the relationship between private wealth and political domination in the context of contemporary financialised capitalism. These proposals include worker-owned and managed cooperatives and democratic control over investment. Far from being obsolete, the Marxian approach is shown to offer valuable lessons for liberal democratic societies that continue to struggle with the normative issues generated by private wealth and political domination.

1 Degrading the State in the Service of Private Power

Marx's early journalistic writings for the *Rheinische Zeitung* have been mostly neglected if not altogether dismissed as the idealistic expressions of a youthful liberal humanist (for recent exceptions, see Bensaïd 2021; Shoikhedbrod 2019; Carver 2018, 269). The rationale for this interpretation can be explained by the canonisation of various Marxist texts at the expense of others, even if some of these texts by Marx and Engels (e.g., *The German Ideology*) were never published as complete monographs, let alone intended as exhaustive treatments by their authors (Carver 2010). While Marx's journalistic writings during this period (1842–1844) are among his earliest reflections on the state, politics and law, they proved integral to the development of his mature work, including his life work, *Capital*. It is no accident that Marx refers in passing to these writings in the 1859 Preface to his *A Contribution to a Critique of Political Economy*, noting the extent to which these writings betrayed his 'embarrassment of having to take part in discussions on so-called material interests' (Marx [1859] 1978d, 3). We also learn that he intended to have these early articles republished in 1851, at the peak of reactionary restoration across Europe (Carver 2018, 269; Leopold 2007, 2). The discussion of Marx's *Rheinische Zeitung* articles that follows will be confined to his reflections on the 'Debates on the Law on the Thefts of Wood,' where one can observe Marx's earliest and arguably most piercing analysis of the relationship between private wealth and political domination.

Recent years have seen a considerable uptake in scholarship on private power and domination among liberal egalitarian theorists, whether conceived through the lens of 'private government' or through the more general framework of 'privatisation.'[1] Such scholarship represents an important step for normative political theory, since it goes some way in problematising the rigid bifurcation of public and private power that is still central to many versions of liberal thought, including liberal egalitarianism. While such scholarly interventions have made important theoretical headways, they nevertheless sidestep important contradictions that Marx and subsequent Marxian thinkers have identified vis-à-vis private wealth and political domination, which will be explored in more detail in the sections that follow.

Marx's earliest discussion of private wealth and political domination is developed in his reflections concerning the 'Debates on the Law on the Thefts of Wood.' While the debates of the Rhineland Provincial Assembly of Estates retained their notorious secrecy, Marx's journalism provided a rare occasion to critically dissect the proposed wood theft law. At the time, Rhenish legislators were considering the adoption of a law that would criminalise the collection of fallen forest wood. Historically, Rhenish peasants were allowed to collect fallen wood and other 'indeterminate' forms of property such as alms. The imposition of the Napoleonic Code in the Rhineland region after Prussia's defeat brought forth a series of modern reforms, in public law as well as in private law. Changes in the domain of private law were accompanied by the expansion of private property rights, specifically in connection with the ownership of forest land. Marx's article examines the political ramifications of this important change. He writes:

> [Legal] understanding therefore abolished the hybrid, indeterminate forms of property by applying to them existing categories of abstract civil law, the model for which was available in Roman law. The legislative mind considered it was the more justified in abolishing the obligations of this indeterminate property towards the class of the very poor, because it also abolished the state of privileges of property. It forgot, however, that even from the standpoint of civil law a twofold private right was present here: a private right of the owner and a private right of the non-owner.
>
> (Marx [1842] 1971, 233)[2]

On the basis of these remarks, one can discern a peculiar change that had begun to take place in the domain of property law. More specifically, Marx observes that far from abolishing the privileges associated with private property, private property was largely depoliticised and given a distinctly private or civil character (Marx [1842] 1971, 233). In other words, private property took the juridical form of a purely private power, but the precondition for the exercise of this private power (i.e., the legally recognised ownership of private wealth) became a basis for political domination. This critical insight is made more forcefully by Marx in *On the Jewish Question*:

> The political suppression of private property not only does not abolish private property; it actually presupposes its existence. The state abolishes, after its fashion, the distinctions established by *birth, rank, education, occupation,* when it decrees that birth, social rank, education, occupation are *non-political* distinctions; when it proclaims, without regard to these distinctions, that every member of society is an *equal* partner in popular sovereignty. [...] But the state

none the less, allows private property, education, occupation, to *act after their own fashion*, namely as private property, education, occupation, and to manifest their *particular nature*.

(Marx [1844] 1978e, 33)

While the new statutory law recognised landlords as the rightful owners of forest land, it did not recognise the customary use rights of peasants to gather fallen wood. Similarly, though there remained an essential difference between ripping branches from a living tree and collecting fallen wood, both came to be regarded as theft and were equally punishable by law (Marx [1842] 1971, 227). In Marx's view, such a transformation in the law had normatively pernicious effects for at least two reasons. First, the new law violated an older customary right by criminalising what amounted to a right of necessity. Second, and more perversely, the wood theft law confirmed the extent to which the political state was being transformed into the servant of the forest owners, while its legislation became increasingly servile to the interests of their private powers. In summary, the wood theft law represented the degradation of the state and the corruption of its laws. While the law punished the customary rights of the poor, it bent the scales of justice in favour of the pecuniary interests of the forest owners, who would profit directly from the mandatory labour and fines that could then be exacted from poor peasants. However, when a law-governed state (*Rechtsstaat*) becomes subservient to the narrow interests of private power, its essence and claims to universality (public interest) are invalidated, leading Marx to insist:

> If the state, even in a single respect, stoops so low as to act in the manner of private property instead of in its own way, the immediate consequence is that it has to adapt itself in the form of its means to the narrow limits of private property. [...] As a result of this, apart from the complete degradation of the state, we have the reverse effect that the most irrational and illegal means are put into operation against the accused [i.e., the poor]; for supreme concern for the interests of limited private property necessarily turns into unlimited lack of concern for the interests of the accused.
>
> (Marx [1842] 1971, 241)

In response to the above predicament, Marx proposes a customary right for the poor of all countries in opposition to the traditional privileges of the landlords, as well as the newfound proprietary privileges of the forest owners (Marx [1842] 1971, 230). As a vociferous critic of the Historical School of Law in Germany,[3] Marx was perfectly aware that appeals to custom often masked entrenched hierarchies and betrayed a broader desire by the wealthy to re-establish the status quo by other means (Bensaïd 2021, 19). Consequently, Marx appeals in the end to the normative standards of 'rational right,' which should have demonstrated to the alleged criminal (the wood pilferer) that the law is just and immortal, whereas the proposed wood theft law taught the very opposite. At its core, Marx's discussion of the wood theft law stands as a powerful case study of how legally recognised private wealth (a manifestation of private power) can transform into political domination by reducing the state to the servant of private power over and against the interests of the poor.[4]

It is important to acknowledge that Marx's critical reflections on the wood theft law were written during his 'pre-communist' period, which goes some way in explaining why he insists upon a 'customary right for the poor of all countries' rather than the abolition of capitalist private property. To be sure, Marx's thinking underwent considerable change between 1842 and 1867, a period spanning his critique of Hegel's *Philosophy of Right*, the revolutions of 1848, the reactionary restoration that paved the way for Louis Bonaparte's coup in France, and the publication of the first volume of *Capital*. The period immediately following Marx's resignation from the *Rheinische Zeitung* was marked by his critical engagement with Hegel's theory of the modern state. The results of Marx's critical study were twofold. First, he recognised that the peculiar nature of the Prussian state (as distinct from Hegel's conception of the modern state) could not be grasped with reference to the abstract idea of rational right. Instead, the truth of that historically specific form of the state and its laws was to be sought in what Marx, following Hegel, called 'civil society,' while the constitution of civil society was to be grasped through a critical study of political economy (see Marx [1859] 1978d, 4). Second, whereas Marx's early journalistic writings appealed to rational right as a standard of normative evaluation, his subsequent writings – from *On the Jewish Question* through the *Grundrisse* – focus on the contradictions between civil society and the state, in particular the extent to which civil society and its market imperatives constrain the constitution of the modern state. However, far from mechanically reducing legal relations to economic relations, Marx emphasised the organic link between concrete forms of production and legal relations. This organic link is expressed most forcefully in the *Grundrisse*, where Marx insists that 'every form of production creates its own legal relations, form of government, etc. In bringing things which are organically related into an accidental relation, into a merely reflective connection, they [bourgeois economists] display their crudity and lack of conceptual understanding' (Marx [1857] 1978c, 226). In the same work, Marx went on to analyse different historical forms of production and the legal relations to which they give rise, including the nascent capitalist mode of production and the liberal constitutional state, characterised as it still is by generalised commodity production with the underlying aim of capital accumulation.

2 The Contradictions of Capital and the 'Faces' of Political Domination

While Marx's *Capital* has traditionally been viewed as a work of economics – or more precisely, a critique of political economy – there have been several important scholarly interventions in recent years that approach it as a work of political theory, abounding with insights for normative political theory more broadly (Roberts 2016; Smith 2019; Shoikhedbrod 2019). When *Capital* is approached in this way, it is easier to discern how Marx's discussion of private wealth and political domination is given a firmer theoretical basis through his analysis of capital's inner dynamics. Incisive as Marx's article on the wood theft law was, it lacked the systematicity and historicity of *Capital*, which remains, among other things, one of the most rigorous attempts to explicate the origins and systemic dynamics of capitalist accumulation. If Marx's formative reflections on the liberal constitutional state brought to bear the persistence of economic inequality in civil society, then the first volume of *Capital* would reveal 'the secret of profitmaking,' and the ways in which capital dominates labour in the 'hidden abode of production,' all against a background of equal rights. Capitalism, for Marx, is a political-economic system in which ownership of the means of production and control over the social surplus becomes concentrated in a few hands. Aside from its systemic tendency towards monopoly and periodic crises, capitalism also produces a reserve army of unemployed labourers and a class structure in which most individuals do not have sufficient access to, or control over, productive property. The formal character of liberal justice abstracts from asymmetries of class power and ignores how these asymmetries translate into political domination in liberal constitutional democracies.

Whereas pre-capitalist political-economic formations were characterised primarily by personal or direct forms of domination, Marx theorised that capitalist production is informed by exchange relations between commodity owners who are not legally bound to the arbitrary will of other individuals. In this sense, Marx recognised that capitalist markets emancipate individuals from ascribed status hierarchies and direct forms of domination that were common in feudal or medieval societies. Capitalism's historical abolition of ascribed hierarchies also gives rise to generalised dependence on impersonal market forces that escape conscious human direction and democratic control. This form of dependence goes hand in hand with a system of class domination in which the owners of private capital dominate non-owners, albeit without recourse to the direct or personal forms of domination that prevailed in pre-capitalist formations. The foregoing reference to impersonal domination does not rule out that individual workers remain *de facto* (as opposed to *de jure*) dependent on individual capitalists.

Private Wealth and Political Domination 91

Retuning to *Capital* provides a renewed opportunity to discern insights that are lacking even in the most sophisticated versions of liberal egalitarianism. The starting point of Marx's analysis in *Capital* is arguably the commodity, while the broader trajectory is the self-valorisation of capital. Both presuppose the necessary buying and selling of a special commodity (i.e., labour power) in the market, founded upon juridical equality between buyer and seller but resulting in *de facto* inequality and domination in the sphere of production. The question that concerns Marx throughout his inquiry is the social reproduction of capital. Capitalist production, whether it takes the form of industrial capital that was common in his time or the financialised capital of our time, is distinguished by several defining features (in non-chronological order). One feature, as we have seen, is the presupposition of juridical equality among rights bearers – workers as much as capitalists. The second involves a socialised form of production that is accompanied by a distinctly private form of appropriation. The third feature, closely connected to the second, yields what Marx termed the 'centralization of existing capital and the concentration of new capital' (Marx [1867] 1976a, 777), which not only reproduces a specific class structure but also helps fuel the business cycle and its reoccurring crises (see Day 2018, 88). The fourth feature of capitalist production is capital's self-valorisation, a process whereby all social and political life is rendered subordinate to the dictates of capital accumulation, primarily as a consequence of the abstract character of labour that prevails in capitalist societies. This process subjugates both owners and non-owners of capital, though obviously not to the same degree, and appears to cement capital's status as 'self-determining subject.'[5]

One can thus discern at least two related but distinct mechanisms of domination that flow from the private appropriation of socially generated wealth. The first and most familiar mechanism is that of class domination, whereby the owners of private capital (the class exercising private power through the ownership of private wealth) dominate non-owners in virtue of their status as non-owners, as well as both classes' respective places in the production process. While the origin of this domination is rooted in the process of production, its consequences are thoroughly *political*. Marx elaborates on this point in *Capital*:

> The specific economic form, in which unpaid surplus-labour is pumped out of direct producers, determines the relationship of rulers and ruled, as it grows directly out of production itself and, in turn, reacts upon it as a determining element. Upon this, however, is founded the entire formation of the economic community which grows up out of the production relations themselves, thereby simultaneously its specific political form. It is always the direct relationship of the owners of the conditions of production to the direct

producers – a relation always naturally corresponding to a definite stage in the development of the methods of labour and thereby its social productivity – which reveals the innermost secret, the hidden basis of the entire social structure and with it the political form of the relation of sovereignty and dependence, in short, the corresponding specific form of the state.

(Marx [1894] 1976b, 772)[6]

The specific political form of the state is therefore closely bound up with the organisation of production, particularly the relationship between the direct producers and the class which controls the means of production and appropriates the surplus generated by these producers. Marx's derivation of the political form of the state from relations of production is bound to strike liberal egalitarian political theorists as suspect for its apparent reduction of politics to economics and the determinism that is usually attributed to such an approach. Critics are likely to point back to the *Communist Manifesto,* written on the eve of the bourgeois revolutions in 1848, where Marx and Engels maintain that 'the executive of the modern State is but a committee for managing the common affairs of the whole bourgeoisie' (Marx and Engels [1848] 1978, 475). However, even this frequently cited passage about the class character of the liberal constitutional state goes beyond a simplistic reduction of politics to economics. It is important to note here that Marx and Engels maintain that a peculiar feature of the modern liberal constitutional state is that the ruling bourgeois class does not actually rule, at least not directly.[7]

The 'relative autonomy' of the state from the economy became an integral part of Marx's understanding of the complex relationship between the state and civil society in *The Eighteenth Brumaire of Louis Bonaparte* (Marx [1852] 1978b). This work was published only four years after the *Communist Manifesto* – that is, after the 1848 revolutions had been defeated. However, Marx continued to regard the relative autonomy of the state as being informed by the broader political balance of class forces rather than resulting automatically from fixed economic relations. Marx's reference to the class character of the liberal constitutional state, as well as his simultaneous acknowledgement of the state's relative autonomy, paved the way for a sustained debate between Nicos Poulantzas (1969) and Ralph Miliband (1970) on the nature of the state in 'late capitalism,' emphasising different poles in Marx's treatment of the state.[8]

In the twenty-first century, John Rawls was among the most formidable liberal egalitarian political philosophers to take on Marx's challenge of class domination in a liberal society that is committed in principle to the freedom and equality of individuals (see Rawls 2001, 135–79). As I have argued elsewhere (Shoikhedbrod 2019), Rawls's discussion of the basic political liberties and their fair value, as well as his proposed regime of property-owning democracy (on which see O'Neill and Williamson 2012), were framed partly as responses to Marx's problematic of capital concentration and class domination. Despite his persistent efforts, Rawls's attachment to private ownership of the means of production, including in the dispersed form of property-owning democracy, is beset with shortcomings in the context of a global political economy (as opposed to an insulated state) which reproduces the principal contradictions of class concentration and domination that his work was meant to redress.[9] What Rawls lacked is a systematic account of capital. Marx was able to overcome this shortcoming because his concept of capital was global in scale and broadly informed by a related but distinct mechanism of domination.[10]

The second mechanism of domination under capitalist production is arguably more elusive. The reason for this is that, unlike class domination, which was discussed in the preceding paragraphs, this form of domination is thoroughly impersonal and systemic, with the important caveat that capital is elevated to the status of a self-determining subject. To be sure, Marx's reference to capital's capacity as a self-determining subject is more metaphorical than literal (in this sense, capital is better understood as a 'pseudo-subject'), but the function of this metaphor is to capture social and political reality under a historically specific form of production, namely, capitalism (see Smith 2019, 120–30). Tony Smith has offered the most sustained explication in recent years of this peculiar mechanism of domination in Marx's social theory, and more importantly, its normative implications. Smith submits:

> The great challenge Marx's concept of capital poses to liberal egalitarianism (and to other positions in normative social theory) is that it provides reasons to include capitalism among the social orders that are inherently flawed from a normative point of view. No less than slavery, no less than feudalism, no less than patriarchy, the systemic subordination of human ends under the end of capital is not, and can never be, consistent with equal concern and respect for persons as ends in themselves.
>
> (Smith 2019, 119)

What distinguishes Smith's analysis from other contemporary Marxian approaches is that it engages critically but also productively with liberal egalitarian perspectives, demonstrating in the end that liberal egalitarians such as John Rawls, Ronald Dworkin, and Jürgen Habermas cannot deliver on their normative ambitions unless they address the challenge of capital and its multilayered forms of domination. At bottom, Smith, following Marx, draws attention to the ways in which the ends or purposes of avowedly self-determining subjects are subjugated to an alien and inhuman subject – the empire of capital – which determines their fates (admittedly, in varying degrees) from cradle to grave. Any normative theory that places value on self-determination must therefore grapple with a social order that reduces individuals and their lives to the playthings of an alien power.

In fairness, Rawlsian-inspired left liberals are not the only ones who must contend with the contradictions identified by Smith. The last twenty years have seen a flowering of interest in theories of non-domination, particularly among neo-republican scholars, who have proposed alternatives to the classical liberal view of freedom as non-interference (see Kimpell Johnson 2022 for further discussion of republicanism in this volume). Neither Quentin Skinner nor Philip Pettit – the two most prominent exponents of neo-republican freedom – have engaged sufficiently with Marx's nuanced understanding of domination, or extended their inquiries to the asymmetrical relation between capital and labour in the twenty-first century. Neo-republicans are arguably as vulnerable to the problems generated by capital as liberal egalitarian theorists. In the neo-republican framework, the critique of domination points back to Roman law, tracing its normative roots to the concept of *sui iuris*. Those who had the privilege of legal personhood under Roman law were recognised as owners of their property and of their person, which meant that they could seek legal redress in a court of law when their private rights were violated by other legal persons. The emphasis on the legal person was integral to the self-understanding of Roman law and continues to be central to neo-republicanism because the *source* of domination must be traced back to an empirically existing legal person who is shown to exercise their arbitrary will over others. Insofar as domination is confined to the actions of persons, neo-republicans cannot explain, let alone address, the various mechanisms of domination identified by Marx's concept of capital and the conversion of private wealth into political domination. Not surprisingly, Pettit has previously argued (2006) against viewing the capitalist market system as a medium of domination.

The impersonal character of capitalist domination has been thoughtfully captured by proponents of radical republicanism, particularly by William Clare Roberts (2016), and more recently by Bruno Leipold (2022), both of whom have tried to present Marx as a proponent of the 'social republic' and as a radical republican in his own right.[11] While I do not take issue with these interpretive breakthroughs, there is a definite sense in which radical republicans have not yet fully come to grips with the Roman law heritage that pervades their treatments of non-domination (the idea that legal personhood is consistent with impersonal domination, which the republican tradition as such has difficulties explaining). Marx was indeed a proponent of the social republic during his lifetime, but he also sought to reach beyond it, philosophically and politically, especially through his original treatment of capital and the distinctive forms of domination to which it gives rise. Engels's prescient account of 'social murder' is also worth quoting at length precisely because it demonstrates how his treatment of impersonal domination overcomes the blind sports that are often shared, albeit in different ways, by liberal and neo-republican accounts of domination:

> When one individual inflicts bodily injury upon another such that death results, we call the deed manslaughter; when the assailant knew in advance that the injury would be fatal, we call his deed murder. But when society places hundreds of proletarians in such a position that they inevitably meet a too early and an unnatural death, one which is quite as much a death by violence as that by the sword or bullet; when it deprives thousands of the necessaries of life, places them under conditions in which they *cannot* live – forces them, through the strong arm of the law, to remain in such conditions until that death ensues which is the inevitable consequence – knows that these thousands of victims must perish, and yet permits these conditions to remain, its deed is murder just as surely as the deed of the single individual; disguised, malicious murder, murder against which none can defend himself, which does not seem what it is, because no man sees the murderer, because the death of the victim seems a natural one, since the offence is more one of omission than of commission. But murder it remains.
> (Engels [1845] 1975, 393–94)

A Marxian approach to private wealth and political domination has several advantages over liberal egalitarian and neo-republican approaches. First, the Marxian approach does not regard the state as wielding the greatest power under all conceivable circumstances. To be sure, the recognition that private wealth (as a manifestation of private power) can trump state power should not lead one to underestimate the threat of state power, for which some Marxists have justifiably been criticised by liberal commentators. As we have seen from Marx's earliest journalistic reflections, state power can become subservient to a mightier power, that is, to private power. In the context of contemporary financialised capitalism, this private power is bound up with the ability of multinational corporations to exert unprecedented political influence and even dictate public policies and legislation. The recognition that private power (in the form of corporate power) can trump state power is also important for considerations of public policy and reform. Liberal egalitarian approaches, such as those of Michael Walzer (1983, 95–128), Jürgen Habermas (2015, 85–102), and Axel Honneth (2017, 76–108), which are concerned with the 'colonisation' of the democratic lifeworld by systematic market imperatives, maintain that the democratic constitutional state can successfully relegate private power to its proper 'sphere.'[12] Such approaches to the problem of private wealth and political domination remain wedded to the classical liberal division between public and private spheres, in which the state remains the 'Leviathan' in the final instance.

The Marxian approach also has the upper hand over its neo-republican rivals in that it brings into critical view specific instances of domination that are not reducible to the arbitrary power of legal persons, including corporations. The idea that political domination is not always directly traceable to specific legal persons provides an alternative basis on which progressive reformers and social activists can conceive of alternative political-economic arrangements in which systemic or structural forms of domination can be seriously constrained and, ideally, abolished. The normative problems generated by capital as a form of private wealth are closely bound up with their political-economic remedies. It is to this matter that I now turn.

3 Confronting the 'Riddle of All Constitutions'

In his 1843 'Contribution to the Critique of Hegel's *Philosophy of Right*,' Marx counterposed democracy to Hegel's preferred regime of constitutional monarchy. The reason for this was that democracy represented for Marx the model constitution. In Marx's view, monarchy is defective because a particular moment of the state (i.e., the monarch) ends up determining and perverting the whole. What distinguishes democracy from monarchy is that the democratic constitution is, in both form and content, the self-determination of the people (the *demos*). It is in this specific sense that 'democracy is the solved riddle of all constitutions.' As Marx put it: 'In democracy the constitution, the law, the state itself, insofar as it is a political constitution, is only the self-determination of the people, and a particular content of the people' (Marx [1843] 1978a, 20). By the time of the 1848 revolutions, Marx and Engels had returned to Cologne with the goal of fighting for a democratic constitution in a unified Germany, which they thought would be ushered in by the ascending liberal bourgeoisie (see Shoikhedbrod 2022). They regarded the achievement of the democratic constitution as the first step towards the resolution of the so-called social question, which was bound up with the problems introduced by the nascent capitalist mode of production. However, the German revolution of 1848 did not come to pass as Marx and Engels had hoped; instead, they were back in exile, awaiting the next democratic opening amidst reactionary restoration. Reflecting in 1892, Engels remarked: 'Marx and I, for forty years, repeated ad nauseam that for us the democratic republic is the only political form in which the struggle between the working class and the capitalist class can first be universalised and then culminate in the decisive victory of the proletariat' (Engels [1892] 1990b, 271).

Marx's account of democracy as the solved riddle of all constitutions did not vanish into thin air. Instead, it took on a more robust and expansive meaning in his life's work, *Capital*, where it was put forward as a necessary solution to the problems generated by private capital and its resultant forms of political domination. More precisely, democracy was to be understood as the *sine qua non* of 'associated production.' In a famous passage in *Capital*, Marx surmised that 'freedom in this field can only consist in socialised man, the associated producers, rationally regulating their interchange with Nature, bringing it under their common control, instead of being ruled by it as by the blind forces of Nature; and achieving this with the least expenditure of energy and under conditions most favourable to, and worthy of, their human nature' (Marx [1894] 1976b, 571). Marx pointed to cooperatives owned and managed by workers as the first sprouts of 'associated production' within actually existing capitalism. Marx wrote that worker cooperatives in particular represent 'within the old form [of production] the first sprouts of the new,' and that 'the capitalist stock companies, as much as the cooperative factories, should be considered as transitional forms from the capitalist mode of production to the associated one, with the only distinction that the antagonism is resolved negatively in the one and positively in the other' (Marx [1894] 1976b, 440; for an illuminating discussion see Hudis 2012; Wolff 2012). In order for associated production to constitute a concrete reality, there would have to exist generalised practices of cooperative solidarity in the productive sphere that build within existing capitalist societies the sprouts of socialist institutions, in which cooperative forms of social property and egalitarian solidarity, rather than competition and domination, would form the basis of social interaction. It is important to reiterate that democratically managed cooperatives were regarded by Marx as transitional institutions en route to a fuller conception of 'associated production'; they did not signal the journey's end. For this and other reasons, contemporary Marxian-inspired socialists differ widely on the role of cooperatives under post-capitalist conditions (Lawler et al. 1998).

The late Erik Olin Wright was one of the most prolific contemporary Marxian-inspired democratic socialists. In his last published book, Wright provided a compelling case for expanding and consolidating the democratic potential of worker cooperatives with the aim of realising such socialist values as justice, freedom, equality, and community (solidarity). Wright's argument is in keeping with his broader challenge for socialists to envision 'real utopias':

> Worker cooperatives are particularly salient for the possibility of economic democracy, for in a worker cooperative, workers own the firm and production is governed through democratic processes. While worker cooperatives produce for the market, *they are organized around values very different from capitalist firms: solidarity, equality, democratic governance, dignity of work, community development.*
> (Wright 2019, 77, my emphasis)

For Wright, worker-owned and democratically managed cooperatives are just one in a range of institutions and social practices that reinforce a 'democratic-conforming market.' On Wright's definition, a 'democratic-conforming' market is one that is 'effectively subordinate to the exercise of democratic power' (2019, 70). Although Wright's analysis needs further elaboration and defence, which would go beyond the scope of the present chapter, it captures an integral dimension of the socialist project that has been largely neglected in recent years (Shoikhedbrod 2021b). Practices of worker self-management within cooperatives, as well as broader processes of democratic control over investment, are structured according to values that are very different from those of capitalist firms. These are values that honour freedom, equality, and community. Wright's work lends itself constructively to broader proposals for economic democracy, such as those theorised by David Schweickart (2011) and Paul Adler (2019), which combine worker self-management, democratic control over investment, and principles of egalitarian solidarity (see Christiano 2022 in this volume on worker co-operatives, and Al Salman 2022 and Bennett and Claassen 2022 on some other institutions for democratic control of the economy). To be clear, I am not claiming that worker-owned and democratically managed cooperatives would be a panacea, especially under the existing constraints of global financial capitalism; they will continually be subject to pressures that are unavoidable under capitalism. However, worker-owned and managed cooperatives remain important first steps towards any version of associated production that might confront the contradictions of private wealth and political domination. More broadly, such proposals help wrest from capital its status as a 'self-determining subject' and transfer this power back to the democratic control of associated producers and the political community more broadly. The politically salient point here is that individuals should be able to exercise democratic control over their economic affairs, which will of course remain a matter of degree and will be subject to considerations of scale. Consequently, rather than abolishing markets *in toto* and replacing them with authoritarian varieties of central planning, the solution to the problem of capital, and of the private power and political domination resulting from it, is to render markets subordinate to democratically determined human ends and needs (Smith 2019, 346; cf. Polanyi [1944] 2001). After all, markets predate capitalism and should not be immediately conflated with either the concept of capital or of capitalism. The goal of subordinating markets to democratic control, including the long-term abolition of capital and its value form, remains an ongoing *political* project.

4 Conclusion

This chapter has offered a distinctly Marxian approach to the contradictory relationship between private wealth and political domination under contemporary financialised capitalism. I began by providing an overview of Marx's early journalistic reflections on the subservience of the political state to private wealth, which was shown to result in the corruption of the state's laws and in the domination of the poor. Marx's formative reflections helped pave the way for his mature understanding of capital and the specific forms of domination to which it gives rise. Focusing on Marx's original conception of capital, as well the contributions of subsequent Marxian thinkers, I outlined the ways in which the Marxian understanding of domination has several advantages over liberal egalitarian and neo-republican accounts. After discussing the relative advantages of the Marxian approach, I concluded by offering a preliminary Marxian-inspired strategy for confronting the contradictory relationship between private wealth and political domination today, that is, by making markets subservient to democratically determined human ends and needs with the broader aim of abolishing capital.

Notes

1 Among classical liberal thinkers, the idea that private power and interest can occasionally undermine public power and public interest was most clearly articulated by Adam Smith (see Smith [1776] 2008, 232). For recent contributions along liberal egalitarian lines, see Cordelli (2020) and Anderson (2017). In this volume, see Richard Arneson's contribution.
2 It is helpful to compare Marx's insights about the wood theft law with E.P. Thompson's parallel treatment of the notorious Black Act of 1723. In both cases, something that was initially regarded (particularly by the poor) as common property for public use was transformed into the object of private property, with its associated rights of exclusion and threats of penal sanction (capital punishment in the case of the Black Act). See Thompson (1975); for a more detailed discussion of this topic, see Shoikhedbrod (2021a).
3 The Historical School of Law was a school of jurisprudence that came to prominence in Germany in the late eighteenth century under the influence of Gustav Hugo and Karl von Savigny.
4 The absence of a sustained engagement with Marx's work has led Katherina Pistor to infer, in an otherwise incisive work, that rational choice theorists and Marxists alike 'ignore the central role of law in in the making of capital and its protection as private wealth. [...] The key to understanding the basis of power and the resulting distribution of wealth lies instead in the process of bestowing legal protection on select assets and to do so as a matter of private, not public, choice' (Pistor 2019, 208). Marx's formative article on the wood theft law sheds valuable light on precisely the problem identified by Pistor, that is, the ways in which private law helps facilitate the accumulation and consolidation of private wealth (in the form of capital).
5 See especially Postone (1993). While Postone develops an innovative reinterpretation of 'social domination' against traditional Marxism, which sheds valuable light on the ubiquity of abstract labour and abstract time under capitalism, his account has the unfortunate tendency of diminishing the relative importance of class domination and underemphasising the role of political agency in counteracting social domination. For a recent intervention that emphasises the importance of class and its implications for grasping contemporary forms of domination and the possibility of collective self-determination, see Cicerchia (2021).

6 One should also consider Engels's extended treatment of the historical origins of the state, including its anticipated 'withering away' under conditions of developed communism in 'The Origin of the Family, Private Property, and the State' (Engels [1884] 1990a).
7 For a well-researched account of the characteristic separation of the political and the economic under capitalism that elaborates on this insight, see Ellen Meiksins Wood (2016, 19–47). Drawing partly on Wood's earlier work, Nancy Fraser (2014) has elaborated on the specific character of financialised capitalism as an administrative political order.
8 For a more detailed examination of this debate and its contemporary relevance, see Clark (1991). For a desired convergence between the best features of welfare liberal and Marxist theories of the state, see Macpherson (2013).
9 See Shoikhedbrod (2019, 141–50). For a favourable interpretation of Rawls's 'reticent' orientation towards liberal socialism, see Edmundson (2017).
10 There are nonetheless innovative scholarly efforts at combining the best of Rawlsian and Marxian insights, such as Reiman (2012). Reiman's earlier work (1987) took as its point of departure the structural coercion that is specific to capitalism.
11 For an original and bold attempt at outlining the institutional nuts and bolts of an anti-oligarchic republic that draws upon the plebeian tradition (including its diverse expression in the works of Karl Marx, Friedrich Engels, Rosa Luxemburg, and Antonio Gramsci), see Vergara (2020; for discussion, see also Bulmer and White 2022).
12 For a recent critique of Honneth's attempted renewal of socialism, see Shoikhedbrod (2021c).

References

Adler, Paul S. 2019. *The 99 Percent Economy: How Democratic Socialism Can Overcome the Crises of Capitalism*. Oxford: Oxford University Press.

Al Salman, Yara. 2022. "Independence in the Commons: How Group Ownership Realises Basic Non-Domination." In *Wealth and Power: Philosophical Perspectives*, edited by Michael Bennett, Huub Brouwer, and Rutger Claassen. London: Routledge.

Anderson, Elizabeth. 2017. *Private Government*. Princeton, NJ: Princeton University Press.

Bennett, Michael and Rutger Claassen. 2022. "Taming the Corporate Leviathan: How to Properly Politicize Corporate Purpose?" In *Wealth and Power: Philosophical Perspectives*, edited by Michael Bennett, Huub Brouwer, and Rutger Claassen. London: Routledge.

Bensaïd, Daniel. 2021. *The Dispossessed: Karl Marx's Debates on Wood Theft and the Right of the Poor*. Translated by Robert Nichols. Minneapolis, MN: University of Minnesota Press.

Bulmer, Elliot, and Stuart White. 2022. "Constitutions Against Oligarchy." In *Wealth and Power: Philosophical Perspectives*, edited by Michael Bennett, Huub Brouwer, and Rutger Claassen, 274–294. London: Routledge.

Carver, Terrell. 2010. "The German Ideology Never Happened." *History of Political Thought* 31, no. 1: 107–27.

———. 2018. *Marx*. Cambridge: Polity.
Christiano, Thomas. 2022. "Why Does Worker Participation Matter? Three Considerations in Favor of Worker Participation in Corporate Governance." In *Wealth and Power: Philosophical Perspectives*, edited by Michael Bennett, Huub Brouwer, and Rutger Claassen. London: Routledge.
Cicerchia, Lillian. 2021. 'Why Does Class Matter?' *Social Theory and Practice*. Online First: September 18, 2021.
Clark, Simon, ed. 1991. *The State Debate*. London: Macmillan.
Cordelli, Chiara. 2020. *The Privatized State*. Princeton, NJ: Princeton University Press.
Day, Richard. 2018. "Why Does Marx Matter?" In *Responses to Marx's Capital*, edited by Richard Day and Daniel Gaido, 1–39. Chicago, IL: Haymarket.
Edmundson, William. 2017. *Rawls: Reticent Socialist*. Cambridge: Cambridge University Press.
Engels, Friedrich. [1845] 1975. "The Condition of the Working-Class in England." In *MECW 4*, 295–596. New York, NY: International Publishers.
———. [1884] 1990a. "The Origin of the Family, Private Property, and the State." In *MECW 26*, 129–276. New York, NY: International Publishers.
———. [1892] 1990b. "Reply to the Honourable Giovanni Bovio." In *MECW 27*, 270–72. New York, NY: International Publishers.
Fraser, Nancy. 2014. "Legitimation Crisis? On the Political Contradictions of Financialized Capitalism." *Critical Historical Studies* 2, no. 2: 157–89.
Habermas, Jürgen. 2015. *The Lure of Technocracy*. Translated by Ciaran Cronin. Cambridge: Polity.
Honneth, Axel. 2017. *The Idea of Socialism: Towards a Renewal*. Translated by Joseph Ganahl. Cambridge: Polity.
Hudis, Peter. 2012. *Marx's Concept of the Alternative to Capitalism*. Leiden: Brill.
Kimpell Johnson, Jessica. 2022. "What About Ethos? Republican Institutions, Oligarchic Democracy and Norms of Political Equality." In *Wealth and Power: Philosophical Perspectives*, edited by Michael Bennett, Huub Brouwer, and Rutger Claassen. London: Routledge.
Lawler, James, Bertell Ollman, David Schweickart, and Hillel Titcktin. 1998. *Market Socialism: The Debate Among Socialists*. New York, NY: Routledge.
Leipold, Bruno. 2022. "Chains and Invisible Threads: Liberty and Domination in Marx's Account of Wage-Slavery." In *Rethinking Liberty before Liberalism*, edited by Annelien de Dijn and Hannah Dawson, 194–214. Cambridge: Cambridge University Press.
Leopold, David. 2007. *The Young Marx*. Cambridge: Cambridge University Press.
Macpherson, C.B. 2013. "Do We Need a Theory of the State?" In *The Rise and Fall of Economic Justice and Other Essays*, 55–75. Toronto: Oxford University Press.
Marx, Karl. [1842] 1971. "Debates on the Law on Thefts of Wood." In *MECW 1*, 224–63. New York, NY: International Publishers.
———. [1867] 1976a. *Capital Volume I*. New York, NY: International Publishers.
———. [1894] 1976b. *Capital Volume III*. New York, NY: International Publishers.
———. [1843] 1978a. "Contribution to the Critique of Hegel's *Philosophy of Right*." In Tucker 1978, 16–25.
———. [1852] 1978b. "The Eighteenth Brumaire of Louis Bonaparte." In Tucker 1978, 606–18.

———. [1857] 1978c. "Grundrisse." In Tucker 1978, 221–93.
———. [1859] 1978d. "On the History of His Opinions." In Tucker 1978, 3–6.
———. [1844] 1978e. "On the Jewish Question." In Tucker 1978, 26–52.
Marx, Karl and Friedrich Engels. [1848] 1978. "Manifesto of the Communist Party." In Tucker 1978, 469–500.
Miliband, Ralph. 1970. "The Capitalist State: Reply to Nicos Poulantzas." *New Left Review* 59: 53–60.
O'Neill, Martin and Thad Williamson, eds. 2012. *Property-Owning Democracy: Rawls and Beyond*. Malden, MA: Wiley-Blackwell.
Pettit, Philip. 2006. "Freedom in the Market." *Politics, Philosophy & Economics* 5, no. 2: 131–49.
Pistor, Katherina. 2019. *The Code of Capital*. Princeton, NJ: Princeton University Press.
Polanyi, Karl. [1944] 2001. *The Great Transformation*. Boston, MA: Beacon Press.
Postone, Moishe. 1993. *Time, Labor, and Social Domination: A Reinterpretation of Marx's Critical Theory*. Cambridge: Cambridge University Press.
Poulantzas, Nicos. 1969. "The Problem of the Capitalist State." *New Left Review* 58: 67–78.
Rawls, John. 2001. *Justice as Fairness: A Restatement*. Cambridge, MA: Belknap.
Reiman, Jeffrey. 1987. "Exploitation, Force, and Moral Assessment: Thoughts on Roemer and Cohen." *Philosophy & Public Affairs* 16, no. 1: 3–41.
———. 2012. *As Free and as Just as Possible: The Theory of Marxian Liberalism*. Malden, MA: Wiley-Blackwell.
Roberts, William Clare. 2016. *Marx's Inferno*. Princeton, NJ: Princeton University Press.
Schweickart, David. 2011. *After Capitalism*. New York, NY: Rowman & Littlefield.
Shoikhedbrod, Igor. 2019. *Revisiting Marx's Critique of Liberalism*. New York, NY: Palgrave Macmillan.
———. 2021a. "Beyond Fetishism and Instrumentalism: Rethinking Marxism and Law under Neoliberalism." In *Research Handbook on Law and Marxism*, edited by Paul O'Connell and Umut Ozsu, 496–510. Cheltenham: Elgar.
———. 2021b. "G.A. Cohen, the Neglect of Democratic Self-Management, and the Future of Democratic Socialism." *Journal of Social Philosophy*. First View: August 23, 2021.
———. 2021c. "Market Morality, Socialism, and the Realization of Social Freedom: A Critique of Honneth's Normative Reconstruction." *Critical Horizons* 22, no. 4: 335–50.
———. 2022. "Marx and the Democratic Struggle over the Constitution in 1848–49." *History of Political Thought*.
Smith, Adam. [1776] 2008. *An Inquiry into the Nature and Causes of the Wealth of Nations: A Selected Edition*, edited by Kathryn Sutherland. Oxford: Oxford University Press.
Smith, Tony. 2019. *Beyond Liberal Egalitarianism*. Chicago, IL: Haymarket.
Thompson, E.P. 1975. *Whigs and Hunters: The Origin of the Black Act*. London: Allen Lane.
Tucker, Robert, ed. 1978. *The Marx-Engels Reader*. New York, NY: Norton.

Vergara, Camila. 2020. *Systemic Corruption: Constitutional Ideas for an Anti-Oligarchic Republic*. Princeton, NJ: Princeton University Press.

Walzer, Michael. 1983. *Spheres of Justice: A Defense of Pluralism and Equality*. New York, NY: Basic Books.

Wolff, Richard. 2012. *Democracy at Work: A Cure for Capitalism*. Chicago, IL: Haymarket.

Wood, Ellen Meiksins. 2016. *Democracy against Capitalism: Renewing Historical Materialism*. London: Verso.

Wright, Erik Olin. 2019. *How to Be an Anti-Capitalist in the Twenty-First Century*. London: Verso.

6 Anarchism and Redistribution

Jessica Flanigan

Anarchists believe that the best society would be a stateless society. Alas, most people do not live in a stateless society. How should anarchists view law enforcement by agents of the state? Of course, anarchists should view most law enforcement as a form of unjustified violence against people because most of the laws that public officials enforce target people who are not liable to be coerced. This means that any laws that go beyond protecting people's enforceable rights are an impermissible exercise of state power.[1]

But we anarchists who find ourselves situated in states can say more about state power beyond 'I'm against it.' In this essay, I argue that anarchists should favour policies that minimise people's exposure to the burdens of state power. Perhaps surprisingly then, anarchists should not necessarily favour policies that aim to lower taxes, nor should they oppose redistribution on principle. In practice, given that existing states uphold and enforce some property conventions, anarchists should be sympathetic to some redistributive policies. This argument is pitched at the level of non-ideal theory. In the world as it is, where wealth and political power is very unevenly distributed within and between states, it would be a mistake for anarchists to complacently accept the current distribution of material resources for the sake of opposing further acts of governmental interference.

My argument for this claim assumes that public officials should not enforce any policies that violate people's natural entitlements.[2] That is, I am assuming that anarchists are correct in claiming that officials lack the authority to enforce most of the laws that they enforce, and that people have no duty to obey most of the laws that are enforced. From that background assumption, I then argue:

1 Public officials will continue to enforce unjust policies.
2 In a system where officials persist in enforcing unjust policies that violate people's natural entitlements, they should structure those policies in ways that reduce the burdensomeness of these rights violations.

3 Redistributive policies can reduce the burdensomeness of state action, relative to the absence of redistributive policies.
4 When public officials enforce unjust policies, they should redistribute resources.

In addition to this argument, we might also add the following argument in favour of redistribution:

5 If a public official enforces an unjust policy, they should compensate the victims of unjust enforcement.
6 Everyone subject to an unjust policy is a victim of unjust enforcement.
7 Officials should compensate the victims of unjust enforcement by structuring the unjust policy (e.g., a property system) in a way that distributes some resources to everyone.
8 When public officials enforce unjust policies, they should do it in a way that distributes some resources to everyone.

In referring to unjust policies, I'm referring to policies that violate people's natural entitlements. These include paternalistic policies, land-use policies, borders, and many property conventions.

Of course, it would be best if officials didn't enforce these policies. But, given that they do enforce unjust policies, not all unjust policies are equally as bad. On my view, it is better if officials enforce laws in ways that redistribute resources to poorer citizens than if they enforce laws that protect the current property distribution and prevent poorer citizens from accessing resources. For this reason, it is better for officials to tax people who are advantaged by the property system in order to redistribute resources to those who are disadvantaged, even if we also grant that officials also don't have the authority to enforce most, if any, of these property conventions in the first place.

In making the anarchist case for a redistribution of resources, I am arguing against anarchists who oppose existing redistributive policies on the grounds that they expand the size of government or increase instances of governmental coercion (Mack 2006; 2018; Friedman 2013; Huemer 2013). On my view, these arguments are mistaken. I grant that lower taxes and less welfare spending would seemingly reduce the size of government and reduce governmental coercion in this narrow sense, thereby bringing a society closer to the anarchist ideal. Yet these policies might nevertheless exacerbate the injustices associated with whatever governmental institutions are left.

In the rest of this essay, I will follow the structure of the preceding arguments. In Section 1, I describe and defend anarchism. There, I argue that public officials unjustly violate people's natural rights when they enforce all sorts of laws, including paternalistic policies, land-use policies, borders, and property conventions. In Section 2, I make the case that, in non-ideal contexts, public officials should try to make it so that whatever unjust policies they do enforce reduce the burdensomeness of these rights violations. In Section 3, I then argue that some redistribution can achieve this goal. In Section 4, I consider a non-instrumental anarchist case for redistribution – compensation. In contrast to the instrumental argument for redistribution, this argument does not make redistribution empirically contingent on its liberatory effects. On the other hand, it is empirically contingent in that it holds that the beneficiaries of redistributive policies will reliably align with the people who are entitled to compensation for unjust policies. I view these two strands of argument as complementary considerations in favour of a presumption of some redistributive policies. In Section 5, I consider the claim that redistribution may unfairly burden people who benefit from the status quo. In response, I argue that this objection assumes that people are entitled to the benefits of the status quo. There, I also note that too much redistribution can backfire. This case for redistribution is purely instrumental, and to the extent that it would not, in practice, have the liberatory effect that I envision, then officials should not redistribute. In Section 6, I consider the best form these policies could take, in light of anarchist values. There, I offer some arguments in support of a basic income programme.

1 Property and Rights

Anarchists believe that public officials do not have the authority to use coercion in ways that violate people's natural rights. Some kinds of law enforcement are not coercive in this way. For example, enforcing a law that prevents people from assaulting or killing other people wouldn't violate anyone's natural rights because people don't have a right to assault or kill others. The same goes for laws against fraud and deception, and laws that uphold contracts, at least on some accounts (Flanigan 2017). In these cases, it's not that anarchists think that public officials have any kind of morally distinctive authority to threaten people with violence, imprisonment or some other policy. It's rather that *anyone* has the authority to interfere with wrongdoers in the service of defending or upholding another person's rights (Brennan 2020).

So, some laws are permissibly enforced. But most laws aren't like this. That's why anarchists oppose the enforcement of most laws. Most of the time, law enforcement involves threatening a person with imprisonment or some other penalty in a way that violates her rights against interference. That's why most instances of law enforcement are unjust. For example, if a migrant crosses a border, which is an invisible line between two countries, she is not liable to be shot or captured in virtue of that fact because walking across an invisible line doesn't violate anyone else's natural rights. When border guards shoot at migrants, they violate migrants' rights against being shot (Huemer 2010; Hidalgo 2018).

Anarchists also think that people have no duty to obey a law *simply* because it is a law (Wolff 1998). Suppose there is nothing morally wrong with selling a drug that that public officials have prohibited. Then, the mere fact it has been prohibited gives a seller no duty to comply with the prohibition.

As I am using the term, anarchism consists in the denial of the moral specialness of the state (Brennan 2020). This is a compelling vision of how people should live together. Public officials don't have any permissions or obligations that private citizens lack (Hasnas 2008). All people are equal with respect to their entitlements to be protected from interference and their entitlements to enforce moral requirements.

Though anarchists agree that a stateless society would be morally best and that the aforementioned laws are unjust, they disagree about other political questions. For the most part, anarchists are sceptical that political processes such as democratic elections or representative government could ever make political power legitimate, but they vary in the degree that they endorse democratic processes for decision-making more generally.[3] Anarchists disagree in their reasons for opposing coercive state policies too. Some argue from a religious tradition (Underwood and Vallier 2020). Some emphasise the importance of social equality. Others think that a system where officials are not permitted to violate people's rights against interference is best because it would promote well-being on balance (Brennan 2018). Anarchists disagree about how feasible a stateless society is too (e.g., Newhard 2016). And they disagree about whether people should try to promote justice through deregulation and anti-statist policy (Simmons 1999; Carson 2018).

It is not my goal in this essay to provide a taxonomy of different kinds of anarchists or to say what all anarchists should believe. Instead, I want to focus on the points of agreement among anarchists, all of whom are advocates for a radical vision of a fully voluntary cooperative society. Though they disagree, anarchist thinkers have collectively developed a broadly coherent theoretical framework that challenges the prevailing view of political authority, and that is the sense of anarchism that interests me here.

With that minimal conception of anarchism in hand, perhaps the greatest area of disagreement among anarchists arises in response to the question of whether people's enforceable natural rights include rights to private property, meaning property rights beyond people's rights to bodily integrity or personal autonomy. On this point, anarchists also disagree about what form property rights might take. Some anarchists argue that people have rights to acquire and transfer property and this fact implies that public officials generally do not have the authority to use force or threats of force to limit people's ability to acquire and transfer property (D. Friedman 1994; 2013; Mack 2006; Huemer 2017). Others think that a stateless society would allow people to acquire and transfer property via markets, but they're sceptical about whether people can acquire rights to natural resources under the current system (Carson 2008; Chartier 2013; Long 2019; Christmas 2021). Other anarchists oppose private property all together (Spafford 2020). Some argue that the ideal society is not only a stateless society but also one where people do not own private property but instead co-own productive resources and engage in mutual aid (Montero and Foster 2017; Graeber 2020).

Here again, for the sake of this argument, I'm not taking a stand on these competing visions of property rights in a stateless society. This is because in the world of existing states, we don't necessarily need to resolve this disagreement. We just need to recognise that there are *some respects* in which the existing enforcement of property rights doesn't align with people's natural rights, if those rights do in fact exist. If people don't have rights to acquire and transfer property, well, that's why the state's enforcement of property rights violates their natural rights (Spafford 2020). But we have reason to think that public officials in *existing* states are not entitled to uphold the property rules that they do, even if there can be rights to acquire and transfer property rights, and even if the just stateless society would have capitalism.

To see this, let's grant for the sake of argument that people can have natural entitlements to external property. Anarchists like Michael Huemer argue that people can have natural rights to things they build using natural resources, such as a house in the wilderness (Huemer 2013; 2017). So, on Huemer's account, if a person builds a home in the wilderness, it would be wrong for an intruder to show up and destroy it, or move into it, and the homebuilder would have a right to protect their home against the intruder. If successful, argument shows that people can, in principle, have enforceable property rights to some external objects outside the context of a state.

Yet within the context of a state, many property rights aren't like Huemer's house. Most of these rights are at least partly conventional rights which public officials define and enforce (Stilz 2017). For example, even if people have rights to their houses, they don't have rights to the legal context that surrounds their houses, such as zoning restrictions that create scarcity in the housing market and artificially inflate the market value of their homes. Or, even if people have rights to acquire and use natural resources to an extent, it doesn't follow that their rights to acquire and use natural resources align with the system of land titles that public officials uphold. And even if people have rights to use natural resources productively and to keep the benefits of that productive use, the political enforcement of land titles doesn't just uphold people's claims to the fruits of their labour. Rather, public officials pre-emptively prevent people from accessing unused land, they prevent people from using their land as productively as possible, and they allow some but not others to access and use natural resources – thereby diminishing competition and distorting the price of these resources (C. W. Johnson 2012).

Or consider property rights in money. The value of money is determined by a convention that people use to coordinate efficient exchanges.[4] In some ways, the monetary system is grounded in people's natural rights to make promises and contracts.[5] But there are a range of efficient coordination mechanisms, and any given system of currency and enforcement is largely decided by public officials enforcing their favoured set of conventions. Additionally, when public officials issue currency and claim a monopoly on the right to govern that currency, they can also determine the value of everyone's holdings (in terms of currency) by setting interest rates and regulating the money supply.

To take another example, intellectual property rights are seemingly entirely divorced from people's natural rights.[6] In these cases, a system of enforceable intellectual property rights consists in upholding a set of conventions through threats of violence, which do violate people's natural bodily rights, for the sake of a potential social benefit (Long 2011; Christmas 2021). For example, if someone invents and sells a cure for an illness, it would not violate her right to use or control that cure if someone else sold the cure at a lower price. Yet public officials enforce laws that prevent people from copying others' ideas in this way.

These examples suggest that even if people have some natural property rights, it's still wrong for public officials to enforce a lot of the property conventions they do, and a lot of people's property holdings are the result of state-backed violations of people's natural rights. Not all law enforcement is unjust. If officials use force or threats of force to protect people's natural rights, these forms of law enforcement are not objectionable. For example, officials (or anyone else) can interfere to protect others' bodily rights, or to protect people from violence and fraud, or to protect whatever property rights are entailed by the exercise of people's natural rights. But since existing property systems go far beyond enforcing people's natural entitlements, even if we grant that people's natural rights to their bodies and their labour entail some property rights, such an argument still would not establish the enforceability of any existing property system.

Property rights enforcement, at least in the context of existing states, involves violations of people's natural rights. In making this case, I've assumed that enforcement of any right always consists in a kind of interference with a person's freedom (Rodin 2014). I also assumed that it is wrong to interfere with a person in this way if they are not liable to be interfered with (Flanigan 2019a, 2019b). Building on these assumptions, I argued that public officials interfere with people who people are not liable to be interfered with when they enforce a lot of existing laws. In so doing, officials enforce a distribution of property that is unjust.

The key takeaway here is that as things currently stand, any system of enforced property rights does not wholly align with people's natural rights. Even if some property rights in natural resources could be enforceable, all political systems of property enforcement infringe on people's rights. The only just property system is a property system outside the state.

2 Anarchists in States

Almost everyone lives in a state. This situation is clearly not ideal, morally speaking, from an anarchist point of view. Almost everywhere, public officials unjustly violate people's natural rights through the enforcement of paternalistic laws, monopoly protections, borders, and some/all property rules. Yet amid these pervasive rights violations, not all regimes are morally equivalent. Public policy can still be better or worse by anarchist standards. In this section, I argue that public officials should try to make it so that whatever unjust policies they do enforce reduce the burdensomeness of the rights violations entailed by law enforcement.

Even granting that a stateless society would be morally best, that doesn't tell us much about how to evaluate the justice of existing institutions. Anarchists should evaluate existing institutions in terms of whether they reduce the injustice associated with the state. This claim can be interpreted in two ways. On one hand, it could mean that anarchists should evaluate existing institutions in terms of whether they reduce the size of the state, on the assumption that reducing the size of the state would reduce the injustices associated with the state. On the other hand, it could mean that anarchists should evaluate existing institutions in terms of whether they reduce the burdensomeness of being subjected to unjust law enforcement. In this section, I defend the second approach. In the next section, I argue that this may require some redistribution of property.

Because public officials lack the authority to enforce most of the laws that they do, one should conclude that it's wrong for public officials to engage in most forms of law enforcement. Officials should stop enforcing paternalistic laws, borders, and so on. On its face, one might think that this also implies that officials should not enforce laws that redistribute property, since these laws are also enforced using threats of force that violate non-liable people's natural rights. After all, if an anarchist society is unavailable, the next-best alternative would be to favour social reforms that reduce the number of times that public officials interfere to violate people's natural rights or to favour a society where public officials have fewer opportunities to violate people's rights.[7]

Alternatively, one might think that if an anarchist society is currently infeasible, then the next-best alternative is to favour social reforms that reduce the *burdensomeness* of law enforcement. It doesn't follow from the fact that governments are unjust that people should aim to limit the size of the government. Public officials have enforced laws that created an unjust distribution of resources. By enforcing these policies, they violated the rights of the relative beneficiaries of those unjust patterns of enforcement as well as those who were disadvantaged by enforcement, but these policies are especially burdensome to people who are disadvantaged by the pattern of enforcement. Reducing the size of government from this point will not necessarily remedy the injustices associated with this unjust pattern of enforcement if people continue to experience the burdens associated with previous governmental injustices.

Consider a morbid medical analogy to illustrate this distinction:

> *Tumour:* Imagine that a patient is suffering from an inoperable malignant tumour. Ideally, the patient would take Drug A, which would eliminate the tumour and all its associated difficulties. Unfortunately, Drug A doesn't exist. The patient has two options. Drug B would shrink the size of the tumour, but it could have severe side effects that would seriously diminish his quality of life. Drug C would leave the tumour in place, and perhaps even cause the tumour to grow. But it would make it so that the tumour was not as much of a hindrance to the patient as he went about his life.

In this case, the patient should take Drug C. If there was a drug, Drug D, that shrunk the tumour and didn't have negative side effects, then the patient might have reason to take it as well. If there was a drug, Drug E, that shrunk the tumour and had beneficial side effects, the patient would have reason to take Drug E, just as he had reason to take Drug C. But, given that only Drug B and Drug C are available, and Drug B risks causing side effects, the patient does not have reason to take it just for the sake of shrinking the size of the tumour.

People who live in states are in an analogous situation. Some policies can minimise the burdensomeness of government *and also* minimise the size of government. Following the analogy, some treatments may have the beneficial effects of Drug E. For example, zoning reform may reduce the government's authority to unjustly enforce burdensome land-use regulations while also making it so that housing policy in general is less burdensome to people. If these policy solutions are available, anarchists have reason to prefer them over alternatives that only reduce the scope of governmental intervention and over alternatives that only address the burdensomeness of being subject to a coercively enforced property system.

Unfortunately, in other domains there is a trade-off between treating the cause of a malady or treating the effects – Drug B or Drug C; reduce the size of government or minimise the burdensomeness of government. For example, say that zoning reform is politically infeasible. Under those constraints, officials may be deciding between policies that raise property taxes on homeowners in order to provide housing vouchers to low-income residents. In cases like this, it could be that officials could make it a lot easier for residents to live in a political community by redistributing property and resources from the wealthy to the disadvantaged, but that these policies would also require further empowering an administrative state and law enforcement to enforce a burdensome tax policy.

When these trade-offs exist, anarchists should favour the policy analogy to Drug C. The reason that people take drugs for tumours is to improve their quality of life, not to fight tumours on principle. Similarly, people who are concerned about the burdensomeness of government, either in terms of well-being, freedom or equality, should favour policies that reduce those burdens over policies that reduce government. This principle is the foundation for the following defence of redistribution.

3 An Instrumental Case for Redistribution

Anarchists should evaluate existing institutions, including the existing system of property, in terms of whether enforcement reduces the burdensomeness of people being subject to unjust law enforcement. This means that anarchists should not reflexively oppose redistributive policies. Given that almost everyone lives in a state, redistributive polices can potentially limit the burdensomeness of being subject to the law. This is an argument about how anarchism as an ideal theory should translate to a world of trade-offs where only second best, third best and nth best options are available. To say that a policy is the best available one in these circumstances is not to say that the policy is itself justly enforced, that officials have the authority to enforce it or that people have duties to comply with the policy.

In practice, this means that when policies that reduce the burdensomeness of law enforcement by limiting the scope of law enforcement are unavailable, anarchists should favour policies that limit the burdensomeness of government. For example, anarchists should support redistributive policies when redistributing resources would reduce the burdensomeness of government, even if the enforcement of a redistributive policy expands the scope of governmental intervention.

Consider another analogy to illustrate this point.

> <u>Thief</u>: A and B know that S is a thief who randomly steals from people. S cannot be stopped. On day one, S steals from A to give to B. B knows this is the case but it's pointless to refuse. On day two, S steals from B to give to A. A similarly knows that this is the case but it's pointless to refuse.

One response to this case is to say that, given that S is stealing, it is morally better if S steals only once, from A to give to B, rather than stealing twice. This is the view that I reject. Rather, on my view, given that S is stealing, it's morally better if S steals in a way that does not disproportionately burden A or B.

In drawing the analogy in this way, I am deliberately granting that A and B have property rights that S violates. This assumption therefore allows that redistribution can violate people's natural rights to property, as critics of redistribution claim. But B does not have a right to whatever S gave them when S stole from A (Wenar 2008; Nozick 2013, 152–153). And likewise, A doesn't have a right to whatever S took from B.

Similarly, I argued earlier that a lot of people's property holdings, and the value of those holdings, are a result of public officials' unjust enforcement of the law. People are not entitled to the benefits of zoning policies that create an inflated value of their homes, even if they do have natural property rights to sell, modify, exclude people from and otherwise control their homes (Chartier 2013, 223–227). People are not entitled to the monopoly protections that intellectual property enforcement provides, even if they do have natural property rights in whatever products they produce (Long 2011; Christmas 2016).

Given that people are not fully entitled to the gains of the property system, many people find themselves in the position of B. Continuing with these examples, People who work for the government, S, violate the rights of some citizens, A, by preventing them from living in a multi-family housing complex in B's neighbourhood or by manufacturing a product when the patent is held by B.

Public officials do not have an entitlement to do these things, but it's unlikely that they will stop. Given that the status quo distribution of resources reflects these patterns of unjust enforcement and given that officials are unwilling to stop enforcing these unjust policies, public officials may either maintain that status quo distribution of property or they might consider enforcing a redistributive policy that makes it less burdensome for people to live under the existing property system.

Some anarchists may argue that S should stop stealing on day one because stealing is wrong, so the less of it the better. These anarchists would oppose redistributive policies on the grounds that any reduction in law enforcement is a reduction in public officials' capacity to unjustly coerce people. On this view, since it is never permissible to violate a person's natural rights in order to bring about a better distributive outcome, it is wrong to violate property-owners' rights in order to make the property system less burdensome to the disadvantaged.

This objection implicitly assumes that the best response to unjust governmental coercion is to favour policies that minimise the number of times that it happens. This is a valuable goal, but it's not clear that redistribution increases the number of times that coercion happens and it's also not clear that minimising the number of times that unjust law enforcement happens is always the best approach.

Redistribution doesn't necessarily involve more instances of unjust law enforcement because, if anything, the situation is even worse than the *Thief* analogy lets on. In existing states, S is continually violating the rights of A and B. So, it's not even the case that S's theft on day one amounts to coercing B to help A and then coercing A to help B on day two. It's that A and B are both coerced on each day by S's enforcement of unjust laws that determine the property distribution. So given that S is doing this, the number of instances of unjust law enforcement is the same whether S redistributes or not. In that context, S should at least make it so that the consequences of S's unjust actions are not excessively burdensome to those who are subject to S.

And even if redistribution does involve more instances of unjust law enforcement, it's not clear that's a bad thing. Consider another analogy:

> *Thief 2:* S is a thief who randomly steals from people and who cannot be stopped. S will either steal a little from A-Y (A and 24 other people), once a day, every day. Or S will steal everything Z owns and prevent Z from ever owning anything ever again.

In this case, S will either choose to steal *more often* by stealing from 25 people, or S will steal less often but the burdens of S's theft will be much greater. The first option will minimise instances of unjust interference and the second will minimise the burdens of unjust interference. Both approaches are, in a sense, consequentialist. They view unjust interference as something to be minimised, rather than as a constraint on action (Smith 2009). Ideally, S would comply with the moral prohibition on violating people's rights. But when S is unwilling to respect people's rights, anarchists have some moral reasons to hope that S's rights violations at least have good consequences.[8] The question here is whether it's better to favour fewer violations or less burdensome violations, when there is a trade-off between the two.

On my view, given that people's rights are being violated either way, it would be better to favour less burdensome violations, because Z has a stronger claim against being interfered with than A-Y do (Scanlon 2000, 235). Or if we are not to consider the pairwise comparison of people's claims, we may also note that the first option would unfairly fail to assign the disproportionately burdened person more moral consideration, but there are moral reasons to give extra consideration to people in Z's position (Kamm 1998). A consequentialist has reason to worry about the first option, to the extent that the cost to Z could be so significant that it could outweigh marginal costs to A-Y.

In wrapping up this argument, I should reiterate that this case for redistribution is empirically contingent. Following Nozick (2013, 198–231), we can imagine a society where public officials continuously redistribute resources for the sake of maintaining an equal distribution. Imagine, for example, that S stole from people continuously, so that no one else could reliably make plans that involved their property because they couldn't anticipate when S would intervene. In such a system, people would not use their property productively out of fear that S would redistribute whatever they gained from it. In this kind of society, S's redistribution would not reduce the burdensomeness of being subjected to unjust law enforcement, it would exacerbate it.

The initial *Thief* example established that public officials *could* use redistribution to reduce the burdensomeness of law enforcement. It did not establish that all redistribution *would* have this effect. Redistribution can backfire if public officials enforce redistributive policies in a way that involves further surveillance and threats of force. This case for redistribution is instrumental to the goal of limiting the burdens of law enforcement. To the extent that redistributing resources would not, on balance, liberate people from the burdens of living under the state, officials should not redistribute.

4 A Non-Instrumental Case for Redistribution

The foregoing case for redistribution appeals to on an empirical assumption that redistributing resources within an existing society can reduce the burdensomeness of being subject to governmental coercion. But it's possible that that's not true. It could be that *any* redistribution involves so much surveillance and enforcement and paperwork that it's more burdensome to people, on balance, than the state-backed enforcement of a property system that doesn't involve redistribution. That is the trouble with instrumentalist arguments for polices. It could turn out that the policy doesn't actually promote the desired end.

In this section, I defend a second, non-instrumental anarchist argument in favour of redistribution in non-ideal contexts. Namely, *even if* a redistributive policy doesn't effectively reduce the overall burdensomeness of being subject to law enforcement, public officials can still have reason to redistribute resources, in some circumstances, as a way of compensating people for the injustice of being subject to law enforcement. This is a non-instrumental argument for redistribution in the sense that redistribution is not justified as instrumental to some other value, rather, it is good to do for its own sake, as a matter of right.

As above, this argument is somewhat contingent. It could be that redistributing resources as a way of compensating people is good for its own sake, but that other moral considerations outweigh this value of providing compensation. Nevertheless, this argument provides further support to the case for redistribution in cases where it's unclear whether redistributing resources would in fact reduce the burdensomeness of an enforced property system on balance, by establishing a presumptive case for effectively redistributing some property to disadvantaged people anyway.

Like the instrumental argument for redistribution, the non-instrumental case for redistribution begins with the observation that no existing property systems are justly enforced and that officials also act unjustly when they enforce paternalistic policies and other polices that are enforced with threats and violence against non-liable people. The next premise is that people should be compensated for the fact that they are subject to law enforcement, including the enforcement of a property system or other unjust policies. Everyone subject to these unjust laws is a victim of unjust enforcement. So, officials should compensate everyone affected by law enforcement. In principle, officials can partly provide compensation through the redistribution of resources. So, when this is practically feasible and there are not sufficient countervailing moral reasons against it, officials should redistribute.[9]

The key premise here is that those who enforce unjust policies should provide some form of compensation for the people who are subject to them in the form of redistribution.[10] This compensation can be understood as a rebate, funded from all the gains that the system brings. Ideally, compensation would not require redistributive taxation. One alternative is that officials could distribute the economic gains from natural resources to citizens. Officials do not have a right to claim a monopoly on natural resources and to exclude people from cultivating and using the resources. But given that they do, they could use the gains from those resources to compensate citizens, not only for the violation that excluding them from accessing natural resources entails, but for all the other rights violations that law enforcement involves too.

But compensation can also take the form of redistributive taxation, following a similar logic as the *Thief* case. As I argued in previous sections, unjust law enforcement violates everyone's rights. Some people are comparatively advantaged by the overall pattern of law enforcement, but they are not entitled to retain the benefits of unjust instances of law enforcement. If this is true, then redistributive taxation as a form of compensation can finance a rebate for everyone who is subject to unjust law enforcement, including the taxpayers, without necessarily violating the property rights of taxpayers.[11]

Another objection to this argument for redistribution is that the property system has been so beneficial to people that additional compensation isn't required beyond the benefits that they've already received (Friedman 2015). But although state-backed property systems provide material benefits to people, it provides these benefits by violating their natural rights to do as they please with their own bodies and (potentially) their rights to use natural resources. Redistributive policies should therefore aim to enable each person to meet their basic needs without being subject to the burdens of coercive property rules (Widerquist 2013).

In this way, a property system could come close to restoring people to the state of freedom where 'every individual was free to work with resources as they pleased, and virtually everyone chose not to have bosses and not to have hierarchies, either political or economic' (Widerquist and McCall 2017, 244). It would achieve this not by eliminating bosses and hierarchies, but by giving people the ability to opt out of participating in them.

Moreover, the case for redistribution as a form of compensation can succeed *even if* a property system promotes well-being on balance, and even if such a system means that fewer people are subjected to hierarchical bosses or violent threats on balance. After all, officials cannot justify subjecting non-liable people to the enforcement of any law merely on the grounds that such a law promotes overall well-being or safety.[12] When officials do enforce laws that violate the rights of non-liable people, they owe those people compensation not solely because compensation will make them better off, but because denying compensation exacerbates the disrespect that unjust enforcement entails (Flanigan and Freiman 2020). This is why the non-instrumental, compensation-based argument for redistribution complements the instrumental argument for redistribution. We can make this case on either non-consequentialist or consequentialist grounds.

Still, even the non-instrumentalist case for redistribution may be limited. If the only way to effectively compensate people for being unjustly subject to law enforcement would be to seriously violate the rights of non-liable people, then compensation is not warranted in these cases. Knowing where to draw the line here is a general problem for any compensation-based argument. If the only feasible way to appropriately compensate the victims of an unjust police shooting is to take money from legitimate public safety efforts, it could be the case that public officials should not aim to appropriately compensate shooting victims. In claiming that officials should redistribute in order to provide compensation to everyone who is subject to unjust law enforcement, I have been assuming that it is possible to enforce a redistributive policy in a way that does not amount to an unacceptable injustice against non-liable people. The assumption that redistribution may not amount to an unacceptable injustice against property holders is grounded in the idea that people are not entitled to the full value of their current property holdings in the first place. If so, then redistributing the status quo distribution would not necessarily violate people's entitlements. In the next section, I will further argue for this point.

5 Objection: Redistribution Violates Property Rights

Some readers may have the intuition that the enforcement of redistributive policies is an unacceptable injustice against property holders for the following reason: even if property holders are not entitled to their existing property, the property holders who benefit from the unjust enforcement of a property system nevertheless aren't liable to be interfered with.[13] For example, maybe natural resources are initially unowned, and when public officials create and enforce a system of entitlements over resources, they are merely providing a benefit to an undeserving few, but not violating the rights of others.

I'm sceptical that law enforcement can ever be characterised as a pure benefit, rather than as a rights violation.[14] Yet even granting, for the sake of argument, that some kinds of law enforcement solely bestow undeserved benefits on citizens, this argument would not weigh against redistribution. Rather, if an advantaged group is receiving an undeserved benefit while others are disadvantaged and experience burdens associated with being disadvantaged, officials have compelling reasons to change course and switch their provision of undeserved benefits to the disadvantaged group to reduce their burdens.

This shows that the case for redistribution doesn't require the premise that law enforcement unjustly coerces people. Rather, if law enforcement is unjustly coercive, then officials have reason to redistribute to minimise the burdens of coercion and to compensate people for injustice. If law enforcement is simply a benefit, then officials have reason to distribute the benefits of law enforcement in ways that minimise the burdens of being disadvantaged in the distribution of benefits.

In response to this argument, a critic of redistributive policies could reply that public officials who redistribute resources don't just fail to provide the benefits that they previously provided to the advantaged. Rather, they enforce redistributive policies by threatening people with incarceration. Here, our imagined critic of redistribution may grant that public officials should find a way to provide benefits and compensation to those who are undeservedly harmed by the enforcement of a property system. But they may then argue that this unfortunate fact does not authorise officials to further interfere with the people who benefit from the existing system.

But this version of the objection builds in the assumption that law enforcement is only violating the rights of the people who are subject to redistribution from the status quo. It overlooks that the status quo also violates the rights of all people who are subject to the initial enforcement of a property system. A critic of redistribution should not assume that the initial enforcement of a property system, which is coercively enforced, violates no one's rights, while *also* assuming that the coercive enforcement of a more redistributive property system would violate rights. Suppose we characterise both property enforcement and redistribution as rights violations, granting that the enforcement of an initial distribution is also unjust. Then, subsequent redistribution is merely unjust in the same way. It is not clearly worse than continuing to enforce the initial distribution.

6 Capitalism, Basic Income, and Borders

So far, I've argued that, to the extent that the enforcement of any property system violates people's natural rights, public officials have moral reasons to prefer the enforcement of property systems that are minimally burdensome to those who are subject to them, and which compensate people for the injustices associated with law enforcement. In this section, I address what this means for public policy.

First, this argument weighs in favour of enforcing a broadly capitalist property system. As far as state-backed property systems go, capitalism is at least especially efficient and capable of generating wealth, which could be diverted to benefit those who are unjustly subject to unjust laws and which could compensate people for unjust law enforcement. A market economy is also less invasive and burdensome than other, more planned property systems. So these are moral reasons to support a broadly capitalist system of property for now, even though the enforcement of these property rules violates people's rights.[15]

Turning to the form that redistribution should take, people who are forced to live within a property system should receive a basic income, just as people who are harmed by the unjust enforcement of other laws that violate their natural rights are entitled to cash compensation. Compensation in the form of a cash transfer or a basic income has several advantages over other redistributive policies (see also Widerquist 2013, 66–70). First, cash is a remarkably efficient way to distribute compensation. And because cash can be used on a wide variety of things, it is more likely to promote the well-being of its recipients, in contrast to in kind benefit programmes which may not give people what they would choose for themselves. Providing compensation in the form of a basic income also limits victims' interaction with the public officials who violate their natural rights via the enforcement of the property system.

Another benefit of a basic income is that it pays compensation to the victims of property rule enforcement in the same coin as the violation. That is, since the injury is the coercive imposition of a currency and natural resource distribution system, then people should be compensated for that with access to currency and resources. In this way, the basic income satisfies the moral desideratum of reciprocity. It aims to restore the relations of equality between the victims and the perpetrators of an unjust property system by imposing a liability on the perpetrators that takes the same form as their injury against the victim (Flanigan 2019a, 2019b). In contrast, a more paternalistic 'in kind' form of compensation would fail to satisfy this desideratum because it would compensate people for the general coercive imposition of property norms with more specific goods.

It's also worth noting that the justifications for redistributive policies I have advanced are not limited to domestic redistributive efforts. Some of the people who are most harmed by the unjust enforcement of laws are those whose rights are violated at a political community's border. To the extent that public officials will continue to enforce immigration restrictions that unjustly exclude people from migrating to their country, the foregoing case for redistribution is also a case for distributing cash assistance to foreigners as compensation for the rights-violation that immigration restrictions involve and to reduce the burdensomeness of being subject to immigration restrictions.

That said, redistributing resources beyond a state's borders is probably less feasible than proposals for more liberal immigration policies. In contrast, proposals to continue enforcing redistributive policies domestically are likely more politically feasible than proposals to stop enforcing all of the aforementioned coercive policies. Yet in both cases, the principle is the same. Given that public officials are unlikely to stop treating people unjustly when they enforce the law, anarchists have reason to support whatever second best or n^{th} best policy that would reduce the burdensomeness of law enforcement and compensate those who are unjustly subject to it.

7 Conclusion

In some ways, the foregoing analysis of property rights and enforcement is similar to the 'myth of ownership' view, which states that property rights are largely conventional (Murphy and Nagel 2004). Like proponents of this view, I have argued that the property distribution is at least partly determined by public officials' decisions about which claims to resources or money they will enforce. The distribution of property also depends on officials' decisions about which natural rights they will violate by enforcing unjust laws. And like proponents of the myth of ownership, I agree that public officials should use property rules to bring about a normatively better distribution of resources.

I reject the myth of ownership view, however, because I deny that public officials have the authority to enforce property conventions in the way they do. All state-backed property systems are unjust, in virtue of the fact that they all violate people's rights. Given that people will continue to live under state-backed enforcement regimes, anarchists should still hope officials change their approach to enforcement in ways that reduce instances of injustice and make the injustices they commit less burdensome to people. And officials should enforce conventions that compensate people, to an extent, for the injustices associated with law enforcement. Yet we should not mistake these reforms for justice. Though redistributive policies can morally improve the unjust status quo, any state-backed system of enforcement will nevertheless remain unjust.

Notes

1 Throughout this essay, I'm sure that some anarchists will disagree with my characterisation of anarchism. And I will sometimes refer to writers who are not always identified as anarchists but who are fellow travellers, as anarchists. For example, I talk about Nozick in this way. But for my purposes I'm less interested in asking 'what is anarchism' and 'who is an anarchist?' Rather, my goal here is to argue that people who reject the claim that public officials have political authority and people who also seemingly view a stateless society as morally preferable (all else equal), should nevertheless be open to redistributive policies. In Flanigan (2019a, 2019b), I develop similar arguments, from a different angle.

2 As I will note going forward, this account is relatively open to competing theories of what people's natural rights are. For those anarchists who are sceptical about 'natural rights,' the argument is still broadly applicable even if anarchism just consists in denying the state's authority to coercively enforce many of the laws that states currently enforce.

3 For an overview of anarchist thought on this topic see Massimino et al. (2020).

4 And as Naomi Zack (1999) points out, monetary systems are presumptively illegitimate to the extent that they are imposed on people who do not consent to them.

5 We can imagine, for example, a system of money that is set apart from central banking, such as free banking (Dowd 1996) or cryptocurrencies.

6 Though see Cwik (2014).

7 Michael Huemer (2013) suggests this when he argues that anarchists should favour broadly libertarian public policies.

8 Here I am following Thomson (1986) in suggesting that people have moral reasons to promote well-being even when they are not morally required to do so as a matter of right (171).

9 Karl Widerquist develops a similar argument in favour of redistribution in the form of a basic income. Widerquist (2013) writes: 'Recipients [of a basic income] are being compensated for not being able to have all the access to resources they might be able to use (alone or in a group of their choosing), for living under rules not entirely of their choice, and for rules that give greater advantages to others' (178). Widerquist is primarily concerned with the fact that the property system 'puts individuals in the position where they are effectively forced to enter the marketplace and serve others' (13), whereas my account is grounded more in the injustice of subjecting someone to violent threats via law enforcement. Still, I view these two accounts as largely complimentary, despite their differing moral foundations.

10 Though he is generally read as a critic of redistribution, even Nozick (2013) is sympathetic to this narrow justification (230–231).

11 Though as Gary Chartier (2013) argues, ending the system where economic and political elites use law enforcement to maintain their existing privilege would be a preferable form of redistribution. On the other hand, Chartier nevertheless supports redistribution in the form of a basic income for other reasons, related to the value of independence (164–167).

12 As Narveson (2008) writes: 'This all comes back once again to the basic idea, the libertarian principle. This rather simple idea is that nobody gets to inflict uncompensated harm or damage on anybody else; and so, only those who have done that are eligible for treatment of the kind proscribed for all others' (106)

13 I am thankful to Jason Brennan for raising this objection.

14 Even if officials do not violate anyone's rights simply by enforcing public safety services that protect people's natural rights, they probably do when they coercively collect taxes to provide these services. Even if no one has an entitlement to natural resources, the enforcement of property rights in natural resources violates people's entitlements to not be threatened with violence and incarceration when they trespass or use resources.

15 Charles Johnson (2008) distinguishes between free market capitalism and corporate state capitalism. In ideal theory, free market capitalism has a lot going for it. Corporate state capitalism is a form of government intervention in the marketplace to uphold an economic order that favours businesses and corporations. Johnson argues that the two cannot coexist, since the free market is defined as an economic order that is free of governmental intervention. But I think we can instead think of these systems on a continuum. Though corporate state capitalism is clearly morally deficient, it can still provide some of the benefits of the gains from trade, in contrast to a more centrally planned economy. In this way, anarchists who hold free market capitalism to be a morally ideal economic order have reason to reluctantly existing instantiations of capitalism, at least relative to alternative governmental arrangements that are even more hostile to free markets.

References

Brennan, Jason. 2018. "Libertarianism after Nozick." *Philosophy Compass* 13 (2): e12485.

———. 2020. "Moral Parity between State and Non-State Actors." In *The Routledge Handbook of Anarchy and Anarchist Thought*, edited by Gary Chartier and Chad van Schoelandt, 235–46. New York, NY: Routledge.

Carson, Kevin. 2018. "Formal vs. Substantive Statism: A Matter of Context." In *The Dialectics of Liberty: Exploring the Context of Human Freedom*, edited by Roger E. Bissell, Chris M. Sciabarra, and Edward W. Younkins, New York, NY: Lexington Books: 293–305.

Carson, Kevin A. 2008. "Organization Theory." *A Libertarian Perspective*. Charleston, SC: BookSurge.

Chartier, Gary. 2013. *Anarchy and Legal Order: Law and Politics for a Stateless Society*. New York, NY: Cambridge University Press.

Christmas, Billy. 2016. "Libertarianism and Privilege." *Molinari Review* 1 (1): 25–46.

———. 2021. *Property and Justice: A Liberal Theory of Natural Rights*. New York, NY: Routledge.

Cwik, Bryan. 2014. "Labor as the Basis for Intellectual Property Rights." *Ethical Theory and Moral Practice* 17 (4): 681–95.

Dowd, Kevin. 1996. "The Case for Financial Laissez-Faire." *The Economic Journal* 106 (436): 679–87.

Flanigan, Jessica. 2017. "Rethinking Freedom of Contract." *Philosophical Studies* 174 (2): 443–63.

———. 2019a. "Duty and Enforcement." *Journal of Political Philosophy* 27 (3): 341–62.

———. 2019b. "An Anarchist Defense of the Basic Income." In *The Future of Work, Technology, and Basic Income*, edited by Michael Cholbi and Michael Weber, 27–48. New York, NY: Routledge.

Flanigan, Jessica, and Christopher Freiman. 2020. "Drug War Reparations." *Res Philosophica* 97 (2): 141–68.
Friedman, David. 1994. "A Positive Account of Property Rights." *Social Philosophy and Policy* 11 (2): 1–16.
———. 2013. "Ideas: Libertarian Arguments for Income Redistribution." December 6, 2013. Retrieved on May 31, 2022, from http://daviddfriedman.blogspot.com/2013/12/libertarian-arguments-for-income.html.
———. 2015. *The Machinery of Freedom: Guide to a Radical Capitalism*. 3rd edition. New York, NY: CreateSpace Independent Publishing Platform.
Graeber, David. 2020. "Introduction." In *The Peter Kropotkin Anthology (Annotated): The Conquest of Bread, Mutual Aid: A Factor of Evolution, Fields, Factories and Workshops, An Appeal to the Young and The Life of Kropotkin*. Independently published.
Hasnas, John. 2008. "The Obviousness of Anarchy." In *Anarchism/Minarchism: Is a Government Part of a Free Country*, edited by Roderick T. Long and Tibor R. Machan, 111–13. Burlington, VT: Ashgate.
Hidalgo, Javier S. 2018. *Unjust Borders: Individuals and the Ethics of Immigration*. New York, NY: Routledge.
Huemer, Michael. 2010. "Is There a Right to Immigrate?." *Social Theory and Practice* 36 (3): 429–61.
———. 2013. *The Problem of Political Authority: An Examination of the Right to Coerce and the Duty to Obey*. 1st edition. New York, NY: Palgrave Macmillan.
———. 2017. "Is Wealth Redistribution a Rights Violation?." In *The Routledge Handbook of Libertarianism*, edited by Jason Brennan, Bas van der Vossen, and David Schmidtz, 259–71. New York, NY: Routledge.
Johnson, Charles W. 2008. "Liberty, Equality, Solidarity: Toward a Dialectical Anarchism." In *Anarchism/Minarchism: Is a Government Part of a Free Country*, edited by Roderick T. Long and Tibor R. Machan, 155–88. Burlington, VT: Ashgate.
———. 2012. "Markets Freed from Capitalism." In *Markets Not Capitalism: Individualist Anarchism against Bosses, Inequality, Corporate Power, and Structural Poverty*, edited by Gary Chartier and Charles W Johnson, 377–84. New York, NY: Minor Compositions.
Kamm, Frances. M. 1998. *Morality, Mortality: Volume I: Death and Whom to Save from It*. New York, NY: Oxford University Press.
Long, Roderick T. 2011. "The Libertarian Case against Intellectual Property Rights." In *Markets Not Capitalism: Individualist Anarchism against Bosses, Inequality, Corporate Power, and Structural Poverty*, edited by Gary Chartier and Charles W Johnson, 187–98. New York, NY: Minor Compositions.
———. 2019. "Why Libertarians Should Be Social Justice Warriors." *The Dialectics of Liberty: Exploring the Context of Human Freedom*, edited by Roger E. Bissell, Chris M. Sciabarra, and Edward W. Younkins, 235–54. New York, NY: Lexington Books.
Mack, Eric. 2006. "Non-Absolute Rights and Libertarian Taxation." *Social Philosophy and Policy* 23 (2): 109–41.
———. 2018. *Libertarianism*. 1st edition. Medford, MA: Polity.
Massimino, Cory, Kevin Carson, Darian Worden, David S. D'Amato, Shawn P. Wilbur, William Gillis, Nathan Goodman, Wayne Price, and Derek Wittorff. 2020. *Anarchy & Democracy: Discussing the Abolition of Rulership*. Independently published.

Montero, Roman A., and Edgar G. Foster. 2017. *All Things in Common: The Economic Practices of the Early Christians*. Eugene, OR: Resource Publications.

Murphy, Liam, and Thomas Nagel. 2004. *The Myth of Ownership: Taxes and Justice*. New edition. New York, NY: Oxford University Press.

Narveson, Jan. 2008. "The State: From Minarchy to Anarchy." In *Anarchism/Minarchism: Is a Government Part of a Free Country*, edited by Roderick T. Long and Tibor R. Machan, 103–10. Burlington, VT: Ashgate.

Newhard, Joseph Michael. 2016. "On the Conspicuous Absence of Private Defense." *Libertarian Papers* 8: 221–34.

Nozick, Robert. 2013. *Anarchy, State, and Utopia*. Reprint edition. New York, NY: Basic Books.

Rodin, David. 2014. "The Reciprocity Theory of Rights." *Law and Philosophy* 33 (3): 281–308.

Scanlon, T. M. 2000. *What We Owe to Each Other*. Revised edition. Cambridge, MA: Belknap Press.

Simmons, A. John. 1999. "Justification and Legitimacy." *Ethics* 109 (4): 739–71.

Smith, Michael. 2009. "Two Kinds of Consequentialism." *Philosophical Issues* 19: 257–72.

Spafford, Jesse. 2020. "Social Anarchism and the Rejection of Private Property." In *The Routledge Handbook of Anarchy and Anarchist Thought*, edited by Gary Chartier and Chad van Schoelandt, 327–41. New York, NY: Routledge.

Stilz, Anna. 2017. "Property Rights: Natural or Conventional?" In *The Routledge Handbook of Libertarianism*, edited by Jason Brennan, Bas van der Vossen, and David Schmidtz, 244–58. New York, NY: Routledge.

Thomson, Judith Jarvis. 1986. *Rights, Restitution, and Risk: Essays in Moral Theory*, edited by William Parent. Cambridge, MA: Harvard University Press.

Underwood, Sam, and Kevin Vallier. 2020. "Christian Anarchism." In *The Routledge Handbook of Anarchy and Anarchist Thought*, 187–204. New York, NY: Routledge.

Wenar, Leif. 2008. "Property Rights and the Resource Curse." *Philosophy & Public Affairs* 36 (1): 2–32.

Widerquist, Karl. 2013. *Independence, Propertylessness, and Basic Income: A Theory of Freedom as the Power to Say No*. New York, NY: Springer.

Widerquist, Karl, and Grant McCall. 2017. *Prehistoric Myths in Modern Political Philosophy*. Edinburgh: Edinburgh University Press.

Wolff, Robert Paul. 1998. *In Defense of Anarchism*. 1st edition. Berkeley, CA: University of California Press.

Zack, Naomi. 1999. "Lockean Money, Indigenism and Globalism." *Canadian Journal of Philosophy Supplementary Volume* 25: 31–53.

PART II
Power in the Economic Sphere

7 Why Does Worker Participation Matter?

Three Considerations in Favour of Worker Participation in Corporate Governance

Thomas Christiano

This chapter argues for a number of considerations that favour worker participation in corporate governance. By 'worker participation in corporate governance' I mean that the workers in a firm have collectively held power over the authoritative direction of the firm, and thus over some of the social world they live in, and consequently workers have responsibility for how the firm develops in a larger market economy. This authoritative direction can be realised by any elements in a tool kit of institutional mechanisms by which employees can participate in governing the firm that employs them. I do not mean to say that workers should necessarily have sole control over the direction of the corporation. I argue that there are a number of mechanisms which give workers a say in the corporation of which they are a part. Workers can be members of a union, which involves collective bargaining with the firm and enforcement of the terms of agreements and the laws regulating the workplace, they can own the firm of which they are a part, they can have part ownership over such a firm, they can have a substantial say over the selection of the board that runs the firm and they can be members of works councils that protect the interests of workers in the firm. Workers often participate through a number of these mechanisms simultaneously. For example, in the German co-determination regime, wages are set on a regional or industry wide basis by collective bargaining while workers are also responsible for choosing some proportion of members of the supervisory boards of the corporation.

We need a tool kit and not just one mechanism because, while all the members of the tool kit enhance the power and responsibility of workers, they are quite distinct, and one form of worker participation may succeed in a particular circumstance where the others do not. It is important to have flexibility in the application of the idea of worker participation to markets. The case for any particular member of the tool kit in a particular set of circumstances requires a great deal of contextual knowledge. Essential to any element of the toolkit is that workers have authoritative power over the firm and responsibility for its fate.

DOI: 10.4324/9781003173632-9

The basic argument is that worker participation in firm governance is a key component in the realisation of equality in a society that relies heavily on the institutions of markets and private property in producing and allocating goods in economic life. I proceed on the assumption that markets and private property are essential institutions for the efficient production of goods and the expression of individuality in persons. In such markets, the presence of worker participation in firms tends to promote equality in the distribution of income without sacrificing efficiency or at least in a way that benefits most persons in the lower half of the income distribution, equality of power in the market, as well as greater and more equal political participation (by enhancing the political capacities of less well-off citizens).

These arguments converge on the importance of worker participation for equality, but they also complement each other. Worker participation enhances political participation for less well-off citizens, thus enabling them to maintain a strong welfare state and the market regulation necessary to achieving worker participation. That markets with worker participation realise a reasonably efficient form of equality is also essential to the support for worker participation because markets are institutions whose purpose is to satisfy human needs and desires and because the principle of equality I deploy here is opposed to levelling down (Christiano and Braynen 2008).

The arguments presented here are distinct from the well-known and widely advanced parallel case argument defended by Robert Dahl (1985). My arguments proceed from the recognition of the importance of voluntary association and exchange in markets as a distinctive form of social organisation that has merit for issues that do not require general collective action. I argue that worker participation is not a direct requirement for the organisation of firms as it is for the state, but rather a remedy to problems that occur in economic markets. Worker participation is instrumentally valuable because it promotes an egalitarian distribution of income that benefits persons in the lower half of the distribution (Section 1); it is a remedy for the inequality of power that less well-off workers have in decentralised economies (Section 2); and it enhances the effective participation of workers in political democracy (Section 3).

1 Efficiency and Equality

We need to start by understanding what a market is. I do not mean 'free markets' when I refer to markets. Nor do I mean perfectly competitive and complete markets, though modelling these can be an important analytical tool for understanding actual markets. Markets are institutions that enable processes of production and distribution of goods to be achieved by means of voluntary exchange among many different parties. They always involve some degree of freedom for the parties; production and exchange are not achieved by command alone. Persons choose to participate in a particular firm and in markets generally. Because the processes are voluntary, the system is coordinated through a set of prices that arise when many engage in exchange. But the process of exchange can be heavily regulated, as they are almost everywhere in modern societies. Free markets are markets that obtain between many persons who possess full liberal property rights and complete freedom of contract. The only regulation that obtains here is a prohibition on involuntary takings of other people's property, force, fraud, and the violation of terms of contract. This is one among many possible ways of organising markets and quite rare since the middle of the twentieth century. I will argue in this chapter that because markets are generally imperfect and incomplete, there are reasons of efficiency, distribution, equality within markets, and political equality for thinking that markets ought legally to be structured to give a significant role to worker participation in the running of firms. In this section, I start with efficiency and equality.

Whatever ideals of social cooperation in the market we endorse, they must be able to satisfy human needs to a high degree, which is the point of markets. My first argument relies on an efficiency sensitive version of the principle of equality, which holds that some losses to overall productivity can be morally justified by gains to those on the lower end of the distribution.

The basic conditions under which a legal regime of worker participation is morally desirable are some degree of monopsony and significant background inequalities under incomplete and imperfect markets (Robinson 1969). There is significant monopsony in the labour market when employees find it difficult to move from firm to firm while employers have less difficulty in securing new employees. Under these circumstances employers mark down the wages of employees and can subject workers to subpar working conditions (Manning 2021). Furthermore, this kind of labour market enables employers to capture most of the rents of the firm due to imperfect markets. Employees in these kinds of markets are often subject to abuses by their employers such as sexual harassment, wage theft, and violations of basic standards of respectful, safe, and clean workplaces. Workers under these circumstances often say that they have no recourse against these practices even though an elaborate system of laws is designed to regulate these practices (Anderson 2017). That these practices are so widespread is a clear indication that these labour markets are not very competitive. There are two kinds of outcome problem with such workplaces. One, workers are not very productive. Two, the welfares of workers, and sometimes basic rights, are set back and the prevalence of these kinds of workplaces tends to lead to increased inequality within the society (Stansbury and Summers 2020).

One key remedy to this inequality of power is worker participation. Collective bargaining greatly increases the bargaining power of workers under conditions of partial monopsony, enabling workers to achieve better wages and working conditions and capture some of the rents of the firm. Unions with collective bargaining rights give voice to workers who are abused, achieving something like the rule of law in the workplace. They aggregate information about the workplace so that the presence of abuse or the violation of health and safety requirements is made amply clear. They make sure that the interests of workers in being in non-abusive, safe, and healthy environments are advanced (Donado and Walde 2012). Furthermore, there is evidence that workers are more productive in workplaces regulated by unions. This seems to be caused by an increase in commitment to the organisation and lower worker turnover (Freeman and Medoff 1984).

One persistent question is whether unions slow down the rates of innovation and capital investment in a society. Here the evidence is clearly mixed. In the United States, it is thought that it does diminish both innovation and capital investment to some degree. This may be due to the element of monopolistic supply that unions realise (Metcalf 2003; Hirsch 2017). At the same time, in Germany, with its mix of union presence and worker participation in election of boards and works councils, there is evidence that unions may enhance the rate of innovation and capital investment in firms (Addison et al. 2017). In what is the most extensive meta-analysis of studies of the effects of unions on productivity, however, the loss in productivity due to lower capital investment and innovation is significantly offset by the gains in productivity from increased worker commitment and lower turnover (Doucouliagos, Freeman, and Laroche 2017).

Finally, there is substantial evidence that unions tend strongly to diminish the overall level of inequality of income in a society. Their decline has been held partly responsible for the great increase in inequality in the United States and other countries (Stansbury and Summers 2020; Freeman 2007; Rosenfeld 2014). This seems to be the result of the most significant effects of unions on firms, i.e., an increase in wages (Card, Lemieux, and Riddell 2003) and a lower level of profitability (Metcalf 2003). Also, as noted above, unions contribute to the welfares of workers by ensuring that workplace health and safety are protected, and other basic rights are respected. The joint surplus, and its growth, seems to be similar between unionised and non-unionised firms but there is a different distribution of that surplus in favour of workers.

On average, unions seem to have a small effect on overall productivity but significant effects on distribution (Doucouliagos, Freeman, and Laroche 2017). So even if there is some hit to overall productivity, it is plausible to say that it is justified in an egalitarian way by the gains in welfare and income among the lower half of the distribution.

It should be noted that the effects noted above are averages over many societies. The effects of unions vary to some extent between different countries with different legal regimes for protecting unions. For example, one study found that in firms with unions in which bargaining takes place at different tiers (national and firm level for instance), capital investment may be higher compared to ordinary firms with only lower tier bargaining (Cardullo, Conti, and Sulis 2020). Hence, this is an area for experimentation with different forms of institutional design.

The effects of worker cooperatives have been less studied, and they are much less prevalent in modern economies than unions. Worker cooperatives are owned and run by the workers (or some very large percentage of them). One major disagreement on worker cooperatives concerns the 'objective function' of these firms, i.e., what exactly they are trying to maximise. Earlier work argued that the objective function of a worker cooperative was to maximise the income per worker of the firm (Ward 1958). A more recent account argues that the objective function is some mix of income and employment (Pencavel, Pistaferri, and Schivardi 2006), while still others argue that worker cooperatives can or do maximise profits (Dow 2003). To be sure, different institutional design can produce different objective functions.

The standard view of the worker cooperative with an objective function of maximising income per worker predicts that the firm will decrease supply when the price for its product goes up (Ward 1958). This would imply a deep inefficiency in worker cooperatives since it suggests that increased demand leads to decreased supply. But this negatively sloped supply curve has not been observed in empirical studies (Bonin, Jones, and Putterman 1993; Dow 2003). There is some tendency towards a more sluggish supply response to increases in product prices (Pencavel, Pistaferri, and Schivardi 2006). On the other hand, cooperatives tend to retain employment in downturns while reducing wages temporarily. This is a major advantage for cooperatives over ordinary capitalist firms. They are more capable of persuading workers to reduce wages during difficult times than capitalist firms; workers trust managers less in capitalist firms than in worker-controlled firms. As a consequence, they don't see nearly as much inefficiencies due to firing workers and then hiring new workers (Burdin and Dean 2009).

Many observe greater productivity or at least no loss in productivity in worker cooperatives (Dow 2003). They give incentives to workers to work harder, and they radically reduce conflict between labour and management. They do, however, tend to invest less in capital (Bonin, Jones, and Putterman 1993). There may be some institutional fixes to the problem of raising capital. For instance, the Mondragon cooperatives have a cooperative bank that ensures a steady supply of capital. This may help with increasing the supply response to increased demand. But it may be that worker cooperatives are better suited to labour intensive firms.

The big question with worker cooperatives is why there are so few of them. The puzzle increases when we observe that worker cooperatives tend to fail no more than other capitalist firms and many say that the failure rate is smaller. Furthermore, there is little reason to believe that they generally degenerate into capitalist firms (Burdin and Dean 2009; Dow 2003). Yet there are not many of them. The main reason seems to be that it is harder for a group of workers collectively to decide on creating such a firm given the heterogeneity of workers and given that they have little capital to start with and are highly risk averse with the little wealth that they possess. Furthermore, Dow has argued that entrepreneurs who have created start-up companies are more likely to be worried about capturing the benefits of the company if it goes to a worker cooperative (Dow 2003).

It is worth considering at this point what may be the most successful effort at worker participation in the firm, which is co-determination. Co-determination occurs to varying degrees throughout much of Europe, but the most commonly studied variants are in Germany and Scandinavia. This is a complex system of worker participation so it can only be very briefly sketched here. The basic system is a combination of collective bargaining and worker participation in electing the members of the board of a corporation. In Germany, in corporations employing between 500 and 2000 workers, the workers elect one third of the members of the supervisory board of the corporation. In corporations with 2000 or more workers, the workers elect 50% of the board, but the owners have control over a tie breaking vote. Only in the coal, steel, and iron industries do workers have full parity with shareholders (Addison 2009). The boards do not determine the basic wage rates; they are determined by industry-wide collective bargaining with unions. But they do participate in choosing the managers, the basic workplace conditions and sometimes the basic investment strategy of the firm. And the unions play a significant role in the running of the board aside from the fact that many of the workers are union members.

The key to co-determination is that it is mandated by law so a firm cannot escape the regime except by moving abroad. It is not a product of the market and it is not merely facilitated by law. Another feature of co-determination is that it includes workers and shareholders as participants in running the firm. This enhances its ability to raise capital above that of worker cooperatives.

As a general rule the assessment of co-determination has been fairly positive. It is reasonably popular in Germany though not as much with shareholders and managers. The initial assessment of co-determination was that it would undermine the value of the firm because workers would 'hold up' capital and 'eat up the firm' (Jensen and Meckling 1979). But subsequent research has found that co-determination is associated with modest gains in productivity in firms (Addison 2009). It is associated with modest improvements in working conditions (Jager, Noy, and Schoefer 2021). It dramatically reduces the conflict between labour and capital; it increases information and therefore trust among workers and managers (Freeman and Lazear 1995). And it has a mechanism for the raising of capital. The collective bargaining part has played a role in limiting income inequality through wage compression. So, if we are thinking in terms of efficiency and equality, co-determination seems to be desirable. But it is a complex system rooted in the experiences of German and Nordic societies so we must be careful in thinking about how it can translate to other countries.

2 Equality of Power in the Market

The second basic standard for evaluating markets is the idea of persons participating as equals in the market. This is a procedural view and is analogous to the democratic idea that persons ought to be able to participate as equals in collective decision-making.

This section lays out and defends the fundamental ideal of equality of power in the market. Then it shows how that ideal is breached in most ordinary labour markets. It argues that worker participation in firm governance is the main remedy for the failure of labour markets to achieve equality of power. It justification is remedial on the account offered here.

Just as democratic decision-making provides a public realisation of equality against the background of disagreement about interests and justice, so equal power in markets provides a public realisation of equality. Persons are given the capacities to stand up for their own interests and values in the context of economic cooperation where there is substantial conflict of interests.

The underlying idea behind the democratic principle is that persons have fundamental interests in being able to shape the social world they live in. They have these fundamental interests because they live in a world where there is a lot of disagreement about how best to shape that world, there is substantial uncertainty about the interests people have and there is serious conflict of interest among them. One treats persons publicly as equals in this context by giving them equal power over the process of collective decision-making. They can then work out their disagreements and decide on a set of institutions in a way that treats each other publicly as equals (Christiano 2008).

Now I am assuming here that there is reason for decentralised decision-making in various spheres of social life, so that not all decision-making ought to, or even can, be made collectively. Decentralised decision-making is desirable because it is a highly productive way of putting resources to their best uses and it is a way of expressing individuality in the process of advancing one's interests.

Nevertheless, there is an important analogy between participation in collective decision-making and participation in economic life. One enters agreements with others to advance one's interests in the social world one lives in. One attempts to shape that social world by recasting one's rights and duties with others and by structuring the division of labour. The sum of one's agreements gives shape to the local world in which one lives. Thus, one advances, in a more localised way, one's morally legitimate interests and idiosyncratic aims.

Moreover, there is a great deal of conflict of interest in negotiating the terms of agreements in the market. For example, each participant in exchange wants to pay less and receive more from the others. And there is unresolved disagreement about the nature of the interests involved. For example, some participate in firms because they value the work and the cooperation while others may simply value the wage. So, persons have rights to participate in this activity as they see fit. But we do not take the interests sufficiently seriously if we are content merely to distribute rights. Persons must have power to advance their interests in this decentralised system of decision-making because of the serious conflict of interest in the making of agreements. We can see this in the case of highly exploitative agreements where persons' rights may be respected but their interests in shaping the world around them are severely hampered by their inferior power and they are treated publicly in a way that is inferior to those of the exploiter.

The ideal of markets among equals involves structuring markets so that persons have equal power to participate in markets. The notion of equal power is not easy to define in the contexts of markets. There are two main elements. One element is equality in the cognitive conditions for participating in the market. I have in mind here equal access to education and training. These conditions are necessary for a person to realise their interests in a complex society. The second element is equality of opportunity, i.e., a robustly equal ability to advance one's interests in a system of social and economic cooperation. The prime determinant of power in economic life is the ability to exit. The amount of opportunity to decline participation in particular agreements is the principal measure of power. When two persons engage in an agreement and one person has very bad alternative options while the other has very good alternative options, the person with the good alternatives will have more power over the agreement-making. The principle of equal opportunity is meant to equalise this distribution of power (Christiano 2018).

The kind of power I am trying to get at here is to be distinguished from 'collaborative power,' which is power one has because one is able to satisfy a desire or need of another. One's power derives from the desires or needs of others. Someone who has a great deal of talent, which means ability to satisfy others' desires, may have more power in this sense. In contrast to that, I am trying to get at 'conflictual power.' This is the power of some to get things at the expense of others, as in monopolistic power and monopsonistic power. Each of these depends not merely on what one has to offer but on whether there are others who offer it or whether one's counterparty has access to the others who offer it. A difference in conflictual power between parties can also involve a lack of power of some due to their lack of ability to enter into agreements, which can occur in cases of great inequality of background resources and asymmetries of information. It is hard for poor people to get credit or insurance in markets because the price of the credit or insurance is driven up by the fact that the lender or insurer doesn't know how serious the risk of default or bad action is and the poor person does not have collateral. Credit and insurance are essential steps to participating fully in markets for production; they give people opportunities to advance their interests and thus empower them in relation to others. Hence, the power of poor people is severely curtailed in economic life.

Though the distinction is intuitive, I still do not have a complete definition with which to distinguish these two notions of power. But three remarks may help. First, this notion of equality of opportunity is very close to Rawls' fair equality of opportunity in which only talent and willingness to put out effort make a difference to what social positions of power one has access to. (Here it is important to be careful and not to confuse the possession of talent with monopolistically held talent.)

Second, this idea is analogous to democratic equality. People often speak of equality of opportunity for influence in democracy, especially with regard to equal participation in processes of discussion and debate. But strictly speaking they do not have complete equality of opportunity for influence. People usually distinguish between one's capacity to participate and one's ability to persuade. The democratic principle permits that some have more influence than others when they are able to make arguments that are more persuasive. In some sense, those with more talent at making good arguments have more power. But this is not an unjust inequality of power. The reason is that the power is a kind of collaborative power, which depends on people accepting the arguments.

Third, one indicator of inequality of power in the sense I am interested in is market power, that is power to mark up the price of one's goods. A natural worry concerning the distinction between collaborative and conflictual power is that both are functions of limited supply. In one case, the supply is relatively small and in the other it is reduced to one or a few colluding suppliers. But here we can make use of the theory of perfect markets as a kind of benchmark. In a perfect market, the supplier is a price-taker, while in monopolistic markets, the supplier is a price-maker and actually restricts supply. The latter is a strong indicator that we are dealing with power in the conflictual sense. The presence of market power seems to me to point to the distinction, though I have not given a rigorous definition of these two notions. Another kind of indicator are inabilities to access markets because of low endowments and asymmetries of information. In contrast, complete and perfect markets with an egalitarian distribution of initial endowments will equalise power in this sense even though some may have some more collaborative power than others because they have more to offer. Market imperfections will create inequalities of power in many cases, that can only be rectified by institutional design. Here concerns of efficiency and equality dovetail since the same problems give rise to problems of both efficiency and equality.

It is important to distinguish collaborative and conflictual power because we do not want to restrict collaborative power but we do want to restrict conflictual power. To restrict collaborative power would in effect be to restrict the ability to satisfy needs and desires. We want those who are most talented to be in the right places in the division of labour since this works to everyone's advantage.

I want to add one more element to the discussion of equality of opportunity. We should distinguish 'competitive' equality of opportunity from 'constructive' equality of opportunity. Competitive equality of opportunity obtains when persons compete for a particular position or set of positions in the division of labour. There is equality when they have the same chances to succeed at achieving these positions given the same talents and willingness to put out effort (Rawls 1971). This kind of equality of opportunity assumes as fixed the division of labour and the criteria for being a good occupant of the positions in the division of labour.

A deeper, constructive conception of equality of opportunity will include not only the ability to compete for positions but also the ability to shape the division of labour itself. This means the ability to play a role in determining what kind of organisation one wants and the criteria of selection for the different positions in that organisation. This is an essential part of a market among equals (Young 1990; Fishkin 2014): people have choices regarding what kind of organisation they want to be a part of and how it works. Possession of merely equal competitive opportunities is compatible with a deeply inegalitarian society. To have equal competitive opportunities merely to occupy roles in deeply hierarchical organisations implies a severe limit to the capacity to shape the social world one lives in, both because the menu of organisations is limited and because one's capacities are limited in the lower parts of the hierarchy.

This allows us now to put together the idea of equality in the market. Equality in the market implies equal power in the market, in the sense of equal conflictual power. This requires that persons have equal access to the cognitive conditions for succeeding well in the market and fair equality of opportunity in the market, in both the competitive and constructive senses outlined above. I think we can say that perfectly competitive and complete markets with an egalitarian distribution of initial endowments will satisfy this principle. Perfectly competitive and complete markets are free markets and are a complete realisation of this idea of equality in the market (as long as endowments are equal), because there are no problems of monopoly or monopsony and information is complete, so there are no problems of credit or insurance and thus no barriers to full participation in the market. Regulation of markets beyond enforcement of contract and property is unnecessary.

Just to illustrate this idea we can invoke the neoclassical equivalence theorems regarding ownership of the firm. In perfectly competitive and complete markets whether capital rents labour or labour rents capital is a matter of no significance. They are both equally efficient, there are no barriers to either of these (Dreze 1989). Here equality of power in the multidimensional sense I outlined above is fully realised. And, it should be noted, there is no reason for the society to intervene.

But, of course, these conditions of perfection and completeness do not obtain in most labour markets. Economic theorists since Adam Smith have recognised and deplored the massive inequality of power in the labour market between owners of firms and workers (Smith 1776). And they recognise that the terms of agreement between labour and capitalist are heavily determined in favour of the capitalist as a result. Hence, in this case, equality in the market is not achieved. There are two ways in which they are not achieved. The first is that workers have unequal power in the market relative to capital and firms. The second is that firms tend rigidly to be structured as hierarchical entities (Christiano 2022). This is not merely a fact about the outcomes of the market but about the market processes themselves.

The toolkit of collective bargaining, worker cooperatives, works councils, and co-determination, as well as combinations of these, are all potential remedies to this kind of inequality of power. They counter the unequal power of the monopsonist and the economic weakness of the poor person with little access to credit or insurance with an institutional design that is meant to remedy the inequality. They substitute one kind of power that is inaccessible to the worker with another kind that is accessible. To see the importance of the idea of worker participation as a remedy for lack of power, it is worth contrasting low skilled workers with very high skilled workers. The latter have a great deal of bargaining power in the market and are able to structure their relations with others more in accordance with their concerns. They usually have worker participation in some form or other, but the legal system does not need to insist on worker participation for them because they already have sufficient power.

But worker participation is not necessarily to be expected in markets where there is a lot of inequality of power. Indeed, some markets may be rigidly biased against this kind of remedy. Monopsony and great inequality of wealth are background conditions that can rigidly bias the labour market against these tools. The very institution that is meant to remedy inequality of power in markets is precluded by those markets where the remedy is necessary. And so, there must be some kind of legal design of markets that includes one or another of these tools to remedy the inequality that normally arises in the market.

To be sure, there are other things a society can do to help remedy inequalities of power. For instance, it can introduce a powerful welfare state, including income support, healthcare provision and social security, to protect people against losses of income. But these are usually not sufficient to counter the inequality of power in the markets that arise from monopsony and inequality of wealth. Economists measure significant markdowns in wages in the United States, e.g., despite its powerful welfare state (Manning 2021). Another set of provisions are occupational health and safety requirements and a minimum wage. But these are also not substitutes for worker participation. Rather, there is complementarity between worker participation and occupational health and safety concerns, since the laws requiring these protections are often ignored by firms that do not have worker participation (Donado and Walde 2012).

3 Participation and Political Equality

The third consideration in favour of worker participation in firms is its contribution to political equality. Here I want to defend what I call the complementarity of participation in firms and political participation. The participation of workers in firms tends greatly to enhance the political participation of those workers and increases its effectiveness. Versions of this thesis have been defended before (Pateman 1970; Cohen and Rogers 1995; O'Neill and White 2019). Carole Pateman argues that worker participation in firms gives workers increased efficacy in politics. Workers learn to engage in argument and debate in the participatory workplace and are then able to think about politics in a more open and receptive way. To be sure, one can get this kind of education from participation in other associations. But work is distinctive, because there is a lot at stake in workplace discussions and also because work occupies more time and energy by far than any other associative activity one can engage with.

I want to add another set of arguments. A number of recent studies have shown two things that would seem to support a very strong role for worker participation. These studies mostly concern unions, so there is a need to draw inferences from these studies for other forms of participation. First, members of unions are very significantly better informed about politics than are other persons in the same jobs but who are not in unions (Kim and Margalit 2017; MacDonald 2021). Second, politicians in legislative districts in the United States that have high union density are substantially more responsive to working-class and lower middle-class interests than are other politicians (Becher and Stegmuller 2021).

Let me explain what I take to be the implications of these two statistical claims. I will start with the second one. Larry Bartels, Martin Gilens, and others have argued that representatives in the United States are highly responsive to the opinions of the upper tercile of the income distribution, only a little responsive to the middle tercile and not at all to the bottom tercile (Bartels 2008; Gilens 2012; for a contrasting view, see Elkjaer 2020). Responsiveness of politicians to the opinions of constituents is the principal mechanism by which political power is secured for people. High levels of responsiveness imply that those constituents have a lot of power. No responsiveness implies that the constituents have no power. Hence these very stark differences of responsiveness imply stark differences in political power. There is a great deal of inequality of power in American democracy. The one thing that bucks this trend is responsiveness to union members in districts with high union density. These are people in the top half of the lower tercile and the bottom half of the middle tercile.

If we look at the larger trends in society, we see that declining unions since the 1970s in the United States are associated with the declining fortunes of the bottom half of the income distribution. And we see that part of the decline occurs because Congress has been less and less friendly to workers. Minimum wage has declined, protection of union organisation has declined, and enforcement and updating of laws protecting workers has declined. A significant part of the increase in inequality is due to the fact that there are far fewer strong organisations promoting the interests of workers in politics (Rosenfeld 2014; Freeman 2007). Unions played a very large role in building and supporting the welfare state in northern Europe (Streeck and Hassel 2003).

How is this connected with the informedness of workers? Democracy, when basic rights are protected (such as the rights to vote, to compete for office, to express one's views and associate freely with others, and to contest free and fair elections) is essentially an information system. It enables the transmission of information and the ability to understand it, synthesise it, and know how to act on it. Politicians pay attention to those who pay attention to them. The more a group of persons knows about politicians, policies, and parties, the more the politicians will pay attention to their distinctive concerns (Downs 1957). Of course, people who are not well informed can still vote on the basis of party identification or personality, but these are fuzzy signals and give politicians a lot of wiggle room in which to make choices. What we see is that the better-off members of society are better educated and better informed about politics. They tend to vote in higher numbers. They also tend to favour programmes that advance their interests. When informed, they tend to disfavour redistribution. The worse-off parts of the population are less well educated and less informed about politics. They tend to turn out less. They tend to favour more redistribution when they are informed. But politicians don't pay much attention to them except perhaps to the big-ticket issues like abortion or gay rights (Erikson 2015). Again, the big exception here is with unionised workers.

Unions contribute to this difference in information in both ways mentioned above. They pool resources from workers and can develop and disseminate information regarding the interests of workers. We see this in the workplace where unions make it possible for the extensive system of occupation and safety laws to be enforced because they aggregate information about violations of these laws (Donado and Walde 2012). They also participate quite extensively in the political system helping broadcast information about the interests of workers and making sure that politicians are aware of these (Rosenfeld 2014).

Unions also play a role in enhancing the information of workers as noted above. Union members are better informed than other similar workers and hold more nuanced views about policy and seem to pursue information more frequently than non-union members. Unions have power in significant part because they can mobilise union members based on their informed preferences both to vote and to get out the vote (Lichtenstein 2013). Mobilisation itself is mostly a process of informing people. Unions don't force people to vote, though they may exert some degree of social pressure. They tell them that they share interests with others and that those interests can be best advanced by voting as a group for a particular set of politicians. Unionised workers are simply more aware on average of what politicians are doing than other similar workers are; this difference holds particularly for low skilled and less well-off workers (Rosenfeld 2010; Bryson, Gomez, Kretschmer, and Willman 2013).

Hence, union participation is a fundamental building block for a democracy that aims to be responsive to the interests of the lower half of the income brackets. There is, in addition, evidence that workplace democracy has a positive effect on political participation. The idea has been a mainstay since Carole Pateman argued that workplace democracy enhanced the workers' abilities to participate in politics (Pateman 1970). There have been critics of what is sometimes called the spill-over effect of workplace democracy (Carter 2006; Adman 2008). But a lot of recent work has argued empirically that workplace democracy both increases workers' motivations to participate in politics and increases their abilities to participate in politics (Budd, Lamare, and Timming 2018; Timming and Summers 2020). Worker participation greatly contributes to the political participation of workers. Since co-determination is a combination of union and worker participation in governance, there is reason to think that it too promotes political participation.

The effect of worker participation on political participation and equality is not a mere desirable by-product of worker participation. It is an essential element in the maintenance of worker participation in societies. Enhanced capacities to participate in politics are essential for workers to protect their interests in economic life (Streeck and Hassel

2003). Worker participation and political participation are complementary goods for workers (Christiano 2019).

4 Conclusion

I have given three considerations in favour of worker participation in the governance of firms. I have not tried to give a definitive answer to the question of the exact form of worker participation. I leave it open to collective choice as to which form is best for the particular markets and communities at issue.

I want to emphasise the qualifications on this approach here. First, I describe a toolkit here because it is likely that different societies with different histories will fit with some of the remedies better than others. Or, in a more fine-grained way, it is likely some tools will achieve greater equality in some markets while maintaining the productivity of those markets while other tools will work better in other markets. This requires testing and trial and error for the society. Second, it may also sometimes be the case that any remedy is worse than the disease, in the sense that the attempted remedy seriously undermines the productivity of the market. I am working here with a conception of equality of power that forbids levelling down. I mean that a market situation which has inequality of power between participants may nonetheless be superior to a situation with equality of power, if everyone (or a substantial proportion of the less well off) is worse off under the situation of equality (Christiano and Braynen 2008). The reason I put the economic arguments in favour of worker participation at the beginning is to provide reason for thinking that these institutions do in fact help the less well-off part of the population. Third, there must be some room available, if possible, for those who simply do not want to participate in the running of firms. This may take several forms even when some kind of participatory firm is mandated. The easiest would be the case that a person might simply prefer not to participate though they have the right. This may still involve some social pressure to participate, so it may not be ideal. Firms that involve worker participation could have quotas for employees who do not wish to participate. They could be non-member employees. This is quite common in the case of worker cooperatives and is often permitted in unionised firms (Burdin and Dean 2009).

These three considerations are importantly interconnected. The economic viability of firms with worker participation is, I believe, an essential support in the argument for worker participation since we are speaking here of one of the main mechanisms by which the needs and desires of persons are satisfied in society. A scheme of worker participation that significantly undermined the ability of society to satisfy human needs and desires would be undesirable. The support that worker participation provides for the political participation of less well-off people in society is an essential support for the maintenance and improvement of the legal regime of worker participation. So, the three attributes of efficient and egalitarian outcomes, equality in the market and enhanced political participation are complementary and mutually reinforcing.

Acknowledgements

I want to thank Rutger Claassen, Michael Bennett, Yara Al Salman, Andrew Williams, Sameer Bajaj, Stuart White, Richard Arneson, Jessica Flanigan, and the participants at the Wealth and Power in Capitalism workshop June 2021 and a session at the Center for Ethics, Law and Public Affairs at the University of Warwick in November 2021.

References

Addison, John T. 2009. *The Economics of Codetermination: Lessons from the German Experience*. New York, NY: Palgrave/MacMillan.

Addison, John T., Paulino Teixera, Katalin Evers, and Lutz Bellmann. 2017. "Collective Bargaining and Innovation in Germany: A Case of Cooperative Industrial Relations?" *Industrial Relations* 56 (1): 73–121.

Adman, Per. 2008. "Does Workplace Experience Enhance Political Participation? A Critical Test of a Venerable Hypothesis." *Political Behavior* 30(1): 115–138.

Anderson, Elizabeth. 2017. *Private Government: How Employers Rule Our Lives (and Why We Don't Talk About It)*. Princeton, NJ: Princeton University Press.

Bartels, L. 2008. *Unequal Democracy*. Princeton, NJ: Princeton University Press.

Becher, M. and Stegmuller, D. 2021. "Reducing Unequal Representation: The Impact of Labor Unions on Legislative Responsiveness in the US Congress." *Perspectives on Politics* 19 (1): 92–109.

Bonin, John P., Derek C. Jones, and Louis Putterman. 1993. "Theoretical and Empirical Studies of Producer Cooperatives: Will Even the Twain Meet?" *Journal of Economic Literature* XXXI (3): 1290–1320.

Bryson, Alex, Rafael Gomez, Tobias Kretschmer, and Paul Willman. 2013. "Workplace Voice and Civic Engagement: What Theory and Data Tell Us about Unions and Their Relationship to the Democratic Process." *Osgoode Hall Law Journal* 50: 965–998.

Budd, John W., J. Ryan Lamare, and Andrew R. Timming. 2018. "Learning About Democracy at Work: Cross-National Evidence on Individual Employee Voice Influencing Political Participation in Civil Society." *ILR Review* 71(4): 956–985.

Burdin, Gabriel and Andres Dean. 2009. "New Evidence on Wages and Employment in Worker Cooperatives with Capitalist Firms." *Journal of Comparative Economics* 37: 517–533.

Card, David, Thomas Lemieux, and W. Craig Riddell. 2003. "Unions and the Wage Structure." *International Handbook of Trade Unions*. Ed. John T. Addison and Claus Schnabel. Cheltenham: Edward Elgar.

Cardullo, Gabrielle, Maurizio Conti, and Giovanni Sulis. 2020. "A Model of Unions, Two-tier Bargaining and Capital Investment." *Labour Economics* 67: 101936.

Carter, Neil. 2006. "Political Participation and the Workplace: The Spillover Thesis Revisited." *British Journal of Political and International Relations* 8: 410–426.

Christiano, Thomas. 2008. *The Constitution of Equality: Democratic Authority and Its Limits*. Oxford: Oxford University Press.

Christiano, Thomas. 2018. "The Wage Setting Process: A Democratic Conception of Fair Market Exchange." *Erasmus Journal for Philosophy and Economics* 11 (2): 57–84.

Christiano, Thomas. 2019. "Democracy, Participation and Information: Complementarity Between Political and Economic Institutions." *San Diego Law Review* 56 (4): 935–960.

Christiano, Thomas. 2022. "Worker Participation and the Egalitarian Conception of Fair Market Exchange." *Social Philosophy and Policy* (forthcoming).

Christiano, Thomas and Will Braynen. 2008. "Inequality, Injustice and the Leveling Down Problem." *Ratio* XXI (4): 392–420.

Cohen, Joshua and Joel Rogers. 1995. *Associations and Democracy*. Ed. Eric Olin Wright. London: Verso.

Dahl, Robert. 1985. *A Preface to Economic Democracy*. Berkeley, CA: University of California Press.

Donado, Alejandro and Klaus Walde. 2012. "How Trade Unions Increase Welfare." *The Economic Journal* 122 (563): 990–1009.

Doucouliagos, Hristos, Richard B. Freeman, and Patrice Laroche. 2017. *The Economics of Trade Unions: A Study of a Research Field and Its Findings*. London: Routledge.

Dow, Gregory K. 2003. *Governing the Firm: Worker's Control in Theory and Practice*. Cambridge: Cambridge University Press.

Downs, Anthony. 1957. *An Economic Theory of Democracy*. New York, NY: Harper and Row.

Dreze, Jacques. 1989. *Labour Management, Contracts and Capital Markets*. London: Blackwell.

Elkjaer, Mad Andreas. 2020. "What Drives Unequal Policy Responsiveness? Assessing the Role of Informational Asymmetries in Economic Policy-Making." *Comparative Political Studies* 53(14): 2213–2245.

Erikson, Robert. 2015. "Income Inequality and Policy Responsiveness." *Annual Review of Political Science* 18: 11–29.

Fishkin, Joseph. 2014. *Bottlenecks. A New Theory of Equal Opportunity*. Oxford: Oxford University Press.

Freeman, Richard B. 2007. *America Works: Thoughts on the Exceptional US Labor Market*. New York, NY: Russell Sage Foundation.

Freeman, Richard and Edward Lazear. 1995. "An Economic Analysis of Works Councils." In *Works Councils: Consultation, Representation, and Cooperation in Industrial Relations*. Eds. Wolfgang Streeck and Joel Rogers. Chicago, IL: University of Chicago Press.

Freeman, Richard and James Medoff. 1984. *What Do Unions Do?* New York, NY: Basic Books.

Gilens, M. 2012. *Affluence and Influence*. Princeton, NJ: Princeton University Press.

Hirsch, B. T. 2017. "What Do Unions Do for Economic Performance?" In *What Do Unions Do? A Twenty Years Perspective*. Ed. James Bennett and Bruce Kaufman. London: Routledge. 193–237.

Jager, Simon, Shakked Noy, and Benjamin Schoefer. 2021. "What Does Co-Determination Do?" *NBER Working Paper Series* n. 28921 (June).

Jensen, Michael and William Meckling. 1979. "Rights and Production Functions: An Application to Labor-Managed Firms and Codetermination." *The Journal of Business* 52 (4): 469–506.

Kim, S. E., Margalit, Y. (2017). "Informed Preferences? The Impact of Unions on worker Policy Views." *American Journal of Political Science* 61 (3): 728–743.

Lichtenstein, Nelson. 2013. *The State of the Union: A Century of American Labor*. Princeton, NJ: Princeton University Press.

MacDonald, D. 2021. "How Labor Unions Increase Political Knowledge: Evidence from the United States." *Political Behavior* 43: 1–24.

Manning, Alan. 2021. "Monopsony in Labor Markets: A Review." *ILR Review* 74 (1): 3–26.

Metcalf, David. 2003. "Unions and Productivity, Financial Performance and Investment: International Evidence." *International Handbook of Trade Unions*. Ed. John T. Addison and Claus Schnabel. Cheltenham: Edward Elgar.

O'Neill, Martin and Stuart White. 2019. "Trade Unions and Political Equality." In *Philosophical Foundations of Labour Law*. Oxford: Oxford University Press.

Pateman, Carole. 1970. *Participation and Democratic Theory*. Cambridge: Cambridge University Press.

Pencavel, John, Luigi Pistaferri, and Fabiano Schivardi. 2006. "Wages, Employment and Capital in Capitalist and Worker Owned Firms." *Industrial and Labor Relations Review* 60(1): 23–44.

Rawls, John. 1971. *A Theory of Justice*. Cambridge: Harvard University Press.

Robinson, Joan. 1969. *The Economics of Imperfect Competition* (2nd ed.). New York, NY: St. Martin's Press.

Rosenfeld, Jake. 2010. "Economic Determinants of Voting in an Era of Union Decline." *Social Science Quarterly* 91(2): 379–396.

Rosenfeld, Jake. 2014. *What Unions No Longer Do*. Cambridge, MA: Harvard University Press.

Smith, Adam. 1776. *The Wealth of Nations*. Indianapolis, IN: Liberty Fund.

Stansbury, Anna and Lawrence H. Summers. 2020. "The Declining Worker Power Hypothesis: An Explanation for The Recent Evolution of the American Economy." *National Bureau of Economic Research*. Working Paper 27193.

Streeck, Wolfgang and Anke Hassel. 2003. "Trade Unions as Political Actors." In *International Handbook of Trade Unions*. Ed. John T. Addison and Claus Schnabel. Cheltenham: Edward Elgar. 335–365.

Timming, Andrew and Juliette Summers. 2020. "Is Workplace Democracy Associated with Wider Pro-democracy Affect? A Structural Equation Model." *Economic and Industrial Democracy* 41(3): 709–726.

Ward, Benjamin. 1958. "The Firm in Illyria: Market Syndicalism." *American Economic Review* 48(4): 566–589.

Young, Iris Marion 1990. *Justice and the Politics of Difference*. Princeton, NJ: Princeton University Press.

8 Taming the Corporate Leviathan

How to Properly Politicise Corporate Purpose?

Michael Bennett and Rutger Claassen

Corporations are increasingly asked to specify a 'purpose.' Instead of focusing on profits, a company should adopt a substantive purpose for the good of society. In the words of an influential report by the British Academy: 'The purpose of corporations is not to produce profits. The purpose of corporations is to produce profitable solutions for the problems of people and planet. In the process it produces profits, but profits are not per se the purpose of corporations' (British Academy 2019, 16). High-profile books (Mayer 2018; Edmans 2020; Henderson 2020), policy-oriented reports (Veldman, Gregor, and Morrow 2016; British Academy 2019; 2020), and academic articles (Levillain and Segrestin 2019; Bebchuk and Tallarita 2020; Rock 2020) have discussed this emerging 'purpose paradigm.'

This chapter analyses, historicises, and radicalises this call for purpose. We schematise the history of the corporation into two main *purpose/power regimes*, each combining a way of thinking about corporate purpose with specific institutions to hold corporate power to account. Under the *special charter regime* of the seventeenth to mid-nineteenth centuries, governments chartered companies to pursue specific public purposes. Under criticism for corruption and lack of competition, the special charter regime gave way to the contemporary *general incorporation regime*. No particular purposes are demanded of corporations, and profit-seeking has become the norm. This regime has come under criticism in turn, and the purpose paradigm has the potential to become a new third purpose/power regime, the *social purpose regime*.

Our analysis of these three regimes focuses on politicisation. We argue that orienting companies to substantive social purposes requires politicising the business corporation, creating meaningful accountability mechanisms to align companies with the goals of the public. The purpose paradigm must overcome its political timorousness and be more institutionally radical. The difficulty is doing this without unacceptable corruption and inefficiency. We need a form of 'proper politicisation.' At the end of the chapter, we discuss some directions for reform which may deliver on that desideratum.

DOI: 10.4324/9781003173632-10

Contemporary ideas about government and society are dominated by a liberal division of labour between an economy of free private contractors on the one hand and a state which regulates them in the public interest on the other. The clearest and most important expression of the contemporary breakdown of this division is the big multinational business corporation. Corporations are the locus of non-state power in the economy, and a major force behind the influence of wealth in the state. The proposals discussed at the end of the chapter import democratic mechanisms familiar from politics to help govern large corporations. In this way, we can attempt to preserve democratic values in our messy, mixed-up reality rather than trying to enforce a neat division between economic and political realms.

We begin by reviewing the current general incorporation regime (Section 1) and the emerging social purpose paradigm (Section 2). We argue that to transform into a new regime the paradigm must politicise corporate purpose (Section 3). In Section 4, we review the special charter regime, which did treat corporate purpose politically. However, in Section 5, we argue that by putting each charter directly in the discretion of the legislature, this regime also invited inefficiency and corruption. Drawing on the historical experience, we put forward desiderata for a better purpose/power regime. Section 6 introduces several directions for reform, which may fulfil these desiderata, extending the social purpose paradigm and giving it potential as an effectual new regime. These rely on either empowering stakeholders through stakeholder boards, dispersing share-ownership amongst citizens, or introducing citizens' juries and citizen assemblies to assess corporate performance on social purpose.

1 Where We Are Now: The General Incorporation Regime

Since the new purpose paradigm emerges as a critique of the current general incorporation regime, it is first necessary to say something about that regime and the purpose paradigm's critique of it.

Four features of the general incorporation regime are particularly salient (for summary, see Table 1). First, incorporation is generally available, to the extent of being little more than a formality. Anyone can start a business; incorporation is part of the open-access orders of modern liberal societies (North, Wallis, and Weingast 2009). Second, as a mere formality, incorporators need not have any particular purpose, with charters often stating that a corporation is for 'any lawful purpose.' This means that most corporate charters have a fairly generic character, allowing businesses to adopt and relinquish purposes as they go. Third, consequently, companies are regulated not according to their particular charters, but according to general rules that apply to any relevant firms. General regulation (such as consumer or environmental regulation) by government applies to specific products or business activities, not to the legal person itself. Regulation operates as an external constraint on the decision-making process proscribed by the corporate governance structure. Fourth, while the law is formally agnostic about corporate purposes, the market context in which businesses operate steers them towards a goal of profit maximisation (more accurately, shareholder value maximisation). This has been justified on the theory that profit-seekers will be led to advance the general welfare by the invisible hand of market competition (Friedman 1970). Since the 1970s, this has been the dominant interpretation of the corporate objective in English-speaking countries. Therefore the general incorporation paradigm is now associated with 'shareholder primacy' as the dominant norm in corporate governance (Hansmann and Kraakman 2001).

The general incorporation regime relies on a liberal division of labour wherein corporations compete and focus on their private interest, while states govern and make rules which embody the public interest (Scherer and Palazzo 2007, 1111). Freedom of incorporation was part of a wider movement to put in place a stricter private/public distinction and understand corporations as firmly on the private side of this dichotomy (Ciepley 2013). However, this should not be understood as licensing corporations to do as they like. Rather, corporate power is subjected to two disciplining forces: market competition and a regulating state.

In the last two decades, increasing doubts have been raised about the tenability of this regime. In particular, globalisation has facilitated the re-emergence of corporations as political actors. Multinationals often operate at a global level which escapes nation-state regulation and in developing countries with weak governance capacities (Scherer and Palazzo 2011). They engage today not only in the 'old' political activities of lobbying and influencing state decisions, but also in 'new' political activities of self-regulation, standards-setting, and public goods provision which effectively bypass states altogether (Hussain and Moriarty 2014; Saunders-Hastings 2022, in this volume). At the same time, many markets have become less competitive and dominated by a small number of big firms. A new technology sector with strong monopolistic tendencies has become more important. Traditional countervailing powers such as labour unions have been weakened. Regulations have been relaxed. As corporations have grown in power, they have burst the banks of market competition and state regulation which were meant to channel their pursuit of profit towards the general welfare.

Consequently, many authors have concluded that we cannot expect companies motivated purely by profits to act in a way that advances the public good. Instead of relying on the invisible hand, companies this powerful should directly pursue the public good and orient themselves towards substantive social purposes. Of course, this reaction has not been universal: some continue to insist that alternatives to the liberal division of labour are specious and that concerned citizens should instead focus on shoring up competition and state regulation (Bebchuk and Tallarita 2020). Rather than engaging in this debate here, we will take the social purpose paradigm's critique of the general incorporation regime as given and ask where it leads us.

2 Proposals for a Social Purpose Regime

In terms of concrete legal reforms, the core of the social purpose paradigm is that a substantive purpose expressing the company's contribution to society should be written into the corporate charter. This purpose does not require state approval. Instead, authorship lies with those mandated to change the charter within the corporate governance structure: directors and/or shareholders in most jurisdictions today. How this core demand is articulated, however, makes a significant difference. We look at three different dimensions, on each of which there are more minimal (reformist) and more demanding (radical) versions of the paradigm.

First, what's the nature of the social purpose, and how far does it stray from the traditional economic purpose of profit-maximisation? While critical of profit-maximisation, social purpose advocates do not envision the supersession of market discipline entirely. These authors still accept profit-seeking as part of, or a means to the realisation of, a corporation's purpose. Exactly how substantive purpose and market discipline should be combined, however, remains disputed. Some purpose advocates prefer to think in terms of win-win situations.[1] Others recognise there may be trade-offs (Mayer 2020, 227). In these cases, the respective weights of social purpose and economic purpose can be conceptualised in a variety of different ways (Lankoski and Smith 2018). At the minimum, one could take profit-maximisation as the goal, and a certain baseline level of social purpose as a constraint in its pursuit. This is often expressed in terms of internalising negative externalities. A more radical version is to take the substantive social purpose as the goal, with a net positive profit balance as a constraint. This can be expressed in terms of creating positive externalities. Between these two extremes there is a continuum of possible trade-offs between purpose and profit.

A second dimension relates to how exactly companies should be incentivised to take on an orientation to purpose. The minimum is an open invitation in law. For example, the 2019 French law (the *Loi Pacte*) makes the adoption of a purpose (*raison d'être*) optional for corporations (Segrestin, Hatchuel, and Levillain 2020). Since nothing has so far actually prohibited corporations from stating a social purpose, such an invitation is above all a symbolic act to emphasise the desirability of doing so. Once a company has a purpose written into its charter, this can have a real impact by changing the content of directors' fiduciary duties and ultimately their legal liabilities. Several jurisdictions have created optional legal forms for the use of corporations with a social purpose. These include the *société à mission* in France, the *Benefit Corporation* in the United States, and the *Special Purpose Company* in the UK. We will say more about some of these forms below (Section 6).

The obvious alternative to these purely optional forms, is to make them mandatory. Colin Mayer, Leo Strine, and Jaap Winter (2020) have argued that something like benefit-corporation status should be required for all firms. Between the purely optional and fully mandatory there is again a continuum of ways states could incentivise companies in the direction of something like the benefit corporation. Such firms could be given preferment in public procurement, tax advantages or other perks.

This brings us to the third dimension, that of corporate governance. Minimally, purpose advocates maintain that directors' fiduciary duty needs to be re-oriented towards the corporation and its purpose rather than towards shareholders. Given that in many jurisdictions this is already the law and shareholder primacy is 'only' a cultural norm, one can question how much of a difference this will make. The strong position of shareholders in the governance structure will remain an obstacle to real change (Strine 2017, 179). At best, investors can be encouraged to put their ethics before their returns (Edmans 2020, 52; Henderson 2020, 124). Along this path, accounting can be reformed so that shareholders get better information about the non-financial performance of their corporations.

More radical proposals aim to change the underlying power structure by empowering other stakeholders in corporate governance. We will discuss some of these proposals further below (Section 6). However, calls for radical institutional reform are still fairly marginal within the purpose paradigm movement. The reason for this, we will argue, is that purpose advocates have generally not yet fully understood that the logical conclusion of the purpose paradigm is to politicise the corporation.

3 Purpose: Politicisation or De-Politicisation?

The potentially unique nature of the social purpose paradigm as a theory of corporate governance can be captured through the analytical lens of 'politicisation.'

To start, consider an argument recently made by Kevin Levillain and Blanche Segrestin (2019). They argue that the emerging attention to 'profit-with-purpose' corporations reflects a re-orientation in corporate governance models from 'primacy' to 'commitment to purpose.' The familiar stalemate in corporate governance discussions, they argue, is between two primacy views: the primacy of shareholders versus the primacy of stakeholders. These two camps have been dominating corporate governance debates for decades. What both models have in common is that they are both 'political'; they lead to 'boiling corporate governance down to the questions of "who elects whom?" and "who monitors whom?".' (Levillain and Segrestin 2019, 642) In contrast, they argue, purpose-driven corporate governance provides something new:

> The existence of a common purpose, explicitly stated in publicly available legal documents, enables derivation of objective and stable criteria for controlling executives' action – for instance through the definition of common standards – independently from the party that is supposed to exert this control.
> (Levillain and Segrestin 2019, 642)

Because of this radical priority of purpose over any constituents' interests, they argue, purpose-driven governance is truly different from both classical antagonists, which each defend and prioritise a particular constituency and its interests, shareholders or wider stakeholders.[2] We think the political nature of the purpose paradigm is a promising line of inquiry, but our analysis is in many respects the polar opposite of Levillain and Segrestin's.

On our analysis, a decision is politicised to the extent that:

1. All members of a group are subject to the decision.
2. Members of the group disagree about what should be done.
3. All members of the group participate in the decision.

This analysis is framed in terms of a single decision, but can easily be generalised to classes of decisions (e.g., corporate strategy) or to decision-making bodies or offices (e.g., the corporate board). As we show below, it can also be reversed to provide an analysis of de-politicisation. We start by taking the three elements of our analysis in turn.

Our first two elements mirror the two parts of Jeremy Waldron's (1999, 101), account of the 'circumstances of politics.' First, the subject matter of politics are common rules or decisions which apply to a whole group of people ('the polity'). Because common rules are imposed and binding for all members, coercion is a central element of politics. When there is no need for a common rule, decision-making about an issue can be 'privatised,' left to group members to decide for themselves. Which issues to politicise (to decide in common) is itself a political question. For example, a topic for local politics might be which colour residents should paint their houses; alternatively, they might decide that there is no need to make house colours a political decision. The 'need' for a common decision is not a feature of the external world, but depends on the interests and preferences of the members of the political community. Our first condition for politicisation is that decisions are collectivised rather than privatised.

The second element is disagreement. Common decisions do not necessarily give rise to politics if everyone is in agreement. In a society of millions, almost every common decision is subject to at least some disagreement. However, some issues are much more controversial than others. Even more than simple disagreement, on our account politicisation implies that decisions are a matter of judgement. The decision cannot be simply reduced to the correct application of a known set of rules, using an established body of technical knowledge. Politicisation in this sense is opposed not to privatisation but to technocracy. A major reason political decisions require judgement is that they depend on disagreements about values as well as facts. Of course, very often authorities make political decisions to create frameworks of rules within which civil servants make more technical decisions. For example, central banking often operates by governments setting an inflation target and then giving civil servants the job of choosing interest rates to hit that target. (De-)politicisation in this sense is a matter of how far decisions can be characterised as a technical question about the correct application of rules, or a matter of judgement on which people disagree.

These two elements can be used to diagnose where politics is present, independently of how we think politics should be organised. Our third element, on the other hand, is a normative statement about how politics should be conducted: those who will be affected by decisions should participate in them. This is the conclusion Waldron (1999) reaches about how to respond to political situations in the first two senses. There are many possible normative foundations for this basic democratic norm. Democratic procedures might be favoured for reasons of procedural fairness and respecting citizens as equals (e.g., Waldron 1999; Christiano 2010). Democracy might be favoured as a way of enhancing the epistemic quality of the decisions (e.g., Landemore 2013; Goodin and Spiekermann 2018). Here, we attempt to stay agnostic on how the basic democratic norm is grounded.

Our account of the three elements of politicisation can be summarised by thinking in terms of the three different ways they can be negated: issues can be de-politicalised by privatising them, by turning them into a technical exercise, and by reserving them to an elite. With this in mind, let's now return to the corporation.

The general incorporation regime is an attempt to depoliticise corporate purpose. In the first sense, it privatises corporate purpose, turning it into a subject on which no collective decision-making is needed. Stakeholders are put in the position of contractors, who, in a competitive economy, can find alternative companies to work with if they disagree with the corporation's decisions. Part of what justified this privatisation is the metaphor of the corporation as a production function quasi-mechanistically obeying market forces. This brings us to the second sense of de-politicisation: genuine disagreement about corporate purpose is denied because market competition is imagined to apply so tightly that companies have no discretion about what to do. All that remains is the technical question of how managers can steer the company to stay in tune with market signals. Finally, de-politicisation in the first two senses justifies de-politicisation in the third. Given that stakeholders are free to work with whomever they like, and given that companies are must bow to the winds of the market, decisions about a company's direction are best taken behind closed doors by board members representing the interests of shareholders.

This extreme version of the liberal division of labour has its attractions as an ideal. However, when used to describe an actual economy in which corporations wield significant power, it is ideological in the pejorative, Marxist sense of obscuring conflicts and power relations, making them harder to contest (cf. Shoikhedbrod 2022, in this volume). The fact that public protests against corporate power have time and again re-emerged over the period covered by the general incorporation regime (Lamoreaux and Novak 2017) is evidence that the general incorporation regime has not successfully depoliticised corporate power. Disagreement about corporate power persists, and without an outlet in regular corporate governance processes, it is taken to the street.

Of course, one might maintain that this disagreement is unfortunate and that we should aim for a more complete de-politicisation of corporate power. However, we do not think this stance would be compatible with the purpose paradigm. This brings us back to Levillain and Segrestin (2019). The corporate purpose statement is the ultimate common rule of the corporation as a polity. Different stakeholders will be advantaged at the expense of other stakeholders depending on which purpose a company commits to and on whether or not that company is judged to be fulfilling that commitment. If anything, then, one would expect the social purpose paradigm to represent a move to politicisation, not – as Levillain and Segrestin argue – de-politicisation. For instead of the one simple goal of profit maximisation, now corporations have to choose between a potentially endless variety of substantive purposes. Of course, Levillain and Segrestin are right that, once adopted, a purpose provides a legal anchor on which corporate constituencies need to focus their actions. But, we contend, both the process of adoption (and periodic revision) and, once adopted, the continual processes of interpretation of that (by its nature rather abstract) purpose cannot avoid politicisation. This suggests a pure idea of purpose-primacy is doomed to failure. The shareholder/stakeholder debate cannot be transcended by a common commitment of all participants to purpose.

We claim that the politicisation of corporate purpose is the logical conclusion of the purpose paradigm. If we want businesses to better serve society, it is important that businesses devote themselves to goals that society values rather than exclusively to the preferences of shareholders and board members. Once we admit the existence of a politics of corporate purpose, we cannot justify restricting decisions to shareholders and board members which clearly concern the general public.

The leading question for the social purpose paradigm should therefore be: how to *properly* politicise corporate purpose? To answer this question, it is important not to repeat historical errors. We will therefore first return to the era before general incorporation, when purpose was at the heart of corporate governance. What can we learn from that previous episode in politicisation of corporate purpose?[3]

4 Back to History: The Special Charter Regime

This section presents the main features of the special charter regime, which began with the first business corporations, the Dutch and English East India Companies, created through special charters from their governments in the seventeenth century. These were a novel adaptation of the general corporate form, which until then had been used only for non-profit purposes (towns, universities, monasteries, etc.). Business corporations remained a relatively rare species until general laws permitting incorporation for business purposes were passed in the nineteenth century. Until then, most commercial enterprises were conducted using unincorporated legal forms such as sole proprietorships or partnerships. Here, we focus on the practice of chartering corporations in the United States, from its independence in 1776 until the advent of general incorporation in the 1850s/1860s. The chartering practice in other countries had similar features, but the United States made more extensive use of the chartering device. We highlight five elements of the chartering practice.

First, in the United States, like other countries, businesses corporations could only be created by a *grant from the state*. This remains formally true today. However, these grants were not administered through a regular bureaucratic process. Instead, each individual charter had to be created by a separate piece of legislation. In the United States, this was handled by State legislatures.

Second, charters required corporations to fulfil a substantive *public purpose*. However, this should not be understood as excluding a private, commercial purpose on the part of the incorporators. According to Pauline Maier (referring, in particular, to Massachusetts), 'that a particular venture would benefit the private estates of individuals seems to have been of no concern – or to have been a positive consideration – as long as the public welfare was also served' (Maier 1993, 56; see also Handlin and Handlin 1947, 130, 132; Seavoy 1982, 6). This is not a surprise given that the initiative for incorporation almost always came from private individuals, not from the state.[4] Incorporation for manufacturing businesses was rare in the first decades of the nineteenth century but became more prevalent in the second half (Hurst 1970, 17; Roy 1997, 49). At first, corporations were approved for public works like canals, bridges, and turnpikes, and services like banking and insurance. In this and other respects, the breakthrough for the business corporation came with railroads in the mid-century.

Third, charters gave corporations a *monopoly position* in their sector and geographic area. It was widely recognised that corporations were 'franchises' of the state, with states giving privileges to specified parties. But we need to carefully distinguish two senses of this term. All corporations are franchises in the sense of having been granted the legal privilege to act as a unified legal person in law. But corporations were also, in this era, 'special-action franchises' (Hurst 1970, 20), chartered to get a specific task done, to the exclusion of others. Only the franchisee had the right to build the bridge or canal or to provide banking and insurance services in a certain area. Such a monopoly position was obviously attractive to investors. As we shall see, it was also a target of criticism.

Fourth, state approval often went hand-in-hand with *charter-based regulation* in the public interest (Handlin and Handlin 1945, 17). A variety of provisions were inserted into corporate charters with the goal of ensuring that companies adequately fulfilled the public purpose for which they had been chartered. One of the most common types of provision were duration limits, limiting the life span of corporations to a specified time period such as ten or thirty years (Hartz 1948, 239). Another example were 'reservation clauses,' giving the legislature the right to alter or revoke charters at will (Hartz 1948, 238). Requirements of rotation for directors and prohibitions on interlocking directorates served as guarantees to prevent private concentrations of power. Charters mentioned production limits for manufacturing companies, gave states the right to purchase public works after they were finished, and covered all kinds of granular local issues. Charter-based regulation needs to be understood against the background of the courts interpreting the power of corporations narrowly. Any powers not expressly granted in the charter were declared beyond the corporation's authority (*ultra vires*) (Hartz 1948, 243; Hovenkamp 1988, 1663).

A fifth feature is less well-known. US states held *visitorial power* over corporations. The idea originated with Catholic church corporations which were visited by their superiors in the hierarchy, who would hold them to account. According to William Blackstone, every corporation was to be held to account by a visitor, because corporations, 'being composed of individuals, subject to human frailties,' were liable 'to deviate from the end of their institution' (Blackstone 2016, 311). In cases of conflict, the visitor would hear the grievances, and 'administer justice impartially' (Holdsworth 1922, 395). Applied to lay corporations, Blackstone held that their visitor was their founder. In a general sense, he claimed, the King was the founder of all such foundations, hence the right would accrue to him (Blackstone 2016, 312).[5] It was this Blackstonian idea which US state courts transplanted to their own context when, in the early nineteenth century, they began to declare that they had visitorial power over corporations (Gluck 2017, 219). Later in the century, the power was ascribed not just to courts, but also to legislatures, as a general right 'to control and superintend corporations' (Glock 2017, 225). According to Glock, this visitatorial power later became the basis for the powers of the regulatory state. Although the origins have been largely forgotten, US state attorneys still hold these powers to inspect corporations (Ciepley 2019, 1005).

These were the main features of the special charter regime. Let's now see which lessons can be drawn from this regime, for the contemporary discussions about the politicisation of corporate purpose.

5 Lessons from History: Properly Politicising Corporate Purpose

In this section, we argue that the special charter regime did politicise purpose. However, it did so in a way with significant drawbacks and should therefore not be directly imitated. Through a discussion of these drawbacks, we derive three desiderata for the proper politicisation of corporate purpose.

We left off our examination of the social purpose regime with Levillain and Segrestin's (2019) argument for moving beyond a 'political,' 'primacy' view towards a 'commitment to purpose' view. Following the logic of this argument, we would expect the special charter regime to be a neat illustration of how purpose-driven organisations function. After all, corporations in that era were legally obliged to pursue only their corporate purpose. These limits were enforced (through *ultra vires* actions, as we saw above) and provided a real sense in which the corporation's mission was more limited and focused than that of companies in the general incorporation regime that venture into any line of business they see fit. However, none of this prevented the special charter corporations from being thoroughly politicised: quite the contrary.

In the nineteenth-century United States, strong opposition arose against corporations, characterised as the 'anticharter doctrine' (Maier 1993, 58) or 'anticharter philosophy' (Roy 1997, 53). Several arguments played a role. One locus of criticism was that corporations in this period were granted *monopolies*. Critics focused not so much on the inefficiency of monopoly as on its inegalitarian distributive tendency, attacking corporations as giving rise to a new aristocratic class. This argument had already been made by Adam Smith, to which anticharter critics readily referred (Maier 1993, 59). A second critique was that corporate privileges were not being allocated fairly because of *political favouritism and corruption*. Access to state legislatures was easier for those with financial means and political connections. Even if it did not involve explicitly bribing legislators, it was objected that unequal access violated the egalitarian spirit of the republic (Mark 1987, 1453; Maier 1993, 72).[6]

Together, these arguments provided a case for general incorporation laws.[7] The monopoly argument is the key one in this respect, since the restriction of privileges to the few can by definition only be resolved by opening up incorporation to all. However, for our purposes, the argument about political favouritism is more instructive. Placing charter decisions directly in the hands of the legislature was an open invitation to corruption and political favouritism. In a recent historical study of incorporation in the state of New York, Eric Hilt writes:

> Although it was the case that the earliest American corporations were seen as public instrumentalities, whether or not they served the public interest was a vigorously contested issue at the time… political discretion over access to charters and their contents often served the interests of incumbent firms and powerful political factions, rather than the public.
>
> (2017, 39–40)

From this point of view, there is no reason for nostalgically putting up the special charter regime as a model to remedy today's discontents with the general incorporation regime. From this history, we suggest, we can pick out three desiderata for a proper politicisation of corporate purpose, under a new social purpose regime (relating to the three senses of politicisation defined in Section 3).

First, such a regime should respect the three elements of politicisation identified earlier in the chapter. It should provide a process for making a common decision about corporate purpose rather than privatising it. It should allow for disagreement and judgement rather than presenting the choice as a technical exercise. It should include all those affected in the decision-making process. On this score, the special charter regime comes out relatively positively, at least compared to the general incorporation regime. Certainly, requiring approval of charters from state legislatures ensured the decision was a collective one that made space for disagreement and judgement. On popular participation there is more room for doubt. In theory, one might expect that elected legislators were appropriately representative of the people. However, anticharter critics lamented the disproportionate political influence of elites.

This brings us to the second desideratum for a corporate purpose regime: the avoidance of corruption. In the eyes of anticharter critics, corruption during the special charter regime reached a level where it harmed the democratic character of that regime. Corruption is not only a problem in democratic terms, but also for its inefficiency and incompatibility with the rule of law. The system should therefore be designed to minimise the incentives and opportunities for an exchange of favours between companies and political decision-makers – an exchange benefiting both parties at the expense of the public. It can be helpful to think of this in terms of the incentives on the supply (companies) and demand (public decision-makers) sides of this corrupt exchange.

On the supply-side, the fact that each company was subject to an individual decision by the legislature meant that there were very strong rewards for shareholders and managers who could corrupt the process. As chapters in this volume by Brian Kogelmann (2022) and Phil (2022) discuss in more detail, the fact that most laws apply to many different companies normally provides a certain degree of security against corruption, because any individual seeking to corrupt the process would be unable to capture all the benefits of doing so. As Kogelmann points out, this is why a prominent theme in normative public choice theory has been the importance of *generality*: ensuring that laws apply to everyone in a diffuse way rather than to a concentrated group in particular. It should be acknowledged that the general incorporation regime essentially brought generality to corporate law, and the consequence was indeed to cut out a whole category of corruption that had flourished in the previous era.

On the demand-side, the special charter regime also encouraged corruption by putting the decision in the hands of elected politicians. Facing regular elections, legislators are in a precarious position, and if extra money for campaigning makes a difference, then politicians who refuse it will in the long run tend to be replaced with politicians who accept it. In addition, campaign donations or offers of employment after leaving office provide relatively sanitised mechanisms of bribery.

Our third desideratum for proper politicisation is that the process should have sufficient administrative capacity. This may seem too trivial to be worth stating, but the lack of administrative capacity was a major weakness of the special charter regime and one which compounded its vulnerability to corruption. As the volume of corporations increased it became impossible for legislators to even attempt proper scrutiny of each charter. Charter-based regulation was often inadequate, and visitorial power was not exercised proactively but only by courts in response to third-party litigation.

With these desiderata in mind, we now move to today's social purpose regime. How can it fulfil these desiderata?

6 Options for Purpose-Driven Corporate Governance

As mentioned at the end of Section 2, the minimal option for corporate governance reform offered by others propagating the social purpose paradigm is to redirect directors' duties towards the corporate purpose. This continues to rely on a trustee model where those subject to corporate power do not have a voice. More radical proposals empower these other constituents, in one way or the other. We think moving in this direction is necessary, given our analysis pointing to the need for proper politisation. But what could this mean in practice? We see three main options.

The first option is to empower stakeholders. The authors of the *International Panel on Social Progress* report articulate the rationale behind this approach:

> Shareholders require some forum in which to make their views known, but so too do other stakeholders. A stakeholder board, which represented employees, shareholders, consumers, and creditors among others, would enable a diverse range of voices to influence the conduct of management. (...) The key concern is that a range of interests should be able to assert real power over the orientation of the company. To that end, devolving the legal powers possessed by shareholders to stakeholders in general would enable a more representative board to exercise such power.
> (Deakin et al. 2018, 246)

This position deserves serious discussion. There are obvious questions to be answered, such as who to include as stakeholders, and how to ensure that stakeholder board members act as faithful representatives of their constituencies. The proposal for stakeholder boards or committees builds on and generalises a longer tradition of thinking about workplace democracy (Malleson 2014; Ferreras 2017). Workplace democracy proposals have tended to originate from authors whose focus is on advancing the interests of labour rather than reconceiving corporate purpose (see Christiano 2022, in this volume). However, instead of representing workers only, a broader range of stakeholders could be empowered to influence corporate decision-making (Moriarty 2010). Some democratically minded authors have explicitly claimed that this is a bad idea, since the interest of non-employee stakeholders in the corporation is 'more tenuous' and their relations with it are 'relatively sporadic' (Hayden and Bodie 2020, 170). Adequately representing diffuse constituencies (such as the victims/beneficiaries of externalities) is likely to be difficult. Nonetheless, in the French context, the new law on purpose driven companies (*sociétés à mission*) has made creation of a stakeholder committee mandatory (Segrestin, Hatchuel, and Levillain 2020). These stakeholder committees are advisory bodies which lack real power, and indeed the *société à mission* form itself is optional rather than mandatory. However, it is easy to imagine how these arrangements could be made stronger, and the *société à mission* may provide valuable experience in the years to come.

A second reform option is to democratise shareholder ownership. For example, Lynn Stout, Sergio Gramitto, and Tamara Belinfanti have proposed a 'Blueprint for Citizen Capitalism' (2019). Under their plan, all citizens would receive shares in a new collective mutual fund. This citizens' fund would acquire shares in a wide variety of corporations, initially through donations from corporations and wealthy individuals. Citizen shares would revert to the fund upon their death. Citizens would not only get dividend payments, but also political rights to direct administrators of the Fund on how to vote the Fund's shares (Stout, Gramitto, and Belinfanti 2019). Similarly, Giacomo Corneo has proposed the establishment of a sovereign wealth fund from which all citizens would receive a 'social dividend,' which would invest on an ethical basis. He also proposes a 'federal shareholder' acquiring a majority stake in key domestic firms to combat plutocratic tendencies (Corneo 2017). These proposals give citizens the power of property to protect their interests in corporate governance. They share some affinities with strategies of dispersing wealth associated with Property-Owning Democracy (on which see Brouwer 2022, in this volume), such as Universal Basic Income, and with certain market socialist proposals (Roemer 1994). They do not reform corporate governance itself and maintain the shareholder-oriented nature characteristic of the general incorporation regime. However, by changing *who* owns shares, they change the power structure within the economy.

The previous suggestions focus on the internal governance of individual corporations. A third option would be to try enhancing external control mechanisms over companies by the political community, yet in a way that reinforces commitment to purpose rather than the traditional liberal division of labour. Gordon Allen has recently proposed 'citizen tax juries': deliberative mini-publics scrutinising tax avoidance by multinational corporations and wealthy individuals (Arlen 2021). In work yet to be published (Bennett and Claassen 2022) we are exploring how this kind of scheme might be applied much more generally in a process we can call the 'Corporate Social Assessment.' Each large company would be assessed on its contributions to the public good every few years by a 'jury' of randomly selected citizens. The juries would apply a marks scheme developed and periodically revised by specially convened Citizen's Assemblies (a larger deliberative body, also composed of randomly selected citizens). Jury assessments would be given teeth by attaching financial consequences: a subsidy for the better-performing companies funded by a tax on the worse-performing companies. In a sense, the Assessment aims to provide an updated version of visitation, more proactive and consequential than the historical practice of the special charter era. It avoids the difficult task of finding people who can represent all the stakeholder groups affected by a company by instead using a representative sample of the citizenry as a whole. Instead of trying to set up a group of stakeholders such that the bargains they reach will constitute a fair compromise between relevant interests, an impartial group of citizens deliberates on the relative value and urgency of different stakeholders' claims.

Comparing these three reform options is beyond the bounds of this paper. We suggest that the choice between these options should be determined by the three desiderata identified earlier. How the purpose paradigm should manifest itself in public policy should depend on how each of these proposals would score on proper politicisation, avoidance of corruption and administrative feasibility.

7 Conclusion

This chapter has compared several purpose/power regimes in the history of the corporation. Table 1 summarises our schematisation of corporate purpose regimes.

Our starting point was the newly developing purpose paradigm, which argues firms should be oriented towards substantive (socially valuable) purposes beyond mere profit-seeking. We argued that this paradigm is too reticent about politicising corporate purpose and too institutionally conservative, and that this frustrates the realisation of its own ambitions. Reflecting on an earlier era in which corporations were very clearly oriented towards substantive purposes, we argued that such an approach cannot avoid politicising the corporation, nor should it. Yet, the manner in which the special charter regime politicised corporations had clear disadvantages. Companies' purposes, and the extent to which they are actually realised, should be meaningfully guided and scrutinised by representatives of the public. However, this should take place in a regular procedure that gives companies some degree of transparency and minimises opportunities for corrupt exchanges of favours. What is needed, is a 'proper politisation' of corporate governance.

Finally, we have put forward several directions for radical reform of corporate governance which may live up to these desiderata. Amongst them are proposals for creating stakeholder boards at corporations, dispersal of shareholder ownership amongst citizens and citizen juries

Table 1 Three corporate regimes compared.

	Special charter regime	*General incorporation regime*	*Social purpose regime*
Corporate creation	State charter as special franchise	State charter as administrative act	State charter as administrative act
Corporate purpose	Public purpose (from the point of view of the chartering authority)	Economic purpose: Profits (legally covered by charter indicating 'any lawful purpose')	Social purpose (with profits as precondition or secondary purpose)
Scope of chartering	Limited (monopoly)	Unlimited (open access)	Unlimited (open access)
Regulation	Charter-based regulation and visitation powers	General laws and market competition	General laws and market competition, plus radical reform of corporate governance

assessing corporate decision-making. Which of these proposals could (best) deliver the demand for a properly politicised corporate governance structure, remains to be debated.

Our reigning ideology today has attempted to depoliticise the corporation, with unpleasant results. If we want companies to pursue valuable social goals, we cannot avoid politicising the question of corporate purpose. Getting big companies to work towards the common good will require thinking of new and creative ways to make them democratically accountable.

Acknowledgements

We would like to thank all the participants at the Wealth and Power workshop for their contributions to this chapter. Also, the anonymous referees provided invaluable feedback. We thank Huub Brouwer and Sam Langelaan for the final editorial suggestions. We thank the Dutch Research Council (NWO) for funding under grant no. 360-20-390, and the European Research Council (ERC) under the European Union's Horizon 2020 research and innovation programme (grant agreement No. 865165).

Notes

1 Here, there are overlaps with earlier proposals for 'enlightened shareholder maximization' (ESV) (Jensen 2002) and 'shared value creation' (Porter and Kramer 2011), although Edmans explicitly distances himself from ESV (Edmans 2020, 42).
2 This ties in with Miller and Gold (2015)'s notion of a fiduciary duty to a purpose rather than to persons.
3 For other analyses going to back to history to throw light on the current corporate purpose debate, (see Guenther 2019; Pollman 2021).
4 Many charters were for public works which allowed states to avoid raising taxes (Hurst 1970, 23; Roy 1997, 48). Toll roads were a common example.
5 In practice, however, Blackstone accepted that the King (acting through the court of king's bench) would visit one species of lay corporations, namely 'civil corporations,' while the other species, 'eleemosynary' (i.e., charitable) corporations, would be visited by their first donor or his heirs.
6 We omit a third argument from anticharter critics, that charters' grants of power posed a *danger to the sovereignty* of the state (Hartz 1948, 72; Maier 1993, 83). Pursued to its logical conclusion, this argument demanded the abolition of the corporate form.
7 However, an alternative faction in the US anticharter movement instead took these arguments as reasons to improve the existing practice, denying incorporation to unworthy candidates rather than expanding it to all (Creighton 1989, 1892; Maier 1993, 75; Roy 1997, 46).

References

Arlen, Gordon. 2021. "Citizen Tax Juries: Democratizing Tax Enforcement after the Panama Papers." *Political Theory*. https://doi.org/10.1177/00905917211018007.

Bebchuk, Lucian, and Roberto Tallarita. 2020. "The Illusory Promise of Stakeholder Governance." *Cornell Law Review* 106 (91): 91–178.

Bennett, Michael, and Rutger Claassen. 2022. "The Corporate Social Assessment. Making Corporate Purpose Pay." Under review.

Blackstone, William. 2016. *Commentaries on the Laws of England. Book I: Of the Rights of Persons*, edited by Simon Stern. Oxford: Oxford University Press.

British Academy. 2019. "Reforming Business for the 21st Century." London.

———. 2020. "Principles for Purposeful Business." London.

Brouwer, Huub. 2022. "Automation, Neutrality, and Property-Owning Democracy." In *Wealth and Power: Philosophical Perspectives*, edited by Michael Bennett, Huub Brouwer, and Rutger Claassen. London: Routledge.

Christiano, Thomas. 2010. *The Constitution of Equality: Democratic Authority and Its Limits*. Oxford: Oxford University Press.

———. 2022. "Why Does Worker Participation Matter? Three Considerations in Favour of Worker Participation in Corporate Governance." In *Wealth and Power: Philosophical Perspectives*, edited by Michael Bennett, Huub Brouwer, and Rutger Claassen. London: Routledge.

Ciepley, David. 2013. "Beyond Public and Private: Toward a Political Theory of the Corporation." *American Political Science Review* 107 (1): 139–58.

———. 2019. "Can Corporations Be Held to the Public Interest, or Even to the Law?" *Journal of Business Ethics* 154: 1003–18.

Corneo, Giacomo. 2017. *Is Capitalism Obsolete? A Journey Through Alternative Economic Systems*. Cambridge, MA: Harvard University Press.

Creighton, Andrew. 1989. "Incorporating the Republic: The Corporation in Antebellum Political Culture." *Harvard Law Review* 102 (8): 1883–903.

Deakin, Simon, Fabian Muniesa, Scott Stern, Lorraine Talbot, Raphie Kaplinsky, Martin O'Neill, Horacio Ortiz, Kerstin Sahlin, and Anke Schwittay. 2018. "Markets, Finance, and Corporations: Does Capitalism Have a Future?" In *Rethinking Society for the 21st Century. Report of the International Panel on Social Progress (IPSP)*, 225–54. Cambridge: Cambridge University Press. https://doi.org/10.1017/9781108399623.007.

Edmans, Alex. 2020. *Grow the Pie. How Great Companies Deliver Both Purpose and Profit*. Cambridge: Cambridge University Press.

Ferreras, Isabelle. 2017. *Firms as Political Entities. Saving Democracy through Economic Bicameralism*. Cambridge: Cambridge University Press.

Friedman, Milton. 1970. "A Friedman Doctrine – The Social Responsibility of Business Is to Increase Its Profits." *The New York Times Magazine*, September 13.

Glock, Judge. 2017. "The Forgotten Visitatorial Power: The Origins of Administrative Subpoenas and Modern Regulation." *Review of Banking & Financial Law* 37 (1): 205–66.

Goodin, Robert E., and Kai Spiekermann. 2018. *An Epistemic Theory of Democracy*. Oxford: Oxford University Press.

Guenther, David. 2019. "Of Bodies Politic and Pecuniary: A Brief History of Corporate Purpose." *Michigan Business & Entrepreneurial Law Review* 9 (1): 1–78.

Handlin, Oscar, and Mary F. Handlin. 1945. "Origins of the American Business Corporation." *The Journal of Economic History* 5 (1): 1–23. https://doi.org/10.1017/S0022050700112318.

———. 1947. *Commonwealth. A Study of the Role of Government in the American Economy, 1774–1861*. Cambridge, MA: The Belknapp Press.

Hansmann, Henry, and Reinier Kraakman. 2001. "The End of History for Corporate Law." *The Georgetown Law Journal* 89: 439–68.

Hartz, Louis. 1948. *Economic Policy and Democratic Thought: Pennsylvania, 1776–1860*. Cambridge, MA: Harvard University Press.

Hayden, Grant, and Matthew Bodie. 2020. *Reconstructing the Corporation. From Shareholder Primacy to Shared Governance*. Cambridge: Cambridge University Press.

Henderson, Rebecca. 2020. *Reimaging Capitalism in a World on Fire*. New York, NY: PublicAffairs.

Hilt, Eric. 2017. "Early American Corporations and the State." In *Corporations and American Democracy*, edited by Naomi Lamoreaux and William Novak, 37–73. Cambridge, MA: Harvard University Press.

Holdsworth, W. S. 1922. "English Corporation Law in the 16th and 17th Centuries." *The Yale Law Journal* 31 (4): 382–407. https://doi.org/10.2307/787883.

Hovenkamp, Herbert. 1988. "The Classical Corporation in American Legal Thought." *Georgetown Law Journal* 76 (5): 1593–690.

Hurst, James. 1970. *The Legitimacy of the Business Corporation in the Law of the United States, 1780–1970*. Charlottesville, VA: The University Press of Virginia.

Hussain, Waheed, and Jeffrey Moriarty. 2014. "Corporations, the Democratic Deficit, and Voting." *The Georgetown Journal of Law and Public Policy* 12: 429–50.

Jensen, Michael. 2002. "Value Maximization, Stakeholder Theory, and the Corporate Objective Function." *Business Ethics Quarterly* 12 (2): 235–56.

Kogelmann, Brian. 2022. "Public Choice and Political Equality." In *Wealth and Power: Philosophical Perspectives*, edited by Michael Bennett, Huub Brouwer, and Rutger Claassen. London: Routledge.

Lamoreaux, Naomi, and William Novak. 2017. "Corporations and American Democracy: An Introduction." In *Corporations and American Democracy*, edited by Naomi Lamoreaux and William Novak, 1–33. Cambridge, MA: Harvard University Press.

Landemore, Hélène. 2013. *Democratic Reason: Politics, Collective Intelligence, and the Rule of the Many*. Princeton: Princeton University Press.

Lankoski, Leena, and N. Craig Smith. 2018. "Alternative Objective Functions for Firms." *Organization & Environment* 31 (3): 242–62.

Levillain, Kevin, and Blanche Segrestin. 2019. "From Primacy to Purpose Commitment: How Emerging Profit-with-Purpose Corporations Open New Corporate Governance Avenues." *European Management Journal* 37: 637–47. https://doi.org/10.1016/j.emj.2019.07.002.

Maier, Pauline. 1993. "The Revolutionary Origins of the American Corporation." *The William and Mary Quarterly* 50 (1): 51–84. https://doi.org/10.2307/2947236.

Malleson, Tom. 2014. *After Occupy. Economic Democracy for the 21st Century*. Oxford: Oxford University Press.

Mark, Gregory A. 1987. "The Personification of the Business Corporation in American Law." *The University of Chicago Law Review* 54 (4): 1441–83. https://doi.org/10.2307/1599739.

Mayer, Colin. 2018. *Prosperity. Better Business Makes the Greater Good*. Oxford: Oxford University Press.

———. 2020. "Ownership, Agency, and Trusteeship: An Assessment." *Oxford Review of Economic Policy* 36 (2): 223–40. https://doi.org/10.1093/oxrep/graa006.

Mayer, Colin, Leo E. Strine Jr., and Jaap Winter. 2020. "50 Years Later, Milton Friedman's Shareholder Doctrine Is Dead." *Fortune Magazine*, September 13.

Miller, Paul, and Andrew Gold. 2015. "Fiduciary Governance." *William & Mary Law Review* 57 (2): 513–86.

Moriarty, Jeffrey. 2010. "Participation in the Workplace: Are Employees Special?" *Journal of Business Ethics* 92 (3): 373–84.

North, Dougless, John Wallis, and Barry Weingast. 2009. *Violence and Social Orders*. Cambridge: Cambridge University Press.

Pollman, Elizabeth. 2021. "The History and Revival of the Corporate Purpose Clause." *Texas Law Review* 99 (7): 1423–1452.

Parvin, Phil. 2022. "Hidden in Plain Sight: How Lobby Organizations Undermine Democracy." In *Wealth and Power: Philosophical Perspectives*, edited by Michael Bennett, Huub Brouwer, and Rutger Claassen. London: Routledge.

Porter, Michael, and Mark Kramer. 2011. "Creating Shared Value." *Harvard Business Review* January–February: 1–17.

Rock, Edward. 2020. "For Whom Is the Corporation Managed in 2020? The Debate over Corporate Purpose." *ECGI Working Paper Series in Law* 515/2020.

Roemer, John E. 1994. *A Future for Socialism*. Harvard: Harvard University Press.

Roy, William. 1997. *Socializing Capital. The Rise of the Large Industrial Corporation in America*. Princeton, NJ: Princeton University Press.

Saunders-Hastings, Emma. 2022. "Corporate Social Responsibility and Philanthropy." In *Wealth and Power: Philosophical Perspectives*, edited by Michael Bennett, Huub Brouwer, and Rutger Claassen. London: Routledge.

Scherer, Andreas Georg, and Guido Palazzo. 2007. "Toward a Political Conception of Corporate Responsibility: Business and Society Seen from a Habermasian Perspective." *The Academy of Management Review* 32 (4): 1096–120. https://doi.org/10.2307/20159358.

———. 2011. "The New Political Role of Business in a Globalized World: A Review of a New Perspective on CSR and Its Implications for the Firm, Governance, and Democracy." *Journal of Management Studies* 48 (4): 899–931. https://doi.org/10.1111/j.1467-6486.2010.00950.x.

Seavoy, Ronald. 1982. The Origins of the American Business Corporation, 1784–855. *Broadening the Concept of Public Service During Industrialization*. Westport, CT: Greenwood Press.

Segrestin, Blanche, Armand Hatchuel, and Kevin Levillain. 2020. "When the Law Distinguishes Between the Enterprise and the Corporation: The Case of the New French Law on Corporate Purpose." *Journal of Business Ethics* 171: 1–13. https://doi.org/10.1007/s10551-020-04439-y.

Shoikhedbrod, Igor. 2022. "Private Wealth and Political Domination: A Marxian Approach." In *Wealth and Power: Philosophical Perspectives*, edited by Michael Bennett, Huub Brouwer, and Rutger Claassen. London: Routledge.

Stout, Lynn, Sergio Gramitto, and Tamara Belinfanti. 2019. *Citizen Capitalism. How a Universal Fund Can Provide Influence and Income to All*. Oakland, CA: Berrett-Koehler Publishers.

Strine, Leo. 2017. "Corporate Power Is Corporate Purpose 1: Evidence from My Hometown." *Oxford Review of Economic Policy* 33 (2): 176–87.

Veldman, Heroen, Filip Gregor, and Paige Morrow. 2016. "Corporate Governance for a Changing World: Final Report of a Global Roundtable Series." Brussels/London.

Waldron, Jeremy. 1999. *Law and Disagreement*. Oxford: Oxford University Press.

9 The Power of Big Tech Corporations as Modern Bigness and a Vocabulary for Shaping Competition Law as Counter-Power

Anna Gerbrandy and Pauline Phoa

The market value of the five largest technology firms is higher than most countries' GDP. In spring 2021, Apple and Microsoft were both worth more than $2 trillion; Amazon was valued over $1 trillion, Facebook (Meta) and Alphabet (Google's parent company) a little under. Each of these companies has a global, or almost global, reach. Each has built its own intricate system around several core digital services – each conglomerate is a 'platform ecosystem' by itself – and between them they dominate markets as diverse as online search, digital advertising, social networking, cloud computing, logistics, wearables and smart phones, gaming, and software-as-a-service. These firms have contributed significantly to the digitalisation of society and the economy, by which we mean the increasing use of digital technologies, as well by their datafication. By datafication we mean the process of turning human actions and behaviours into digitised data. In aggregated form big tech, and other firms, can use these data for analyses and predictions to profit-making ends. Big tech firms are branching out into robotics, healthcare, and education, and in response to the COVID-19 pandemic, they were invited to 'share skills and talent with the government' in order to tackle the pandemic (Volpicelli 2020). Much innovation in the current digital age comes from these conglomerates, and if it doesn't, it often gets snapped up by them. Also, their (former) CEOs are among the richest men in the world. Conglomeration and wealth are concentrated within these 'big tech' companies. It seems safe to assume that there is power too. This chapter's first goal is to tease out how the corporate wealth of the big techs translates into power.

Power in *markets* can be countered by, inter alia, competition law, called 'antitrust law' in the United States. Currently, it is contested how competition law (ought to) function(s) with respect to the digital platform economy. Generally, competition law is a set of legal rules and institutions supporting the market mechanism. Market theory posits that markets deliver the greatest economic welfare when competition is

DOI: 10.4324/9781003173632-11

unhindered. Market power is assumed to be reined in by the competitive process itself, but where market power becomes problematic, competition law can step in. It aims to keep companies disciplined to compete 'on the merits' so that the market can deliver its promise of optimal economic welfare. Competition rules support the market mechanism by preventing companies from engaging in anti-competitive behaviour, prohibiting anti-competitive agreements or concerted practices ('cartels') and checking against the abuse of powerful ('dominant') positions.[1] In this sense, competition rules are held to be neutral and non-political, based on the purely economic-factual logic of market theory, and applied within the boundaries of the market sphere. However, the question is whether competition law works well (enough) in the platform economy. Considering the possibly far-reaching power of big tech platform companies (big techs in short), this chapter's second goal is to show how the market-theory's interpretation of the aim of competition law might become difficult to uphold.

This chapter hence focuses on one arena in which the wealth-power nexus that is central to this book has appeared in recent times: the platform economy. We show how the power of big techs, while related to their wealth-generating functions, manifests itself beyond market power in non-economic spheres of society. Second, adding to the other institutional pathways suggested in this book, we focus on competition law and show how it needs to be changed if it is to be able to counter this power. To this end we first provide a general introduction of the debate on the aims of competition law (Section 1). Then we focus on the corporate power of big techs and argue that it is much more than mere market power felt in the economic domain. We show that the power of big techs is a combination of instrumental power, structural power, and discursive power, and manifests also in the political, social, and personal domain (Section 2). This leads to a position of Modern Bigness, which is a complex form of corporate power based in the digitalised and datafied society (Section 3). Finally, we show how the Modern Bigness theory of power of big techs leads to a recalibration of competition law (Section 4).

1 The Debate over the Aims of Competition Law

Precisely because of the rise of big tech companies, both the concept of power and what competition law ought to do about it is hotly debated (Lancieri and Sakowski 2021). Competition law has not been able to prevent a high degree of concentration (and even monopolisation) on the tech market. Moreover, lengthy procedures in the EU make for slow responses to abusive behaviours, and the fines and remedies imposed seem to make little difference, since new abuses keep occurring (Cafarra 2021). In the United States, antitrust authorities' response to big tech was, until recently, largely non-existent. Consequently, a fundamental discussion is taking place on whether competition law is indeed merely an instrument to support the economic logic of the market mechanism (Andriychuk 2017; Ezrachi 2018). This is a complex discussion, with in some instances century-old roots. It takes place in academia, enforcement practice, legislative institutions and political arenas across the globe. It is both theoretical and practical, both global and bound to local jurisdictions. We provide here only a condensed version of the current debate in the EU and the United States, the leading competition law jurisdictions globally. This focus is also justified given that the big techs under scrutiny are based in the United States, and the (albeit not always successful) competition law effort to curb that power has until recently mostly been coming from the EU.

In the current debate in the United States about the function of antitrust law, the main voices are those of the 'Chicago School-rationalists' and those of the 'neo-Brandeisians' (sometimes also pejoratively called the 'populists'). These two positions are quite polarised, with a third position in between, that of the 'modernists,' who are proposing a slight update to the rationalists' position but not changing their fundamentals (see also Shapiro 2021). The debate is not merely technical-legal in nature, but takes place in the political arena too, as we saw both during the election campaigns of 2020 and around appointments in leading antitrust positions in Biden's government (Waller and Morse 2020).

The *rationalists* base themselves on Chicago-school economics, which came to bloom in post-war academic and regulatory settings and deeply influenced economics, politics, and society. Its central thought is that it is best to let the market mechanism function with minimal interference by the government. The premise of a free-market economy is not just that it delivers the greatest (public) benefits in terms of economic welfare, but also that it is an expression of individual freedom and autonomy. A free-market economy is presumed to lead to a fair (if not equal) distribution of welfare, since everyone has equal access to the market, participating on a level playing field (on egalitarianism, see also Arneson 2022, in this volume). Chicago-school economics shaped the United States' competition policies. As the market leads to economic benefits and government interference often gets it wrong, competition law should be used only in (very) limited circumstances: only if a negative effect on consumer welfare, in the sense of a lowering of quality of service or charging of above-competitive prices, can be proven (Medvedovsky 2018; Crane 2019; Sokol 2019). Hence, the rationalists applaud the hands-off position towards the rise of big techs by American antitrust enforcement in the past decades.[2]

The rationalists distrust the 'neo-Brandeisians,' who are inspired by the work of Judge Brandeis in the early twentieth century (Crane 2019). They argue that the power of big corporations is not merely bad news for markets, but also for democracy: the *political power* of big companies is a threat (Stucke 2012; Khan 2017). Neo-Brandeisians thus consider the consumer welfare standard of the Chicagoans inappropriate to deal with the intricate platform power of the big techs. Long predating Chicago-school economics, Judge Brandeis indeed focused on the broad impact of corporate power and its relationship with politics (Brandeis 1933). Neo-Brandeisians criticise the rationalists' analysis of market-based problems in isolation from their political aspects and effects. This weakens the ability to assess either area correctly. In their view, while some corporate activities may pass the consumer welfare standard, they might be questionable when viewed through the neo-Brandeisian lens. For example, in the digital healthcare sector, it led to a disregard for the public interest when judging Amazon's leveraging of its logistics power to gain carve out a position in the medical supplies distribution market (Business Insider 2022). Thus, the neo-Brandeisians argue against the Chicagoans for a broadening of the aims of antitrust, to include a wider range of societal harms that follow from powerful market positions.[3]

In light of these opposing camps in the competition law community, it is no surprise that the Biden administration's appointments of academic proponents of political antitrust to key positions in government has led to controversies, but also to new investigations against some big techs (Federal Trade Commission 2021).

The European Union's competition law debate might seem somewhat less entrenched or polarised than its counterpart in the United States, but it is no less complex – also because the debate is held in many languages at the same time. Here too, historic roots and subsequent economic-legal developments provide a backdrop for current positions. Competition law was included in the original EEC-treaty, for example, on the basis of both the ordo-liberal notions of protecting the functioning of markets and individual economic freedom (Gerber 1998), and on the integrationist notion of shaping an internal market without national boundaries. It also encompassed notions of workable competition and the protection of economic freedom (Monti 2002). However, following the US-led Chicago school turn to economics, its market theory also became the basis of much of the EU's competition law enforcement actions from the 1990s onwards. Competition law became based on market theory, with a focus on protecting consumer welfare by protecting efficiently working markets within the integrated internal market (Monti 2007). This worked well enough for several decades, but also in the EU, renewed discussions on fundamentals have emerged, mostly in light of the twin challenges of sustainability and digitalisation (Gerbrandy and Claassen 2016).

As to the digital economy, the EU has levied the highest competition law fines ever against big techs – not once but several times. However, many feel this was still too little too late, and not terribly effective as deterrent for the big techs to change their behaviour (Gal and Petit 2021). Like in the United States, there are arguments in the EU not to stray from economics-based logic, set within the debate on reconsidering the effectiveness and scope of competition rules in the digital economy (Crémer, de Montoyem, and Schweitzer 2019; Lancieri and Sakowski 2021). Meanwhile, several Member States (and the UK) are in the process of recalibrating their national competition rules. The European Commission is proposing legislative (regulatory) action – separate from competition law enforcement – focusing on platforms (European Parliament and Council 2020).

Many of the voices in the European debate seem to chime in with the *modernists'* perspective. The proposals for tweaks to competition law (and other regulatory tools) are mostly market-based, though with specific twists. The context of creating a European 'internal market' is always in the background, and issues relating to fundamental rights protected by the EU Charter, such as privacy, are never far away. More recently, the debate has also shifted to discussing more fundamental corrections or overhauls of the market-based focus of competition law.

The premise underlying the dominant economic interpretation of both the EU's competition rules and those in the United States is that the free-market mechanism is both an expression of individual freedom and autonomy and an instrument to deliver the greatest public welfare benefits. However, outside competition law circles the notion that the capacity of a market system to achieve fair and equitable distribution has been contested in the last decade, both in public debates and in academic work (Piketty 2014; Pistor 2019). In this new setting, it is relevant to better understand the (nature of the) corporate power of big tech companies and to develop the (linguistic) tools for a discussion on the fundamentals of the use of competition law in the digital age.

2 Corporate Power across Economic and Other Domains

In this section, we set out the foundations for our theory of the corporate power of big techs. When considering how competition law should be shaped in response to the wealth and power of big techs, let us first repeat that its focus (in the past decades) has been almost exclusively on how power plays out in the *economic domain* where the market mechanism, competitive pressures, and producer and consumer interactions reign. Our analysis starts there too.

To grasp the power of any company, competition law focuses first on its market power. As corporations are market-based entities, market power is the *foundation* of a company's power. In competition law market power is usually expressed in terms of *market shares*. Simply put, the higher the captured market shares, the greater the company's market power. High market shares make it possible for a company to behave independently from competitors, which, in a monopoly-situation, are non-existent. In EU competition law, market shares over 40% can give rise to a 'dominant' position, while over 70% will almost always mean dominance. This triggers the application of the rule not to *abuse* this dominance. The economic logic is clear, as a dominant company can easily extract monopolistic prices or hinder competition.

The platform economy makes this analysis slightly more complex. The market power of platform companies such as Amazon, Google, Facebook, Microsoft, and Apple, is grounded in the economics of *multi-sided* platforms. Here the logic of network effects (where users flock to users) creates tipping points, which create one or two winners capturing close to the whole market. This changes the market from having many competing companies into a market with one or two that 'win' (Poniatowski et al. 2022). Moreover, multi-sided platforms are prone to lock-in strategies, which entice and/or force users to stay within the boundaries of the bundled services offered by the platform company. The outcome of these economic logics is the emergence of the 'super-platforms' of the five largest tech companies (Ezrachi and Stucke 2017), governing a large part of the platform economy. Each of them offers one or more core services around which other services are built. A layered and intricately interdependent conglomerate structure – an ecosystem – has taken shape (van Dijck 2020). The current platform economy can thus be characterised as an ecosystem of ecosystems.

Market power, however, provides only the first foundational tile. The corporate power of big techs moves beyond just the power to behave independently on a market. Even competition lawyers and economists will also consider that a platform ecosystem rests upon the gathering of data and that data streams tie the interwoven services together (Bedre-Defolie and Nitsche 2020). However, though *having* data and being able to *gather* data strengthens the market power foundation of big techs, it is the *capability* to do something useful with these data that moves their power beyond only market-power. The capability to obtain information from data and feed that information back into the ecosystems businesses strengthens the corporate power of big techs in a continuous loop. This informational loop is important for all big tech ecosystems, but is indispensable for systems that rely (mostly) on advertising as a business model (Teece 2010). The combination of amassing data and having data capabilities not only strengthens market power but is foundational for the complex form of corporate power that big techs possess.

A further foundation of big techs' power lies in their ability to acquire (competing) businesses and start-ups. Here is where the monetary *wealth* of big tech-corporations funnels into acquiring innovation, which then translates into consolidation of their conglomerate positions. Apart from investing in their own innovations and continuous technical updates of existing services, these corporate giants can acquire developing competitors or promising new ventures. Many start-ups also want to be noted by big techs: it gives the 'start-up guys in a garage' (though almost never:

start-up gals) a chance to share in the riches (Daniel 2021). Thus, the big techs *envelop* adjacent markets into their system, further strengthening the position of the *conglomerate* (Eisenmann, Parker, and Van Alstyne 2011).

These platform-economic logics are the foundations on which the corporate power of big techs rests. To disentangle how the resulting power manifests, we build upon the work of Fuchs, who distinguishes three dimensions to corporate power: instrumental, structural, and discursive (Fuchs 2007). The *instrumental* dimension of power is about the direct influence of one actor over another – such as a corporation lobbying to influence the outcome of a parliamentary decision (see Parvin 2022, in this volume). The *structural* dimension of power relates to influencing the input side of the political process, such as agenda-setting, making options available and acceptable, but also has a dynamic aspect in which corporate actors govern themselves, for example through self-regulation. The *discursive* dimension of power catches an even deeper layer to power, in which norms, ideas and discourse, communicative practices, and cultural values are shaped by corporate power. As Fuchs points out here: 'power not only pursues interests, but also creates them' (Fuchs 2007, 10) (for an historical view on corporate power, see Bennett and Claassen 2022, in this volume).

These dimensions of power are at play in relation to the power of big techs as well. But where Fuchs is mostly concerned with how corporate power engages the *political* domain, we propose to add three other domains, to map how big techs' power manifests: the *economic*, *social*, and *personal* domain. Though not separated neatly – companies act across all domains, sometimes at the same time – it is useful to distinguish between these four domains to grasp how the power of big techs may manifest.

Simplifying, let us assume that the *economic* domain covers activities that in many jurisdictions are (mostly) governed by the market mechanism: decisions about production, distribution, consumption of goods or services and all the concomitant wealth transfers that occur are up to the market. While the market is constituted by institutions, the market mechanism itself is the primary disciplining mechanism for the behaviour of market actors. This is a familiar domain to competition lawyers and economists, as this is where competition rules apply and are enforced: against the negative welfare effects of market power. As to the *political* domain, we use the term to indicate the realm of power structures and decision-making by governments. It is the public domain of citizens and governments. Public power is disciplined, in democracies, by political processes of election, representation, and legislation, and in many jurisdictions, by the specific safeguards of the rule of law. By the *social* domain we mean the sphere of interactions between people(s), groups, and networks of relationships. Many foundational works on 'power' relate to power in the social domain: within and between groups and networks (in a sense this also encompasses both the economic and political domain) (Foucault 2003; Lukes 2005). In a society with great social capital, the shared values, norms, and understandings and the networks of relationships allow individuals to work together to achieve a common purpose to function effectively (Putnam 1993). The *personal* domain is that of individuals; the domain which relates to or affects a particular person. For our purposes we include in the personal domain also the *private* element of the personal domain, meaning that which belongs or pertains to (only) that individual person, including that which is (intended to be) secret.

Combining Fuchs' three dimensions of power with the four domains in which we expect corporate power of big techs to manifest, generates a fine-grained image of the width and depth of their power.

For example, the *instrumental dimension* of big techs' power is manifested in the political domain by their direct lobbying and campaign financing (Cao and Zakarin 2020; Yanchur, Schyns, Rosén Fondah, and Pilz 2021). In the social domain big techs exercise their power instrumentally by shaping online interactions into groupings, factions, and like-minded spheres (Pariser 2011; Sunstein 2018). In the economic domain they exclude competitors from a market and acquire innovators (Competition and Markets Authority UK 2021). In the personal domain, the instrumental dimension of power is felt in specifically tailored and timed content, taking the form of 'hypernudges': an individually tailored series of targeted content, adjusted in real-time, and aimed at steering the user towards a certain behaviour. This might be a steering towards buying into a certain service, towards creating distrust, or towards voting in favour of a political outcome. This means that even when a person is in her home or on an inconsequential errand, she may be steered in her behaviour simply by using platform services, such as maps, smart gear or home assistants (Morozovaite 2021).

The *structural dimension* also manifests across the four domains. For example in shaping legislation by providing boundary-setting briefs and pre-emptively engaging in legislative processes, or in directing forms of self-regulation (The Economist 2021); in creating the social norms of online interactions; the way platform-work is shaped (Aloisi and Gramano 2019); in setting the structures for interaction between the companies, developers, and consumers on the different sides of a multi-sided market; in reshaping institutions as old as 'property' in relation to data (Purtova 2015); and by entering our homes with digital assistants, introducing tracking devices for our things, our pets, and perhaps our children or elderly parents, and by bringing smart glasses to the market and defining what is private (West 2019).

The *discursive dimension* of the power of big tech platforms also ranges across all domains. In the political domain we find it in online political campaigning and newsfeeds, and in defining what is on the political agenda. In the social domain an example is the first introduction of smart glasses; unsuccessful, but nonetheless setting the stage for what will become acceptable in the future (Kernaghan 2016). In the economic domain it manifests in how data is perceived, which services are marketable, etc. In the personal domain, in how we inform ourselves and shape our opinions. Intuitively, discursive power may seem easy to grasp, because most information is now brought to us digitally, often by way of the platforms within the ecosystem of big techs: from breaking news and background stories to conspiracy theories, from literature and movies to immediate clips of what is happening elsewhere, from academic articles to tweets, from encyclopaedias to cat-memes, from recipes to instructions on how to change a flat tire, and from coverage of global disasters to family pictures of beach-outings. Importantly, when online, we are both user-citizen, user-consumer, user-daughter (or mother, or sister, or aunt), and user-interactor with self-chosen or random others in a delineated or random group. This information and how we process or consume it, shapes how and what we think.

However, the discursive power of big techs is more difficult to grasp than this suggests. For much of that information is not generated *by* the big tech companies themselves, but to a large degree by others, both individuals and (semi-organised) organisations (Thorson and Wells 2016). Indeed, the notion of discursive (political) power in contemporary hybrid media systems seems focused on individuals (Chadwick 2017; Jungherr, Posegga, and An 2019). Users provide, post, and generate information. Some of these users – political parties, governments, businesses, interest groups, and other intermediaries – also use the available (sometimes very granular) data to tailor information specifically to other users, mostly private individuals. This makes it more difficult to uphold the thesis that the big techs *themselves* shape discourses across domains. But we need to remind ourselves that without the platform services, the reach of discursive power would be much more insulated. The way the platforms' algorithms influence which content is shown, means that, indeed, 'social media platforms [are] active political actors in their own right' (Helberger 2020). In this sense, it is the big techs who wield discursive power.

The resulting picture of this exposé of power dimensions across domains, is that of powerful corporations shaping markets, democracies, social interactions, and our personal lives.

3 Big Techs' Corporate Power as 'Modern Bigness'

At this point, one may object that all large corporations exert a certain power in the political, economic, social, and personal domain (think of oil corporations, banks, pharmaceuticals, agri-food conglomerates). So, what is new? We posit that there is a difference of pervasiveness, scope, precision, and invasiveness between 'normal' corporate power and the corporate power of big techs. The difference stems from a combination of these factors and the way they interact.

First, consider the *pervasiveness* of digitalisation and datafication of society. The impact of digitalisation and connectedness are so all-encompassing that an overview is impossible. Digital technologies, including algorithms, now mediate much of our daily activities. They affect how we live and how we work; they are now 'entangled in the structures of society' (Dufva and Dufva 2019). There is as yet no end to this technological development in sight. For example, at the moment the notion of creating the metaverse – science fiction when first masterfully introduced (Stephenson 1992) – promises a next step in which the digital and physical in our social reality will seamlessly entwine. The pervasiveness of the digitalisation of society is staggering and leading these developments are, for a large part, now the innovations of the big techs.

Also, second, consider the *scope* of platform ecosystems' services. The ever-changing balance between public services provided by government and those provided by the market has shifted, in the past decades, towards much more market services (Crouch 2011). Now the leading role of market parties in providing digital services and concomitant devices brings further shifts. Market-based digital(ised) services enter previously publicly domains such as (in the Netherlands, for instance) intramural healthcare, extramural patient care, and education. Also, fundamental infrastructural services such as internet access, digital identification services, and the 'green passes' used during the current COVID-19 pandemic are provided through market logic and profit-making, using proprietary technology, resulting in further datasets that are market actors' property. Part of this shift is, furthermore, that governments are becoming dependent for both day-to-day governing activities – including the provision of public services they do offer – on platform companies, for example for cloud computing services. Governments or NGO's have so far not been able, or have not tried, to provide alternatives that would make them less dependent on big techs for pivotal governmental services and systems. The result is a heavy dependence of government on the platforms of mostly the big techs, while, at the same time, these companies provide services such as internet access and access to information that are very much like public utilities (Lalíková forthcoming), however, without the guarantees that accompany traditional public utilities.

Third, consider the *precision* with which big tech companies can reach individuals. The use of data generally, and personal (and private) data specifically, for the personalisation of targeting audiences has never been as all-encompassing as in today's platform economy. The concept of a 'surveillance economy' has been raised in this regard (Zuboff 2019), but even if one rejects that notion, the manifestation of corporate power is clearly more invasive, pervasive, and persuasive now that digital services are ubiquitous and for a large part built on datafication and personalisation.

These are not separate factors. They interact in a flywheel effect across the four domains. Though the economic, political, social, and personal domains were never completely separated from each other, the platform economy has provided a further waning of clearly defined roles. For example, a user of platform services can be a consumer of services, a friend engaged in forging new friendships, a reader of news to shape her political views, a target of political and commercial advertisements, and a co-producer of online content. In doing all this, she produces and thus immediately shares data with both the platform and other parties tracking her online activities. She has 'hyphenated' roles that may change shape while she moves seamlessly from one activity to another, while spanning multiple domains. Again, there is a flywheel effect as the instrumental dimension of power is amplified in the discursive power dimension, in which the roles of actor and object become confused. And, of course, the possible *future* uses of digital, data-driven, and personalised technology are endless, which – in theory – stretches and deepens the manifestation of corporate power of big techs further. In sum, although other big transnational corporations have power across the instrumental, structural, and discursive dimensions, the power of the big tech platform companies is significantly amplified by the inherent characteristics of the platform economy and its structuring of our datafied social interactions.

This amplification is so significant that we posit that it goes beyond the kind of power wielded by traditional corporations, leading to a new kind of power we have labelled 'Modern Bigness': a four-dimensional corporate power of big techs that is all-encompassing, shaping current and future markets and democracies.

So far, we have shown the foundations of the power of big techs and how its dimensions manifest across different domains. However there are some caveats to the conclusion that this is a power to shape current and future markets and democracies. For example, it is more difficult to uphold if the big tech corporations do not *each* and *separately* manifest their power in all dimensions across all four domains. For instance, the kind of power in the structural and discursive domains that the network ecosystems of Google and Facebook create, seems different from the kind of power that Amazon holds. Amazon is less directly involved in the advertisement-driven social network structures that impact the discursive shaping of political opinion (even though it wields power through its algorithmically curated recommendations in its 'everything store' and through the recommendations made by its voice assistant Alexa). The power of Microsoft and Apple seems to manifest in a different manner than Google, Facebook, and Amazon, as being predominantly based in software licensing and cloud services (Microsoft) and a vertically integrated chain of hardware, operating system and app store (Apple).

We acknowledge that the above model of Modern Bigness is a theoretical construct, and we have not (yet) mapped all manifestations of power of the platform corporations onto all domains. We would, however, argue that the power of big techs is a *combined* construct – a collective power – governing much of the economy and society precisely because the economy and society have digitised. This is not a collective power in the sense of a 'cartel,' which is based on express understandings between companies, agreeing to anti-competitive practices such as price-agreements. It is a collective power in the sense that almost no human activity escapes the reach of the big techs. In this ecosystem of ecosystems the branches sometimes overlap, build upon each other, and lead to contradictions and synergies. Such a collective power is a difficult construct to be handled in competition law practice. There is often competition from (smaller) companies for specific services. Furthermore, the platform companies themselves are also competitors to (some of) each other, which means that – in theory – the way their power plays out might counterbalance each other. Yet, cooperation between them, specifically where services are complementary or interests align, also exists. The question (for us) is whether (and how much) it matters for shaping a regulatory response in relation to their impact on democracies and citizens, if big tech's corporate power is (conceptualised as) the sum of their positions or (also) separately as individually powerful corporations.

There is another important caveat. The conclusion that big techs can shape current and future markets and democracies is true only if there is no (imminent) threat to their positions stemming from the market mechanism itself. This is what the big techs themselves point out: that disruptive innovation is around the corner, that competition is one click away, that their positions are never secure. Indeed, TikTok, for example, is a competitor for (part of) Facebook (Newton 2021). However, disruptive innovation theory seems not to be able to explain what has been happening in the past decades (and Facebook has, of course, launched a TikTok competitor, though it has yet to become successful) (Hutchington 2021). What is called 'dominant design theory' seems a more relevant perspective (Hummel forthcoming). Applied to markets in which aggressive strategies of mergers and acquisitions are prevalent, this theory implies that at least in more mature markets, an imminent threat to the core platform services of the big techs seems unlikely.

Finally, our conclusion would be less encompassing if the corporate power of big techs could be countered by other institutions. These can be the institutions of democracy itself, including the rules and laws governing how voting and law-making happens. They can also be the regulatory frameworks of economic law, including competition law. The latter was traditionally shaped as a hammer to be used against the negative welfare effects of economic power, as we saw above. The question is whether it can also be (effectively) used against the negative manifestations of Modern Bigness. This is what we turn to now.

4 A More Precise Legal Vocabulary to Shape Competition Law as Counter-Power

The question then, for us as competition lawyers, is this: if Modern Bigness transcends the economic domain, should competition law's focus equally transcend the market, by including the political, the social, and the personal? This is undeniably a normative and political question. It also underlies the discussions in the United States' and European competition law fields (Section 1). Our findings as to pervasiveness, scope, precision, and invasiveness of power of big techs have implications for this normative question of how to shape a possible regulatory-legal reaction. Competition law is equipped to counter negative effects of corporate power, though it is mostly used today to counter the negative effects of market power only. This is not necessarily problematic *if* the effects of market power stay within the economic domain. It is also less problematic if the premise of personal autonomy underlying much of economic law, holds true in all domains. And it would not be as problematic if possible spill-over effects in, e.g., the political domain can be kept in check by democratic processes and the traditional institutions of democratic, open societies. If all these assumptions hold true, then economic law can be focused on well-functioning markets, and ignore the political, social, and personal domains.

However, the theory of big techs' power as Modern Bigness questions these premises, and hence also question competition law's exclusive focus on consumer welfare. Above we have shown, first, that big techs' power further disrupts a neat division between the four domains (economic, political, social, and personal). The notion of Modern Bigness connotes not merely a vast market-based instrumental power, but also, perhaps more importantly, a structural and discursive power, which – even though big tech corporations are built upon a market-based, profit-making business logic – also has significant impact on political and social relations and on our personal lives. Second, as discussed above, though implicit in most competition law regimes is a trust in the market mechanism to deliver public benefit, this presumption is contested. Moreover, third, also as explained above, the specifics of data-driven digital technologies, and our increasing dependency on them, fundamentally challenge the concept of personal autonomy. For example, the way in which the big techs wield *instrumental* power vis-à-vis platform-users raises the question whether the users of digital services are still autonomous individuals, or whether they have lost (part of) their agency (Gal 2018; Vold and Whittlestone 2019). The multiple ways in which corporate power manifests itself also raises the question whether consumers are turned into a commodity (Lynskey 2015; Phoa 2021). The already contested capacity of the market to deliver on important public benefits is thereby hampered even more seriously. Another important factor that makes competition law regimes fall short is, fourth, the encroachment of private actor's platform ecosystems upon the public sphere and government systems. The public sphere then becomes governed by commercial priorities rather than public interest and values. Ironically, as the role of big tech in these domains grows, states increasingly encourage self-regulation. This, however, also leads to unclear norms, expectations, and liabilities, and a veritable shift in institutional roles (Jorgensen and Zuleta 2020). Big techs' Modern Bigness therefore increasingly compromises and confuses the conditions for the functioning of the market itself. This confusion also includes the roles of the actors and objects that are assumed by the legal system.

The discussion on how to shape a competition law regime in light of the power of big techs, however, rarely analyses the precise character of power that big techs possess, and what that characterisation means for the foundational assumptions of competition law. A more refined *vocabulary* is needed to discuss this power, how that power manifests itself, and how it impacts on the foundations of competition law. While the economics-focused rationalists have the language of economics to fall back on for a more precise analysis of what ought (not) to be prohibited by competition law, the political, social, and personal domains remain mostly 'unspeakable' for them. Though the neo-Brandeisians in the antitrust debate are concerned about broader effects of corporate power, their analysis often lacks precision, including in vocabulary.

A possible way forward lies in what seems, to its critics, the weaker point of the neo-Brandeisian position: in its basis in social values, which can be made much more explicit. Note that the economic approach of the rationalists is also based on a value, i.e., efficiency, which is given great precision through economic analysis. The neo-Brandeisian approach, being 'not-just-economics,' is mostly *implicitly* value-based (Polański forthcoming), and lacks precision. However, an explicit value-based analysis, we propose, could deliver a stronger and more fully developed alternative interpretation of competition law. We see at least three ways in which these values might be designed to play a role. First, one might add to the economic values other *counterbalancing* values, and then weigh economic welfare against other social values. Second, one might *incorporate* economic values within a wider value-based concept. Third, one might use other social values, in specific circumstances, as an *additional* lens to view practices as anti-competitive. Whichever way one chooses, support for such a wider conceptualisation of competition law's values can be found in the roots of both American and European competition law systems, for both visibly include notions of economic freedom. However, an updated version, fit for the twenty-first-century version is needed. The relevant values can be construed as components of 'citizen welfare' or the 'well-being of citizens.' We believe that such a values-based approach gains substance, by using existing metrics included in, e.g., broad welfare concepts (e.g., van Dijck, Nieborg, and Poell 2019). These are still very broad concepts, and their application in competition law – unlike the current practice based on the notion of economic efficiency – might at first lead to less clarity, since it may be unclear when a lessening of, or harm to, citizen welfare or well-being occurs. However, we are confident that over time, courts will establish authoritative interpretations of these concepts, and legal certainty will increase.

There are a number of further points for debate to come to a recalibrated theory of competition law, with tools to deal with the manifestations of power of Modern Bigness. For example, in a value-based approach that is built around a concept of citizen welfare, infringements upon fundamental citizens' rights and values, such as autonomy of decision-making, privacy or equality, that occur through the power of Modern Bigness, can be countered by competition law. This would hold even if there is no negative effect on consumer welfare. The point of debate is whether the link with the big tech business' model, in which there is no difference between negatively impacting consumer welfare or negatively impacting citizen autonomy, continues to be relevant.

In our view, a broadening of competition law would not dilute or weaken it. Its central focus would still be on corporate *power*, countering its negative effects. Competition law is an addition to other regulatory instruments, as well as the actions of civil society institutions, which together need to shape a regulatory landscape covering the negative effects of Modern Bigness across domains. But the role of competition law could be even broader. Is it relevant above a certain threshold of power, as is currently the case with the notion of market power leading to a position to behave independently of other market actors? Could we construe such thresholds for power in the other domains, for example by focusing on the number of users, or the scope of offered services? Or does labelling a specific firm's corporate power as 'Modern Bigness' in itself contain the threshold above which competition law applies? There is also the debate on whether competition law should be used to only counter the negative *effects*, both within and beyond the economic domain, or can be used to dismantle the Modern Bigness position of power directly.

Without a (legal) vocabulary, it is difficult to account in law for the effects of Modern Bigness outside the economic domain (and it is even more difficult to account for structural or discursive power effects within the economic domain). A more refined vocabulary leads to a more precise discussion. It could lead to a more refined toolkit, and invite a change in current practices. It might not radically replace competition law's focus on the economic domain, but it could at the very least lead to a keener eye for aspects of big techs' power and behaviour beyond the market domain. Alternatively, and more ambitiously, a refined vocabulary could lead to a more fundamental change in the system of competition law, flanked by other forms of economic regulation, to counter the (negative effects of) instrumental, structural, and discursive cross-domain power.

5 Conclusion

As mentioned in the introduction, these have been our aims: to make explicit the shape of the power of big techs and to show how competition law's current vocabulary fails to grasp it. In doing so, we have offered a more detailed taxonomy for the foundations and manifestations of the power of big techs in the digital society. This has provided conceptual room to acknowledge and analyse the changing distributions of actorship and hyphenated roles in society as a consequence of the rise of big tech. Finally, we have argued that much of what is held to be competition law's foundational assumptions, is shifting, and needs to shift further, to take account of these transformation in power in the digital economy.

Acknowledgements

The authors are grateful for Lisanne Hummel, Laura Lalíková, and Viktorija Morozovaite for assistance in shaping this chapter, and to Marleen Kappé for her editing assistance. This chapter draws upon the 'Power in the digital society' paper presented at Ascola conference (July 2021), of Gerbrandy, Hummel, Lalikova, Morozovaite, and Phoa (https://law.haifa.ac.il/index.php/en/ascola). It is part of the Modern Bigness ERC project (Gerbrandy), funded by the European Research Council (grant agreement No. 852005).

Notes

1 Most jurisdictions have competition laws, often also including a review of mergers. The EU includes rules limiting state aids. As academics based in the EU, our starting point is the EU's competition rules included in the Treaty on the Functioning of the European Union. Many countries have used the EU or the United States' rules as models. Though there are differences, the EU and US competition rules are similar on a general level.
2 There *modernists* agree with this (Chicago-school based) economic theory of markets. Enforcement action needs to stay focused on assessing (negative) economic effects of *market* power. However, they concede that enforcement of competition law could have been more vigorous and needs to be more market specific. Thus, they acknowledge that a more active interference by competition enforcement-actors is useful (Shapiro 2021).

3 The rationalists and modernists argue that this political interpretation of the aim of antitrust will lead to losing the rationality of an economics-based application of the rules, and hence to a harm to economic welfare. Political antitrust, it is brought forward, would mirror the irrational way competition provisions were used before the introduction of Chicago-school economics.

References

Aloisi, Antonio, and Elena Gramano. 2019. "Workers Without Workplaces and Unions Without Unity: Non-Standard Forms of Employment, Platform Work and Collective Bargaining." In *Employment Relations for the 21st Century, Bulletin of Comparative Labour Relations*, eds. Valeria Pulignano and Frank Hendrickx. Alphen aan den Rijn: Kluwer Law International.

Andriychuk, Oles. 2017. *The Normative Foundations of European Competition Law: Assessing the Goals of Antitrust through the Lens of Legal Philosophy*. Strathclyde: Edward Elgar.

Arneson, Richard. 2022. "Two Liberal Egalitarian Perspectives on Wealth and Power." In *Wealth and Power: Philosophical Perspectives*, eds. Michael Bennett, Huub Brouwer, and Rutger Claassen. London: Routledge.

Bedre-Defolie, Ozlem, and Rainer Nitsche. 2020. "When Do Markets Tip? An Overview and Some Insights for Policy." *Journal of European Competition Law and Practice* 11 (10): 610–622.

Bennett, Michael, and Rutger Claassen. 2022. "Taming the Corporate Leviathan. How to Properly Politicize Corporate Purpose?" In *Wealth and Power: Philosophical Perspectives*, eds. Michael Bennett, Huub Brouwer, and Rutger Claassen. London: Routledge.

Brandeis. 1933. "Louis K. Liggett Co. v. Lee, 288 U.S. 517."

Business Insider. 2022. "Big Tech in Healthcare." *The INsider*. Last modified January 12, 2022. https://www.businessinsider.com/big-tech-in-healthcarereport?international=true&r=US&IR=T.

Cafarra, C. 2021. "Google Shopping: A Shot in the Arm for the EC's Enforcement Effort, But How Much Will It Matter?" *Concurrences* (Art. No. 104053). December 13, 2021. https://www-concurrences-com.proxy.library.uu.nl/en/bulletin/special-issues/big-tech-dominance/google-shopping-a-shot-in-the-arm-for-the-ec-s-enforcement-effort-but-how-much-en.

Cao, Sissi, and Jordan Zakarin. 2020. "Big Tech and CEOs Poured Millions Into The Election. Here's Who They Supported" *Observer*. November 2, 2020. Accessed August 24, 2021. https://observer.com/2020/11/big-tech-2020-presidential-election-donation-breakdown-ranking/.

Chadwick, Andrew. 2017. *The Hybrid Media System: Politics and Power*. Oxford: Oxford University Press.

Competition and Markets Authority UK. 2021. *cma-cases*. 12 June. Accessed August 25, 2021. https://www.gov.uk/cma-cases/facebook-inc-giphy-inc-merger-inquiry.

Crane, Daniel A. 2019. "How Much Brandeis Do the Neo-Brandeisians Want?" *The Antitrust Bulletin* 64 (1): 531–539.

Crémer, Jacques, Yves-Alexandre de Montoyem, and Heike Schweitzer. 2019. *Competition Policy for the Digital Era*. European Commission. Luxembourg: Publications Office of the European Union.

Crouch, Colin. 2011. *The Strange Non-Death of Neoliberalism.* Cambridge: Polity Press.

Daniel, Kim. 2021. "Startup Acquisitions, Relocation, and Employee Entrepreneurship." *SSRN.* March 1. Accessed August 24, 2021. https://papers.ssrn.com/sol3/papers.cfm?abstract_id=3568153.

Dufva, Tomi, and Mikko Dufva. 2019. "Grasping the Future of the Digital Society." *Futures* 107 (3): 17–28.

Eisenmann, Thomas, Geoffrey Parker, and Marshall Van Alstyne. 2011. "Platform Envelopment." *Strategic Management Journal* 32 (12): 1270–1285.

European Parliament and Council. 2020. "Proposal for a Regulation on Contestable and Fair Markets in the Digital Sector (Digital Markets Act)." *COM(2020)842 final.*

Ezrachi, Ariel. 2018. "EU Competition Law Goals and the Digital Economy." Oxford Legal Studies Research Paper No. 17/2018. https://ssrn.com/abstract=3191766.

Ezrachi, Ariel, and Maurice E. Stucke. 2017. "Emerging Antitrust Threats and Enforcement Actions in the Online World." *Competition Law International* 13 (2): 125–136.

Federal Trade Commission. 2021. "FTCC Alleges Facebook Resorted to Illegal Buy-or-Bury Scheme to Crush Competition After String of Failed Attempts to Innovate." *Federal Trade Commission.* August 19, 2021. Accessed August 20, 2021. https://www.ftc.gov/news-events/press-releases/2021/08/ftc-alleges-facebook-resorted-illegal-buy-or-bury-scheme-crush.

Foucault, Michel. 2003. *Power: Essential Works of Foucault, 1954–1984.* New York, NY: The New Press.

Fuchs, Doris. 2007. *Business Power in Global Governance.* Boulder: Lynne Rienner Publishers.

Gal, Michal S. 2018. "Algorithmic Challenges to Autonomous Choice." *Michigan Technology Law Review* 25 (1): 59–104.

Gal, Michal S., and Nicolas Petit. 2021. "Radical Restorative Remedies for Digital Markets." *Berkeley Technology Law Journal* 37 (1), https://ssrn.com/abstract=3687604.

Gerber, David J. 1998. *Law and Competition in Twentieth Century Europe: Protecting Prometheus.* Oxford: Oxford University Press.

Gerbrandy, Anna, and Rutger Claassen. 2016. "Rethinking European Competition Law: From a Consumer Welfare to a Capability Approach." *Utrecht Law Review* 12 (1): 1–15.

Helberger, Natali. 2020. "The Political Power of Platforms: How Current Attempts to Regulate Misinformation Amplify Opinion Power." *Digital Journalism* 8 (6): 842–854.

Hummel, Lisanne M.F. Forthcoming. "Dominant Positions or Dominant Designs?" (unpublished manuscript, February 18, 2022), Microsoft Word File.

Hutchington, Andrew. 2021. "Can Facebook Work Out How to Slow the Momentum of TikTok?" *Social Media Today.* March 14, 2021. Accessed August 24, 2021. https://www.socialmediatoday.com/news/can-facebook-work-out-how-to-slow-the-momentum-of-tiktok/596681/.

Jorgensen, Rikke Frank, and Lumi Zuleta. 2020. "Private Governance of Freedom of Expression on Social Media Platforms." *Nordicom Review* 41 (1): 51–67.

Jungherr, Andreas, Oliver Posegga, and Jisun An. 2019. "Discursive Power in Contemporary Media Systems: A Comparative Framework." *The International Journal of Press/Politics* 24 (4): 404–425.

Kernaghan, Sheilagh. 2016. "Google Glass: An Evaluation of Social Acceptance." PhD Dissertation, School of Engineering and Digital Arts, University of Kent.

Khan, Lina. 2017. "Amazon's Antitrust Paradox." *Yale Law Journal* 126 (3): 564–907.

Lalíková, Laura F. Forthcoming. "Public Services, Essential Facilities and Platform Infrastructures" (unpublished manuscript February 18, 2022), Microsoft Word file.

Lancieri, Filippo, and Patricia Morita Sakowski. 2021. "Competition in Digital Markets: A Review of Expert Reports." *Stanford Journal of Law, Business & Finance* 26 (1): 65–170.

Lukes, Steven. 2005. *Power: A Radical View*. Basingstoke: Palgrave Macmillan.

Lynskey, Orla. 2015. *The Foundations of EU Data Protection Law*. Oxford: Oxford University Press.

Medvedovsky, Konstantin. 2018. "Hipster Antitrust – A Brief Fling or Something More." *CPI Antitrust Chronicle* 1 (1): 2–7.

Monti, Giorgio. 2002. "Article 81 and Public Policy." *Common Market Law Review* 39 (5): 1057–1099.

——. 2007. *EC Competition Law*. Cambridge: Cambridge University Press.

Morozovaite, Viktorija. 2021. "Two Sides of the Digital Advertising Coin: Putting Hypernudging into Perspective." *Markets and Competition Law Review* V (2): 105–145.

Newton, Casey. 2021. "Social Networks Are Finally Competitive Again: Facebook's Surprising New Challengers Across Adio, Video, Photos and Text." *The Verge*. February 23, 2021. Accessed August 28, 2021. https://www.theverge.com/2021/2/23/22296520/social-networks-competition-facebook-tiktok-twitter-clubhouse-snap.

Pariser, Eli. 2011. *The Filter Bubble: What the Internet Is Hiding from You*. London: Penguin UK.

Parvin, Phil. 2022. "Hidden in Plain Sight: How Lobby Organisations Undermine Democracy." In: *Wealth and Power: Philosophical Perspectives*, eds. Michael Bennett, Huub Brouwer, Rutger Claassen. London: Routledge.

Phoa, Pauline. 2021. *EU Law as a Creative Process*. Groningen: Europa Law Publishing.

Piketty, Thomas. 2014. *Capital in the Twenty-First Century*. Cambridge, MA: Harvard University Press.

Pistor, Katharina. 2019. *Code of Capital: How the Law Creates Wealth and Inequality*. Princeton, NJ: Princeton University Press.

Polański, Jan. Forthcoming. "A Positive Program for Antitrust? Enforcing Law in Times of Political and Economic Tides" (unpublished manuscript, February 18, 2022), Microsoft Word file.

Poniatowski, Martin, Hedda Luttenberg, Daniel Beverungen, and Dennis Kundisch. 2022. "Three Layers of Abstraction: A Conceptual Framework for Theorizing Digital Multi-sided Platforms." *Information Systems and e-Business Management* 20: 257–283.

Purtova, Nadezhda. 2015. "The Illusion of Personal Data a No One's Property." *Law, Innovation and Technology* 7 (1): 83–111.

Putnam, Robert. 1993. *Making Democracy Work: Civic Traditions in Modern Italy*. Princeton, NJ: Princeton University Press.

Shapiro, Carl. 2021. "Antitrust: What Went Wrong and How to Fix It." *Antitrust Magazine* 35 (1): 33–46.

Sokol, Daniel D. 2019. "Antitrust Curse of Bigness Problem." *Michigan Law Review* 118 (6): 1259–1281.

Stephenson, Neal. 1992. *Snow Crash*. New York, NY: Bantam Books.

Stucke, Maurice E. 2012. "Reconsidering Antitrust's Goals." *Boston College Law Review* 53 (2): 551–630.

Sunstein, Cass R. 2018. *Echo Chambers*. Princeton, NJ: Princeton University Press.

Teece, David J. 2010. "Business Models, Business Strategy and Innovation." *Long Range Planning* 43 (2–3): 172–194.

The Economist. 2021. "Facebook Tries to Pre-empt Regulation by Squeezing Anti-vaxxers." *The Economist*, February 13, 2021.

Thorson, Kjerstin, and Chris Wells. 2016. "Curated Flows: A Framework for Mapping Media Exposure in the Digital Age." *Communication Theory* 26 (3): 309–328.

van Dijck, José. 2020. "Seeing the Forest for the Trees: Visualizing Platformization and Its Governance." *New Media & Society* 23 (9): 1–19.

van Dijck, José, David Nieborg, and Thomas Poell. 2019. "Reframing platform power." *Internet Policy Review* 8 (2): 1–18.

Vold, Karina, and Jessica Whittlestone. 2019. "Privacy, Autonomy, and Personalised Targeting: Rethinking How Personal Data Is Used." In *Report on Data, Privacy, and the Individual in the Digital Age*, eds. Carissa Véliz. Oxford: Center for the Governance of Change.

Volpicelli, Gian M. 2020. "Inside Dominic Cummings's Coronavirus Meeting with Big Tech." *Wired*, March 12, 2020. https://www.wired.co.uk/article/dominic-cummings-coronavirus-big-tech.

Waller, Spencer Weber, and Jacob Morse. 2020. "The Political Face of Antitrust." *Brooklyn Journal of Corporate, Financial, and Commercial Law* 15 (1): 75–96.

West, Emily. 2019. "Amazon: Surveillance as a Service." *Surveillance & Society* 17 (1/2): 27–33.

Yanchur, Alina, Camille Schyns, Greta Rosén Fondah, and Sarah Pilz. 2021. "Computer Says No: How the EU's AI Laws Cause New Injustice." *euobserver*. August 23, 2021. Accessed August 24, 2021. https://euobserver-com.proxy.library.uu.nl/investigations/152695?utm_source=euobs&utm_medium=email.

Zuboff, Shoshana. 2019. *The Age of Surveillance Capitalism*. London: Profile Books.

10 Economic Power and Democratic Forbearance

The Case of Corporate Social Responsibility and Philanthropy

Emma Saunders-Hastings

In the spring of 2021, executives from Major League Baseball, Coca-Cola, Delta, and other corporations criticised a restrictive new voting law adopted by the state of Georgia. These interventions drew rebukes from politicians generally more solicitous of corporate political speech. Senator Mitch McConnell commented that 'My warning, if you will, to corporate America is to stay out of politics. It's not what you're designed for. And don't be intimidated by the left into taking up causes that put you right in the middle of America's greatest political debates.' Asked to specify what kinds of corporate activities were out of bounds, the senator clarified: 'I'm not talking about political contributions' (Thrush 2021).

McConnell is not alone in attempting to define a boundary between acceptable and unacceptable forms of corporate influence – nor in inviting the suspicion that his distinction is ad hoc and unprincipled. Some exercises of private influence are democratically objectionable; others represent the exercise of legitimate rights, powers, and prerogatives; some may be cases of an agent doing her duty. The difficulty is deciding which is which. Especially in an age of partisan polarisation, one person's act of corporate social responsibility (CSR) is another's exercise of malign private influence. Similar difficulties arise in normative evaluations of elite philanthropy, which often track judgments about the motivations or substantive policy agendas of particular donors. Philanthropic donations allow the rich to exercise important forms of influence over public outcomes and matters of common concern. But how troubling this is will, for many, depend on which billionaire donor's name is front of mind.

As a matter of democratic principle, it is unsatisfactory to say that corporations or wealthy individuals may exercise public influence so long as they do so in ways that promote justice or good outcomes: democratic theory is supposed to supply principles to govern political contestation in the context of disagreement about important substantive political and policy questions. In this chapter, I argue that forbearance from undemocratic action is a responsibility of both

DOI: 10.4324/9781003173632-12

corporate managers and philanthropists and show how this links concerns in democratic theory and business ethics. I also consider the complexities of practicing democratic forbearance in existing democratic societies.

CSR and philanthropy are often treated as comparatively benign exercises of economic power. Compared with campaign contributions and lobbying activities, CSR and philanthropy may seem less consequential, less harmful, and less threatening to political equality. They can therefore be helpful cases for isolating and assessing the different factors that might make a form of influence undemocratic. If we focus on the degree to which elite influence is self-interested or self-serving, CSR may look more problematic than philanthropy, since there is good reason to think that many CSR activities are superficial and aimed primarily at benefitting firms and their owners.[1] On the other hand, if we focus on the degree to which economic elites are exerting consequential forms of social and political influence, in ways insulated from public accountability, philanthropy may look more democratically threatening than CSR (though not than corporate influence writ large). When we focus on influence and its operation, it seems likely that CSR is (or will often be) doing something rather different than elite philanthropy. This is true even if – indeed, because – we can expect that corporations are motivated by economic gain to a greater degree than individual philanthropists. In their CSR activities, corporations often act in ways responsive to (what they take to be) the preferences of ordinary citizens: they engage in CSR in part as a way of seeking support from a broad audience of people. On the other hand, elite philanthropists often use donations to promote their preferred outcomes in ways that are less deferential to public goals and that bypass strategies of public legitimacy-seeking. CSR is not a democratic panacea, but it can often be downgraded as a democratic threat, for reasons that do not apply in the same way either to elite philanthropy or to corporate influence generally.[2]

I begin by defining CSR and philanthropy, highlighting the areas of conceptual overlap between them and some important distinctions (Section 1). I then develop a preliminary framework for assessing when these exercises of private power violate democratic norms and principles. CSR and philanthropy are unavoidably exercises of *nondemocratic* power. But they can avoid being exercises of *undemocratic* power if they avoid distorting the inputs or subverting the outputs of democratic institutions and processes (Section 2). Applying and further developing this standard, I show how both CSR (Section 3) and philanthropy (Section 4) can threaten political equality and when they can be compatible with it. Finally, I consider some complexities that arise, for the evaluation and regulation of private influence, once we relax idealising assumptions about public democratic institutions (Section 5).

1 Corporate Social Responsibility and Philanthropy

This chapter deals with two topics that raise many parallel issues but which should be distinguished at the outset. One immediate difficulty lies in the malleability of both CSR and philanthropy as concepts. Philanthropy can be defined as a kind of activity, or in terms of motivations, or as a matter of legal or tax status (Saunders-Hastings 2019). CSR is perhaps even more amorphous, to the point where it may be better understood as a discourse than as a clearly defined set of actions or policies. Nevertheless, for the purposes of comparing CSR and philanthropy, and their potential threats to political equality, it is worth attempting to specify definitions focused on activities and practices.

Drawing on the work of Nien-hê Hsieh (2017, 188), I will use *corporate social responsibility (CSR)* to refer to (1) activities or constraints on the activities of business corporations and their managers that (2) explicitly aim or purport to benefit people other than the business's owners or shareholders,[3] in ways that are (3) not legally required and (4) not mere by-products of ordinary commercial activity (so that, for example, contributions to a rising GDP do not count). As Hsieh emphasises, CSR can refer 'to a variety of business policies, standards, and activities, ranging from policies to refrain from certain harmful actions to activities that aim to benefit parties directly' (2017, 188n2). Examples of the former include 'over-compliance' with government regulation and the voluntary adoption of environmental sustainability goals or labour standards beyond what the law requires; examples of the latter include donations to local food banks or children's sports teams. More recently, advocates of extended conceptions of 'corporate citizenship' and 'political CSR' have argued that corporations have political responsibilities that go beyond either self-restraint or philanthropy: for example, to 'take over the administration of citizenship rights' in contexts where governments are unwilling or unable to do so (Matten and Crane 2005, 172) or 'to contribute to the development and proper working of global governance' (Scherer and Palazzo 2008, 414) (see also recent discussions of 'corporate purpose,' as discussed in Bennett and Claassen 2022, in this volume).

I use *philanthropy* to refer to voluntary donations of private money (or other goods) for broadly public purposes (Saunders-Hastings 2019; 2022, 2). Philanthropy can be practiced by individuals or other kinds of agents and so its neatest overlap with CSR occurs in the case of corporate philanthropic donations, which count as both CSR and philanthropy on the definitions used here.

In neither case are agents' motivations central for classifying the activities of interest: philanthropy may be motivated by altruism or by a desire for reputation and enhanced social status; practices of CSR may be adopted for public-spirited reasons or more cynical ones. CSR and philanthropy also need not conflict with the economic interests of firms or individuals: To describe policies or activities as instances of CSR does not exclude the possibility that they also serve a commercial function (e.g., by helping to improve a business's reputation or building customer loyalty), and philanthropy can benefit donors in economic as well as social terms (e.g., by reducing their tax liability). However, philanthropy must at least aim or claim to benefit people other than the donor and her immediate circle of family and friends: a gift to one's child does not count as philanthropy, while a gift to the child's school does count (even if the motivation to benefit one's own child is constant across the two cases). Similarly, what distinguishes CSR is an explicit appeal to benefits to others when explaining, justifying, or promoting business practices, either in decision-making within the firm or in public-facing communications. Benefits to others need not exhaust the reasons for adopting a practice. Both CSR and philanthropy are therefore best understood as activities undertaken on a voluntary basis by private actors, and which at least purport to benefit others.

Despite the areas of overlap between the two practices, some people who tolerate or even embrace (non-corporate) philanthropy nevertheless reject CSR, arguing that it misconstrues the purpose of business corporations and the responsibilities of their managers. Milton Friedman famously argued that 'The Social Responsibility Of Business Is to Increase Its Profits.' According to Friedman, corporate executives are agents of the business's owners and have duties 'to conduct the business in accordance with their desires, which generally will be to make as much money as possible while conforming to the basic rules of the society' (Friedman 1970). In donating corporate money or voluntarily forgoing profits, a manager is 'in effect imposing taxes' on shareholders or any other owners for whom he acts as agent. Even if such a manager does good, he does so with his hand in other people's pockets. This principle-agent argument against CSR (except perhaps to the extent that it is profitable) does not apply in the same way to philanthropy, where individuals really are spending their own money[4] or where foundation officials act as agents promoting the avowedly philanthropic goals of their principals.[5] On the other hand, Friedman also argues that managers lack the expertise required to promote the common good competently or responsibly (Friedman 1970; see Lechterman 2021, 164–90, for a reconstruction and qualified defence of Friedman's argument). Here, the distinction with philanthropy is less clear cut: it seems possible to object that philanthropists too lack the qualifications or expertise required to pursue some social outcomes. Self-appointed and unaccountable promoters of the public good can be unreliable, whether or not they are or ought to be oriented to profit-seeking.[6]

Something along the lines of Friedman's argument might be the most charitable way of interpreting Mitch McConnell's criticism of (some) corporate political activity. To whatever extent he is not simply claiming a unique legitimacy for corporate support of Republican political objectives, perhaps he is calling for corporations to restrict their attempts at political influence to activities instrumental to their pursuit of profit. From this point of view, corporations have a legitimate stake and the competence to intervene in debates about (say) tax policy and environmental regulation, which entitles them to contribute to campaigns and to make independent expenditures that they expect to advance shareholder value. But perhaps they lack similar standing to 'take up causes' that do not directly implicate their economic activities and interests ('It's not what you're designed for'). Interestingly, an understanding of businesses as fundamentally oriented towards profit-seeking contributes to suspicion and rejection of CSR on the political left as well. The left critique takes the profit orientation of business as an empirical rather than normative premise and worries that CSR will be used to give ethical cover to corporate wrongdoing (e.g., that highly publicised environmental initiatives will present a misleading picture of an airline or oil company's overall environmental impact, contributing to 'greenwashing'). Sometimes, this critique extends to (non-corporate) elite philanthropy and its potential to contribute to the social legitimation of inequality (e.g., Giridharadas 2018).

All these objections notwithstanding, many people see both CSR and philanthropy as comparatively benign or unimportant aspects of elite influence.[7] The most prominent criticisms of contemporary 'oligarchic' power focus on the influence that corporations and wealthy individuals can exercise over elected officials through campaign contributions and lobbying. By contrast, less overtly political exercises of economic power may seem to present less of a threat to democracy. Other chapters in this volume examine elite political influence in more depth (Destri 2022; Parvin 2022); however, there are important reasons for seeing CSR and philanthropy as continuous with corporate and elite political activity rather than wholly distinct from it. As I have argued elsewhere (Saunders-Hastings 2018; 2022), a striking feature of elite influence today is the degree to which donors deploy (formally) political and philanthropic instruments in tandem. Many wealthy individuals use campaign contributions, investments in for-profit companies (e.g., 'impact investing') and donations to non-profits as a coordinated set of strategies for promoting their goals (whether those goals are self-interested, altruistic, or ideological). Corporations, too, can use formally philanthropic donations to promote political goals (although not all of these donations are likely to be counted or publicised as examples of CSR). For example, the American Legislative Exchange Council (ALEC) – a 501(c)(3) non-profit eligible to receive tax-deductible contributions – uses its library of model bills and its popular meetings for state legislators to promote anti-union and anti-regulatory legislation. ALEC receives most of its financial support from corporate donors – including, in the past, companies such as Amazon, Facebook, Google, Walmart, McDonalds, and Visa (Hertel-Fernandez 2019, xii). It is difficult and potentially misleading to draw sharp distinctions between CSR, philanthropy, and politics. Rather, we need democratic principles that can be used to evaluate the diverse portfolio of strategies by which economically powerful actors can shape outcomes of common concern.

2 Assessing Undemocratic Practices

Democratic political institutions and practices distribute opportunities to influence or control group decisions according to some principle of equality. This principle may be formal or substantive and more or less demanding: it may require merely formal equality of opportunity for influence (e.g., in the form of one-person-one-vote) at a specific procedural stage; more substantively equal expectations of influence over some set of social outcomes; or even institutions and practices that promote the collective empowerment of a group's less powerful members (e.g., McCormick 2011; Vergara 2020). On most views, democratic procedures are not morally required in all collective decision-making contexts (e.g., within religious institutions or voluntary associations). The term *nondemocratic* is therefore morally neutral: it simply describes institutions and practices that do not aim to equalise people's opportunities or power to affect collective decisions or outcomes of common concern. The term *undemocratic*, on the other hand, describes *objectionably* nondemocratic institutions, practices, or norms: ones that represent a dereliction of the kinds of political equality that ought to obtain between members of some group (paradigmatically, between members of society).

CSR and philanthropy are nondemocratic exercises of economic power, occurring at the discretion of business managers and rich donors. Even when practiced by internally democratic groups (e.g., a workers' cooperative or philanthropic 'giving circle,' rather than a hierarchically organised firm or foundation), CSR and philanthropy do not give those affected by them a say – much less an equal say – in the relevant decisions or outcomes (on worker participation, see Christiano 2022, in this volume). Rather, both CSR and philanthropy generally aim or purport to promote (or avoid harm to) the substantive interests of beneficiaries, 'stakeholders,' or other affected parties on unilateral and voluntary rather than reciprocal and accountable terms. The question, then, is when such nondemocratic practices constitute a threat to political equality.

As a starting point, I will suggest that the exercise of economic power in the form of CSR or philanthropy is *undemocratic* when it allows economic elites (1) to exercise disproportionate power in *choosing* the policies and social outcomes to be pursued through collective institutions and practices[8] or (2) to *undermine* the pursuit of democratically selected aims or policies (including by blocking some policy options, rendering them unrealisable, or acting to prevent democratic deliberation and action on some public problems). My intention is for this to be a broad standard, capable of cutting across a range of more specific conceptions of democracy. The standard recognises that democracy can be subverted in at least two different ways: when appropriately egalitarian decision-making procedures become less equal in their inputs (e.g., because of some people's disproportionate influence within them) and when egalitarian procedures become less binding or effective in their outputs (e.g., because some people can exempt themselves from or otherwise subvert the results of collective decisions).

Importantly, this standard applies whether or not an exercise of power promotes the substantive interests of the people affected. Respect for political equality requires powerful economic actors to avoid promoting (even) good outcomes in ways that usurp or subvert democratic authority. While the standard presupposes conditions of economic inequality, it does not rely on the claim that the rich hold their wealth unjustly: background distributive injustice would exacerbate democratic concerns, but the use of economic power to usurp or subvert democratic decision-making can be objectionable even if economic inequalities themselves are not.

Both legislative responses and ethical self-restraint have a role to play in the avoidance of undemocratic action. While legislation and enforcement can and should close some channels of undemocratic influence, economically powerful actors are likely to have opportunities to usurp or subvert collective decisions under any feasible regulatory regime. Forbearance from undemocratic action is therefore an important ethical responsibility that should condition and constrain the promotion of (other) good outcomes by businesses and philanthropists.

3 Corporate Social Responsibility and Democracy

I will begin by considering some corporate activities, from *outside* the category of CSR, that are widely understood to be democratically objectionable. By explaining why these forms of corporate activity are objectionable, we will be in a better position to assess whether similar objections apply to CSR and under what conditions CSR could avoid democratic objections.

Many people object to familiar corporate political activities (e.g., campaign-related expenditures and lobbying) on the grounds that they give businesses and managers objectionably unequal influence over the aims that political institutions pursue. Often, the worry is that unequal influence will lead to forms of capture that will undermine the instrumental value of democracy. But corporate political influence is not undemocratic only to the extent that its exercise harms people's substantive interests: rather, it is undemocratic when it distorts or usurps valuable egalitarian procedures for making collective decisions and setting policy objectives. While familiar kinds of corporate influence may indeed result in outsized consideration for business owners' *interests*, one can equally object that they give outsized influence to business managers' *judgments* (in matters that lie beyond their authority or competence). The latter objection can apply even where the former does not.

Importantly, the concern for preserving valuable egalitarian procedures for influencing common outcomes does not apply only to corporations' *external* actions or influence over elected officials. Some activities *within* firms can be undemocratic (even if one doubts that the internal organisation of firms must itself be thoroughly democratic). Alex Hertel-Fernandez (2018) has shown that managers view the political recruitment and mobilisation of their employees as an important tool for influencing elections and policy outcomes. Such practices are objectionable in part because they taint the inputs of collective decision-making processes, by manipulating workers' political participation (or chilling political activities that bosses disapprove of). The workplace can function as a lever for undemocratic influence in the broader society. Democracy requires restraining some ways that economically powerful actors might seek to influence others – in this case, people whom they are in a position to coerce economically.

Corporations and their managers can also act undemocratically without intervening directly in democratic decision-making processes or silencing and manipulating ordinary citizens' exercise of political voice. As Thomas Christiano (2010) has argued, capitalists can subvert political equality by exercising their property rights in ways that undermine democratic aims. Some (actual or anticipated) exercises of property rights by corporations and their managers shrink the space of policy options that can realistically be pursued. Christiano argues that 'commitment to democratic norms implies that private capitalist firms must cooperate with a democratic assembly and government in the pursuit of the aims of a democratic assembly,' in ways that go beyond the mere requirement of complying with the law, and even at some cost to firm profits (Christiano 2010, 196). Democratic norms – and the challenge of making the division of democratic labour consistent with the ideal of political equality – require that citizens participate as equals in choosing the aims of their society, while politicians, interest groups, and administrators decide the means for pursuing those aims. Public actors can subvert political equality when they 'substitute their own aims, in part, for those that have been chosen by citizens,' rather than promoting citizens' aims as well as possible within the 'feasible set' of policy options available (Christiano 2010, 201). But private actors can also subvert democratic policy-making: by affecting the content of the 'feasible set,' uncooperative capitalists can undermine the pursuit of citizens' chosen aims. For example, corporations might threaten to engage in layoffs or outsourcing in response to proposed regulatory measures (or government might anticipate such a response from corporations, even absent any overt threats). In many cases, an uncooperative corporate response could render even an otherwise popular policy excessively costly or self-defeating, and government might therefore decide against adopting it. Rather than co-opting legislators in order to substitute their own aims for those of other citizens, capitalists can make some democratic aims unrealisable by exercising or threatening to exercise their property rights in ways that run counter to democratic aims and purposes. When they do so, Christiano argues, they will often act undemocratically.

Of course, Christiano's argument focuses on capitalists' *self-interested* exercises of property rights in ways that might undermine democratic equality. Could 'socially responsible' exercises of property rights likewise subvert political equality and the pursuit or realisation of democratic aims? It depends on the kind of CSR being envisioned. If CSR is understood to require businesses to expand their involvement in processes of political decision-making and governance, or to promote the interests of 'stakeholders' directly as a substitute for government action, the risk of undemocratic consequences seems serious. As critics have argued, some versions of 'political CSR' seem inappropriately to treat business corporations as agents for holding other actors accountable rather than as powerful agents who must themselves be held to account (Hussain and Moriarty 2016). For example, scholars of political CSR have embraced 'the movement of the corporation into environmental and social challenges such as human rights, global warming, or deforestation' and its 'more intensive engagement with transnational processes of policy-making and the creation of global governance institutions' (Scherer and Palazzo 2008). It might be tempting to say that businesses can permissibly exercise their influence when they do so in ways that promote substantive justice. But from a democratic perspective, the problems with such a sweeping authorisation are obvious: democracy is supposed to constrain the ways that one may impose (even) one's sincere convictions about justice on other people. Political equality is threatened when economic power is exercised in ways that distort the inputs or subvert the outputs of democratic procedures.

But not all forms of CSR present this kind of threat to democracy. Compared with versions of CSR that specify extensive governance responsibilities for businesses, versions that specify obligations of *forbearance* and ethical restraints on profit-seeking are more likely to avoid undemocratic action. When business managers decline to profit from gaps in regulation (e.g., by avoiding pollution, even when polluting would be legally feasible or financially advantageous), the objection that they have usurped or subverted the democratic determination of policy objectives need not apply. In Joseph Heath's 'market failures approach' (MFA) to business ethics (Heath 2014), social responsibility centres on the avoidance of imposing negative externalities (even where imposing them is not illegal). Attempts to realise profits by displacing costs onto others (e.g., by exploiting market failures or engaging in rent-seeking) undermine the purpose of business in a just society (which is, roughly, to promote well-being through individually competitive behaviour within a market system that maximises efficiency overall – in part by virtue of being constrained by justice-promoting public institutions). Although he defines businesses' ethical responsibilities in relation to the value of Pareto efficiency (and not democracy), Heath's argument has clear affinities with Christiano's: both focus on the importance of capitalist forbearance and call for upholding a democratic division of labour, rather than assigning businesses a more sweeping responsibility to promote stakeholders' interests. A conception of CSR as forbearance therefore provides a bridge between important work in business ethics and in democratic theory.

Heath's MFA specifies much more significant ethical responsibilities for managers than Friedman does. But it nevertheless keeps those responsibilities closely tied to the purpose of *business*, markets, and profit-seeking (again, within an overall scheme of social cooperation, i.e., where state institutions promote justice through their regulatory and redistributive activities). Heath's most contentious claim is that 'efficiency imperatives' are 'pretty much all there is to business ethics, at least with respect to market transactions' (2014, 174); he cautions against the temptation to add additional obligations derived from principles of justice or fairness (but cf. Singer 2018, discussed below). A business is (on this view, and within the right institutional context) the right kind of entity to contribute through competitive (and suitably constrained) market behaviour to the promotion of efficient and welfare-enhancing outcomes; it is the wrong kind of entity to benevolently promote all stakeholder interests or assume governance responsibilities.

From a democratic point of view, there is a great deal to be said for this division of institutional labour. By adopting the kinds of restraints on profit-seeking that the MFA calls for, firms would often avoid undermining not only the substantive interests of other people but also the aims of democratic legislation. Some of Heath's proposed restraints call specifically for forbearance vis-à-vis *democratic* institutions and processes: for example, he argues that managers have obligations to refrain from rent-seeking and from opposing regulations aimed at correcting market failures. When CSR takes the form of refraining from exercising economic power to influence or thwart democratic legislation, it seems to that extent supportive rather than subversive of political equality. Other CSR activities, such as attempts to minimise negative externalities or to avoid deceptive advertising, are less obviously oriented towards political institutions and processes: forbearance in these cases takes the form of restraints on harm to people's substantive interests rather than on unequal influence. Nevertheless, such activities will not in general involve *undemocratic* action: they can be fully consistent with respect for the authority of democratic legislation and with citizens' freedom to decide as equals on the aims they will pursue in common.

Not all CSR activities can be conceived as cases of forbearance.[9] A forbearance-focused approach to CSR is unlikely to emphasise corporate philanthropy as an ethical requirement. (Heath's book does not discuss it.) But, while not a democratic *requirement* like forbearance, a great deal of corporate philanthropy – at least of the kind that gets counted as CSR – may nevertheless be unthreatening from a democratic point of view.[10] It seems significant here that the causes that most firms promote under the auspices of CSR tend to be different and considerably more popular than those for which they lobby and fund issue ads. Corporate philanthropy is often directed to uncontentious or even banal causes: not everyone will be enthusiastic about them but few are vociferously opposed (so, for example, companies like Disney and Macy's are enthusiastic donors to the Make-A-Wish Foundation, which arranges 'wish experiences' for children with life-threatening illnesses; and corporations typically signal their support for women by making donations to fight breast cancer rather than funding reproductive health services). This tells us little about the substantive merits of corporate donations. But it does indicate, I think, that in their CSR activities corporations are often aiming to follow (sometimes at a distance) rather than to steer public opinion. Compared with corporations' campaign-related and lobbying expenditures, CSR often looks more reactive: it seeks less to change the political aims that citizens are pursuing than to signal support for those aims (whatever they may be) and so gain loyal customers.

None of this is to say that we should expect too much from CSR or that it should be allowed to pre-empt the public, democratic regulation of corporations. But no capitalist society could regulate away all of the opportunities for corporations to undermine democratic aims and people's substantive interests. CSR in the form of forbearance therefore has a role to play in upholding whatever degree of political equality can be realised under capitalism. Importantly, this line of defence will not vindicate all activities that might fall under the CSR label. It fits most comfortably with the voluntary adoption of constraints on profit-seeking (e.g., minimising negative externalities, and refraining from opposing regulation aimed at correcting market failures). It is less clear that 'political CSR' can be defended on the same basis, i.e., if it calls for businesses to shape or even assume responsibility for governance arrangements. On a forbearance conception, the point is not to make business *democratic*, but to prevent it from acting in *undemocratic* ways.

4 Philanthropy and Democracy

Like CSR, large-scale philanthropy is a fundamentally nondemocratic practice. It is an exercise of economic power by wealthy citizens and the private institutions they create. Scholars who recognise the prima facie tension between democracy and concentrated, unaccountable power have nevertheless argued that some kinds of elite philanthropy can be consistent with or even supportive of democracy. Reich (2018) argues that the comparative advantage of philanthropy, in relation to majoritarian democratic decision-making, lies in the values of pluralism and 'discovery': broadly speaking, in the promotion of minority, long-term, or experimental public goods. Philanthropy can be supportive of democracy when it successfully contributes to such goods. However, as I have already argued, good substantive outcomes are not an adequate *democratic* justification for exercises of elite influence: it needs also to be shown that influence avoids usurping or subverting egalitarian procedures for setting the aims of public policy. Like CSR, philanthropy compatible with democracy must avoid *undemocratic* action. Nor is this constraint a simple one to observe; it stands in tension with many philanthropists' ambitious agendas for transformative social and political influence.

Unlike CSR, philanthropy always involves positive action (i.e., contributions of money or other goods) rather than forbearance from action. But this does not mean that philanthropy necessarily usurps or undermines democratic aims. Sometimes, philanthropy funds non-public goods that do not aspire or appear to have significant public effects. Philanthropy can also help to supply public or semi-public goods (e.g., funding for arts and sciences) beyond the level desired by the median voter, without undermining existing public goods or democratic decision-making about them.[11] And sometimes, philanthropic activity provides new or supplementary public goods in ways that then 'audition' for public approval and uptake (Beerbohm 2016, 222–23). Andrew Carnegie's funding of public libraries can serve as an example of philanthropy operating in the latter mode. Because Carnegie's gifts generally covered only the construction of libraries and not their maintenance, they could achieve lasting influence only to the degree that communities were persuaded of the value of providing libraries as a public good. The Russell Sage Foundation, too, developed a model of 'exerting influence ... through the creation of public demands' – for example, by offering expertise to local groups mobilising to support the construction of community playgrounds (Turner 2001, 134). Here again, influence was exerted through 'demonstration projects' whose success required reaching and persuading a broad public of the projects' value (Turner 2001, 134). While this remains an exercise of elite influence, it becomes less democratically threatening to the extent that it avoids circumventing (and may even stimulate) democratic deliberation about matters of common concern.

On the other hand, some philanthropy engages much more straightforwardly in setting social and political aims *for* other citizens (in exchange for partially funding the pursuit of those aims). Moreover, it can do so in ways that bypass the strategies of public approval-seeking that characterise the examples just discussed (and, indeed, many CSR activities). While philanthropy can supplement publicly funded goods and services, it also often aims to redirect public funds and influence the ways that they are spent. Studies of educational philanthropy in the United States (e.g., Reckhow 2013; 2016; Tompkins-Stange 2016) have shown how large-scale educational philanthropists aim to 'leverage' their donations into influence over public education policy, including through conditional or restricted gifts to public agencies. Such practices give economic elites undemocratic influence over public policy. Even when such gifts are accepted by democratically elected officials, they transform relationships of authority and accountability in undemocratic ways: officials often promote *donors'* policy preferences rather than democratically decided ones or constrain their pursuit of democratically decided policy objectives in conformity with donor conditions. Some policy options may be permanently removed from democratic consideration and contestation. For example, as part of the 'Grand Bargain' that resolved the city of Detroit's bankruptcy proceedings, philanthropic foundations contributed resources to shore up city workers' pension plans. One condition on these philanthropic contributions was the privatisation of the Detroit Institute of Arts: the museum and its collection were transferred from city ownership to an independent non-profit (in part to avert any future risk of art being sold to help fund public pensions). Art lovers might value this outcome, but it represented a deliberate curtailment of democratic authority and control. Philanthropic practices that usurp public policy-making or constrict the policy options open to democratic publics are antithetical to the demands of forbearance.

Even without explicit conditions that constrain future public policy options, philanthropic influence can shape deliberation in undemocratic ways. The Broad Center, financed by the Eli and Edythe Broad Foundation, 'develops leaders to help transform America's urban public schools.'[12] Here, the orientation of philanthropic influence is much less public-facing than in the library and playground examples considered above. The aim is instead to develop and influence a class of public employees who will be able to help shift the direction of public policy, without the need to appeal directly to the public. Similarly, discussing the Rockefeller Foundation's efforts to professionalise public administration, Stephen Turner identifies a type of philanthropic activity whose 'primary audience is not the public, but individuals with discretionary power, usually in bureaucracies' and whose legitimacy is often not even a matter of public discussion (Turner 2001, 136). Philanthropy of this kind aims to influence officials, bureaucrats, and administrators directly, and can therefore avoid recourse to strategies of public persuasion and legitimacy-seeking.

This seems to me to be a crucial difference between some elite philanthropy and the kinds of corporate philanthropy that are commonly counted as examples of CSR: very little 'socially responsible' corporate philanthropy occurs without publicity.[13] But philanthropy by individuals and foundations often *does* occur without publicity and in ways that deliberately evade public scrutiny. This points us to an important difference between these two forms of influence and their relationship to democracy. I have suggested that, notwithstanding pervasive rhetoric about responsible corporate 'leadership' on issues of social responsibility, corporate philanthropy typically involves uncontroversial stances for popular and/or relatively depoliticised causes, with corporations seeking to fall in line with public attitudes rather than to transform them. This characterisation does not hold, or not to the same extent, for many philanthropic activities; perhaps counterintuitively, this may make elite philanthropy a greater *democratic* concern than CSR. This argument does not rely on the claim that elite philanthropy is more self-interested than CSR, or that its substantive outcomes are worse. Compared with businesses engaging in CSR, philanthropic individuals and foundations may be more inclined to bypass appeals to a wider public. To that extent, they may sometimes impose donors' judgments on beneficiaries and the wider community to a greater degree than corporate philanthropists. These differences become clearer when we focus on the different ways that public influence can operate, rather than only the range of motives that can underlie it.

5 Undemocratic Private Power in Ideal Theory and the Real World

I have developed a claim about forbearance as an important democratic obligation for powerful economic actors like business managers and elite philanthropists. It is often permissible and even desirable for such actors to take steps to benefit others. But the democratic obligations of CSR and philanthropy function mostly as constraints rather than as obligations to promote specific substantive outcomes. In this final section, I want to consider the complexities that arise in applying this guidance in actually existing democracies.

The crux of the issue is that, in the real world, we cannot equate deference to *legislative* outcomes with respect for citizens' decisions, on suitably equal terms, about what public outcomes to promote or pursue. If we suspect that democratic deficits taint electoral and policy processes, it becomes less clear *how* to respect democratic constraints on the activities of private actors. This objection arises most obviously when businesses and philanthropists operate in countries that lack democratic government, but one can also object that *most* countries lack the kind of *robustly* democratic government that idealised conceptions of democracy describe. To the degree that we doubt (a) that electoral processes are sufficiently egalitarian, and electoral competition sufficiently well-informed and transparent, for the results to count as meaningful rankings of citizens' shared aims and/or (b) that accountable government actors are trying in good faith to realise citizens' shared aims, the net effect of private influence on the articulation and realisation of citizens' shared aims becomes more difficult to specify.

While Christiano rightly anticipates that capitalists will be quickest to exercise property rights to protect their profits, some companies have engaged in similar *actions* (e.g., decisions to relocate commercial operations or events) as a way of taking a social or political position. Consider Major League Baseball's decision to move its All-Star Game in the wake of Georgia's new voting law. As in the cases that Christiano considers, this was an example of capitalists exercising property rights in ways that they were legally entitled to do: as a private corporation, MLB may hold its All-Star Game where it likes. However, in this case, the decision signalled displeasure with a law enacted by the Georgia state legislature, and the decision was interpreted as intended to create incentives in favour of repealing the law (for state legislators) or (failing that) for citizens to vote against politicians who supported the law. Because of this, some critics characterised MLB's decision as an undemocratic exercise of economic power to influence citizens' political choices. How should we evaluate MLB's decision?

At issue here is not only the substantive justice of the Georgia law (i.e., whether it violates political liberties in ways that would make it illegitimate even if enacted through democratic procedures) but its procedural authority (i.e., whether it represents government's good-faith effort to pursue aims chosen by citizens through egalitarian procedures). By exercising economic power in order to create incentives in favour of repealing the law, would corporations be undermining the pursuit of *democratic* aims? Or has government already abridged political equality by pursuing aims that were not chosen by citizens on equal terms? Once we recognise the risk of inflating the democratic authority of electoral and legislative outcomes, it may seem more difficult to demand deference and forbearance from corporate actors.

Some scholars of business ethics have argued that, where there are democratic deficits in political institutions, private actors may justifiably engage in forms of influence that would be impermissible if political institutions were fully just and democratic. Abraham Singer extends Heath's approach in order to argue that firms have obligations to avoid profiting from 'justice failures' as well as market failures. Singer argues that the ability of corporations to exercise outsized political influence results from a 'justice failure': the failure of political institutions to secure equal citizenship. Corporations and managers ought to refrain from exploiting this and other justice failures, which entails 'a general principle to refrain from contributing to electoral campaigns or attempting to undo laws and regulations curtailing corporate campaign contributions, even if doing so is legal and would be advantageous for one's business' (Singer 2018, 109). However, Singer recognises complexities that might push responsible corporations in the opposite direction. He thinks that the requirement to refrain from political activity 'can be lifted when corporations are participating in such a manner so as to eliminate the underlying political justice failure'; that is, corporate actors can permissibly 'work toward curtailing their own outsized effect on politics, even if doing so requires using that outsized effect' (109). Importantly, Singer's claim is not that corporate influence is justified whenever it promotes substantive justice. Rather, his claim applies much more narrowly to cases 'where the justice failure lies precisely in the ability of businesses to affect politics at the expense of democratic equality' (110). On this view, corporate action in the Georgia case might therefore count as the impermissible exploitation of economic power, even if it were to promote political equality (i.e., by helping to secure citizens' voting rights), since the interventions did not aim to erode the power of *corporations* relative to other social actors.

The narrowness of the exception that Singer makes to corporations' general obligation to abstain from political activity aims in part to keep the focus on procedural values, rather than granting corporations a more sweeping permission to promote substantive justice. But even procedural values might seem to license MLB's action: MLB might claim that its exercise of corporate speech and property rights did not subvert *democratically* chosen aims in the first place (i.e., because the new voting restrictions were themselves the product of an undemocratic process, subject to complaints of voter suppression and racial gerrymandering). Of course, there are strong reasons against inviting corporations to make their own interpretations about how much democratic legitimacy different laws and policies enjoy. Nevertheless, in existing democratic societies, accounts of when corporate or philanthropic influence is undemocratic cannot presuppose that all government policy enjoys robust democratic authority. This makes it considerably more difficult to specify the ways that procedural values should constrain private influence. In evaluating CSR and philanthropy, I think that we can begin to make progress by applying a publicity heuristic[14]: asking whether influence is oriented towards seeking legitimacy from the public or rather attempting to bypass the need to persuade and engage citizens. A publicity heuristic can be useful in evaluating the seriousness of departures from democratic forbearance. Some forms of influence (including some that would be ruled out if formal political institutions were fully just and democratic) are more compatible than others with respect for citizens' status as equals and their shared authority over matters of common concern.

6 Conclusion

Considering CSR and philanthropy together presses us to specify our reasons for objecting to some uses of economic power. Is the problem that some putatively beneficial activities are covertly self-serving, allowing the wealthy to reap more ethical credit than they deserve? Is it that some agents, because of their distinctive purposes or special obligations to principals, cannot or should not be charged with 'socially responsible' action? Or is the problem the exercise of public influence insulated from mechanisms of accountability to ordinary people? These questions affect not just how we rank the relative threats of CSR and elite philanthropy, but how we understand the grounds of democratic objections to elite power more generally.

Of course, CSR and philanthropy raise practical as well as theoretical questions for people committed to the value of democracy. I have argued that many of the most important democratic demands on corporations and philanthropy consist of restraints rather than positive obligations. Even when attempting to confer benefits on particular people or on society, donors, corporations, and managers should refrain from subverting the development, articulation, and realisation of democratic aims. But what this entails in practice is a complex matter: private actors in the real world may not confront public institutions so robustly democratic that the demands of political equality can be satisfied by deference to government policy. These complexities argue in favour of greater attention to the direct influence of corporations and donors over other social actors.

Notes

1 Although some critics make parallel claims about elite philanthropy (e.g., Giridharadas 2018).
2 To claim that CSR is often democratically unthreatening is not to provide a justification of the capitalist economies within which CSR is practiced; it leaves open the possibility that market socialism or a Rawlsian 'property owning democracy' would be preferable to capitalism (including on democratic grounds). I bracket that broader question here, in order focus on some specific threats to political equality as they present themselves in existing democratic societies.
3 Here I modify Hsieh's characterisation of CSR as 'activities that benefit parties beyond routine commercial transactions' (2017, 188n2), to leave open the possibility that some CSR practices fail actually to benefit people other than the business's owners or shareholders (just as some philanthropy may fail actually to help its intended beneficiaries).

4 At least from a legal point of view; Cordelli (2016) argues that wealthy donors in circumstances of background distributive injustice lack moral entitlements to their property and should therefore be regarded as spending money that is not really their own.

5 As Lechterman (2021, 171) recognises, the principal-agent argument against CSR also seems to lack force in the case of 'social enterprises' that explicitly orient their commercial activities to social aims or companies funded by 'impact investors' who pursue social goals alongside financial returns.

6 Warren Buffett, a prominent philanthropist, criticises CSR in terms that hew closely to Friedman's. He argues, 'This is the shareholders' money,' which it would be wrong on principle for managers to 'donate.' He also expresses scepticism about managers' ability to know and promote what's good for society: 'It's very hard to do. If you give me the 20 largest companies, I don't know which of the 20 behaves the best, really … I think it's very hard to evaluate what they're doing … it's very, very hard. I like to eat candy. Is candy good for me or not? I don't know' (Armstrong 2019). The interviewer does not appear to have asked, nor Buffett to have explained, whether this epistemic argument about the difficulty of doing good also applies to non-corporate philanthropy.

7 Of course, many non-wealthy people make philanthropic contributions, but elite philanthropy (by millionaire or billionaire donors and private foundations) raises distinct concerns. On the differences between elite and ordinary philanthropy, see Saunders-Hastings (2018; 2022, chapters 3 and 5).

8 What counts as 'disproportionate' power will of course depend on how substantive and demanding a conception of political equality one adopts. On some views, any departure from strict equality of substantive influence may count as outsize power; others will only object to inequalities that are dramatic and/or entrenched. The standard here is meant to be open-ended but to rely only on the uncontroversial claim that democracy is undermined if putatively collective institutions in effect allow powerful economic actors to impose their preferred policies on others.

9 Crane, Matten, and Spence (2014, 67) distinguish between 'Traditional CSR,' where 'value-distribution' activities (e.g., charitable donations) occur as a supplement to regular business practices, and 'Contemporary CSR,' where 'value-creation' activities are integrated into regular business practices (e.g., decisions about labour practices and environmental impact). In this framework, many obligations of democratic forbearance would fall into the category of contemporary CSR. However, that category also seems to include some activities that conflict with the demands of forbearance (e.g., assuming governance responsibilities on behalf of various 'stakeholders').

10 I have in mind here some of the most common and generic forms of corporate philanthropy. Lechterman (2021, 185–86) gives a less tepid endorsement of a narrower category of corporate philanthropy: contributions of in-kind goods, where firms have important assets to share and can do so on a neutral basis, without crowding out the public provision of important goods.

11 This is not to say that there is never a democratic concern in such cases (they may, for example, raise worries about externalities and the 'crowding out' of public funding). I simply mean to grant that some philanthropy can supplement rather than undermine government provision of public goods.

12 https://broadfoundation.org/about-us/#.
13 The qualifications here are meant to exclude donations to organisations like ALEC, which corporations generally *are* keen to avoid publicising. On American billionaires' strategies of (self-interested) political influence through 'stealth politics,' see Page, Seawright, and Lacombe (2019).
14 Thanks to Michael Bennett for suggesting this framing.

References

Armstrong, Robert. 2019. "Warren Buffett on Why Companies Cannot Be Moral Arbiters." *Financial Times*, December 29, 2019. https://www.ft.com/content/ebbc9b46-1754-11ea-9ee4-11f260415385.

Beerbohm, Eric. 2016. "The Free-Provider Problem." In *Philanthropy in Democratic Societies: History, Institutions, Values*, eds. Rob Reich, Chiara Cordelli, and Lucy Bernholz, 207–25. Chicago, IL: University of Chicago Press.

Bennett, Michael and Rutger Claassen. 2022. "Taming the Corporate Leviathan. How to Properly Politicize Corporate Purpose?" In *Wealth and Power. Philosophical Perspectives*, eds. Michael Bennett, Huub Brouwer, and Rutger Claassen. London: Routledge.

Christiano, Thomas. 2010. "The Uneasy Relationship between Democracy and Capital." *Social Philosophy & Policy* 27(1): 195–217.

Christiano, Thomas. 2022. "Why Does Worker Participation Matter? Three Considerations in Favor of Worker Participation in Corporate Governance." In *Wealth and Power. Philosophical Perspectives*, eds. Michael Bennett, Huub Brouwer, and Rutger Claassen. London: Routledge.

Cordelli, Chiara. 2016. "Reparative Justice and the Moral Limits of Discretionary Philanthropy." In *Philanthropy in Democratic Societies: History, Institutions, Values*, eds. Rob Reich, Chiara Cordelli, and Lucy Bernholz, 244–265. Chicago, IL: University of Chicago Press.

Crane, Andrew, Dirk Matten, and Laura J. Spence. 2014. *Corporate Social Responsibility: Readings and Cases in a Global Context*. 2nd ed. New York, NY: Routledge.

Destri, Chiara. 2022. "No Money, No Party: The Role of Political Parties in Electoral Campaigns." In *Wealth and Power. Philosophical Perspectives*, eds. Michael Bennett, Huub Brouwer, and Rutger Claassen. London: Routledge.

Friedman, Milton. 1970. "A Friedman doctrine: The Social Responsibility Of Business Is to Increase Its Profits." *New York Times Magazine*, September 13, 1970.

Giridharadas, Anand. 2018. *Winners Take All: The Elite Charade of Changing the World*. New York, NY: Knopf.

Heath, Joseph. 2014. *Morality, Competition, and the Firm: The Market Failures Approach to Business Ethics*. Oxford: Oxford University Press.

Hertel-Fernandez, Alex. 2018. *Politics at Work: How Companies Turn Their Workers Into Lobbyists*. Oxford: Oxford University Press.

Hertel-Fernandez, Alex. 2019. *State Capture: How Conservative Activists, Big Businesses, and Wealthy Donors Reshaped the American States—and the Nation*. Oxford: Oxford University Press.

Hsieh, Nien-hê. 2017. "Corporate Moral Agency, Positive Duties, and Purpose." In *The Moral Responsibility of Firms*, eds. Eric W. Orts and N. Craig Smith, 188–205. Oxford: Oxford University Press.

Hussain, Waheed and Jeffrey Moriarty. 2016. "Accountable to Whom? Rethinking the Role of Corporations in Political CSR." *Journal of Business Ethics* 149: 519–34.
Lechterman, Theodore M. 2021. *The Tyranny of Generosity: Why Philanthropy Corrupts Our Politics and How We Can Fix It*. Oxford: Oxford University Press.
Matten, Dirk and Andrew Crane. 2005. "Corporate Citizenship: Toward an Extended Theoretical Conceptualization." *Academy of Management Review* 30(1): 166–79.
McCormick, John P. 2011. *Machiavellian Democracy*. Cambridge: Cambridge University Press.
Page, Benjamin I., Jason Seawright, and Matthew J. Lacombe. 2019. *Billionaires and Stealth Politics*. Chicago, IL: University of Chicago Press.
Parvin, Phil. 2022. "Hidden in Plain Sight: How Lobby Organisations Undermine Democracy." In *Wealth and Power. Philosophical Perspectives*, eds. Michael Bennett, Huub Brouwer, and Rutger Claassen. London: Routledge.
Reckhow, Sarah. 2013. *Follow the Money: How Foundation Dollars Change Public School Politics*. Oxford: Oxford University Press.
Reckhow, Sarah. 2016. "More that patrons: How Foundations Fuel Policy Change and Backlash." *PS: Political Science and Politics* 49(3): 449–54.
Reich, Rob. 2018. *Just Giving: Why Philanthropy Is Failing Democracy and How It Can Do Better*. Princeton, NJ: Princeton University Press.
Saunders-Hastings, Emma. 2018. "Plutocratic Philanthropy." *Journal of Politics* 80(1): 149–61.
Saunders-Hastings, Emma. 2019. "Philanthropy." In *International Encyclopedia of Ethics*, ed. Hugh LaFollette. Hoboken, NJ: John Wiley & Sons.
Saunders-Hastings, Emma. 2022. *Private Virtues, Public Vices: Philanthropy and Democratic Equality*. Chicago, IL: University of Chicago Press.
Scherer, Andreas Georg and Guido Palazzo. 2008. "Globalization and Corporate Social Responsibility." In *The Oxford Handbook of Corporate Social Responsibility*, eds. Andrew Crane et al., 413–31. Oxford: Oxford University Press.
Singer, Abraham. 2018. "Justice Failure: Efficiency and Equality in Business Ethics." *Journal of Business Ethics* 149: 97–115.
Thrush, Glen. 2021. "McConnell, Long a Defender of Corporate Speech, Now Suggests Executives 'stay out of politics.'" *The New York Times*, online edition, April 6, 2021. https://www.nytimes.com/2021/04/06/us/politics/mitch-mcconnell-voting-rights.html.
Tompkins-Stange, Megan. 2016. *Policy Patrons: Philanthropy, Education Reform, and the Politics of Influence*. Cambridge, MA: Harvard Education Press.
Turner, Stephen. 2001. "What is the Problem with Experts?" *Social Studies of Science* 31(1): 123–49.
Vergara, Camila. 2020. *Systemic Corruption: Constitutional Ideas for an Anti-Oligarchic Republic*. Princeton, NJ: Princeton University Press.

11 Independence in the Commons

How Group Ownership Realises Basic Non-Domination

Yara Al Salman

Republicans have long recognised that property institutions profoundly impact power relationships between citizens. On the one hand, these institutions can stand at the basis of the two problems associated with the wealth-power nexus analysed in this volume. That is, property has the potential to subvert democracy on the national level (McCormick 2006), and to support domination in the social domain by making some people highly economically dependent on others (Gourevitch 2013). On the other hand, and more optimistically, property can play a key role in realising political equality and social independence for all citizens. One way to achieve this, which has been amply discussed in the republican literature, is to ensure that everyone has equal *individual* property holdings (Domènech and Raventós 2008; Pettit 2008; Lovett 2009; Casassas and De Wispelaere 2016; Kimpell 2022, in this volume). A different method, and one that has received far less attention, is to secure non-domination through institutions of non-hierarchically organised *group* ownership. This strategy is mainly researched in the context of firm governance, where collective worker ownership can replace the hierarchies of shareholder business corporations (Gourevitch 2014). What is still lacking in the literature on property and non-domination, however, is a general theory of group ownership, that explains when and why this institution can realise non-domination not just in the context of firm governance, but in other spheres as well.

This essay aims to provide two of the starting points for such a theory. First, I develop a normative framework for the analysis of ownership institutions. I shall argue that to realise basic non-domination, ownership institutions must enable people to use resources to resist arbitrary power relationships. In addition, they must give people equal control over the resources they need to be able to resist such relationships. Second, I develop a conception of group ownership that can satisfy these criteria. The resulting account can be used to analyse sharing arrangements in their own right, but it can also be used to compare sharing with non-sharing ownership institutions, to see which is best able to realise non-domination.

DOI: 10.4324/9781003173632-13

The essay is structured as follows. I first outline a conception of basic non-domination and explain briefly why it is of value. People enjoy basic non-domination when they are able to withstand power asymmetries, and are in control of the decisions that structure that ability (Section 1). I then specify two criteria that ownership institutions must meet to help secure basic non-domination. The *basic capability criterion* states that such institutions must enable people to use resources to strengthen their ability to withstand power asymmetries. Furthermore, ownership institutions must place the people who rely on a resource for that reason, equally in charge of how that resource may be used. This is the *control* criterion. I show that there is no reason to suppose that only institutions of individual ownership can meet these criteria. Nor is there a reason to think that means of obtaining a livelihood – such as land and firms – are the only types of resources that are of interest here. This clears the path for a defence of group ownership in different types of resources (Section 2). Finally, I develop a conception of group ownership, called *sharing in common*. This is an arrangement in which members of a private group determine democratically how their shared object may be used. I first explain in a general sense when and how group ownership succeeds in realising basic non-domination (Section 3). This is illustrated by a discussion of actual sharing arrangements in natural resources (Section 4) and informational resources (Section 5).

1 Basic and Full Non-Domination

Before outlining my conception of *basic* non-domination, it is worth expanding very briefly on the ideal of non-domination itself, in particular the place of collective control as part of this ideal. The concepts of domination and non-domination evaluate relationships of power. On Phillip Pettit's seminal definition, you are dominated if an agent has the capacity to interfere with you on an arbitrary basis (Pettit 1997, 52; see also Kimpell 2022, in this volume, for a discussion of Pettit). Interference is arbitrary, and therefore unjustified, if it's not under the control of whoever may be subjected to it (Pettit 1997; 2012; Forst 2013).[1] Conversely, you enjoy non-domination when you are in control of the power to which you are subjected, equally with everyone who is in the same position. You then possess a degree of anti-power: robust control over how others may act towards you, making the power relationship symmetrical (Pettit 1996).

The ideal of non-domination is morally grounded in a commitment to securing people's social status (Pettit 1997, 87; Gädeke 2020, 25–30), meaning the standing they ought to occupy in a society in virtue of their personhood. Very briefly, the view is that this status is negated when people have no or no equal say over the forces that bind them. Human beings are capable of practical reason; they can set their own goals and evaluate their own reasons for action, as well as the rules by which such actions are governed. It is wrong to treat them as if they do not have that capacity, and decide *for them* what they may and can do, or determine for them – for example, through manipulation – what they will or want to do. Republicans stress, moreover, that it's not just actual arbitrary interference that is objectionable, but also the capacity thereto. Just the fact that someone *can* interfere with your life entirely at their own discretion, and that you consequently depend on their goodwill, means that your will is treated as if it is of no consequence. Though a dominating agent may refrain from interfering with you, they do not recognise this as an obligation they have in virtue of your status (Pettit 2007).

People's equal social status is affirmed, however, when they are equally in control of the power relationships that govern their actions. This is what it means to be treated 'properly as a person,' as 'a voice that cannot be dismissed without independent reason' (Pettit 1997, 91). It means that interference must be justified to you, and that you – together and equally with everyone who is in a similar position – decide whether it takes place (Forst 2013). It is worth stressing, given the present interest in group ownership and collective control over resources, that the type of control that is required for non-domination on this understanding of the term, is usually *collective democratic* control, not individual control. That is to say, power is justified when the people subjected to it have an equal and effective opportunity to influence its exercise (Pettit 2012, chap. 4).

Different theorists have objected to this way of understanding non-domination, and argue that the emphasis on democracy is misguided (see, e.g., List and Valentini 2016; Arnold and Harris 2017). However, their objections are often based on a misunderstanding of the reasons that republicans ought to value democratic collective control. This misunderstanding is invited by Pettit's own defence of non-domination, for which he uses the following illustration:

> Suppose you wish to restrict your alcohol consumption and hand over the key of your alcohol cupboard to me, making me promise to return the key only at twenty-four hours' notice and not in response to a request for its immediate return. When I refuse a request for immediate return of the key, I interfere with your choice, removing the option of having a drink now. I deny you the possibility of choosing according to your current will. But do I subject you to my will? Do I impose my will on you, for example, in a way that might reasonably trigger resentment? Surely not.
>
> (Pettit 2012, 57)

Interference in this case seems justified because it conforms completely to the will of the individual subjected to it. This individual is able to ensure that the interference tracks their subjectively defined interests entirely.

As critics have noted, however, this example does not explain why power is justified when its exercise is controlled by a collective, in a democracy (List and Valentini 2016; Arnold and Harris 2017). After all, individuals who have to take a decision together can disagree with one another. Though they may have an equal opportunity to influence any decision, the end result will not accord with all of their individual views. Consequently, their subjectively defined interests are not automatically promoted through their participation in a collective control mechanism. In short: non-domination as the robust capacity to take part in a collective decision-making mechanism, cannot be defended by showing that it necessarily promotes people interests (Arnold and Harris 2017) or that it gives effect to people's individual will (List and Valentini 2016).

But that is not how non-domination ought to be defended in the first place. As I said, the ideal of non-domination is rooted in a commitment to securing people's proper status, that is, the status they ought to enjoy as beings capable of practical reason. And it is precisely this status that is affirmed when people are included in democratic decision-making mechanisms. They are then treated as a person, to whom you have to justify the power to which they are subjected (Forst 2013), rather than as a thing with which you can do what you want. To quote Pettit again:

> To have the full standing of a person among persons, it is essential that you be able to command their attention and respect: if you like, their authorisation of you as a voice worth hearing and an ear worth addressing.
> (Pettit 2002, 350)

To be sure, individuals may not always get their way in a democracy, but then that is not necessary to ensure that they are treated properly as a person among persons. To the contrary, it is precisely by ensuring that people have *equal* control over power that their equal status is recognised. The upshot, as I will show later, is that the control that individuals gain through individual ownership, is not always necessary to realise non-domination. Group ownership can do the job just as well, by realising democratic control over resources.

You enjoy *full non-domination* when no agent has the capacity to interfere with you arbitrarily; you are in control – together with others in a similar position – of how others may act towards you. This is a difficult ideal to attain even in the best of circumstances. It is therefore worth establishing what the priorities should be from a republican perspective. In which relationships is it most important that people enjoy non-domination? Articulating this priority will come down to articulating a concept of *basic non-domination*, understood as the minimal standard that a society ought to secure in organising its power relations (for similar conceptions of a minimal standard of non-domination, see Forst 2001;

ohman 2005; Laborde 2010). This priority should not – in the first instance – be defined by standards external to the ideal of non-domination, but by the central concern that animates it: the concern with subjection to an arbitrary will. Basic non-domination involves having the reasonable ability to withstand subjection to an arbitrary will and being in control of the decisions that structure that ability. This may sound like a circular standard, but I aim to show now that it is not.

A person's reasonable ability to withstand arbitrary subjection consists of a number of capabilities and functionings.[2] If you lack the capabilities to satisfy basic human needs, you may come under the power of someone who can let you satisfy those needs (Lovett 2009). The capabilities to seek adequate nourishment, healthcare, and shelter are like that. If I am hungry and unable to do something about it myself, I may submit – seemingly voluntarily – to someone's will, just to get some food. In addition, there are capabilities and functionings that one needs to be able to recognise and address arbitrary power relationships. These include the capability to access non-biased information and the functioning of being literate, for example. Without them, you would be vulnerable to manipulation and possibly unable to check the power that is exercised over you, whether by politicians or private parties (see also Laborde 2010, 53). Of course, people have often been able to resist power asymmetries even when they lack the types of capabilities and functionings just mentioned. My focus, however, is not on the very possibility of resisting power – which does indeed exist even under desperate conditions – but on what people might *reasonably* require to be able to do that.

It matters how these basic capabilities, as I shall refer to them, are secured. For basic non-domination, it's not enough that a person has access to a basic capability by leave of someone else, since this would just make them dependent on an arbitrary will. Instead, people should be in charge of those decisions that affect and structure the provision of their basic capabilities. Citizens should not only be able to access healthcare, for example, but should also be in charge of the rules and regulations concerning whether care is provided at all, what sort of care that is, and so on. They must be in control of such decisions together and on an equal basis with everyone else whose capability to access healthcare is similarly at stake. When all basic capabilities and functions are so protected, a person enjoys basic non-domination. They are then equally in control of the preconditions of their own empowerment.

This account of basic non-domination is admittedly sketchy. That is to some extent a necessary feature of the idea. What exactly counts as a reasonable ability to withstand subjection – and which capabilities and functionings make up that ability – is not something that can be entirely determined in theory. This is both because republicans believe citizens should formulate the standards that govern their society themselves, and because what counts as a requirement for not being vulnerable to subjection will vary depending on contextual factors (Pettit 1997, 158). However, for my present purpose it suffices to lay out the very general idea of basic non-domination, rather than specify what it looks like exactly. This is because the capabilities that I shall focus on in this essay are uncontroversially basic in the sense I have outlined here, and concern people's livelihood and access to adequate information. Before I get to the discussion of group ownership, however, I will first say more about the link between non-domination and ownership in general.

2 Ownership, Independence, and Basic Non-Domination

Ownership gives agents the right to decide how an object may be used, within limits set by the law (Waldron 1988, 39; Katz 2008). As a part of that prerogative, owners enjoy liberties to derive income from and use their property, and the right to determine when and under which conditions non-owners may do the same.

As such, ownership plays an important role in securing socioeconomic independence (Domènech and Raventós 2008; Jackson 2012). Alex Gourevitch (2014) shows how throughout history, different republican authors have recognised that if people own the means by which they can secure their own livelihood, then they don't have to rely on anyone's capricious will for their most basic needs. Socialist republicans in the nineteenth century recognised this ideal of social independence as valuable in itself (Leipold 2022). It meant that they would not have to submit to a master, but were in control of their own work, the profits they kept and the amount of leisure time afforded to them (Gourevitch 2014). More traditionally, republican authors valued socioeconomic independence for its effects on political independence (Jackson 2012; Casassas and De Wispelaere 2016). People who could secure their own livelihood could speak for themselves, while dependents might parrot the views of their benefactors.

These historical views raise the question of whether ownership can only contribute to non-domination by securing control over one's livelihood. My view is that the historically recognised link between the capability for self-preservation, ownership in the means of production and socioeconomic independence is only *one* instance in which capabilities, resources, ownership, and the non-domination of owners are linked. A more general statement of the link between these factors looks as follows: ownership realises non-domination insofar as it places people in control of resources they rely on to do or be something. This relation obtains for instance when, as James Harrington advocated (1992), an individual owns (the property institution) a plot of land (the resource) that they rely on to make a living (the capability), making them independent with respect to that capability. But it also obtains when the residents of a neighbourhood own (the property institution) their local swimming pool (the resource), and are therefore in control of whether they can swim close to their home (the capability). In both cases, a degree of non-domination is realised, but the arrangement in the first case is more important because it helps to realise *basic* non-domination. It places people in control of the resources they require to withstand arbitrary power. There is a strong argument, I posit, in favour of ownership institutions that contribute to this minimal social standard.

Generalising from this, we can say that ownership institutions realise basic non-domination if they satisfy two criteria. First, they must promote the use and production of resources in such a way that owners can rely on these resources for their basic capabilities and functionings. I call this the *basic capability* criterion. Second, ownership institutions must place the people who rely on resources for their basic capabilities equally in control of how those resources may be used. That is, people who rely on resources in this way must have an equal opportunity to influence decisions about how the resource may be used. This *control* criterion, as I shall call it, explains who the constituents of an ownership regime should be and, in the case of multiple constituents, how they ought to organise power within their ownership regime. Combined, the criteria ensure not only that people gain the capabilities and functionings needed to withstand power asymmetries, but also that people are in control of the decisions that might affect these basic capabilities. The criteria thereby give specific content to the idea of socioeconomic independence that has been so central in republican thought. As I see it, having a minimally acceptable degree of resource-based independence requires people to be in control of those resources, where a lack of control would leave them unable to withstand subjection to arbitrary power.

An example of a group ownership arrangement that fits the two criteria is a shared fishery, where the people who rely on the resource for their daily income are in charge of the rules relating to fishing spots, times, gear, and other relevant use rules, and are thus able to manage the fishery sustainably and efficiently. Under these circumstances, their livelihood is neither subject to the arbitrary will of a superior, nor is it threatened by overexploitation or underuse of the resource. Their livelihood is secure and they are the ones who secure it, and this is (part of what) secures their status as an equal among all persons in their society.

In articulating the idea of minimal resource-based independence in this way, I attempt to modify traditional republican approaches to this topic in two ways. First, my framework broadens the range of capabilities and resources comprehended in resource-based independence. The historical focus in the republican literature on socioeconomic independence is on the capacity for self-preservation, and on how control over means of production can secure that. Thus, there is a venerable tradition of arguments in favour of land ownership, allowing wealthy land owners and the independent peasantry to satisfy their basic needs (Jackson 2012).

These arguments subsisted during and after the Industrial Revolution, when, in response to the domination labourers suffered under capitalism, republican agrarian reformers advocated a return to the independence of small free-holders (Gourevitch 2014, 94). Socialist republicans in that era, by contrast, argued in favour of collective ownership over the means of production, but here too the critique was directed at a property system that did not allow everyone to obtain their livelihood, and therefore means of *subsistence,* independently (Leipold 2022; on socialism, see also Shoikedbrod 2022, in this volume).

By contrast, the two criteria I have set out above allow for a concern with capabilities beyond those required for subsistence, and therefore also beyond the resources needed for that. They also include, for example, the capability to obtain non-biased information with which people can orient themselves in the world in a basic way, and the information resources that people require access to for that capability. It matters for people's basic non-domination who owns such information resources, and who therefore decides on their content, conditions for access, and so on. Subsistence capabilities are, after all, only part of what it takes to reasonably be able to withstand alien subjection. Other capabilities contribute to this aim as well, and they may require ownership over different sorts of resources than have often been the focus in the republican literature.

Second, my framework is open on the question of who should be owners: individuals, private groups or states. Prior to socialist understandings of republicanism, republicans generally defended *individual* ownership of means of production, mainly land (Gourevitch 2014). This tradition is largely continued today, as many contemporary authors defend a basic income for individual citizens to secure their socioeconomic independence (Domènech and Raventós 2008; Pettit 2008; Lovett 2009; Taylor 2013; Casassas and De Wispelaere 2016). With the recovery of socialist republican perspectives, however, and a renewed interest in justice in production in political philosophy, we see more and more defences of collective worker control over the means of production (see on this, e.g., Hsieh 2005; González-Ricoy 2014; Anderson 2015; Gourevitch 2016; Breen 2017; Muldoon 2019; O'Shea 2019; see also Christiano 2022 in this volume). The present essay aims to add to that literature, and explain with respect to an array of resources how group ownership can help to realise basic non-domination.

Indeed, there are no reasons internal to republican thought that wed it only to individual ownership. Two misconceptions might convince one otherwise, however. First, it might be thought that the republican opposition to dependence implies a commitment to complete self-sufficiency (see, e.g., Friedman 2008). Harrington may evoke just such an idea by claiming that 'the man that cannot live upon his own must be a servant; but that can live upon his own may be a free man' (1992,

269). To achieve such self-reliance, individuals have to own the resources they rely on individually, and not depend on the cooperation of any fellow-owners. However, self-sufficiency is neither a realistic goal, nor one that is required for non-domination. People must constantly rely on others to help them, to refrain from harming them, or generally to engage in a complex web of interactions that makes all sorts of activities possible. They nevertheless enjoy non-domination if their interactions are governed by rules over which they have an equal say. They are then independent in the sense of not depending on another agent's arbitrary will, not in the sense of depending only on themselves. And it is only this type of independence that is required to affirm people's equal status as practical reasoners.

Second, one might think that individual ownership can better protect individuals from in-group domination. It could be argued, for example, that it's better to give a basic income to an individual woman, than to give it to the household she belongs to. This is because in the latter case, there is a risk that her access to the income depends on the goodwill of her more powerful male family members. More generally, it seems that group property comes with the risk of creating dependencies within that group, a risk that can be avoided by placing individuals in control of the resources they need. Note, however, that I have not argued that all forms of group ownership are acceptable from a republican point of view. To the contrary, the control criterion states that such ownership regimes must be internally democratic. Power must be held equally by all the group members. It may be difficult to make sure that groups are organised in this way, but it is certainly not a conceptual impossibility. What is more, I shall show in Sections 4 and 5 that there are circumstances in which group ownership is even *preferable* to individual ownership, because it can better satisfy the basic capability criterion.

In sum, republicans should not just prize individual ownership in the means of production. Any ownership institution that satisfies the basic capability and the control criterion, helps to realise basic non-domination. This includes, as I shall now demonstrate, group ownership institutions.

3 Sharing in Common

I will now outline a conception of group ownership that can satisfy the two criteria for non-domination. I will refer to this conception as *sharing in common*. It denotes an arrangement in which a private group of persons decides democratically how an object may be used, both internally by all the member-owners, and externally by non-owners. Use is a capacious term here, meant to cover changing an object, maintaining it, deriving an income from it, and so on. Any individual rights with respect to that object are, then, authorised, defined and subject to change by the group's democratic decisions. The same goes for individual obligations; these are also democratically determined and may concern, for example, the maintenance tasks that member-owners have to perform. This collective control over individual rights and obligations makes group ownership as sharing in common irreducible to individual property rights.

Sharing in common differs from several other types of sharing. It is different, first, from an *open access regime* as the concept has been defined in the literature on natural resources (Eggertsson 2003). Such regimes typically have no regulation of use. Everyone is allowed to use the resource at their own discretion. In that minimal sense they do share it, but there is no structure for binding collective decision-making in place. The high seas may qualify as an example. Group ownership as sharing in common is also different from *voluntarist sharing*. This type of sharing is based on the willingness of an owner to allow non-owners to make use of their property. This can occur on a highly informal level, as when I lend you my book, or in more structured environments typical of collaborative consumption. Here individuals share their cars, couches, and other property with strangers, but in a way that is governed by norms that apply to and are sometimes also created by the entire community of sharers (Benkler 2004). However, these communally defined norms have no fundamental bearing on individual rights to use the pooled property. The individual owners who make their property available to others can at any time withdraw with no change to their property rights. This makes voluntarist sharing different from sharing in common, where the group determines what individual use rights are. Finally, sharing in common is different from *hierarchical* sharing arrangements, where, although multiple people can make use of an object, they are not equal in their power to decide how the resource may be used.

Group ownership understood as sharing in common is an ideal type, that is approached by many actually existing sharing arrangements. In what follows I shall briefly discuss two such arrangements, namely common property regimes (CPRs) in natural resources and knowledge commons. I will explain for both arrangements whether they can (1) promote ways of using and producing resources, that will allow people to rely on these resources for their basic capabilities (the basic capability criterion) and (2) place the people who rely on a resource for that reason, in control of what may be done with that resource (the control criterion). The discussion is to some extent hypothetical, sketching the possibilities that these types of sharing may offer, if they could resemble the idea of sharing in common more.

In focusing on these cases, I aim to move the discussion on shared control of resources away from the arena in which it is usually addressed in the republican literature, namely the literature on workplace democracy. It is certainly worthwhile to discuss whether worker-governed corporations can help to realise basic capabilities and the right type of control, but the danger of focusing too much on this question is that the more general discussion on group ownership is inhibited. As long as researchers only investigate the value (or lack thereof) of collective control over one type of resource or in one area of life, it will remain unclear whether such control could be of value in other areas as well.

4 Common Property Regimes in Natural Resources

The first illustration of how sharing in common works in practice comes from CPRs in natural resources. These are property arrangements in which a bounded group of interdependent users of a resource manage that resource themselves by collectively setting up use-rules and monitoring compliance with those rules. The term was coined by Elinor Ostrom in her ground-breaking studies on governance institutions for shared natural and agricultural resources, including fisheries, crop land, pastures, forests, irrigation systems and water basins (Ostrom 1990; 2000). What is shared in these cases is the resource system, not the units appropriated from that system. To illustrate, shepherds may share a pasture together, but once they have – according to collectively determined procedures – obtained fodder from that land, this fodder is usually owned individually (Ostrom 1990, 30).

CPRs resemble sharing in common because individual rights and obligations on resource use, maintenance, and so on are determined collectively by the group. Where they differ is that democratic governance is not part of the definition of a CPR. Though users govern the rules for their resource themselves, they don't always all have an equal say in the creation of these rules. This is not to claim that CPRs *cannot* be democratically organised; some of them certainly are. Rather, the point is that they don't have to be so organised to count as a CPR. The focus in this essay is therefore on the subset of democratic CPRs.

Can CPRs satisfy the basic capability criterion? Different theories predict that CPRs are either incapable of this or that they can only do so in a way that is much less efficient than individual property ('efficiency' refers here to a high conversion rate of resources to basic capabilities). These predictions are based on two main assumptions. First, there is the assumption that the use, production, and maintenance of shared resources is subject to adverse incentives, which will lead to overuse and underinvestment. This was Gareth Hardin's thesis in his famous 'The Tragedy of the Commons' (1968). He argued that when resources are shared, there is no way for individuals to isolate the effects of their decisions. If they restrain themselves in using the resource or contribute to its upkeep, then the created benefits are open for every user to enjoy and will therefore quickly dissipate. Nor is there a way of isolating the harmful effects of overuse or a lack of maintenance to the individual who commits them. Under these circumstances, Hardin assumed, individuals have no incentive to restrict themselves from overusing the resource or to provide the necessary upkeep, a problem which is compounded by their awareness that fellow resource users don't have these incentives either. Hence, the 'rational' thing to do is to maximise one's short-term gains from the resource before its certain destruction. Sharing a resource thus makes it impossible to use it for one's basic capabilities. Why Hardin assumed that this outcome was unavoidable is unclear. Even if one agrees with his view of human motivation, the question remains why resource users cannot come to a mutual agreement about what sort of use they want to allow, and monitor compliance with these rules.

This brings us to the second assumption that underlies the prediction that CPRs fail to satisfy the basic capability criterion. This is the idea that people who share a resource will either be unable to form agreements on use together, or will only be able to do so at high cost. Harold Demsetz (1967) famously defended this thesis, albeit – like Hardin – through theoretical speculation rather than empirical analysis. Demsetz argued that groups sharing a resource will not create use-rules, because the costs of multiple people coming to an agreement outweigh the benefits that can be obtained through it. Monitoring costs also increase with the presence of multiple users. Hence, Demsetz argued that the evolution of property rights always moved in the direction of individual rather than shared property. Individual owners can decide for themselves how they will use their property; they do not have to agree with co-owners on such decisions and therefore face little decision-making costs, let alone monitoring costs. Hardin, too, defended a division of natural resources into individual parcels, though he also saw a role for strong government regulation of resource use (1968). Individual owners can reap the benefits from their forbearance in using their property, as well as from their investments, so that they face no adverse incentives that lead to resource destruction.

If these predictions were correct, then group ownership would either leave people without their basic capabilities, or would only allow a few persons to attain them. However, empirical evidence on CPRs shows that the predictions are misguided. The many examples of long-lasting CPRs that Ostrom (1990) studied show that it is possible for people who heavily depend on a resource for their livelihood to share a natural resource in a durable way, while also obtaining benefits from it. Thus, fishers were able to rely on a sustainably managed fishery, farmers on a dependable irrigation system, communities on the timber they could obtain from their forests in a durable way, and so on. In the language of my framework, CPRs *can* help people to gain some of their basic capabilities. The CPR members in the case studies could all gain and be assured of the future attainment of the capability to be nourished, sheltered, and other capabilities that require a dependable income. The resource users could and did come together to make collective decisions about what use they allowed, and they devised cost-effective ways of monitoring use (Ostrom 1990).

In fact, CPRs are not only viable, but sometimes *more efficient* institutions for securing basic capabilities, compared to individual property regimes. Under certain circumstances, sharing can lead to a higher conversion rate of resources to basic capabilities than can be achieved under individual ownership. In particular, R.M. Netting (1976) argued that group ownership of natural resources is more efficient than division into individual property when the value of per-unit production of a resource, the frequency and dependability of the yield, and/or the possibility of improvement of a resource are low. Sharing resources then functions as an insurance mechanism. Rather than relying on one small plot of land with a not very dependable yield, for example, farmers can work together and work a bigger plot of land. In this way, they spread the risk of relying on it (Netting 1976; Ellickson 1993; Smith 2002; De Moor 2015). They can then depend on at least a part of that land yielding sufficient produce. Group ownership is also a more efficient strategy than individual property when the area required for effective use, or the size of the group needed to make capital investments is large. Under these circumstances, sharing natural resources enables users to benefit from economies of scale (Netting 1976; Ellickson 1993), both through sharing capital and through sharing the benefits of their labour.

To be sure, some of these efficiency benefits can also be realised in a hierarchically organised firm. Capital and labour are then also pooled. The problem from my republican point of view, however, is that hierarchical organisations don't satisfy the *control criterion* for basic non-domination. Members of such organisations are not equally in control of the resources they rely on. CPRs, however, can satisfy this criterion.

What is more, research suggests that the success of CPR members to gain basic capabilities is not hindered when they use democratic collective decision-making procedures. In fact, Ostrom argued that the success of long-enduring CPRs is partly due to the fact that these regimes include most resource users in collective decision-making processes (Ostrom 1990, 90). This finding is corroborated by other case studies and reviews of the literature (Ribot 2008; Cox, Arnold, and Tomás 2010; De Moor 2015). Researchers have suggested different reasons for why it's beneficial that people govern the resources they rely on themselves. To begin with, users have a great degree of expertise on a resource, which they make use of when devising their usage and maintenance rules (Ostrom 1990, 20). Moreover, by including everyone in their decision-making processes, CPR members are able to make use of each other's different specialised knowledge (Agarwal 2001), which can lead to better use rules. In addition, users also perceive rules they make themselves as more legitimate than rules imposed by an external party, making compliance with these rules more likely (Dietz, Ostrom, and Stern 2003).

5 Knowledge Commons

Knowledge commons are another example of arrangements that approach the idea of sharing in common. The concept of knowledge commons refers to the institutionalised sharing and co-production of information resources in bounded or unbounded groups, according to social or formal norms (Frischmann, Madison, and Strandburg 2014a). I use the term information resources loosely, to refer to things like news articles, encyclopaedias, software, scientific discoveries, technological innovations, theories, ideas, and datasets. These commons can either be open for everyone or only accessible to a bounded group of users. As an example of an open type of common, one can think of Linux: an open-source operating system that everyone may use, obtain source code from, and contribute to for free. Another example is the digital encyclopaedia Wikipedia. Patent pools, in which researchers and innovators share their findings with a select group of others, are an example of closed knowledge commons. Here I focus only on the open types.

Work on the knowledge commons has so far mainly focused on shared access to information, paying less attention to the rules under which individuals jointly use and produce information (see, e.g., the contributions in Frischmann, Madison, and Strandburg 2014b). Though it is recognised that norms are in place and are necessary, it is not yet clear whether knowledge commons have a unified way of creating those norms, and whether they practice democratic decision-making or not. It is unclear, in other words, whether and to what extent knowledge commons satisfy the control criterion for basic non-domination. However, the governance mechanism characteristic of Wikipedia shows that there certainly is room for some kind of equal collective decision-making. Articles on Wikipedia may be edited by everyone, giving users of the encyclopaedia first-order control over content. More significantly, users/editors may also propose, discuss, and adopt the second-order norms that guide content production as well as the general aim of Wikipedia. These proposals are not voted on, but are adopted by consensus. Everyone can state their reasons for why a certain proposal ought to be adopted or not and suggest amendments.[3] Wikipedia and similar projects can therefore be said to approach the idea of sharing in common, at least on paper.[4]

While there is a rich and rigorous literature on CPRs in natural resources, research on knowledge commons is still at a relatively early stage of development, and includes many pioneering papers about the promise of the Internet, which are only recently being supplemented by rigorous case studies (Frischmann, Madison, and Strandburg 2014a). What is well established, however, is that evidence on knowledge commons challenges an influential view in theories on knowledge production (Madison, Frischmann, and Strandburg 2010; Hess 2012). This view holds that knowledge, as a public good, is subject to provision dilemmas.

It is difficult to exclude people from knowledge, and the use of knowledge does not detract from its quality (Hess and Ostrom 2007). Because of these features, the standard argument continues, it's unattractive for private persons to produce knowledge. They would have to invest in something that they could not reap the profits from. Hence, the only two solutions to this problem are – according to this dominant view – to either ensure through intellectual property law that private producers can exclude users from their products and thus reap the benefit of what they create, or to have governments produce knowledge themselves or pay for its production. The first solution is clearly opposed to sharing, while the second allows for something like a public domain of information only when it is publicly funded. Neither recognises a conception of private persons producing and sharing information among themselves. If correct, then the standard view would imply that people cannot rely on shared information resources for their basic capabilities.

However, it turns out that the standard narrative is too pessimistic in evaluating people's incentives to produce knowledge. Projects like Linux and Wikipedia show that people have many reasons to contribute to the production and dissemination of information. They find it interesting, seek a creative outlet or want to contribute to a larger project (Benkler and Nissenbaum 2006). Volunteers have the opportunity to contribute because the work is divided into small tasks that do not take too much time and are therefore not too costly (ibid.). Together, they can achieve something that no individual could do on their own. Yet it is doubtful that volunteers would put in the same effort for information resources that are not made freely accessible.

There are reasons to be optimistic, then, about the potential of knowledge commons to satisfy the basic capability criterion. Examples such as Wikipedia show that it is possible to create and maintain a shared information resource that people can rely on for their basic capabilities. I am not arguing that knowledge commons already do satisfy this requirement (which I am not in a position to judge). Rather, we need to recognise their potential, especially if they are also democratically governed. As noted above, having access to information is crucial for a person's ability to secure themselves against subjection to an arbitrary will. But how do you ensure that information is not biased, not infiltrated by private interests, or even politically coloured? How do you ensure that the information you need to orient yourself freely in the world is also created with that purpose in mind? Democratic open knowledge commons, in which producers and users are the same persons, would try to achieve this by placing control over information production squarely with the people who rely on it. It would be through their eternal vigilance, so to speak, that the quality of information would be assured. In other words, democratic open knowledge commons place people in control of the preconditions of their own empowerment. By sharing knowledge resources in common, an important component of basic non-domination is realised.

6 Conclusion

This essay aimed to explain when and how group ownership can help realise basic non-domination. For this, ownership institutions must promote the use and production of resources in such a way that people can rely on them to attain their basic capabilities. This in turn is required to be reasonably able to withstand subjection to an arbitrary will. But that is not enough; to realise basic non-domination, ownership institutions must also place people in control of decisions concerning the resources they rely on. Group ownership, understood as sharing in common, can satisfy both criteria. Thus, it places people in charge of their own empowerment. Group ownership therefore has an important role to play in policy as well as theory, where it deserves more attention than it has received until now.

Acknowledgements

For their many helpful questions and comments, I would like to thank Huub Brouwer, Michael Bennett, Rutger Claassen, Dorothea Gädeke, Colin Hickey, Emma Saunders-Hastings, and Dick Timmer.

Notes

1 This is not the only understanding of arbitrary power that has been defended in the republican literature. For discussions of alternative understandings, see, e.g., Richardson (2003, chap. 3); Lovett (2010, chap. 4; and Arnold and Harris (2017).
2 On the concepts of capabilities and functionings, see, e.g., Robeyns (2016).
3 See: https://en.wikipedia.org/wiki/Wikipedia:How_to_contribute_to_Wikipedia_guidance; https://en.wikipedia.org/wiki/Wikipedia:Centralized_discussion; https://en.wikipedia.org/wiki/Wikipedia:Consensus.
4 One might agree with that assessment, without also wanting to claim that Wikipedia is based on any form of *ownership*. Yochai Benkler (2014), for example, explicitly pits knowledge commons against the concept of property. Two things are worth noting in response. First, Benkler sees exclusion from and asymmetric control over resources as the central features of property. Yet that is only one conception of property, and one that has been subjected to important criticisms (see, e.g., Katz 2008). On the perspective I adopt, property refers simply to a system of rights and obligations with respect to objects, and ownership refers to control over how things may be used (Katz 2020). This understanding is much more amenable to including knowledge commons as property institutions. Secondly, even if knowledge commons cannot be conceptualised as a traditional form of ownership, they can still be said to approach the idea of sharing in common, that is, a sharing arrangement in which the collective decisions

of the participants determine the rules under which a good is shared. My point about the link between sharing in common and non-domination would therefore still stand.

References

Agarwal, Bina. 2001. 'Participatory Exclusions, Community Forestry, and Gender: An Analysis for South Asia and a Conceptual Framework.' *World Development* 29 (10): 1623–48.

Anderson, Elizabeth. 2015. 'Equality and Freedom in the Workplace: Recovering Republican Insights.' *Social Philosophy and Policy* 31 (2): 48–69.

Arnold, Samuel, and John R. Harris. 2017. 'What Is Arbitrary Power?' *Journal of Political Power* 10 (1): 55–70.

Benkler, Yochai. 2004. 'Sharing Nicely: On Shareable Goods and the Emergence of Sharing as a Modality of Economic Production.' *The Yale Law Journal* 114 (2): 273–358.

———. 2014. 'Between Spanish Huertas and the Open Road: A Tale of Two Commons?' In *Governing Knowledge Commons*, edited by Brett M. Frischmann, Michael J. Madison, and Katherine Jo Strandburg, 69–98. Oxford: Oxford University Press.

Benkler, Yochai, and Helen Nissenbaum. 2006. 'Commons-Based Peer Production and Virtue.' *Journal of Political Philosophy* 14 (4): 394–419.

Bohman, James. 2005. 'The Democratic Minimum: Is Democracy a Means to Global Justice?' *Ethics & International Affairs* 19 (1): 101–16.

Breen, Keith. 2017. 'Non-Domination, Workplace Republicanism, and the Justification of Worker Voice and Control.' *International Journal of Comparative Labour Law and Industrial Relations* 33 (3): 419–40.

Casassas, David, and Jurgen De Wispelaere. 2016. 'Republicanism and the Political Economy of Democracy.' *European Journal of Social Theory* 19 (2): 283–300.

Christiano, Thomas. 2022. 'Why Does Worker Participation Matter? Three Considerations in Favor of Worker Participation in Corporate Governance.' In *Wealth and Power: Philosophical Perspectives*, edited by Michael Bennett, Huub Brouwer, and Rutger Claassen. London: Routledge.

Cox, Michael, Gwen Arnold, and Sergio Villamayor Tomás. 2010. 'A Review of Design Principles for Community-Based Natural Resource Management.' *Ecology and Society* 15 (4): 38–57.

De Moor, Tine. 2015. *The Dilemma of the Commoners: Understanding the Use of Common-Pool Resources in Long-Term Perspective*. Cambridge: Cambridge University Press.

Demsetz, Harold. 1967. 'Toward a Theory of Property Rights.' *The American Economic Review* 57 (2): 347–59.

Dietz, Thomas, Elinor Ostrom, and Paul Stern. 2003. 'The Struggle to Govern the Commons.' *Science* 302 (5652): 1907–12.

Domènech, Antoni, and Daniel Raventós. 2008. 'Property and Republican Freedom: An Institutional Approach to Basic Income.' *Basic Income Studies* 2 (2): 1–8.

Eggertsson, Thráinn. 2003. 'Open Access versus Common Property.' In *Property Rights: Cooperation, Conflict, and Law*, edited by Terry Lee Anderson and Fred S. McChesney, 73–89. Princeton: Princeton University Press.

Ellickson, Robert C. 1993. 'Property in Land.' *The Yale Law Journal* 102 (6): 1315–400.
Forst, Rainer. 2001. 'Towards a Critical Theory of Transnational Justice.' *Metaphilosophy* 32 (1–2): 160–79.
———. 2013. 'A Kantian Republican Conception of Justice as Nondomination.' In *Republican Democracy: Liberty, Law and Politics*, edited by Andreas Niederberger and Philipp Schink, 154–68. Edinburgh: Edinburgh University Press.
Friedman, Marilyn. 2008. 'Pettit's Civic Republicanism and Male Domination.' In *Republicanism and Political Theory*, edited by Cécile Laborde and John W. Maynor, 246–68. Malden, MA: Blackwell.
Frischmann, Brett M., Michael J. Madison, and Katherine Jo Strandburg. 2014a. 'Governing Knowledge Commons.' In *Governing Knowledge Commons*, edited by Brett M. Frischmann, Michael J. Madison, and Katherine Jo Strandburg, 1–43. Oxford: Oxford University Press.
———, eds. 2014b. *Governing Knowledge Commons*. Oxford: Oxford University Press.
Gädeke, Dorothea. 2020. 'From Neo-Republicanism to Critical Republicanism.' In *Radical Republicanism: Recovering the Tradition's Popular Heritage*, edited by Bruno Leipold, Karma Nabulsi, and Stuart White, 23–46. Oxford: Oxford University Press.
González-Ricoy, Iñigo. 2014. 'The Republican Case for Workplace Democracy.' *Social Theory and Practice* 40 (2): 232–54.
Gourevitch, Alex. 2013. 'Labor Republicanism and the Transformation of Work.' *Political Theory* 41 (4): 591–617.
———. 2014. *From Slavery to the Cooperative Commonwealth: Labor and Republican Liberty in the Nineteenth Century*. Cambridge: Cambridge University Press.
———. 2016. 'The Limits of a Basic Income: Means and Ends of Workplace Democracy.' *Basic Income Studies* 11 (1): 17–28.
Hardin, Gareth. 1968. 'The Tragedy of the Commons.' *Science* 162 (3859): 1243–48.
Harrington, James. 1992. *The Commonwealth of Oceana and A System of Politics*, edited by J. G. A. Pocock. Cambridge: Cambridge University Press.
Hess, Charlotte. 2012. 'The Unfolding of the Knowledge Commons.' *St. Anthony's International Review* 8 (1): 13–24.
Hess, Charlotte, and Elinor Ostrom. 2007. 'Introduction: An Overview of the Knowledge Commons.' In *Understanding Knowledge as a Commons: From Theory to Practice*, 3–26. Cambridge, MA: The MIT Press.
Hsieh, Nien-hê. 2005. 'Rawlsian Justice and Workplace Republicanism.' *Social Theory and Practice* 31 (1): 115–42.
Jackson, Ben. 2012. 'Property-Owning Democracy: A Short History.' In *Property-Owning Democracy: Rawls and Beyond*, edited by Martin O'Neill and Thad Williamson, 33–52. Malden, MA: Blackwell.
Katz, Larissa. 2008. 'Exclusion and Exclusivity in Property Law.' *University of Toronto Law Journal* 58 (3): 275–315.
———. 2020. 'Property Law.' In *The Cambridge Companion to the Philosophy of Law*, edited by John Tasioulas, 371–88. Cambridge: Cambridge University Press.

Kimpell, Jessica. 2022. 'What About Ethos? Republican Institutions, Oligarchic Democracy and Norms of Political Equality.' In *Wealth and Power: Philosophical Perspectives*, edited by Michael Bennett, Huub Brouwer, and Rutger Claassen. London: Routledge.

Laborde, Cécile. 2010. 'Republicanism and Global Justice: A Sketch.' *European Journal of Political Theory* 9 (1): 48–69.

Leipold, Bruno. 2022. 'Chains and Invisible Threads: Liberty and Domination in Marx's Account of Wage-Slavery.' In *Rethinking Liberty before Liberalism*, edited by Annelien de Dijn and Hannah Dawson, 194–214. Cambridge: Cambridge University Press.

List, Christian, and Laura Valentini. 2016. 'Freedom as Independence.' *Ethics* 126 (4): 1043–74.

Lovett, Frank. 2009. 'Domination and Distributive Justice.' *The Journal of Politics* 71 (3): 817–30.

———. 2010. *A General Theory of Domination and Justice*. New York, NY: Oxford University Press.

Madison, Michael J., Brett M. Frischmann, and Katherine Jo Strandburg. 2010. 'Constructing Commons in the Cultural Environment.' *Cornell Law Review* 95 (4): 657–709.

McCormick, John P. 2006. 'Contain the Wealthy and Patrol the Magistrates: Restoring Elite Accountability to Popular Government.' *American Political Science Review* 100 (2): 147–63. https://doi.org/10.1017/S0003055406062071.

Muldoon, James. 2019. 'A Socialist Republican Theory of Freedom and Government.' *European Journal of Political Theory*, 1–25.

Netting, Robert M. 1976. 'What Alpine Peasants Have in Common: Observations on Communal Tenure in a Swiss Village.' *Human Ecology* 4 (2): 135–46.

O'Shea, Tom. 2019. 'Socialist Republicanism.' *Political Theory* 48 (5): 548–72.

Ostrom, Elinor. 1990. *Governing the Commons: The Evolution of Institutions for Collective Action*. Cambridge: Cambridge University Press.

———. 2000. 'Private and Common Property Rights.' In *Encyclopedia of Law and Economics*, edited by Boudewijn Bouckaert and Gerrit de Geest, 332–79. Cheltenham, UK/Northampton, MA: Edward Elgar.

Pettit, Philip. 1996. 'Freedom as Antipower.' *Ethics* 106 (3): 576–604.

———. 1997. *Republicanism: A Theory of Freedom and Government*. Oxford: Oxford University Press.

———. 2002. 'Keeping Republican Freedom Simple: On a Difference with Quentin Skinner.' *Political Theory* 30 (3): 339–56.

———. 2007. 'Free Persons and Free Choices.' *History of Political Thought* 28 (4): 709–18.

———. 2008. 'A Republican Right to Basic Income?' *Basic Income Studies* 2 (2): 1–8.

———. 2012. *On the People's Terms: A Republican Theory and Model of Democracy*. Cambridge: Cambridge University Press.

Ribot, Jesse C. 2008. 'Building Local Democracy through Natural Resource Interventions: An Environmentalist's Responsibility.' *Policy Brief*. World Resources Institute.

Richardson, Henry S. 2003. *Democratic Autonomy: Public Reasoning about the Ends of Policy*. Oxford Political Theory. Oxford: Oxford University Press.

Robeyns, Ingrid. 2016. 'Capabilitarianism.' *Journal of Human Development and Capabilities* 17 (3): 397–414.

Shoikedbrod, Igor. 2022. 'Private Wealth and Political Domination: A Marxian Approach.' In *Wealth and Power: Philosophical Perspectives*, edited by Michael Bennett, Huub Brouwer, and Rutger Claassen. London: Routledge.

Smith, Henry E. 2002. 'Exclusion versus Governance: Two Strategies for Delineating Property Rights.' *The Journal of Legal Studies* 31 (2): S453–S487.

Taylor, Robert S. 2013. 'Market Freedom as Antipower.' *The American Political Science Review* 107 (3): 593–602.

Waldron, Jeremy. 1988. *The Right to Private Property*. Oxford: Clarendon Press.

PART III
Wealth and Democratic Institutions

12 Hidden in Plain Sight

How Lobby Organisations Undermine Democracy

Phil Parvin

What role, if any, should lobbyists play in a democracy? More specifically, how much power should unelected individuals and organisations have to influence the course of politics in democratic states? The question is crucial and urgent: the story we are used to telling ourselves about democracy is simplistic and untrue. According to that story, power is held by citizens who voluntarily entrust it to professional representatives who wield it on their behalf through institutions bound by constitutional rules which hold them in check. In reality, vast power is held by unelected organisations which exist beyond the scope of democratic checks and balances and scrutiny. Democratic institutions were primarily designed to scrutinise and regulate the exercise of a certain kind of power: power which is unitary, legitimated through democratic mechanisms like the vote, and exercised by elected politicians. They were not designed to police the exercise of power which is disaggregated across numerous majoritarian and non-majoritarian institutions, not legitimated by votes, and not exercised by politicians. They were not designed to curb the kind of power held by unelected organisations that can, over the long term, warp our democratic norms in ways which concentrate power and influence among the wealthy, structurally entrench social and economic inequalities, and stifle opposition.

But this is what has happened in democracies across the world. If we adopt Chari and Kritzinger's standard definition of a lobbying organisation, 'whether motivated by economic, professional, or public concerns, as 'any group, or set of actors, that has common interests and seeks to influence the policy making process in such a way as their interests are reflected in public policy outcomes,' we can see just how widespread the practice is (Chari et al. 2019, 3). There has been an explosion in the number and influence of lobby groups in the UK and elsewhere over the past half-century, and a concurrent explosion in the amount that these organisations spend on influencing decision-makers. In 2002, Google spent less than $50,000 on lobbying Washington. 15 years later, in 2017, they spent $18 million, more than any other organisation in the world. In 2018, they spent $21 million lobbying Washington, and a further

DOI: 10.4324/9781003173632-15

€6 million lobbying EU institutions. Similar rises are visible across all sectors, across a diverse and growing range of issues, from energy, to healthcare, to financial and technology regulation, and beyond. In the decade from 2010 to 2020, organisations in the USA spent in excess of $37 billion dollars on lobbying Congress and federal agencies (OpenSecrets.org 2021). Organisations representing corporate interests account for the vast majority of this figure. In 2015, organisations representing business interests in the USA spent 34 times as much on lobbying as labour unions and public interest groups *combined* (Drutman 2015). Between 2010 and 2020, the US Chamber of Commerce alone spent $1 billion lobbying for business interests, and in 2019, the ten biggest spenders on lobbying in the USA – all of whom represent private sector interests – spent over $94 million in a *single three month period*. These figures are in addition to the lobbying that takes place at the level of state legislatures and even county level.

Companies spend so much on lobbying because it *works*. Lobby groups which represent elite interests in particular are overwhelmingly successful in securing change. This isn't just because they can throw more money at an issue, although that is a factor. It is because the lobbying community so strongly reflects elite interests (Baumgartner et al. 2009). Lobby groups are extremely influential and are capable of wielding considerable power to change the course of policy debates or, just as important, to halt policy change where change would be unwelcome. But the lobbying community is overwhelmingly dominated by groups which represent the concerns of social and economic elites: it does not reflect average citizens' concerns. A recent survey of US citizens, for example, revealed that the issues they cared most about were crime, tax, and foreign aid. The vast majority of federal lobbying activity is not in these areas, however, but rather in technology and energy (which each scored very low among citizens' interests) and in foreign trade, banking, and finance – none of which figured among citizens' interests at all (Baumgartner et al. 2009). The fact that lobbyists are central to the democratic system and wield significant power *and* that the lobbying community is dominated by groups which lobby on issues which are important to wealthy elites (but not to the majority of citizens) means that these groups have a significant advantage in securing favourable policy outcomes for elites, and ensuring that the concerns of non-elites are side-lined. The power wielded by lobbyists is overwhelmingly directed at entrenching elite interests while the 'economically disadvantaged continue to be under-represented in pressure politics' (Skocpol 2003, 54).

Developing a coherent position on lobbying in a democracy requires us to balance two competing yet reasonable positions. On the one hand, lobbying is positive and necessary. It can enrich democracy. It can increase the representation of diverse interests and provide information and expertise to generalist policy makers (Chari et al. 2019; Parvin 2018a). It is also a consequence of wider commitments to democratic freedoms, as we will see. On the other hand, lobbying poses an urgent threat to democracy: it entrenches social, economic, and political inequalities, and enables well-resourced organisations and individuals to leverage their wealth to skew the political agenda towards their own interests at the expense of others' (Cave and Rowell 2014; Grant 2018). The case for or against lobbying is therefore not straightforward. However, I suggest that that while lobbying is in theory an important part of democracy, its legitimacy is undermined by its *in practice* tendency to entrench, perpetuate, and even worsen social, economic, and democratic inequalities within and between states in ways that are often visible (but difficult to combat), but sometimes also invisible.

I do not present a decisive solution to the challenge posed by lobbying to democratic theory and practice in this chapter. Instead, I make three claims. First, that lobbying is a central aspect of democratic decision-making and of the democratic state, both at the level of principle and practice. Second, that – given its centrality in real world democracy – it needs to be more central in debates among political philosophers about the current challenges facing democracies. And third, that lobbying is a threat to democracy in ways that go far beyond what can be resolved through institutional or legal reform. I suggest that the power of lobby groups resides at least partly in their 'capture' of elite institutions in ways which make reform structurally difficult, but also in their capture of the background norms and ideas implicit in the political culture of modern democratic societies. Drawing on libertarian and egalitarian critiques of lobbying, I suggest that lobby groups have been instrumental in shaping the political culture and norms of democratic states over the long term, shifting the debate but, more importantly, shifting the background social and political values in which these debates take place. The *in practice* concentration of political power among socioeconomic elites delivered by lobbying over the long term via the bending of social norms and values towards their interests raises profound normative, not just empirical, questions about its place in our theories of democracy, of the democratic state and the interconnection between democratic institutions and capitalist markets and suggests the need for radical change.

1 The Democratic State as a Site of Disaggregated Power

The question of what role, if any, lobbyists should play in democratic politics is one of the most urgent questions facing contemporary liberal democratic states. Lobbying is *everywhere*. It is not merely the preserve of big business or corporations: it is practised by a wide range of organisations in the public, private, and third sectors – including NGOs, think tanks, campaign organisations, charities, and trade associations (Parvin 2016). It is also not something done only by 'lobbyists': lawyers, company directors, journalists, corporate media teams, and people working in public relations, advertising, and countless other professions often work explicitly to influence politicians and the political agenda, and to represent sectional interests. It is also not a niche activity. Lobbying has become a central aspect of democratic decision-making in Britain, Europe, and the USA, and the conduct of politics at a global and international level. There are currently over 22,000 registered interest groups and advocacy organisations based in Washington DC, and over 40,000 individuals and groups across the USA who lobby at the state legislature level. According to the EU Transparency Register, 12,500 groups and organisations from the private, public, and charity sectors are currently 'engaged in activities seeking to influence the EU policy and decision making process' (European Commission 2021).

Considerable lobbying activity is also visible at the local and national levels in EU member states, particularly in the major financial and political centres like Berlin, Geneva, and Madrid. Exact numbers are hard to find, however. In Britain, the political consultancy sector employs around 14,000 people and has been valued at over £1.9 billion (Parvin 2007). However, this figure doesn't include the activities of a wide range of professionals working in a diverse range of overlapping areas including public affairs, government relations, policy research, media relations, strategic communications, crisis management, finance, and law. It also doesn't include lobbyists who work *outside* of the private sector in trade associations, think tanks, and so on, or in international organisations who are based outside of the UK, but who seek (and are able) to influence UK policy decisions.

States have afforded lobby groups greater and greater formal access. MPs in the UK may be approached upwards of 100 times a week by lobbyists from a range of organisations and sectors in Britain and beyond, and the government regularly consults outside groups when developing policy (Bache and Flinders 2004; Parvin 2007; 2016). In the USA, think tanks and 'special interest groups' occupy a very influential place in the legislative process through the donations they are able to make to politicians' election campaigns, their networks, and their lobbyists at the national, state, and local levels (Medvetz 2012). States increasingly draw upon the expertise of international NGOs, charities, and voluntary bodies in the formation and implementation of policies concerning aid, trade, human rights, development, and regularly work with professional bodies, intra-governmental organisations, and research institutes on constitutional questions arising out of relations with other nation states and European institutions. Furthermore, states increasingly rely on non-state organisations to *deliver* policy: international organisations and charities do not just lobby the UK government for certain policies over others, they also lobby to implement them, just as private businesses do not simply lobby for increased private provision of public services like border controls and healthcare, but also lobby to be the ones who implement these policies in return for public money.

Taken together, hundreds of millions of dollars a year are spent by organisations of various kinds across the world on influencing policy, gaining access to decision-makers, and raising awareness of issues among legislators, the media, and 'stakeholder groups.' Lobbying is now so ingrained in the majority of democracies around the world, and so central to the core activities of the modern state on the domestic and global stages, that it has forced many political scientists to re-think their understanding of democracy, and of the democratic state, from the ground up (Baumgartner et al. 2009; Bevir 2010; Rhodes 2017).

Political philosophers have not, on the whole, followed suit. In the rapidly growing Anglo-American political theory literature on the problems facing democracy, one issue in particular dominates all others: the disconnect between institutions and practices on the one hand, and the citizens which, in a democratic system, afford them authority, on the other. Democrats of many stripes have argued, and continue to argue, for democratic 'innovations' aimed at better incorporating ordinary citizens into the democratic process (e.g., Fishkin 2018; Fung 2015; Landemore 2020). They have done so in an attempt to address what they take to be the central question of contemporary democratic theory: how to more fully incorporate citizens into the democratic system in order that democracy can discharge its founding responsibility of ensuring legitimacy to institutions and governments, and protecting individual freedom and equality.

The decline of citizen participation, the widespread disaffection with politics characteristic of many democratic states like the UK and the USA, and the wider debilitating effects that these can have on the rate and quality of democratic deliberation are not trivial. Indeed, changing patterns of citizen participation have played an important role in driving the growth and influence of unelected lobby groups: citizens have increasingly rejected traditional forms of political activity like voting, and looked instead to campaign organisations and interest groups to represent them, leading to a rise in the fortunes of unelected groups like Friends of the Earth, Oxfam and Amnesty International, as well as their centrality (Parvin 2018b; Skocpol 2003). But the overwhelming preoccupation among Anglo American democratic theorists on the role of citizens in a democracy, and the specific challenge of how to better incorporate citizens' voices into decision-making, has skewed debates about democracy away from other important issues.

The vast majority of democratic governance in the contemporary era is not conducted by states in conversation with citizens, and was not designed to be. It is conducted by states in conversation with other elite actors who represent sectional interests. Power is 'disaggregated' across numerous majoritarian and non-majoritarian bodies, institutions, agencies, and organisations (Bevir 2010; Rhodes 2017). We might reasonably disagree as to whether this is a good thing. But we should not assume that it represents a *failure* of democracy. The fact that in a representative democracy 'the people' are only one actor among many is by design. Representative democracy is, in Manin's words, a 'mixed' system, in which some decisions are appropriately made by the people (or their representatives), while others are not (2010; see also Landemore 2007). The fundamental question is not how we might ensure greater public control over all the decisions that modern states are required to make, but which decisions should be made by citizens and their representatives, and which should be made by unelected bodies of one kind or another, many of which are explicitly and deliberately insulated from the public will (Urbinati 2006). Constitutional and institutional machinery exists specifically to circumscribe the power of citizens to influence democratic practice: separation of powers, judicial review, and the idea that there should be 'checks and balances' on the activities of governments and legislatures on the one hand, but also of citizens on the other, all exist to delineate the appropriate bounds of the public will, and hold in balance the powers of majoritarian and non-majoritarian institutions. To put it a different way, democrats need to be clear in what circumstances the state must be responsive to the public will, and in what circumstances it should not.

Understanding democracy this way, we can see that focusing on the narrow question of how we include citizens more fully into our democratic system addresses one – but only one – important question. Acknowledging that citizens are only one among many other actors in a democracy by design offers a different perspective on the contemporary democratic predicament than that offered by many political philosophers. Low rates of participation among citizens are not, as so many believe, indicative of a *crisis* of representative democracy. Representative democracies are designed to ensure good governance in a context of widespread political disengagement and political ignorance, and that political power is not concentrated in the hands of particular groups or individuals but distributed appropriately across multiple sites which hold one another in check. The fact that the people are not directly involved in decision-making, that states are disaggregated, and that power is wielded by unelected groups, bodies, and appointees is not in itself a failure to live up to democratic principles so much as an attempt on the part of the system to manage the complexities of the world in which democratic principles are applied. So before we tackle the question of how citizens could be better included in decision-making, we need first to ask what the appropriate limits of citizens' involvement in decision-making should be.

This shift in emphasis better enables us to grasp the trajectory of democratic change in liberal democratic states over the past half-century, and provides a useful perspective from which to analyse whether actually existing states have got the balance right. In the UK, for example, many political decisions are not made by elected representatives, but by non-majoritarian organisations which are not directly accountable to the people (Bevir 2010). The UK affords the unelected House of Lords the power to revise, amend, and delay legislation emanating from the elected House of Commons. Furthermore, Britain, like the USA, increasingly relies on the courts, and judges in particular, to determine the outcome of policy dilemmas by recourse to constitutional law and precedent. Similarly, UK monetary policy is currently set by the Bank of England which, since 1998, has been formally independent of government. Finally, in 2010, the coalition government created the Office of Budgetary Responsibility to provide independent scrutiny and analysis of economic policy.

The Civil Service employs almost half a million public servants who exercise considerable power across the full range of government business at all levels. These powers are expressly designed to be insulated from the public will in order that civil servants can be impartial rather than subject to electoral pressure. Significant powers have also been afforded to regulators and other independent public bodies to help develop policy as well as monitor their delivery. In 2010, the UK coalition government identified 901 'quangos' or 'arm's length bodies' – bodies funded, but not run, by government departments – with responsibility for all kinds of functions across the full range of policy areas (Public Administration Committee 2010).

Meanwhile, many powers once held by the nations of Europe are now held by the institutions of the EU, which are not straightforwardly accountable to the electorates of its member states but which affect many millions of people within and beyond the EU's borders. International politics is conducted by and through a dense network of unelected organisations. Relations between states are mediated by international institutions like the International Monetary Fund, the World Bank, and the United Nations. Development goals are decided and delivered via a global NGO and not-for-profit sector, comprising charities, campaign groups, voluntary bodies, professional organisations and more. There are around 'seventy international bodies that have universal or intercontinental memberships,' most of which are opaque, exist only to those citizens who have heard of them at all as acronyms and 'do not fall within the orbit of democratic politics' (Vibert 2007, 5–6).

Decisions at the local, national, and international levels, then, are made within closed communities of elite actors whose populations include, but are not limited to, state officials, government advisers, and lobbyists from a range of organisations who provide expert advice but who also represent particular interests (Chari et al. 2019; Grant 2018). If the hallmark of a functioning democracy is – as critics like Landemore contend – that the state is directed by the public will, and that decisions are made by politicians in conversation with citizens, we would need to conclude that the UK, the USA and the vast majority of European nation states are not democracies. But again, in framing the debate about the nature and future of democracy as almost entirely about the relationship between citizens and the state, many democratic theorists miss the bigger picture. States are disaggregated, non-monolithic – with power centres spread across different institutions, some of which are appropriately responsive to the public will, others of which are not (Rhodes 2017). And the world beyond the state is populated by organisations of various kinds which have no straightforward democratic mandate conferred by, for example, the vote but which are central to policy-making process and wield significant power within it.

2 The Case for Lobbying

The challenge posed by lobby groups cannot simply be that they are unelected, then: a great many organisations and bodies within and beyond the state are unelected yet exercise great power. Many are explicitly designed to be insulated from public opinion, yet have a considerable range of powers to, for example, alter policy, influence decisions, constrain the actions of elected politicians, enforce regulations and deliver public services. Furthermore, many democratic theorists have written in defence of unelected groups and the role they play in representing citizens' interests, connecting citizens and the state, and fostering citizens' democratic capacity (Knight and Johnson 1998; Putnam 2001). Governance in democratic societies is largely a process of elected and unelected groups of one kind or another engaging with other elected and unelected groups across a web of interconnected institutions, bodies, and organisations. Elected politicians are one – and only one – component of this process.

To grasp the true nature and scale of the challenge posed by lobbying, we need to analyse in more detail the role lobby groups play, and have played, in our democratic culture. The first step in doing *that* is to make lobbying as central to our democratic *theory* as it is to our democratic *practice*. Doing so reveals a fundamental tension. On the one hand, lobbying occupies a central and important role in both the practice *and theory* of democracy. On the other, it poses a significant challenge to them both. Let me state more clearly the positive case first, before explaining in more detail its negative role in the rest of this chapter.

Many democrats have emphasised the need for individuals to be able to affect change through collective action and pressure politics (e.g., Dryzek 2012; Habermas 1996; Young 2002). Many political scientists have emphasised the positive role of interest groups in democratic politics (e.g., Dahl 1989; Fraser 2004; Hirst 1994), and even lobbying's harshest critics acknowledge that the ability of groups and individuals to lobby their elected representatives as well as other organs of the state, is 'central to a healthy democratic system' (Cave and Rowell 2014, 9). Dahl's vision of democracy as a polyarchy comprising multiple sites of power – some elected, some not – in fact looks similar to the picture of the disaggregated state that I sketched in Section 1. In ideal circumstances, disaggregation of power can enrich and deepen democracy, ensuring checks and balances across the system, and warding against undue concentrations of power in any one individual or institution. It may also provide practicable solutions to two democratic challenges: deficits produced by declining citizen participation and by widespread political ignorance. Pluralist like Dahl, for example, have emphasised the potential of unelected groups to plug democratic deficits of the first kind: in a society in which a considerable proportion of the citizen body are either unwilling or unable to exercise their political power through participation, non-state organisations, and bodies of different kinds can exercise it on their behalf, bridging states and citizens and fulfilling an important representative role (Dahl 1989).

Meanwhile, representative democrats and also epistocrats have emphasised the ability of unelected bodies to resolve deficits of the second kind: a lack of the kind of political knowledge that is needed to resolve complex policy dilemmas (Brennan 2016). Democracies need expertise. Politicians are generalists; they cannot possibly be expected to be experts in all the numerous areas of public policy in which they are required to legislate. Some democrats seek to capture this expertise among citizens via democratic innovations and increased opportunities for deliberation (e.g., Fung 2015; Landemore 2020). But an alternative approach is to look to expert organisations to provide this knowledge. Indeed, this approach has the benefit of providing a response to epistemic shortfalls in the citizen population in a way that takes seriously the first deficit: that of declining citizen participation. Good governance requires decision-making to be grounded in facts and experience which, in a democracy, are ideally provided by citizens through their participation. As citizen participation declines, lobby organisations of different kinds can fill (and have filled) the vacuum (Parvin 2018a). Professionals with knowledge and experience in different areas of public policy can therefore provide invaluable information for politicians and, in doing so, improve governance. Lobbyists themselves have often defended their role in providing important information to politicians in this way (Chari et al. 2019; Lessig 2011).

More generally, lobbying by unelected groups seems to flow from more fundamental commitments to the kind of constitutional rights that democrats tend to support. The commitment to liberal freedoms of assembly and speech, which are generally supported by democrats, necessarily combine to permit citizens to join with like-minded others and to collectively seek to influence decision-makers. Furthermore, democratic citizens are broadly assumed to be able to contribute financially to support these groups' ability to influence politicians on their behalf. Citizens are free to join with one another in an attempt to pressure governments to advance their interests, just as they are free to pay a pressure group, trade association, or trade union to do so on their behalf.

The philosophical case for lobbying, then, is that it is protected by wider commitments to rights to, for example, free speech and assembly, and that unelected lobby groups can plug into the disaggregated state, connecting citizens with states (and connecting different parts of the state together) in a way that is important for democratic functioning and representation.

3 Two Critiques? The Problem with Lobbying

Having argued that lobbying is central to democratic practice and, hence, should be central to democratic theory, and having presented a broad philosophical justification for lobbying's place in a democracy, I now suggest why it is such a problem. I do so through the lens of two critiques – one from egalitarianism and one from libertarianism – which are widely seen as very different but in fact stem from the same root: a shared rejection of the practice of real-world capitalism.

The egalitarian critique of lobbying focuses on the threat to social justice posed by organisations who defend private over public interest. Lobbying is, egalitarians say, a practice which enables powerful private interests to skew democratic decision-making away from requiring corporations and other private entities to satisfy their moral obligations to ensure a more just society (by improving the conditions of their workers, for example, or paying a fair share of tax) towards allowing them to merely satisfy their own private interests instead. This is indeed a concern. States in which corporations and corporate lobby organisations have the power to influence policy decisions have, in general, proven themselves less hospitable to reforms grounded in liberal egalitarian claims about redistribution, economic intervention, and the alleviation of inequality through reforms in, for example, labour laws, tax laws, minimum wage legislation, and the provision of welfare than states in which the ability of corporations to influence political decision-making is weakened (e.g., Drutman 2015; Lessig 2011). The fact that business taxes are so low in the USA, that workplace democracy, labour unions and workers' rights are weak, and that large corporations benefit from so many opportunities to insulate their wealth through complex legal and economic mechanisms, cannot be disaggregated from the fact that business corporations in the USA are allowed relatively easy access to elected politicians and are able to influence policy-makers through direct lobbying and the financing of election campaigns (Thomas 2016). Similarly, the fact that in the UK and the EU more generally have stronger labour unions and workers' rights is at least partly due to the fact that lobbying and campaign finance are governed by much stricter rules than in the USA.

The worry for egalitarians is that current institutional, economic, and legal arrangements give disproportionate voice to elite interests over others, and concentrate power in the hands of socioeconomic elites at the expense of everyone else. They are, again, right to be worried. While the disaggregated state might work in theory to provide appropriate checks and balances across the system, it in fact does no such thing: the in-built dominance of organisations representing elite interests both within and beyond the state concentrates power in the hands of these organisations, and makes it easier for them to control the policy-making process. The disaggregated state has the theoretical capacity to ensure political equality, but in practice elites have captured democratic institutions in ways which render them less accessible – and less responsive – to non-elites. The 'revolving door' between the state and the private sector ensures a cross-pollination of people and expertise: corporate lobbyists hired by government as consultants or permanent state officials on the basis of their industry experience, and public officials and former politicians hired or re-hired for their inside knowledge and contacts. Large, well-resourced organisations like the Confederation of British Industry, the Institute of Directors, corporate trade bodies, and industry representatives in the UK, and the Chambers of Commerce, pro-business think tanks, and industry groups in the USA, are able to leverage their powerful insider status, as well as their formidable networks and spending power, to over-populate the various organs of the disaggregated state in ways which enable them to shut down policy change and dominate policy debates, as, for example, large technology companies have done recently in the USA in the debate about data privacy, and as Uber and Lyft (in the USA) and Deliveroo (in the UK) have recently done in debates over employment rights.

Egalitarian liberals tend to see this as an intrinsic problem with market capitalism. But many libertarians and classical liberals are just as concerned about lobbying. For them, lobbying is an inevitable consequence of having an over-powerful state. The more areas of policy the state has control over, and the more power it has in each of these policy areas, the more it will attract vested interests who will try to influence the state in exercising its power in ways which benefit them (Badhwar 2020; Munger and Villarreal-Diaz 2019).

Libertarians believe lobbying is pernicious because it subverts the operation of free markets, for two reasons. The *first* is that it worsens some of the problems that already plague real-life (as opposed to theoretically ideal) capitalism. Existing capitalist states do not have free markets in the way that most libertarians and classical liberals would defend, they operate 'crony capitalism': a system which allows organisations to leverage their economic advantage for political gain (Friedman 2002; Hayek 1944). Under crony capitalism, rich organisations can use their wealth to lobby for laws which help them maintain their own dominance, but which are incompatible with a true free market. Lobbying, therefore, results in government 'playing favourites,' bestowing privileges on 'particular firms or particular industries ... [including, but not limited to] monopoly status, favourable regulations, subsidies, bailouts, loan guarantees, targeted tax breaks, protection from foreign competition, and non-competitive contracts' (Mitchell 2012, 3–4). From the bailout of the banks in the wake of the 2008 financial crisis, to the millions in state aid given to the airline industry and multi-million dollar food and hospitality chains in the wake of the COVID-19 pandemic, governments use tax-payers' money to insulate wealthy corporate interests from risk, while often also insulating them for having to pay tax in those jurisdictions (Shaxson 2011).

It is therefore irrational under crony capitalism for a business to choose not to engage in lobbying; even organisations which might otherwise choose not to engage in it feel compelled to do so, partly because everyone else is benefiting from it (Holcombe 2013). In a society in which the state is directly involved in the economy, profitability over time becomes less dependent on innovation and more dependent on lobbying the state.

> [E]xisting firms, making existing products, over time find decreasing returns to continued investment in plant and equipment. They also find it increasingly difficult to innovate. At some point ... it becomes more profitable ... to use the power of the state to extract resources from others or to protect those existing products from competition ... As a consequence ... firms focus less on new products or better manufacturing and spend their money instead on lobbyists and political influence.
>
> (Munger and Villarreal-Diaz 2019, 340)

Their goal in lobbying, then, is to co-opt the coercive power of the state that already exists in the economy for their own ends, to 'thwart innovation before it happens, to slow down the dynamic processes that animate capitalist development,' and create barriers to competition (Munger and Villarreal-Diaz 2019, 340). This redirection of state powers by powerful vested interests towards the narrow interests of certain industries and/or individual companies is a form of market failure that should worry libertarians *and* egalitarians: wealth is translated into power in ways which stifle market competition, amplify certain voices at the expense of others, and undermine political equality. Governments select the companies and/or industries they favour and leave the ones they don't – the smaller and less connected ones – to the true rigours of market competition. Becoming a favoured company largely depends on establishing strong networks with as wide a range of state bodies and institutions as possible. Becoming an 'insider' organisation – a regular at the policy-making table, a trusted expert organisation – pays dividends, especially in a crisis. During the financial crisis in 2008 and the COVID-19 pandemic in 2020/2021, for example, when decisions needed to be made quickly and information was scarce and fluid, organisations with already-established links with the state disproportionately benefitted (Abramson 2020).

The *second* reason is that interest group pluralism constrains economic efficiency, stifles growth, and leads to bad governance. These concerns were most obviously raised by Mancur Olson in *The Rise and Decline of Nations*, and directly challenged the view that lobby groups enrich democratic governance by providing necessary expertise and experience (1982). In that book, Olson claimed that 'political lobbying adversely affects the economic performance of the state' because lobby groups create competing demands on the state's time and resources (Olson, as cited in Horgos and Zimmerman 2009, 303). Resources that could be spent on facilitating production and industrial growth are instead spent meeting the demands of special interest groups. Governments have to meet with them all, listen to their concerns, and make difficult and often time-consuming decisions about which 'side' wins, who gets what, and when. As a result, governance slows down, congested by competing interests. Time and money is wasted. The state gets *bigger*, in order to deal with the extra work created by the competition of special interests, and also *less powerful*, its ability to make decisions and pursue a vision of society chipped away and undermined by its need to appease a multitude of competing groups. Olsen believed that something like this process accounts for the decline of nations throughout history, where potential greatness is squandered by internal squabbling and fragmentation. Again, we can see this as a problem associated with the rise of the disaggregated state: while such a state has the theoretical capacity to improve governance by balancing the popular will with sources of expertise as well as sectoral interests, in practice it often leads to deadlock, stalemate, and – consequently – watered-down policies which favour the status quo.

So, liberal *egalitarians* criticise lobbying for undermining democracy while *classical* liberals and libertarians criticise it as an inevitable byproduct of democracy. But both are united in understanding lobbying as a negative consequence of broken capitalism. It enables certain organisations, and businesses in particular, to secure favourable treatment from elected governments to stifle market competition and get exemption from laws which apply to everyone else. Furthermore, the need for lobbying grows according to an internal logic of crony capitalism. As more organisations secure their profitability and success through lobbying, it is only rational for more and more organisations to engage in more and more of it. And as more businesses engage in it, the more it is necessary for organisations representing other interests – consumers, workers, etc. – to engage in it too. The imbalances of power characteristic of the contemporary disaggregated state are exacerbated by the internal logic of crony capitalism to expand the role of lobbying and are left untouched by this expansion. Lobbying begets lobbying. The only hope for less powerful organisations to make an impact, is to play the lobbyists at their own game: a game in which elite organisations enjoy an overwhelming structural advantage.

4 The Scale of the Problem: Norm Capture and the Structural Barriers to Reform

How, then, do we lessen the disproportionate power held by lobby groups for elite and corporate interests? While libertarians and egalitarians agree that the cause of the problem is the lived practice of capitalism, they propose different solutions. Classical liberals and libertarians, after all, seek to *minimise* the role of lobbying in democracy by *restricting* the scope of democracy and reducing the size of the state. Egalitarians, on the other hand, generally seek to *expand* the scope of democracy and *increase* the size of the state. Libertarians seek to remove the problem at source, avoiding the need to increase state regulation and rules which serve to stifle the operation of free markets. Egalitarians seek to constrain the activities of lobbyists *and* markets more generally through democratically enacted laws. That is, libertarians and classical liberals see democracy as an *unjust* constraint on markets which enables monopolies to translate wealth into power, while egalitarians see democracy as a *just* constraint on markets which can, if structured correctly, impose limits on the activities of lobbyists and corporate interests, as well as secure greater equality through various state initiatives aimed at redistributing wealth.

For libertarians, the solution is a radical reconfiguration of political institutions and a dramatic reduction in the size and scope of the state. Abolishing as much regulation as possible and ensuring that limited states are kept out of as much of the economy as possible would ensure that lobbyists for corporate interests would become redundant: profitability would no longer depend on securing links with government and the state, and so the need for lobbying and lobbyists would dry up (Badhwar 2020; Mitchell 2012). Corporations would need to stand on their own two-feet: they would know that they would not be bailed out in times of crisis and that their profitability would depend on innovation, not government favouritism (Munger and Villarreal-Diaz 2019).

The solution for egalitarians is actually less radical, as it involves the augmentation of existing democratic institutions (rather than their abolition or replacement) and legislative measures aimed at tightening lobbying rules. Egalitarians believe that passing laws which ensure transparency, limit spending, regulate fairly and firmly, ensure strict penalties for groups which break the rules and impose steeper taxes on corporations with a view to alleviating inequalities and creating a more level playing field would, if done correctly, strike a balance between ensuring the democratic right of all to lobby elected politicians and state bodies on the one hand, and ensuring that lobby groups representing elite interests do not have disproportionate influence on the other.

I do not want to evaluate either approach here. Instead, I want to make a different, deeper point: that both libertarians *and* egalitarians face the same fundamental challenges in resolving the problem. I have written elsewhere of the obstacles which stand in the way of legislative or institutional reform: changes to laws and regulations, as well as institutional reforms, are hampered by the fact that they would first need to pass through institutions and processes which have already been 'captured' by powerful lobby groups (Parvin 2021). In order for change to be actioned, it would need to be agreed by lobby groups who would stand to lose out from the changes. Lobby groups have generally proven unwilling to relinquish any of their power, leading to ineffective regulation as in, for example, the UK 2014 Lobbying Act, or no regulation at all: of all the world's 'major states' (including 'all OECD countries, plus major democracies in Europe, Asia and Latin America') only 17 political systems had lobbying laws in place in 2017, a figure which remains the same today (Chari et al. 2019).

The fact that legislative and institutional reform must be proposed within, and must withstand scrutiny from, democratic institutions can be seen to be a huge obstacle to reform once the nature and scope of those institutions, and their composition, is fully understood. In Section 1,

I described how unelected bodies and organisations are central to policy formation and delivery in contemporary democracies, and wield significant power. In Section 3, I then discussed some of the ways in which this policy making process is dominated by, and disproportionately composed of, organisations which lobby for the interests of wealthy elites. Lobbying is, in the words of Baumgartner et al., a process of 'mobilising bias' that exists within mainstream democratic politics, its institutions, and its discourse (2009). The lobbying community is dominated by large, well-resourced organisations – businesses, think tanks, trade associations, industry groups – which argue for private interests. The structure of the modern state thus works in the favour of those groups who possess the resources and human capital to establish strong networks across the different sources of power and responsibility to be found within it. This is not to say that businesses always get what they want. Environmental groups, consumer groups, and other non-corporate organisations have had some success in shifting the agenda and holding corporations to account, but examples of such are notable because they are rare. Smaller groups representing the concerns of non-elites and minorities are constantly faced with having to push against the weight of the in-built bias in the system in ways that elite lobby groups do not. While it is true that many different organisations and bodies lobby the state, those representing wealthy elites find that they do so more easily than other groups and have greater success in securing or halting policy change (Bartels 2017; Baumgartner et al. 2009).

But the problem is not merely institutional. The deeper problem is that, over the long term, lobby groups representing elite interests have – through their dominance in the lobbying community and in wider processes of policy-making and decision-making – been able to 'capture' the political culture, and to help shape the norms and values of citizens in democratic societies in ways which foreground and entrench elite interests (and the political initiatives necessary to advance them) as mainstream, natural and feasible, and cast the interests of non-elite citizens (and their associated political programmes) as radical, impracticable, and often dangerous.

Social norms are important subjects of analysis for political philosophers. Their importance is most obviously emphasised by theorists working in the Marxist and Hegelian traditions, but they are also central to communitarian, liberal, feminist, and other traditions too. Norms provide the background context in which we understand ourselves and the world. We choose and act and live our lives situated in dense networks of values and ideas which are not always visible, but which provide structure to our lives and to the wider society: through generations of socialisation, individuals absorb the values of the society in which they live, they learn the rules and find their place, and, in doing so, reinforce these values and ensure their survival (Bourdieu 1990; Okin 1989).

Prevailing ideas and established norms also determine the limits of what is possible, both for individuals in their life-choices and also for a society. They determine the limits of what is seen as politically feasible and define which ideas are mainstream and which are radical. In the UK, arguments in favour of universal healthcare, which is free at point of use, are entirely mainstream. In the USA, they are radical. In the USA, arguments in favour of gun ownership are mainstream. In the UK, they are radical. The capacity for a society to change is not constrained merely by formal laws and institutions, but also the imagination of the people and the values which constitute the political culture. Neither an individual nor a society can alter its course unless they or it believe that altering its course is possible.

Activists throughout history have known all too well the stifling energy of widespread assumptions about what is 'true' or 'normal' or 'inevitable' in politics. A central task facing any movement for political change is causing a disruption in the public culture, to encourage people to 'think different,' to step outside of the social and normative context in which they live, and to challenge normalised beliefs and patterns of behaviour. We can see this in the women's movement of the 1960s and 1970s, which sought to reveal that many supposed 'facts' about women and society which were seen at the time as natural (and therefore, immutable) were actually socially constructed (and therefore, changeable) (e.g., Friedan 1963). The result was a dramatic shift in the rights and status of women, but also in the political culture more widely: a situation that was viewed by the political mainstream as 'naturally' or 'obviously' true and correct was revealed by the radical periphery to be untrue. Where change was seen as impossible and unneeded, it became seen as possible and necessary.

Similarly, the civil rights movement succeeded in shifting generations of settled attitudes about the 'natural' or 'inevitable' inferiority of people of colour and expanded people's horizons about what in US society was possible or feasible. The women's movement and the civil rights movement provided a point of perspective from outside the dominant normative structure from which to observe overarching norms and values. They showed that, despite appearances to the contrary, other ways were possible and necessary.

Social norms and values are extremely important, therefore. They have the power to define people, and to constrain or liberate them, by presenting them with the world in which they live and act and choose. Sexist values reified and entrenched through ongoing patterns of behaviour can constrain the lives and the aspirations of women, shape men's attitudes to women, and cultivate in both men and women the 'knowledge' that these 'facts' are unchangeable (Mackinnon 1989). Racist norms can oppress people of colour by holding them in place and teaching them that the place in which they are held is immutable and natural. The radical shifts in political culture ushered in by activists for civil rights and gender equality show that change is possible but that it is difficult, involving sacrifice and bravery and imagination. Change has to begin with a radical claim that seems, in the context of wider entrenched social norms and prevailing values, wrong, impossible, and perhaps nonsensical.

In democracies around the world, including the UK and the USA, lobby groups representing elite interests have not only engaged in the elite capture of state institutions and the broader policy making process, they have also engaged in what I call 'norm capture': they have, over many years, gradually but systematically helped to shape the values and ideals of the political culture in ways which establish elite interests as mainstream and natural and feasible and rule contrary interests off the table as infeasible, inadmissible and dangerous.

They have not done so deliberately, or at least my claim does not rest on the fact that they did. The problem is structural. Arguments which favour elite interests by concentrating wealth and privilege among an ever-diminishing number of high-net-worth individuals, and, by foregrounding the interests of businesses and their owners over workers, become assimilated into the background culture such that their function in entrenching and perpetuating inequality becomes lost. Ideological or partial statements become absorbed into the mainstream culture and reframed as non-ideological and impartial declarations of facts. Language matters, and the language of mainstream political discourse – the way we come to describe and understand political challenges and even identify them – has been shaped at least partly by organisations like the Institute for Economic Affairs and business interests in the UK, and the Heritage Foundation and other conservative think tanks and interest groups in the USA, which have been instrumental in mainstreaming crony capitalist ideology in those countries since the 1980s and establishing it as the de facto natural standard for economic and political success (Medvetz 2012). Organisations which champion elite interests have had particular success in the USA, largely through their ability to leverage the founding mythology of that country (as one grounded in meritocracy, the claim that American markets distribute wealth fairly on the basis of hard work and talent, rather than – as egalitarians argue – unfairly on the basis of luck). Against such a background, but also in the context of demographic shifts put in motion by Thatcherism in the UK, elite groups have been able to establish crony capitalism as a natural consequence of a commitment to freedom and responsibility, in which the wealthy are held to be deserving of their wealth, which was achieved through hard work and talent, and the poor are seen as deserving of their poverty.

In a context in which the norms of crony capitalism have been widely internalised and are taken as given, in which it is widely seen as inevitable that we should prioritise the freedom of businesses to pursue their economic interests, to maximise their profits, and in which the profit motive is seen as a central and reasonable engine of wealth creation and freedom, arguments that question these things, or which suggest that a different way is possible or necessary, are often seen as radical or bizarre, or harmful. Initiatives designed to alleviate inequalities become reframed as expensive insurance schemes, or as disincentives to work, or even as unpatriotic (Thomas 2016). Increases in corporation tax on multibillion dollar companies are criticised for their negative impact on entrepreneurialism and innovation. Companies and their lobbyists meet calls for greater fairness with threats. They will be forced relocate to different countries, they say, or to lay off workers or reduce production. Increasing businesses taxes will, with regret, mean fewer vaccines, fewer cars, more expensive food and medicine and clothes. In the USA, arguments in favour of extending free healthcare provision are met by the argument from insurance companies, private health providers and Republican politicians that doing so would be too costly, too soft on the poor or too un-American. In the USA (and less so in the UK) labour unions are seen as a threat to democracy and economic growth. In the UK and the USA economic success is increasingly measured narrowly in terms of the success of the stock market, even though the majority of stocks and shares are overwhelmingly owned by the wealthiest in society. In 2021, 51% of all directly held stocks in the US stock market were owned by the top 1% by net-worth, while the bottom 50% owned none. The US government's $1.5 trillion injection into the stock market in 2020 represented one of the single largest upward redistributions of wealth from public to private hands in history. Between March 23rd and April 20th 2020, $7 trillion was added to the capital wealth of US stockholders. In the same month, 20.5 million Americans lost their jobs.

The problem is not simply that states like the UK and the USA are, with the help of elite lobby organisations, designing policies and making decisions which satisfy the interests of the wealthy. It is that these trajectories of worsening inequality are considered by so many to be normal, inevitable or immutable. Crucially, they are seen as such by the people who have the most to lose: the poor. Data gathered by political scientists over the past half-century show clearly how citizens of low socioeconomic status act and form political preferences in response to wider social norms which harm their wider interests (e.g., Achen and Bartels 2017; Bartels 2017). In the USA, for example, the poorest have historically voted against measures like the extension of Medicaid, social security, and legislation aimed at strengthening labour unions. In states like Kentucky, which have become increasingly dependent on federal funding for their economic stability, citizens have increasingly voted for conservative policies which would roll back federal funding, decimating the very services they have come to rely on (Mettler 2018). In the UK, low socioeconomic groups have consistently rejected tax increases and other measures aimed at alleviating economic inequalities. Crony capitalist norms shape the values and expectations of citizens, even to the point of convincing them to act in ways which are harmful to them. The real challenge posed by lobbying is the role it plays in entrenching and shaping these wider norms and ideals about politics, what is feasible and what is not, what is radical and what is not, in ways which shape citizens' choices, expectations, and sense of self. Lobby groups help shape and reify the prevailing form of broken capitalism which fits neither libertarian nor egalitarian politics, but which characterises capitalist states across the world, a form of capitalism which harnesses the power of the state (distributed across its numerous majoritarian and non-majoritarian institutions and shared in complex ways with non-state organisations of numerous kinds) to entrench patterns of behaviour across the political culture and encourage citizens to believe that crony capitalism is the best, or the most natural, or the inevitable way to organise a society.

5 Conclusion

The challenge posed by lobbying is thus bigger than lobbying itself, and concerns the norms, ideals and values which provide the context in which lobbying operates and makes sense. It is to reveal the non-natural, non-immutable nature of these values, to reveal that they can be changed and to convince those at the bottom with the most to lose that the world with which they are presented is not the only one or the natural one. This, I suggest, is a central task of democratic theory and practice: to roll back the prevailing background values that support and justify a form of democracy and a form of capitalism which work to entrench power and wealth at the top and allow wealthy elites, through the organisations that represent them, to control the political culture.

It is difficult to know how such a thing might be possible. It may be impossible. At the very least, the large and complex nature of the problem suggests the need for a similarly large and complex solution: there will be no quick fixes through mere legal or regulatory reform of lobbying. If caps on campaign spending were introduced in the USA tomorrow, for example, or if tighter lobbying rules had been introduced in the UK in the wake of the recent government inquiry into lobbying, the disproportionate influence of wealthy elites would remain (Allegretti 2021). It would be found in the centrality of elite organisations in the democratic system, and in the broader values of the public culture in which they are mainstream. The dominance of lobby groups representing elite interests, and the background values and norms which explain these elites and see them endure, has been built over the long term, and lobby groups themselves have been involved in this process: leveraging their wealth to establish disproportionately strong and close networks with states, publicly espousing the virtues of crony capitalism from positions of disproportionate prominence, harnessing the energies of the disaggregated state for their own purposes. Institutions and laws need to be changed. But so do the background values of the public culture which tend to serve and insulate elites, and ensure their continuation.

References

Abramson, Alana. 2020. "'No Lessons Have Been Learned'. Why the Trillion Dollar Coronavirus Bailout Benefited the Rich." *Time Magazine*. Retrieved on 10 May 2021 from <https://time.com/5845116/coronavirus-bailout-rich-richer/>.

Achen, Christopher. H. and Larry M. Bartels. 2017. *Democracy for Realists: Why Elections Do Not Provide Responsive Government*. Princeton, NJ: Princeton University Press.

Allegretti, Aubrey. 2021. "Audit Office Sets Up Seventh Inquiry Into Government Lobbying." *The Guardian*. Retrieved on 23 May 22 from <https://www.theguardian.com/politics/2021/apr/16/audit-office-sets-up-seventh-inquiry-into-government-lobbying>.

Bache, Ian and Matthew Flinders. 2004. *Multi-Level Governance*. Oxford: Oxford University Press.

Badhwar, Neera K. 2020. "Cronyism: The Toxic Friendship Between Business and Government." Retrieved on 10 May 2021 from <https://www.libertarianism.org/columns/cronyism-toxic-friendship-between-business-government>.

Bartels, Larry. 2017. *Unequal Democracy: The Political Economy of the New Gilded Age*. Princeton, NJ: Princeton University Press.

Baumgartner, Frank R., Jeffrey M. Berry, Marie Hojnacki, David C. Kimball, and Beth L. Leech. 2009. *Lobbying and Policy Change: Who Wins, Who Loses, and Why*. Chicago, IL: University of Chicago Press.

Bevir, Mark. 2010. *Democratic Governance*. Princeton, NJ: Princeton University Press.

Bourdieu, Pierre. 1990. *Logic of Practice*. Cambridge: Polity.

Brennan, Jason. 2016. *Against Democracy*. Princeton, NJ: Princeton University Press.

Cave, Tamasin and Andy Rowell. 2014. *A Quiet Word: Lobbying, Crony Capitalism, and Broken Politics in Britain*. London: Bodley Head.

Chari, Raj, John Hogan, Gary Murphy, and Michele Crepaz. 2019. *Regulating Lobbying: A Global Comparison*. 2nd edition. Manchester: Manchester University Press.

Dahl, Robert A. 1989. *Democracy and Its Critics*. New Haven, CT: Yale University Press.

Drutman, Lee. 2015. "How Corporate Lobbyists Conquered American Democracy." *The Atlantic*, April 20. Retrieved on 23 May 2022 from <http://theatln.tc/2s0x9Bg>.

Dryzek, John. 2012. *Foundations and Frontiers of Deliberative Governance*. Oxford: Oxford University Press.

European Commission. 2021. *Annual Report on the Operations of the Transparency Register 2021*. Brussels: European Commission.

Fishkin, James. 2018. *When the People Are Thinking: Revitalizing Our Politics Through Public Deliberation*. Oxford: Oxford University Press.

Fraser, Nancy. 2004. *Redistribution or Recognition? A Political-Philosophical Exchange*. London: Verso.
Friedan, Betty. 1963. *The Feminine Mystique*. New York, NY: W. W. Norton.
Friedman, Milton. 2002. *Capitalism and Freedom: 40th Anniversary Edition*. Chicago, IL: Chicago University Press.
Fung, Archon. 2015. "Putting the Public Back Into Governance: The Challenges of Citizen Participation and Its Future." *Public Administration Review* 25: 1–10.
Grant, Wyn. 2018. *Lobbying: The Dark Side of Politics*. Manchester: Manchester University Press.
Habermas, Jürgen. 1996. *Between Facts and Norms*. Cambridge: Polity.
Hayek, Friedrich. 1944. *The Road to Serfdom*. London: Routledge.
Hirst, Paul. 1994. *Associative Democracy: New Forms of Economic and Social Governance*. Cambridge: Polity.
Holcombe, Randall G. 2013. "Crony Capitalism: By-product of Big Government." *The Independent Review* 17 (4): 541–559.
Horgos, Daniel and Klaus W. Zimmerman. 2009. "Interest Groups and Economic Performance: Some New Evidence." *Public Choice* 138: 301–315.
Knight, Jack and James Johnson. 1998. "What Kind of Political Equality Does Deliberative Democracy Require?" In *Deliberative Democracy: Essays on Reason and Politics*, edited by James Bohman and William Rehg, 279–319. Cambridge, MA: MIT Press.
Landemore, Helene. 2007. "Is Representative Democracy Really Democratic? Interview of Bernard Manin and Nadia Urbinati." *La Vie des Idees*. Retrieved on 24 May 2022 from <https://laviedesidees.fr/IMG/pdf/20080327_manin_en.pdf>.
———. 2020. *Open Democracy: Re-Inventing Popular Rule for the 21st Century*. Princeton, NJ: Princeton University Press.
Lessig, Lawrence. 2011. *Republic, Lost: How Money Corrupts Congress – And a Plan to Stop It*. New York, NY: Twelve.
MacKinnon, Catherine A. 1989. *Towards a Feminist Theory of the State*. Cambridge, MA: Harvard University Press.
Manin, Bernard. 2010. *The Principles of Representative Government*. Cambridge: Cambridge University Press.
Medvetz, Thomas. 2012. *Think Tanks in America*. Chicago, IL: Chicago University Press.
Mettler, Suzanne. 2018. *The Government-Citizen Disconnect*. New York, NY: Russell Sage.
Mitchell, Matthew. 2012. *The Pathology of Privilege: The Economic Consequences of Government Favouritism*. Arlington, VA: Mercatus Center.
Munger, Michael. C. and Mario Villarreal-Diaz. 2019. "The Road to Crony Capitalism." *The Independent Review* 23(4): 331–344.
Okin, Susan M. 1989. *Justice, Gender and the Family*. New York, NY: Basic Books.
Olson, Mancur. 1982. *The Rise and Decline of Nations: Economic Growth, Stagflation, and Social Rigidities*. New Haven, CT: Yale University Press.
Opensecrets.org. 2021. "Lobbying Data Summary." Retrieved on 10 May 2021 from <https://www.opensecrets.org/federal-lobbying>.
Parvin, Phil. 2007. *Lobbying: Friend or Foe*. London: Hansard Society.
———. 2016. "Silencing the Critics: Charities, Lobbyists, and the Government's Quiet War on Dissent." *Renewal* 24(3): 62–75.

———. 2018a. "Representing the People: British Democracy in an Age of Political Ignorance." *Political Studies Review* 16(4): 265–278.
———. 2018b. "Democracy Without Participation: A New Politics For a Disengaged Era." *Res Publica* 24: 31–52.
———. 2021. "The Participatory Paradox: An Egalitarian Critique of Participatory Democracy." *Journal of Representative Democracy* 57 (2): 263–285.
———. 2022. "The Ethics of Political Lobbying: Power, Influence, and Democratic Decline." In Political Ethics: A Handbook, edited by Edward Hall and Andrew Sabl, 236–264.
Public Administration Committee. 2010. *Smaller Government: Shrinking the Quango State*. London: UK Parliament. Retrieved on 24 May 2022 from <https://publications.parliament.uk/pa/cm201011/cmselect/cmpubadm/537/537vw08.htm>.
Putnam, Robert D. 2001. *Bowling Alone: The Collapse and Revival of American Community*. New York, NY: Simon & Schuster.
Rhodes, Roderick. A. W. 2017. *Network Governance and the Differentiated Polity: Selected Essays Volume 1*. Oxford: Oxford University Press.
Shaxson, Nicholas. 2011. *Treasure Islands: Tax Havens and the Men Who Stole the World*. London: Bodley Head.
Skocpol, Theda. 2003. *Diminished Democracy: From Membership to Management in American Civic Life*. Norman, OK: University of Oklahoma Press.
Thomas, Alan. 2016. *Republic of Equals*. Oxford: Oxford University Press.
Urbinati, Nadia. 2006. *Representative Democracy: Principles and Genealogy*. Chicago, IL: Chicago University Press.
Vibert, Frank. 2007. *The Rise of the Unelected: Democracy and the New Separation of Powers*. Cambridge: Cambridge University Press.
Young, Iris M. 2002. *Inclusion & Democracy*. Oxford: Oxford University Press.

13 No Money, No Party
The Role of Political Parties in Electoral Campaigns

Chiara Destri

Money works its way through all aspects of the democratic process and may be thought to represent its biggest threat (Dworkin 1996), but nowhere is its role as noticeable as in campaigns, often seen as *the* democratic moment *par excellence*. Through elections, citizens put candidates in office and authorise their exercise of political power. Through campaigns, candidates (compete to) put themselves on the ballot. There are different democratic values at stake in a campaign (Lipsitz 2004), and more importantly there are various political actors involved (individuals, parties, corporations, unions, and nonprofit organisations) and multiple ways in which money influences electoral results (Christiano 2012).

While concerns about corruption, political equality, and fair competition have generally pervaded the debate about campaign finance regulations, this chapter focuses on the neglected role of political parties. It advances three claims: (1) that parties are ideally suited to organise campaigns in accordance with the democratic principle of collective self-rule, because they realise campaigns' epistemic, justificatory, and motivational functions; (2) that campaign finance scholars ought to include parties in their normative accounts because these regulations affect parties' capacity to fulfil campaign functions; and (3) that political theorists working on parties should consider the effect of different financing schemes on parties' internal structure, because the former may either worsen or counteract possible drawbacks of the latter. If political parties are vital to our democracies, as I argue, and if campaign finance regulations affect parties' functioning and internal structure, normative scholars working on these issues should talk to each other.

The chapter is organised as follows. The next section introduces the normative debate on political parties, while the second one zooms into parties' capacity to fulfil campaigns' three functions. The third section covers the normative debate over campaign finance. Since this is complex and highly contextual (Dawood 2015), I only offer admittedly simplistic silhouettes of the main arguments in favour of public funding. The fourth section explains why political parties matter for a normative account of campaign finance and vice versa: different financing schemes enhance

DOI: 10.4324/9781003173632-16

or hinder parties' capacities to fulfil the three campaign functions and affect their internal structure. Parties' proper functioning qualifies then as another *pro tanto* reason in favour of public funding. While this may seem underwhelming as globally 69.5% of countries already provide direct public funding to parties, either regularly or for campaigns or both, according to the International IDEA database,[1] looking at the effect of state subsidies on parties' internal structure helps us see how a specific type of public funding, namely the voucher system, seems particularly beneficial to enhance intraparty democracy.

1 Political Parties

While political science has always looked at parties in representative mass democracy as non-replaceable (Sartori 2005, 24), political philosophy has been investigating parties and partisanship only for the last fifteen years (Muirhead and Rosenblum 2020), after long neglecting them (Schattschneider 1942, 16; Van Biezen and Saward 2008). Important contributions have bolstered a sense of partisanship's intrinsic value (White and Ypi 2016; cf. Efthymiou 2018) and its compatibility with public reason (Muirhead and Rosenblum 2006; Bonotti 2017) and deliberation (Rosenblum 2008; White and Ypi 2011; 2016; Wolkenstein 2016; cf. Muirhead 2010).

Despite its internal differences, this burgeoning literature aims to vindicate the value of parties in representative democracies by adding normative content to political scientists' minimal definition. Empirically, a political party is 'any political group that presents at elections, and is capable of placing through elections, candidates for public office' (Sartori 2005, 57). An organisation's political goals, its electioneering style and its internal structure have no import: so long as it contests elections by placing candidates for office, that organisation is a party.

Normatively, though, this is not enough because this definition cannot discriminate between proper parties and factions. Factions, as White and Ypi (2016) argue, are rightly seen as disruptive of democracy because they pursue mere aggregations of sectoral interests at the expense of society's common good. Parties, in contrast, offer 'principled visions of what society should look like for the benefit of all' (51). They provide partisan conceptions of the common good and aspire to harness political power to govern *in the name* and *for the benefit of* the people.

According to the normative literature, proper parties have two core features: (1) they offer a (partisan) view of the common good (White and Ypi 2016), as already mentioned; (2) they accept pluralism (White and Ypi 2016; Urbinati 2019; Herman and Muirhead 2020). Hence, 'at the core of the idea of party' is 'the pursuit of political visions irreducible to the self-centred aims of sectoral groups or to personal interests' (White and Ypi 2016, 13); such political visions include generalisable aims and principles (5) articulated on the basis of reasons all citizens can accept (60; see also Bonotti 2017, 108). Furthermore, since parties recognise the contestability of their claims and the legitimacy of other contestants, they also abide by a fundamental democratic ethos, being committed to regulated rivalry and peaceful rotation in office (Muirhead and Rosenblum 2020).[2]

So understood, not only are parties not a threat to democratic institutions, but they are also 'agents of popular sovereignty' (Wolkenstein 2019). First, parties on the ground bring likeminded individuals together and enable them to shape public affairs by connecting their values and views to legislation (Wolkenstein 2020, 27). Second, parties in office provide political justifications for policy proposals that are supposed to be publicly accessible to all citizens in virtue of their being anchored to a conception of the common good (Bonotti 2017). In this respect, the result of democratic decision-making is justified to citizens even though they do not elaborate proposals directly (Biale and Ottonelli 2019, 508).

If parties differ from factions in the way described, it is not simply a matter of definition that they contest elections; rather, it is desirable that they do so because they make the systematic pursuit of principled politics possible (Goodin 2008, 211). The next section illustrates parties' role in elections by showing how they satisfy three functions that campaigns serve as preparatory stage for elections.

2 Parties and Electoral Campaigns

Campaigns are run by a candidate or party and cover the ensemble of activities and practices, such as rallies, door-to-door and social media outreach, political advertising, and public debates, that aim at supporting that candidate's bid for office. Campaigns are mainly composed of a 'string of speech acts' with a communicative intent (Beerbohm 2016, 383; see also Lipsitz 2004, 170–71; Thompson 2019) and generally cover a more or less officially specified period of time preceding an election (Thompson 2004).[3] Hence, they contribute to 'the most fundamental institution of representative democracy': the electoral process (Kateb 1981, 357). Elections serve at least two purposes: (1) they provide the means for 'selecting representatives from among a slate of candidates' (Thompson 2002, 23) and (2) they give citizens the opportunity to hold officeholders accountable (Bovens 2007; Mansbridge 2014). By preparing citizens for elections, campaigns enable them to exercise their political agency and impress their views on the law-making process, according to the democratic principle of collective self-rule.[4]

Importantly, campaigns are a highly contextual matter, as they are affected not only by various socioeconomic circumstances, but also by a country's political institutions. Electoral incentives differ from one system to another depending on the electoral law (proportional representation versus first-past-the-post), the way constituencies are organised (single-member versus multimember districts), and the number of parties contesting elections (two parties or more) (Thompson 2019, 229), as well as the broader democratic setup (parliamentarianism versus presidentialism) and constitutional essentials (Dawood 2015, 330). That said, it seems reasonable to require that all campaigns fulfil at least three functions, regardless of the different context in which they take place.[5]

First, campaigns are 'information environments' (Lipsitz 2004, 163; see also Beerbohm 2016, 390–91): they are meant to provide citizens with the necessary knowledge to make their choice at the voting booth. Even though the way campaigns are run may seem to disprove campaigns' *epistemic* function, evidence shows that campaigns significantly increase citizens' political knowledge, especially for those who begin with the least information (Coleman and Manna 2000; Freedman, Franz, and Goldstein 2004; Jacobson 2015). In fact, voters' right to be correctly informed is an important concern in the campaign finance discussion (Beitz 1989, 212–13; Thompson 2002, 109ff).

Parties discharge this function by reducing informational complexity; they develop comprehensive and coherent programmes that select and articulate societal demands around a principled vision of society (Beitz 1989, 184ff; Christiano 1996, 222–23; White and Ypi 2010). By marshalling competing concerns that pervade political debates, and by clarifying the stakes and implications for citizens, parties help them process information to make autonomous decisions.

This function is particularly important in the context of the moral division of labour characterising modern democracies (Christiano 1996; 2012). Citizens do not have the time and resources to competently assess disparate issues, ranging from climate change to pension schemes, and from healthcare to geopolitics. Nevertheless, the democratic principle of collective self-rule expects them to take a leading role in the decision-making process, at least with respect to society's fundamental aims (Christiano 2012). All of this requires knowledge and competence. Parties supply these by acting as coordination agencies: their internal division of labour allows them to turn to trusted experts in these fields and to personnel specialising in illustrating problems and stakes to the public (Christiano 1996, 223).

Information is not enough, as the point of campaigns is ultimately to persuade voters to support a candidate's bid for office. The second function of campaigns is thus *justificatory*. From the candidate's point of view, electioneering serves to advertise and defend her political views, programme, and character (Beerbohm 2016). The currency of electoral campaigns is reasons: by appealing to reasons that voters may share, challengers aim to convince them of the soundness of their proposals; incumbents aim to do likewise and to give an account of what they did in office. These reasons may be unsatisfactory, but they are essential in campaign efforts. Voters cannot be bought, they can only be persuaded (cf. Brennan 2011). Like all justificatory endeavours (White and Ypi 2016, 62–65), campaigns are comparative and adversarial. Since candidates compete against each other, their political programme is assessed based on a comparison with other available programmes. In principle, this trait should contribute to satisfying their epistemic function, since letting candidates confront each other enhances citizens' political knowledge (Manin 2017), to the point that negative campaigning has been defended as an abrasive but nevertheless effective way to increase citizens' competence close to elections (Sides et al. 2010; Mattes and Redlawsk 2015). A renowned poster distributed by the Democratic Party in the 1960 electoral campaign, for instance, reported a less than flattering picture of the Republican candidate, Richard Nixon, with the following catchphrase underneath: 'Would YOU buy a used car from this man?'

Parties satisfactorily fulfil this justificatory function because they provide justifications for their programmes that are *addressed at* and *accessible to* all citizens (White and Ypi 2011; Bonotti 2017).[6] Furthermore, because partisans are meant to realise their own programmes (Muirhead 2014, 69), they have 'an inherent tendency to articulate their claims and programs in adversarial terms calling for the public to constantly compare, assess, and redefine' their arguments (Biale and Ottonelli 2019, 505). This ambition compels parties to be 'bilingual' (Muirhead and Rosenblum 2006): they operate as a two-way channel of communication and expression (Sartori [1976] 2005, 24) by gathering demands from citizens and by organising them on a principled platform meant to affect political decisions. This is crucial to the democratic ideal because citizens need to recognise collective decisions as justifiable according to their own lights (Lafont 2019), and parties help them understand when, why, and how this is the case.

The third function of campaigns is *motivational*. Many things go on in people's lives that they must pay attention to – and politics does not always comes first. The purpose of campaigns is to mobilise citizens, thereby enabling them to exercise their political agency. While campaigns aim to include citizens in the active electorate, parties tend to keep citizens engaged even beyond the electoral moment. They give citizens membership in a political community that has shared values and ideals and a history of achievements and struggles, all of which determine their political identity and a related sense of purpose that prompts them to exercise their agency effectively at and beyond elections (White and Ypi 2011; 2016; Ypi 2016; Biale and Ottonelli 2019). In other words, parties boost citizens' motivation and enable them to effectively participate in politics.

To see why parties are ideally suited to fulfil these functions, let us compare them with campaigns run by individuals, as it was the case in the earlier stages of parliamentarism (Manin 1997). As Goodin's (2008) thought experiment of a 'No-Party Democracy' illustrates, without parties, politics would be a lot more personalistic, as individual candidates 'would commend themselves to voters, first and foremost, on the basis of their own personal characteristics' (209). A focus on personality would also make coalition building with other elected officials ad hoc and personal, thereby favouring clientelism. According to Goodin, identity and patronage politics would be even more on the rise because presumably having only individual candidates running for office would increase the importance of demographically shared characteristics and sectoral interests (2008, 210).

Even if individual candidates did manage to offer political values as structuring commitments for selecting and articulating societal demands, they would end up complicating the issue space. Epistemically, the tendency to fragmentation and multiplication of cleavages would produce 'a lot of extra noise in the electoral process' (Christiano 1996, 222) and the political landscape would be too complex for citizens given their limited cognitive resources. It would also be more difficult for citizens to keep track of all available justifications and to hold elected officials accountable. Motivationally, in the absence of associative practices of the like of parties, citizens would not share a sense of belonging to the same political project, and their electoral participation, which is importantly driven also by partisanship (Bartels 2000; Weinschenk 2013), would probably decrease.

Parties seem then to play a crucial role in fulfilling the three campaign functions, which in turn help citizens select and hold officeholders accountable, thereby realising the democratic ideal. It is important to point out, however, that these functions are not always achievable at the same time in the same way. Rather, they may be in tension and the need for trade-offs between them may arise.

To mention the starkest conflict: the motivational function of campaigns may lead to behaviours that undermine their justificatory and epistemic function. The potentially self-enforcing relation between informing citizens and giving them reasons has led scholars to consider the electoral process not only as part of a deliberative system, but as deliberative in itself (Christiano 1996, 244; Lipsitz 2004). This seems unwarranted. The point of deliberative interactions, and the aim that participants in such interactions ought to have, is either to achieve agreement (Gutmann and Thompson 1998) or to correctly identify justice and the common good (Martí 2006). Neither constitutes the candidates' goal while electioneering, since campaigning involves adversarial and strategic interactions in which various candidates compete for citizens' votes (Thompson 2013; 2019; Bagg and Tranvik 2019). While in the spirit of a systemic approach to deliberative democracy (Parkinson and Mansbridge 2012) this will hopefully lead to a more knowledgeable public, a highly polarised context may well prompt candidates seeking to win elections to lie about their opponents' views, and to forms of pandering and manipulation. If this electioneering style is adopted by important competitors, it may end up poisoning the entire electoral debate, to the disadvantage of voters that campaigns are meant to inform.

According to a deliberative and public-reason-driven reading (Muirhead and Rosenblum 2006; White and Ypi 2016; Bonotti 2017), one may think that partisanship is at odds with campaigns' non-deliberative environment. This is not the case, though. While deliberation may develop among fellow partisans (Wolkenstein 2016; 2020), a partisan conception of agency does not require citizens to examine political issues in an *impartial* and *detached* way all the time, as deliberative accounts do (Muirhead 2010; Biale 2018). The entire point of partisanship is that partisans are free to be partial towards their own viewpoints, so long as they recognise others' viewpoints as legitimate, though not as equally valid (Biale 2018, 137). Naturally, this still means that partisans should avoid factionalism, in the sense of a staunch defence of purely sectoral interests in a biased and fact-insensitive manner, as this would be incompatible with their acceptance of pluralism. Yet this requirement does not translate into an obligation to assume an impartial perspective on political issues. Independents who listen to partisans' debates may assess facts impartially, but partisans typically do not.

When they conform to these normative expectations, parties satisfy the three functions of campaigns in that they are particularly well positioned to inform citizens, offer them reasons, and mobilise them. In so doing, parties contribute to preparing citizens for the exercise of their agency at elections. The extent to which parties satisfy these functions depends on three aspects: the inter-party system, parties' internal structure, and parties' financial resources.

As a matter of fact, the time in which each citizen could simply stand up in the agora and offer to run for an elected office by declaring his willingness to do so is long gone if it was ever there at all. In contemporary mass democracies, no candidate can hope to inform, persuade, and motivate her prospective voters without having money to reach them. Financial resources pay for advertising, printing flyers, buying airtime on national radio and TV broadcasts[7] and of course organising events (to raise more money). As Michael Bloomberg's 2020 campaign bid shows, throwing money at campaigns does not *guarantee* electoral success (Amorós and Puy 2010). Nevertheless, a minimal financial endowment is necessary and even seems to affect a candidate's chances of winning (Alexander 2005).

Parties pool resources from different sources, like membership dues, private donations and public funds (van Biezen and Kopecký 2017), and use them to support their candidates' bid for office. In so doing, they offer a structure for political competition that does not simply reproduce citizens' economic inequalities in the political sphere.[8] And yet normative theorists working on parties do not interact with normative theorists working on campaign finance. To remedy this lack of communication, the next section outlines the scholarly debate over campaign finance, while the fourth explains what party and campaign scholars can learn from each other.

3 Campaign Finance

While often making the headlines of many countries' political debate, campaign finance has rarely been scrutinised by democratic theorists. Most scholars who examine it have the US Supreme Court's rulings in mind and tend to overlook other countries' funding schemes. Since in the US parties are best understood as 'loose alliances' rather than proper organisations (Katz and Kolodny 1994, 24), the normative literature on campaign finance has failed to properly consider them. This exclusive focus on the US, furthermore, is partly explained by the fact that campaign finance is at the same time a very sensitive issue in American public discourse and highly contextual, connected as it is to the broader set of circumstances in which campaigns take place.

Campaign finance situates itself in a middle ground position between the institutions of the electoral system and campaign ethics, which govern political actors' electioneering conduct. Offering a normative account of campaign finance that is justifiable across various electoral systems is therefore difficult. And yet the problem of private money skewing the democratic process sadly characterises various democracies around the globe (Cagé 2020). This chapter follows the blueprint laid out by US scholars, but also makes reference to other Western European countries.[9]

According to Dennis Thompson (2002, 105), regulations of campaign finance involve three related questions: (1) *the object of regulation* (contributions, expenditures, or both); (2) *the subject whose contribution is regulated* (wealthy individuals, parties, unions, interest groups); and (3) *the objective of regulation* (fighting inequity, corruption, lack of competitiveness, etc.). Before moving on to the third question, which constitutes the normative core of the debate about campaign finance, a few terminological clarifications are needed.

The use of private money in campaigns can be divided into two broad categories: contributions (the money that individuals and legal entities donate to candidates) and expenditures (the money candidates spend on their campaign). Although clearly connected, these have been traditionally kept separate in the US public debate (Issacharoff and Karlan 1999), because of a US Supreme Court's ruling that banned limits on expenditures but not on contributions (*Buckley v. Valeo*). According to the court's reasoning, both limits on expenditures and contributions constitute infringements on the First Amendment rights of free speech and association. However, while limits on contributions are justified because they prevent corruption or its appearance, limits on expenditures lack such a strong justification and are therefore unacceptable (Sunstein 1994; Dawood 2015, 333). Clearly, this position is not universally shared, as European countries such as France, the UK, and Italy feature limits on candidates' spending and countries such as Spain, the UK, and Italy also limit political parties' expenditures.[10] To give an example of how consequential expenditure limits can be, compare the US, on the one hand, where no limits apply, and France and the UK, on the other, where they do. The average candidate for the US House of Representatives spent about 1.7 million dollars in 2018 (Sides et al. 2019, 85), whereas in France and the UK the average parliamentary candidate contented herself with spending around 18,000 euros in 2012 and 4,000 euros in 2015, respectively (Cagé 2020, 22). Even accounting for population differences, the spending difference is significant.

This chapter focuses on direct contributions, called *hard money* in the US, which are campaign-related funds given directly to a candidate or party. Indirect contributions, by contrast, are funds given to political parties for nonpartisan goals, such as encouraging people to vote, and funds given to third parties for influencing public opinion (Sides et al. 2019). Among third parties we count interest groups, faith-based organisations, charities and, in the US context, political action committees (PACs) and 'independent expenditure committees' (known as Super PACs).[11] The lack of restrictions on third-party spending is an increasingly serious problem for democratic campaigns, as other spending limits can be eluded by rerouting money through third-party channels (Issacharoff and Karlan 1999). In *Citizens United v. FEC*, the US Supreme Court, for instance, maintained the limit on third parties' direct contributions but lifted the one on indirect ones (Dawood 2015, 333). Yet the issue also concerns many other democratic countries, as third parties are rarely banned from spending on campaign activities (only 13.3% of all states reported in the International IDEA database ban them) and 42.8% of reported countries have no limitation on third-party spending at all, including Germany, France, and Italy.[12]

The distinction between direct and indirect contributions maps onto Christiano's salient distinction between 'gatekeeping' money and money as 'influence on public opinion' (2012, 244ff).[13] Money acts as a gatekeeper when paying individuals or legal entities can set the agenda by funding their preferred candidates (what happens with direct contributions). By financing certain candidates, wealthy individuals and interest groups obtain protection of their interests at the decision-making level (Gilens 2012; Bartels 2016). In contrast, money influences public opinion when paying individuals or legal entities can broadcast their opinions to the public more extensively. This is what happens with indirect contributions and related expenditures, which sway public opinion in one way or another by making wealthy actors' interests and their conception of justice more pervasive in public debate (Christiano 2012, 247). Naturally, the two phenomena are intertwined: just as donations to candidates can end up influencing the public sphere through candidates' speeches, so can indirect expenditures affect candidates' electoral chances by swaying public opinion.

Since contributions affect elections in intertwined ways, a thorough normative account of campaign finance ought to consider both money as gatekeeper and money as influence. However, as Pevnick (2016a; 2016b) observes, all three most important rationales that have been invoked to regulate campaign finance may either threaten citizens' right to free speech (if they require a strict cap on both gatekeeping and influence money), or end up being ineffective (if they only apply to money as gatekeeping). The justification of a system of floors, i.e., public funding, takes then precedence over justifying a system of ceilings (Thompson 2002, 113). This chapter does the same for three reasons. First, gatekeeping money is what is primarily at stake when political parties are involved. Second, all three main rationales for campaign finance regulations support public funding.[14] Finally, the case of European countries, most of which bestow generous public provisions on parties, show that when state subsidies are predominant, 'other sources of income tend to be relatively insignificant' (van Biezen and Kopecký 2017, 88).

The first and virtually undisputed concern in campaign finance debates is the threat of corruption. At the basic level corruption involves public power used to realise private gains (Thompson 2005) and so-called *quid pro quo* corruption happens when donors use hard money with the aim of getting specific favours in return (Sunstein 1994). *Quid pro quo* corruption, or its appearance, plays a central role in US Supreme Court's decisions (Dawood 2015, 334) as it is considered the only valid reason to limit wealthy donors' right of free speech by imposing limits on their contributions (Pevnick 2016a, 1185). Interestingly though, such a limit on natural persons' direct contributions, while present in countries such as Canada, France, and Belgium (the limit applies also to legal persons in Italy and Ireland), is missing in other European democracies such as Germany, Spain, Switzerland, Austria, the Netherlands, and most Scandinavian countries.[15]

Since the crux of this argument depends on the conception of corruption one endorses (Dawood 2015, 335), Thompson (1995) draws a distinction between individual corruption, concerning personal gains and institutional corruption, which takes place when the institutional setting provides the wrong incentives to players, thereby damaging the integrity of the democratic process (see also Warren 2004). The problem then becomes distinguishing between legitimate responsiveness to citizens' interests and wrongful dependence on a subset of wealthy donors. To this end, Lessig proposes to look at what he calls 'dependence corruption' (2011, 17). When candidates need a certain amount of financial support from their donors to be considered viable, it is difficult to see how they can be relied upon to govern in ways that are not disproportionately favourable to those donors (Sides et al. 2019, 119). Hence, instead of depending 'on the people alone,' Congress becomes dependent on wealthy contributors.

Avoiding corruption is not the only admissible goal. Unlike the US Supreme Court, the German constitutional court has regularly struck down political finance laws when they violated explicit constitutional guarantees of (relatively) equal opportunities for political influence for citizens (Scarrow 2018, 104). The German constitutional court's preoccupation is with a different goal: protecting citizens' political equality. Dominant in campaign finance discussions in political theory (Dawood 2015), the principle of political equality requires that citizens enjoy equal opportunity to exercise their political influence (Beitz 1989; Sunstein 1994; Christiano 1996; Dworkin 1996; 2002; Cohen 2001; Rawls 2005). Accordingly, political equality cannot be limited to equal voting rights, but must also include equal broader influence over political affairs (Brighouse 1996).[16] As Ronald Dworkin (1996) succinctly puts it, 'Each citizen must have a fair and reasonably equal opportunity not only to hear the views of others as these are published or broadcast, but to command attention for his own views' (19–24).

The last rationale for campaign finance regulations rests on the principle of fair competition (Pevnick 2016a; 2019). At first, this goal may seem indistinguishable from the previous one. After all, as Joshua Cohen (2001) emphasises, egalitarians hold that 'in a democracy, citizens are also agents, participants, speakers, who may aim to reshape both the terms of political debate and its results, *by running for office* or seeking to influence the views of candidates, the outcomes of elections and the inter-election conduct of politics' (72, my italics). Nonetheless, equality-based arguments concern lay citizens' opportunity for political influence *in their role as participants* in the public deliberation around viable candidates. By contrast, competition-based arguments look at the opportunities citizens have *to become viable candidates*, if they so intend, and aim at levelling the playing field (Beitz 1989, 200; Pevnick 2016a).[17]

As said, all these three rationales justify a system of floors aimed at limiting the import of private money in politics by ensuring public support for candidates and parties. Interestingly however, they may support significantly different schemes of public subsidies, because their goals (reducing corruption, enhancing political equality and ensuring fair competition) do not overlap completely (Pevnick 2016a; pace Lessig 2011). Any public system works for corruption scholars, as long as it is effective at limiting officeholders' undue dependence on private donors (Pevnick 2016a, 1187). This can be realised successfully without also equalising citizens' political influence, which is instead required by egalitarians (Beitz 1989; Christiano

1996; Cohen 2001; Dworkin 2002; Thompson 2002). Similarly, the type of public funding that advocates of fair competition favour is one that gives all *competitors* equal resources, rather than giving all *citizens* equal opportunities to determine the results (Brighouse 1996).

The voucher system acts as a litmus test because it shows how these three rationales have conflicting implications concerning the type of public funding they support. This system, proposed by Hasen (1996) and supported also by other scholars (Ackerman and Ayres 2002; Cagé 2020), allows citizens to finance their preferred candidate by employing state-funded vouchers that are equally distributed. If all direct contributions to campaigns were given exclusively through these vouchers, citizens would enjoy equal opportunity to select candidates for elections, thereby equalising gatekeeping money. This system is different from the ways most European democracies implement some form of public funding, since European parties often must pass a certain threshold of support, quantified in terms of antecedent votes or seats in parliament, to qualify for public resources (Cagé 2020).[18] Accordingly, parties are proportionally reimbursed for their expenses based on the level of support they receive at prior elections. This not only favours the status quo, but also prevents citizens from discriminating between the party they want to subsidise and the one they intend to vote for. However, vouchers too may end up disproportionally benefiting candidates who enjoy widespread support at new contestants' expense. As such, they are strongly favoured by egalitarians, possibly favoured but not required by corruption scholars and clearly opposed by advocated of fair competition (Pevnick 2016a). In fact, levelling the playing field would require distributing public funds in an equal way across candidates, regardless of the share of votes and seats allocated in previous elections (Christiano 1996).[19]

Despite their differences, there is one further feature that these three normative approaches share. They conceive of campaign finance regulations as an institutional setting of incentives for *individual* political actors. Approaches based on corruption and fair competition look at candidates and how they can enjoy equal chances to win without the support of a handful of wealthy donors. Equality-based views concentrate on citizens' opportunities to be part of the election process, either as selectors of candidates, through their use of gatekeeping money, or as participants in the public deliberation around that process, through influence money. As a result, all three perspectives fail to properly consider the role of political parties.

4 Parties and Campaign Finance

While political scientists have extensively written about party finance, normative theorists have largely ignored it. On the one hand, those coming from party studies have focused on parties' internal structure, asking whether this structure ought to be democratic and/or deliberative (Wolkenstein 2016; 2018; 2020; Invernizzi-Accetti and Wolkenstein 2017; Biale and Ottonelli 2019; Bagg and Bhatia 2021). On the other hand, theorists who have sought to provide a normative account of campaign finance have only acknowledged parties as responsible for structuring political competition, without pondering the implications of their role (Beitz 1989, 180–87; Christiano 1996, 222, 244–48; Thompson 2002, 67).

Yet, since parties, as we have seen, are ideally suited to organise campaigns, the effect of campaign finance schemes on their functioning gives us at least a *pro tanto* party-based reason in favour or against such schemes. The way money is raised and distributed among parties affects not only the party system and its level of polarisation (La Raja and Schaffner 2015), but also parties' capacity to discharge their three functions and their internal structure. Since this topic is highly contextual, prescriptions for a campaign finance system must be sensitive to each country's specific institutional (particularly electoral) and sociopolitical conditions. While this broader task cannot be achieved in this chapter, a few general observations may still be advanced.[20]

First, like the party system and parties' internal structure, financing schemes also affect parties' capacity to fulfil campaign functions. Parties that do not raise membership dues and are left with little or no public subsidies, like Democrats and Republicans in the US,[21] are presumably under a much higher pressure to collect voluntary private contributions, which make them more dependent on wealthy donors (Lessig 2011). This may engender a starker tension between the justificatory and epistemic function on one side, and the motivational function on the other. For parties may be pushed to adopt manipulative techniques that ensure wider electorate's support while actually pursuing their wealthy donors' interests, as in the case of oligarchic agenda capture (Winters and Page 2009). Hence, the motivational function will be fulfilled at the expense of parties' capacity to inform and give reasons to all citizens. By comparison, public funding provisions seem to strain big parties less because they ensure minimal financial support for their electoral activities. Since similar observations may be true of each function taken individually, campaign finance scholars ought to evaluate financing schemes also on the grounds of their effect on parties' campaign functioning.

Second, campaign finance regulations affect both a party system and parties' internal structure by either exacerbating or countervailing some of their problematic features. Consider the debate on intra-party democracy (henceforth IPD).[22] Empirical party scholars have long discussed the desirability and feasibility of IPD (Carty 2013). In principle, parties need not be internally democratic to fulfil campaign functions, as polity-level democracy may only require free choice among parties rather than active participation within them (Schumpeter [1942] 2008; Sartori 1962; Rosenbluth and Shapiro 2018). However, if parties develop a rigidly oligarchic structure (Michels 1962), citizens' political agency is curtailed (Wolkenstein 2020) and the party agenda can be captured by the elites (Bagg and Bhatia 2021). Furthermore, even parties' satisfaction of the three campaign functions can be set back, thereby limiting the contribution they offer to the realisation of collective self-rule through the electoral process. For example, if parties' policies are entirely determined by party leaders interested in being re-elected as officeholders, these policies may be less coherently structured around a principled view of the common good (Kirchheimer 1966; c.f. Rosenbluth and Shapiro 2018).

IPD may seem the perfect remedy to this problem, but some of its forms have been denounced as counterproductive, because by including lay citizens in parties' selection processes (i.e., open primaries), they end up concentrating more power in party elites' hands at the expenses of rank-and-file members (Katz and Mair 1995; 2009, 759; Carty 2013, 17–19). This and other objections[23] to IPD have been answered by political theorists who defend a deliberative, rather than aggregative, model of IPD (Wolkenstein 2016; 2018; 2020; Invernizzi-Accetti and Wolkenstein 2017; Ebeling and Wolkenstein 2018; Biale and Ottonelli 2019), according to which party members at local branches should have the opportunity to deliberate and participate in the process determining their party's policy programme, its electoral strategies and candidates, as well as its executive elites. Other scholars offer a qualified defence of IPD as mass organised engagement in party decision-making, aimed at resisting oligarchic agenda capture under conditions of a rigid party system (Bagg and Bhatia 2021).

Campaign finance schemes also play a role in this debate around IPD because they can contribute to counteracting parties' oligarchic tendencies. As a matter of fact, these tendencies may be exacerbated when parties benefit from state subsidies because reliance on public funds makes party elites less dependent on citizens' support and more inclined to inter-party collusion (Katz and Mair 1995; Hopkin 2004). At the same time, we have seen that there are good reasons to favour public funding over private donation schemes. As a result, the way state subsidies are distributed acquires crucial importance. While most countries featuring public funds assign them directly to parties based on their prior electoral support, a two-staged voucher system seems preferable to enhance IPD. In this system, state subsidies are distributed directly to citizens in the form of equal vouchers that they use to fund the party of their choosing. Resulting resources are then further divided in two. Part of them serves to run parties' everyday activities and events, such as conferences and primaries. Another part is further equally divided among all party members, who can use these second vouchers to finance both internal candidates at party primaries and local branch delegates sent to party conferences. In such a way, it would be possible to further counteract the inherent tendency of party organisations to steer towards oligarchy, because party members would enjoy further control over candidate and executive selection by deciding whom they want to finance and whom they want to vote for.

While these are just two small examples, they illustrate how campaign finance regulations affect both parties' capacity to fulfil campaign functions as well as their internal structure, and how these effects provide campaign finance and party scholars in political theory compelling reasons to talk to each other.

5 Conclusion

This chapter has defended three related claims. The first one is that political parties are ideally suited to organise electoral campaigns because of a functional convergence between parties and campaigns: the former satisfies the latter's epistemic, justificatory, and motivational functions. While this enables parties to contribute to the realisation of collective self-rule because they enable citizens to exercise their agency at elections, their contribution is significantly affected by campaign finance regulations.

The second claim that I have defended is that scholars seeking to offer a normative account of campaign finance should consider the effects of different financing schemes on parties' capacity to fulfil campaign functions, because this, in turn, enhances or undermines citizens' electoral agency. While the three main rationales offered in the debate (anti-corruption, political equality and fair competition) may be seen to favour state subsidies, parties' campaign functioning gives another independently valid reason to support public funding.

The third claim of this chapter is that party scholars in political theory ought to include campaign finance regulations in their reflections, because these either exacerbate or counteract parties' oligarchic tendencies. Since risks of cartelisation are not entirely offset by forms of IPD, the two-staged voucher system that I have sketched in the last section offers an alternative way to empower citizens and rank-and-file party members with respect to party elites. Reasons of space prevent me from developing this argument further, but I hope this shows that normative theorists working on political parties and those working on campaign finance would highly benefit from mutual interactions.

Acknowledgements

I would like to thank all participants to the 2021 online Wealth and Power workshop with other contributors to this volume, as well as to a 2020 ECPR GC Panel, for their helpful comments. Special thanks go to the three anonymous referees, the editors of this collection and Carlo

No Money, No Party 267

Burelli. This research was possible thanks to a European Grant H2020-MSCA-IF-2018, project number 836571, and Goethe University's ConTrust Initiative.

Notes

1. However, only 15% of countries provide public funding to all registered parties without requiring a threshold of support, necessary for eligibility in most countries. See https://www.idea.int/political-finance-tool-new (accessed on April 15, 2022).
2. Naturally, partisanship and civic commitment may be in tension (Ypi 2016, 602).
3. While there is no natural distinction between regular and electoral politics (Pevnick 2016b), the fact that a distinction is somehow arbitrary does not entail that we should not draw it (Thompson 2002). Furthermore, even though campaigns are not strictly speaking necessary for elections to be democratic (Abizadeh 2005), they usually precede them in the context of mass democracies.
4. That parties and campaigns contribute to the realisation of the democratic ideal remains true even if citizens' ignorance and motivated reasoning are thought to undermine that ideal (Achen and Bartels 2016).
5. I take these functions from Biale and Ottonelli (2019) but they apply them to parties.
6. The electoral context plays an important role in parties' capacity and willingness to do that, since parties in PR systems will likely appeal to narrower segments of the citizenry.
7. Though access to media is subsidised by the state in most Western countries, with the notable exception of the USA: https://www.idea.int/data-tools/question-view/552 (accessed on April 15, 2022).
8. By contrast, with individual candidates only the wealthy and well-connected would stand a chance at presenting themselves as viable candidates.
9. Unfortunately, campaign finance being such a contextual issue, this chapter cannot credibly address all democratic countries, such as India and those in Latin America and Eastern Europe, which would have to feature in a lengthier analysis.
10. According to the International IDEA database, 31.7% of all countries impose limits on parties' expenditures and 46% on candidates' expenditures. The USA is included among the countries that limit candidates' expenditures, but this limit only concerns candidates for presidential elections who have received public funding. See https://www.idea.int/political-finance-tool-new (accessed on April 15, 2022). Since spending limits reduce fundraising pressure for contestants, they can also be seen as a tool to reduce big donors' influence (Scarrow 2018, 107ff).
11. PACs and Super PACs are organisations that pool campaign contributions from members and use these funds in political campaigns. Super PACs have no spending limits, but they must not privately coordinate with a candidate's campaign (Dawood 2015, 339).
12. Notable exceptions are Spain, Portugal, Canada, and the UK: https://www.idea.int/data-tools/question-view/284599 (accessed on April 15, 2022).
13. The other two ways in which money influences politics are not directly related to the purpose of this chapter (Christiano 2012, 242–244, 250) and concern money as independent political power and money illegally used to bribe elected officials.

14 A third dimension shifts attention from the type and amount of money spent on campaigns to the transparency of contributions and expenditures (Ackerman and Ayres 2002). For instance, most states (54.4%) in the International IDEA database prohibit political parties from accepting anonymous donations (https://www.idea.int/data-tools/question-view/538, accessed on April 15, 2022), though interestingly fewer (41.9%) ban anonymous donations to candidates (https://www.idea.int/data-tools/question-view/539, accessed on April 15, 2022). While this strategy is largely independent from the other two, a comprehensive outlook at campaign finance would need to take this into account too.
15 See the International IDEA database: https://www.idea.int/data-tools/question-view/546 (accessed on April 15, 2022).
16 For the distinction between impact and influence, see Dworkin (1987, 9).
17 Both Beitz (1989, 200–201) and Pevnick (2019) deny that fair competition has intrinsic moral value.
18 See the International IDEA database: https://www.idea.int/data-tools/question-view/550 (accessed on April 15, 2022). Since public funding is distributed proportionally, it appears to be incompatible with fair competition. Nonetheless, public subsidies have often been shown to help new contestants, even in systems that favour incumbents (Scarrow 2006; van Biezen and Rashkova 2014).
19 This is how so-called clean-election reforms work in the US: candidates publicly funded must renounce any private fundraising; in return they get *equal* funds and matching funds if they need to compete with a privately funded candidate who has more financial resources (Pevnick 2016a, 1189).
20 I leave aside campaign finance effects on party system but a draft paper by Matteo Bonotti and Zim Nwokora tackles this issue.
21 In 1971 the Federal Election Campaign Act provided public funding in the form of matching funds for presidential campaigns. However, since public funds come with a spending limit, almost no major-party presidential candidate in the last primaries and general elections accepted them (Sides et al. 2019, 110).
22 While the definition of IPD is 'essentially contestable' (Cross and Katz 2013, 3), I will consider as internally democratic a party whose candidate and elite selection are taken through an egalitarian procedure including all party members.
23 Other objections raised against IPD concern conflicts of responsiveness between party members and the larger electorate (Cross and Katz 2013, 172); threats to a party's electoral viability as elites are forced to take positions that are further away from the median voter (Rosenbluth and Shapiro 2018); and decrease of inclusion and representativeness in candidate selection (Hazan and Rahat 2010).

References

Abizadeh, Arash. 2005. 'Democratic Elections without Campaigns? Normative Foundations of National Baha'i Elections'. *World Order* 37 (1): 7–49.

Achen, Christopher H., and Larry M. Bartels. 2016. *Democracy for Realists: Why Elections Do Not Produce Responsive Government*. Princeton, NJ: Princeton University Press.

Ackerman, Bruce A., and Ian Ayres. 2002. *Voting with Dollars: A New Paradigm for Campaign Finance*. New Haven, CT: Yale University Press.

Alexander, Brad. 2005. 'Good Money and Bad Money: Do Funding Sources Affect Electoral Outcomes?' *Political Research Quarterly* 58 (2): 353–58.
Amorós, Pablo, and M. Socorro Puy. 2010. 'Indicators of Electoral Victory'. *Public Choice* 144 (1/2): 239–51.
Bagg, Samuel, and Udit Bhatia. 2021. 'Intra-Party Democracy: A Functionalist Account'. *Journal of Political Philosophy*, Online First.
Bagg, Samuel, and Isak Tranvik. 2019. 'An Adversarial Ethics for Campaigns and Elections'. *Perspectives on Politics* 17 (4): 973–87.
Bartels, Larry M. 2000. 'Partisanship and Voting Behavior, 1952–1996'. *American Journal of Political Science* 44 (1): 35–50.
——. 2016. *Unequal Democracy: The Political Economy of the New Gilded Age*. New York, NY: Russell Sage Foundation.
Beerbohm, Eric. 2016. 'The Ethics of Electioneering'. *Journal of Political Philosophy* 24 (4): 381–405.
Beitz, Charles R. 1989. *Political Equality: An Essay in Democratic Theory*. Princeton, NJ: Princeton University Press.
Biale, Enrico. 2018. *Interessi Democratici e Ragioni Partigiane: Una Concezione Politica Della Democrazia*. Bologna: Il Mulino.
Biale, Enrico, and Valeria Ottonelli. 2019. 'Intra-Party Deliberation and Reflexive Control within a Deliberative System'. *Political Theory* 47 (4): 500–26.
Biezen, Ingrid van, and Petr Kopecký. 2017. 'The Paradox of Party Funding: The Limited Impact of State Subsidies on Party Membership'. In *Organizing Political Parties*, edited by Susan E. Scarrow, Paul D. Webb, and Thomas Poguntke, 84–105. Oxford: Oxford University Press.
Biezen, Ingrid van, and Ekaterina R. Rashkova. 2014. 'Deterring New Party Entry? The Impact of State Regulation on the Permeability of Party Systems'. *Party Politics* 20: 890–903.
Biezen, Ingrid van, and Michael Saward. 2008. 'Democratic Theorists and Party Scholars: Why They Don't Talk to Each Other, and Why They Should'. *Perspectives on Politics* 6 (1): 21–35.
Bonotti, Matteo. 2017. *Partisanship and Political Liberalism in Diverse Societies*. Oxford: Oxford University Press.
Bovens, Mark. 2007. 'Analysing and Assessing Accountability: A Conceptual Framework'. *European Law Journal* 13 (4): 447–68.
Brennan, Jason. 2011. 'The Right to a Competent Electorate'. *The Philosophical Quarterly* 61 (245): 700–24.
Brighouse, Harry. 1996. 'Egalitarianism and Equal Availability of Political Influence'. *Journal of Political Philosophy* 4 (2): 118–41.
Cagé, Julia. 2020. *The Price of Democracy: How Money Shapes Politics and What to Do about It*. Cambridge, MA: Harvard University Press.
Carty, R. Kenneth. 2013. 'Are Political Parties Meant to Be Internally Democratic?' In *The Challenges of Intra-Party Democracy*. Oxford: Oxford University Press.
Christiano, Thomas. 1996. *The Rule of the Many: Fundamental Issues in Democratic Theory*. Boulder: Westview Press.
——. 2012. 'Rational Deliberation among Experts and Citizens'. In *Deliberative Systems: Deliberative Democracy at the Large Scale*, edited by John Parkinson and Jane Mansbridge, 27–51. Cambridge: Cambridge University Press.

Cohen, Joshua. 2001. 'Money, Politics, Political Equality'. In *Fact and Value: Essays on Ethics and Metaphysics for Judith Jarvis Thomson*, edited by Alex Byrne, Robert Stalnaker, and Ralph Wedgwood, 47–80. Cambridge: MIT Press.

Coleman, John J., and Paul F. Manna. 2000. 'Congressional Campaign Spending and the Quality of Democracy'. *The Journal of Politics* 62 (3): 757–89.

Cross, William P., and Richard S. Katz. 2013. *The Challenges of Intra-Party Democracy*. Oxford: Oxford University Press.

Dawood, Yasmin. 2015. 'Campaign Finance and American Democracy'. *Annual Review of Political Science* 18 (1): 329–48.

Dworkin, Ronald. 1987. 'What Is Equality – Part 4: Political Equality'. *University of San Francisco Law Review* 22: 1–30.

——. 1996. 'The Curse of American Politics | by Ronald Dworkin | The New York Review of Books'. *The New York Review of Books*, 17 October 1996.

——. 2002. *Sovereign Virtue: The Theory and Practice of Equality*. Cambridge, MA: Harvard University Press.

Ebeling, Martin, and Fabio Wolkenstein. 2018. 'Exercising Deliberative Agency in Deliberative Systems'. *Political Studies* 66 (3): 635–50.

Efthymiou, Dimitrios. 2018. 'The Normative Value of Partisanship: When and Why Partisanship Matters'. *Political Studies* 66 (1): 192–208.

Freedman, Paul, Michael Franz, and Kenneth Goldstein. 2004. 'Campaign Advertising and Democratic Citizenship'. *American Journal of Political Science* 48 (4): 723–41.

Gilens, Martin. 2012. *Affluence and Influence*. Princeton, NJ: Princeton University Press.

Goodin, Robert. 2008. *Innovating Democracy: Democratic Theory and Practice After the Deliberative Turn*. Oxford: Oxford University Press.

Gutmann, Amy, and Dennis F. Thompson. 1998. *Democracy and Disagreement*. Cambridge, MA: Harvard University Press.

Hasen, Richard L. 1996. 'Clipping Coupons for Democracy: An Egalitarian/Public Choice Defense of Campaign Finance Voucher'. *California Law Review* 84 (1): 1–59.

Hazan, Reuven Y., and Gideon Rahat. 2010. *Democracy within Parties: Candidate Selection Methods and Their Political Consequences*. Oxford: Oxford University Press.

Herman, Lise Esther, and Russell Muirhead. 2020. 'Resisting Abusive Legalism: Electoral Fairness and the Partisan Commitment to Political Pluralism'. *Representation*, Online First.

Hopkin, Jonathan. 2004. 'The Problem with Party Finance: Theoretical Perspectives on the Funding of Party Politics'. *Party Politics* 10 (6): 627–51.

Invernizzi-Accetti, Carlo, and Fabio Wolkenstein. 2017. 'The Crisis of Party Democracy, Cognitive Mobilization, and the Case for Making Parties More Deliberative'. *American Political Science Review* 111 (1): 97–109.

Issacharoff, Samuel, and Pamela S. Karlan. 1999. 'The Hydraulics of Campaign Finance Reform'. *Texas Law Review* 77: 1705–38.

Jacobson, Gary C. 2015. 'How Do Campaigns Matter?' *Annual Review of Political Science* 18 (1): 31–47.

Kateb, George. 1981. 'The Moral Distinctiveness of Representative Democracy'. *Ethics* 91 (3): 357–74.

Katz, Richard, and Robin Kolodny. 1994. 'Party Organization as an Empty Vessel: Parties in American Politics'. In *How Parties Organize*, edited by Richard S. Katz and Peter Mair, 23–50. London: SAGE Publications.

Katz, Richard, and Peter Mair. 1995. 'Changing Models of Party Organization and Party Democracy: The Emergence of the Cartel Party'. *Party Politics* 1 (1): 5–28.

———. 2009. 'The Cartel Party Thesis: A Restatement'. *Perspectives on Politics* 7 (4): 753–66.

Kirchheimer, Otto. 1966. 'The Transformation of the Western European Party Systems'. In *Political Parties and Political Development*, edited by Joseph LaPalombara and Myron Weiner. Princeton, NJ: Princeton University Press.

La Raja, Raymond J., and Brian F. Schaffner. 2015. *Campaign Finance and Political Polarization: When Purists Prevail*. Ann Arbor, MI: University of Michigan Press.

Lafont, Cristina. 2019. *Democracy without Shortcuts: A Participatory Conception of Deliberative Democracy*. Oxford: Oxford University Press.

Lessig, Lawrence. 2011. *Republic, Lost: How Money Corrupts Congress – and a Plan to Stop It*. New York, NY: Twelve.

Lipsitz, Keena. 2004. 'Democratic Theory and Political Campaigns'. *Journal of Political Philosophy* 12 (2): 163–89.

Manin, Bernard. 1997. *The Principles of Representative Government*. Cambridge: Cambridge University Press.

———. 2017. 'Political Deliberation & the Adversarial Principle'. *Daedalus* 146 (3): 39–50.

Mansbridge, Jane. 2014. 'A Contingency Theory of Accountability'. In *The Oxford Handbook of Public Accountability*, edited by Mark Bovens, Robert Goodin, and Thomas Schillemans, 56–69. Oxford: Oxford University Press.

Martí, José Luis. 2006. 'The Epistemic Conception of Deliberative Democracy Defended'. In *Deliberative Democracy and Its Discontents*, edited by José Luis Martí and Samantha Besson, 27–56. Aldershot: Ashgate.

Mattes, Kyle, and David P. Redlawsk. 2015. *The Positive Case for Negative Campaigning*. Chicago, IL: University of Chicago Press.

Michels, Robert. 1962. *Political Parties*. New York, NY: Collier.

Muirhead, Russell. 2010. 'Can Deliberative Democracy be Partisan?' *Critical Review* 22 (2–3): 129–57.

———. 2014. *The Promise of Party in a Polarized Age*. Cambridge, MA: Harvard University Press.

Muirhead, Russell, and Nancy Rosenblum. 2006. 'Political Liberalism vs. "The Great Game of Politics": The Politics of Political Liberalism'. *Perspectives on Politics* 4 (1): 99–108.

———. 2020. 'The Political Theory of Parties and Partisanship: Catching Up'. *Annual Review of Political Science* 23 (1): 95–110.

Parkinson, John, and Jane Mansbridge, eds. 2012. *Deliberative Systems: Deliberative Democracy at the Large Scale*. Cambridge: Cambridge University Press.

Pevnick, Ryan. 2019. 'Should Campaign Finance Reform Aim to Level the Playing Field?' *Politics, Philosophy & Economics* 18 (4): 358–73.

———. 2016a. 'Does the Egalitarian Rationale for Campaign Finance Reform Succeed?' *Philosophy & Public Affairs* 44 (1): 46–76.

———. 2016b. 'The Anatomy of Debate about Campaign Finance'. *The Journal of Politics* 78: 1184–95.
Rawls, John. 2005. *Political Liberalism*. New York, NY: Columbia University Press.
Rosenblum, Nancy. 2008. *On the Side of the Angels: An Appreciation of Parties and Partisanship*. Princeton, NJ: Princeton University Press.
Rosenbluth, Frances McCall, and Ian Shapiro. 2018. *Responsible Parties: Saving Democracy from Itself*. New Haven, CT: Yale University Press.
Sartori, Giovanni. 1962. *Democratic Theory*. Detroit: Wayne State University Press.
———. [1976] 2005. *Parties and Party Systems: A Framework for Analysis*. Colchester: ECPR Press.
Scarrow, Susan. 2006. 'Party Subsidies and the Freezing of Party Competition: Do Cartel Mechanisms Work?' *West European Politics* 29: 619–39.
———. 2018. 'Political Finance Regulation and Equality: Comparing Strategies and Impact'. In *Handbook of Political Party Funding*, edited by Jonathan Mendilow and Eric Phélippeau, 103–24. Cheltenham: Edward Elgar Publishing.
Schattschneider, Elmer Eric. 1942. *Party Government: American Government in Action*. New York, NY: Farrar and Rinehart.
Schumpeter, Joseph A. [1942] 2008. *Capitalism, Socialism, and Democracy*. New York, NY: Harper Perennial.
Sides, John, Keena Lipsitz, and Matthew Grossmann. 2010. 'Do Voters Perceive Negative Campaigns as Informative Campaigns?' *American Politics Research* 38 (3): 502–30.
Sides, John, Daron Shaw, Keena Lipsitz, and Matt Grossmann. 2019. *Campaigns and Elections*. New York, NY: W. W. Norton & Company.
Sunstein, Cass. 1994. 'Political Equality and Unintended Consequences'. *Columbia Law Review* 94 (4): 1390.
Thompson, Dennis. 1995. *Ethics in Congress: From Individual to Institutional Corruption*. Washington, DC: Brookings Institution Press.
———. 2002. *Just Elections: Creating a Fair Electoral Process in the United States*. Chicago, IL: University of Chicago Press.
———. 2004. 'Election Time: Normative Implications of Temporal Properties of the Electoral Process in the United States'. *American Political Science Review* 98 (1): 51–63.
———. 2005. 'Two Concepts of Corruption: Making Campaigns Safe for Democracy Law and Democracy'. *George Washington Law Review* 73 (5 and 6): 1036–69.
———. 2013. 'Deliberate about, Not in, Elections'. *Election Law Journal* 12 (4): 372–85.
———. 2019. 'The Political Ethics of Political Campaigns'. In *The Routledge Handbook of Ethics and Public Policy*, edited by Annabelle Lever and Andrei Poama, 240–52. New York, NY: Routledge.
Urbinati, Nadia. 2019. 'The Phenomenology of Politics as Factionalism'. *Constellations* 26 (3): 408–17.
Warren, Mark. 2004. 'What Does Corruption Mean in a Democracy?' *American Journal of Political Science (Wiley-Blackwell)* 48 (2): 328–43.
Weinschenk, Aaron. 2013. 'Polls and Elections: Partisanship and Voting Behavior: An Update'. *Presidential Studies Quarterly* 43 (3): 607–17.

White, Jonathan, and Lea Ypi. 2010. 'Rethinking the Modern Prince: Partisanship and the Democratic Ethos'. *Political Studies* 58 (4): 809–28.

———. 2011. 'On Partisan Political Justification'. *American Political Science Review* 105 (2): 381–96.

———. 2016. *The Meaning of Partisanship*. Oxford: Oxford University Press.

Winters, Jeffrey A., and Benjamin Page. 2009. 'Oligarchy in the United States?' *Perspectives on Politics* 7 (4): 731–51.

Wolkenstein, Fabio. 2016. 'A Deliberative Model of Intra-Party Democracy: Deliberative Model of Intra-Party Democracy'. *Journal of Political Philosophy* 24 (3): 297–320.

———. 2018. 'Intra-Party Democracy beyond Aggregation'. *Party Politics* 24 (4): 323–34.

———. 2019. 'Agents of Popular Sovereignty'. *Political Theory* 47 (3): 338–62.

———. 2020. *Rethinking Party Reform*. Oxford: Oxford University Press.

Ypi, Lea. 2016. 'Political Commitment and the Value of Partisanship'. *American Political Science Review* 110 (3): 601–13.

14 Constitutions against Oligarchy

Elliot Bulmer and Stuart White

> But although it never seems to make it into Hansard
> The question at some point must still be answered ...
> Oh, what are we going to do about the rich?
> What are we going to do about the rich?
> (Pet Shop Boys, *Agenda* EP, 2019)

When protestors filled streets and squares around the world in 2011 and 2012, frequently under the banner of 'Occupy,' two issues stood out. One was economic inequality and austerity. A second, as Mary Kaldor and Sabine Selchow note in their discussion of assembly movements in Europe at this time, was 'extensive frustration with formal politics as it is currently practiced ... current protests are not so much simply about austerity but about *politics*' (Kaldor and Selchow 2013, 84). For example, Italian protestors against a new high-speed rail link between Turin and Lyon spoke of 'political and economic oligarchies ... inflicting contested choices on local populations and institutions' (Kaldor and Selchow 2013, 85). This frustration was linked to 'projects of collective re-imagining of democracy' (Kaldor and Selchow 2013, 88).

In this chapter, we address this concern with oligarchy in the spirit of supporting a collective reimagining of democracy. Our focus is how *constitutions* can address oligarchy. Ganesh Sitaraman notes how constitutional theory often does not address this problem, perhaps because, as he also argues, such theory often assumes a 'middle-class' society characterised by a broad spread of wealth (Sitaraman 2016a, 2016b).[1] This leaves constitutional theory ill-equipped to address problems of real-world capitalist democracies with substantial wealth inequality. Addressing this gap, we ask: how can we use a constitution – a codified and entrenched set of fundamental laws – to limit the problem of oligarchy?

First, in Section 1, we clarify the problem. Fundamentally, the problem is of oligarchic *power*: an oligarchy holding undue opportunity for political influence. The consequence of oligarchic power, however, is likely to be oligarchic *impact*: a skewing of policy away from the interests of

DOI: 10.4324/9781003173632-17

those whom we term, without pejorative intention, 'commoners.' If oligarchic power was one of the concerns of the Occupy protesters, then oligarchic impact – arguably reflected in economic inequality and austerity – was another. Section 1 also explains how we understand the term 'oligarchy' and identifies some mechanisms which produce oligarchic power in formally democratic politics.

In Sections 2 and 3 we consider how constitutions can help democracies mitigate the problem. One strategy is to use a constitution to anticipate and restrain potential oligarchic impact. For example, if we anticipate that oligarchic impact will weaken a welfare state's protections then we can use a constitution to make such protections harder to challenge. This strategy has limitations, however. Set the bar of protection too high, or define it too precisely, and we arguably have an undue limitation on democratic decision-making as well as on oligarchic impact. In Section 3 we therefore consider a second strategy: to structure the political process itself to counter oligarchic power, for example through special 'plebian' or 'commoner' institutions. In Section 4 we conclude that a pluralistic approach, addressing oligarchic impact and power, and addressing oligarchic power in multiple ways, is most promising.[2]

1 Oligarchic Power and Impact as Constitutional Problems

We begin by clarifying the criteria for oligarchy, oligarchic power, and oligarchic impact.

Democracy does not require that people have equality of actual political influence. If some exert more influence through more political participation, where all have equal opportunity to participate, this is not necessarily undemocratic. But if some exert less influence due to their race or gender, for example, or because poverty limits their participation, then they have less opportunity for influence, and this is undemocratic. To capture this thought, we shall say that individuals in a democracy should have substantive (not merely formal) *equality of opportunity for political influence* (Cohen 2009).

We understand the term 'oligarch' in three analytically distinct, but not mutually exclusive, ways. First, it refers to *the wealthy, broadly construed* – say, those in the top few percentages of the income or wealth distribution. This is an elite group, but a large one: the 'mass affluent' (Winters 2011). Second, it refers to the *very rich*, a small subset of the first group: perhaps the top 0.01%, or the 'billionaire class.' The mass affluent fly business class; the billionaire class can own an airline. Third, it refers to *business corporations*. The political influence of corporations links back to that of the wealthy and the very rich as they are more likely to hold corporations' assets.

In contrast to these overlapping definitions of oligarchy, we identify the 'non-oligarchs,' or 'plebians' (Vergara 2019) or 'commoners.' This group includes 'the working class,' 'the proletariat,' and 'the poor' but, crucially, it also includes 'the middle class,' 'the petit bourgeoisie,' and others who might enjoy moderate prosperity but are not in the oligarchic elite. This analysis treats all non-oligarchs (whether the 'bottom 90%' or the 'bottom 99%') as fellow-commoners – as members of 'the people' as against the oligarchs. The distinction between oligarchs and commoners therefore mirrors imperfectly distinctions between patricians and plebians in republican Rome or *grandi* and *popolo* in medieval and early modern Florence (Vergara 2019, 255).

Oligarchic *power* arises when the wealthy and/or the very rich and/or business corporations have greater opportunity to exercise political influence than is compatible with the principle of equal opportunity for political influence. This is a direct violation of democratic principle. It can also have undesirable impacts on policy, e.g., by making the economy work less effectively for the good of all. We refer to these policy effects as oligarchic *impact*.

How can oligarchic power and impact arise? In any democracy citizens will possess equal votes and equal rights to stand for elected office. How do the wealthy, the very rich, and business corporations gain undue power in spite of this equality? Let's consider four possible mechanisms.

1.1 Opportunity of Oligarchs to Shape the Preferences of Elected Representatives

Election, as opposed to choosing representatives by lot, has been long recognised as an inherently oligarchic form of representation, in which those who are wealthy – and who enjoy the other advantages that flow from wealth, such as independence from employment, time, contacts, public profile, and education – have systematic advantages, in standing for office and winning elections, over the non-wealthy (Manin 1997). Where elections have costs, and candidates rely on private donors for funding, candidates are pressured to become more attuned to the policy preferences of those who give them funds. These will tend to be richer citizens who have more capacity to donate funds. Some argue that the skew in policy towards wealthy preferences in the USA is rooted in this mechanism (Lessig 2015). Other costs, not fully met by public sources, such as those related to research and staffing, increase the potential for the wealthy, very rich, and business corporations, to shape elected representatives' preferences.

Wealthier citizens will also have more resources to support lobbying activity. In addition, business corporations can offer incentives to politicians in terms of positions outside of politics. If a corporation relies on politicians' decisions for business, then it might seek to influence their decisions by offering them (or hinting at the future offer of) paid positions within the firm. This 'revolving door' can reinforce the business's lobbying efforts as former politicians use their connections to promote the business's interests.

1.2 Opportunity of Oligarchs to Shape the Preferences of Other State Officials

In most representative democracies, representatives are reliant on professional civil servants for advice (Weber 1948, 196–244). Judicial review of policy can give the judiciary an effective policy-making role. A government's ability to enforce its will ultimately depends on the police, military, and intelligence services. All these officials occupy a place in society. What if they share a social background with the wealthy or the very rich? Even where leading state officials are drawn from a wider demographic base, they can come to share a social milieu with oligarchs (Miliband 1969). This makes it more likely that they favour their interests. They might do their job with conscientious commitment to the public good. However, their assumptions about what serves the public good are likely shaped by their relative social proximity to oligarchs. 'Revolving door' mechanisms will tend to reinforce this bias.

1.3 Opportunity of Oligarchs to Shape Popular Preferences

Oligarchs can use their wealth to influence popular preferences. This might happen within economic enterprises, for example if business owners present employees with information to influence how they vote and forbid trade unions from entering the premises to give an alternative view (Anderson 2017). Oligarchs can use resources to support media outlets and thereby exert influence on public opinion. Social media platforms offer possibilities for contesting dominant political narratives, but oligarchs can seize these opportunities too. Public broadcasting might offer 'balance' in media coverage. But if leading officials in public broadcasting are socially close to the wealthy and very rich, their conception of what 'balance' is might be skewed towards the views of the wealthier. The social and cultural influence of the very wealthy is exercised also through 'think tanks,' gifts to universities, and by funding 'astroturf' campaigns to shift the terms of political discourse.

1.4 'Business Confidence'

Elected politicians generally wish to get re-elected. Their chances diminish if the economy performs poorly. The economy will perform poorly if capital-owners withhold investment, and they might withhold investment if they judge policies to be against their interests. Even if a policy has public support, the prospect of a negative reaction from capital-owners will act as a constraint (Lindblom 1977, Christiano 2010, Bennett 2021). Given a very unequal distribution of capital, this effectively puts a degree of veto power in the hands of wealthier citizens and business corporations.

This source of oligarchic power seems ineliminable in a society that is both 'liberal' and capitalist: a society in which private property rights confer control over investment on property-owners and the state is committed to uphold private property rights (Block 1987; see Bennett 2021, for a qualified counterargument). In this respect, one can argue that all capitalist democracies are in practice a form of 'mixed constitution' combining democratic elements with oligarchic (Aristotle 1984).

This, however, is not grounds for fatalism. Constitutional provisions can have a major effect on the degree of oligarchic power and impact. How, then, might the constitution – understood as a codified and entrenched, supreme and fundamental law – help address oligarchic power and impact? We consider this question in the next two sections.

2 Constitutional Defences against Oligarchic Impact

If we anticipate that oligarchs will potentially wield undue power, and that this will impact policy, we might try to limit the potential impact through constitutional provisions that restrain some policy outcomes while mandating or encouraging others. The constitution may provide the impetus for actions or policy choices aimed at the public good, while outcomes favouring oligarchic interests are prohibited or made more difficult.

Such constitutional provisions can operate: (a) positively, by encouraging or requiring certain public-regarding policy choices or (b) negatively, by discouraging, hindering or prohibiting pro-oligarchic policy choices. Positive provisions can be permissive (granting a power to act), directive (creating a moral duty or expectation to act), procedural (making it easier to act in particular ways, through removal of procedural obstacles that would otherwise apply) or prescriptive (requiring and entrenching policy choices). Negative provisions can be prohibitive (denying a power to act) or procedural (making it harder to act in particular ways through procedural obstacles). Let's review these possibilities.

2.1 Positive (Public-Regarding) Policy Prescriptions

Permissive provisions can be found in many constitutions. In a unitary state, the national legislature may be broadly empowered to act for the public good under a formula such as 'parliament may enact all laws for the peace, order and good government' of the country. In a federal or regionalised country, the constitutional division of powers between levels of government means that the provisions will be vested at the national level only if agreed through an appropriate process. For example, section 52 of the Australian constitution was amended in 1946 to enable the federal Parliament to legislate for the 'provision of maternity allowances, widows' pensions, child endowment, unemployment, pharmaceutical, sickness and hospital benefits, medical and dental services [...], benefits to students and family allowances.' This provision does not itself create a right to any of those policies. However, the fact that these powers have been conferred and are explicit in the constitution creates a public expectation that they be used. It also protects the exercise of these powers against judicial challenge.

Directive Principles are values that the constitution directs the state to pursue. They entered the corpus of Westminster Model constitutionalism via Ireland, where initially they were used, in the constitution of 1937, to embed principles of Catholic Social Teaching into the institutional framework of a liberal democracy (Keogh and McCarthy 2007). In India, Directive Principles were first used in an explicitly anti-oligarchic, and, indeed, pro-poor, way (Austin 1966, Khaitan 2018, Gavai 2021). Directive Principles have been used in other Commonwealth countries, including Bangladesh, Pakistan, Malta, Nigeria, and Sri Lanka.

Some Directive Principles may be framed as socioeconomic rights or entitlements – such as the right to housing, education, healthcare, sanitation, decent wages, and working conditions. For example, the Constitution of Malta states that workers are 'entitled to a weekly day of rest and to annual holidays with pay' (art. 13) and to 'reasonable insurance on a contributory basis for their requirements in case of accident, illness, disability, old-age and involuntary unemployment' (art. 15).

Other Directive Principles may be framed as positive obligations on the state. Taking Malta again, the Constitution does not include a 'right to culture,' but gives the state an obligation 'to promote the development of culture' (art. 8) and to 'safeguard the landscape and the historical and artistic patrimony of the Nation' (art. 9). Either way, Directive Principles are non-justiciable: the rights conferred by them are not directly enforceable in a court, and the obligations placed on the state – while genuinely *constitutional* obligations – are morally and politically, rather than legally, binding. As the Constitution of Malta states (in wording very similar to that found in other countries using Directive Principles), 'The provisions of this chapter shall not be enforceable in any court, but the principles therein contained are nevertheless fundamental to the governance of the country and it shall be the aim of the State to apply these principles in making laws' (art. 21). The constitutional obligation therefore falls chiefly upon the legislature to translate these principles, by ordinary legislation, into enforceable rights or government programmes.

Directive Principles are not mere verbiage. They create expectations and can legitimate certain policies while de-legitimating others. Constitutions are addressed not only to courts, but also to Ministers, civil servants, parliamentarians, and the public. There can also be forms of non-judicial enforcement of Directive Principles. For example, many constitutions establish an independent Human Rights Commission, whose remit is to monitor the country's human rights situation, to conduct investigations into complains, and to report to Parliament (see, for example, the Constitution of Fiji, section 45). Such a commission could also have responsibility for reporting on progress towards the fulfilment of Directive Principles.

Moreover, while Directive Principles are not directly enforceable, courts do not simply ignore them. In India, the Supreme Court has asserted the relevance of the Directive Principles, regarding them as part of the 'the conscience of the constitution'; they are distinct from justiciable Fundamental Rights but nevertheless on a par with them, such that the constitution as a whole should be applied and interpreted in ways that are consistent with the Directive Principles (Gavai 2021). It is a speculative point of constitutional design, but there is scope in an anti-oligarchic constitution for a fuller recognition of the judicial role in the application of Directive Principles. In the UK, under the Human Rights Act 1998, there is a mechanism that, while it does not give the courts the power to annul Acts of Parliament that infringe guaranteed rights, does require the courts to read ordinary legislation in ways that are, if possible, consistent with those guaranteed rights and, where this is not possible, to issue a Declaration of Incompatibility which triggers a fast-track to parliamentary rectification (Young 2017). Such a process might provide the courts with a flexible means of promoting adherence to Directive Principles.

Finally, we come to directly judicially enforceable socioeconomic provisions. These might be socioeconomic *rights*, but they can also be framed as state obligations. However, given the nature of these rights – and the demands they place upon both the state's fiscal resources and its governance capacity – the rights themselves are not always absolute and their enforcement is not always directly applicable. For example, the South African constitution establishes enforceable rights to social goods such as housing (art. 26). As interpreted by the Constitutional Court in the Grootboom case (*Government of the Republic of South Africa & Ors v Grootboom & Ors 2000*), this provision places an enforceable constitutional obligation on the government to develop and implement a housing strategy to give effect to the right, but does not necessarily mean a person has a right to be provided with a house (Klug 2010). In practice, therefore, even enforceable socioeconomic rights depend not only upon the willingness of courts to give legal effect to them, but also upon the ability of Parliaments and Governments to deliver the goods.

2.2 Negative Policy Prohibitions

A constitution might also address potential oligarchic impact by placing certain policy choices 'off-limits.' Just as a liberal-democratic constitution prevents an Act of Parliament from unduly restricting freedom of speech, an anti-oligarchic constitution could contain provisions limiting Parliament's capacity to shift the tax burden from oligarchs to commoners, or to privatise public assets. Any legislation attempting to do this could be challenged in court and, if found unconstitutional, annulled.[3]

Another form of negative policy provision places procedural hurdles in the way of certain policies. For example, instead of prohibiting privatisation of the National Health Service, the constitution might provide that no healthcare services may be privatised except with the approval of a two-thirds majority in Parliament or by means of a referendum. There are already examples of such procedures applied to civil and political rights. In Sweden, an Act of Parliament limiting certain constitutionally protected rights can be delayed for a year – to give time for a rethink, and for civil society opposition to organise – at the request of ten members of Parliament. This delay may be over-ridden only by a 5/6ths majority vote of the members of Parliament. Such provisions, extended to policy areas such as tax, welfare, and privatisation, could protect public-regarding policies from oligarchic impact.

2.3 Implications and Limitations

This policy-embedding approach to restraining oligarchic impact affects how we understand the nature of the constitution. The myth of 'constitutional neutrality' is rejected in favour of a substantive 'national covenant' that pre-commits the state to certain values and, broadly speaking, policies and outcomes (Bulmer 2015). What are the implications of this, and what are the limitations of the approach?

First, if the constitution is to have such policy commitments, then it is crucial that the constitution-making and amendment processes are themselves deeply democratic. This follows from the underlying principle of equal opportunity for political influence and, more specifically, is likely to be instrumentally important to weakening oligarchic power in making the constitution itself. In a recent judgment, the High Court of Kenya held that the 'essential features of the constitution that form the basic structure can only be changed through the people by exercising the primary constitutive authority' (Roznai 2021). The court held that an adequate amendment process must therefore have four stages: civic education, public discussion, deliberation in a constitutional assembly, followed by a referendum on the assembly's proposals (*David Ndii and Others v Attorney-General and Others*, para. 4740). Mandating popular participation in this way helps to ensure commoners a greater say in constitution-making (see also Landemore 2021, chapter 7).

A second issue is that it may not be desirable for a constitution to lock-in specific policy measures. Reasonable citizens can disagree about whether a 'social minimum' to end poverty is best achieved through universal basic income, a negative income tax, or by various other means. These sorts of policy questions are not best answered by the constitution. In seeking to limit oligarchic impact, we should be careful not to unduly limit the discretion of democratic politicians and citizens to make inevitable choices and trade-offs. Otherwise, our effort to limit oligarchic impact will constrain democracy as well.

Third, attempting to pre-commit the state to specified policies through constitutional mandates might be ineffective if the implementation of these provisions is left to institutions – judicial, administrative, or parliamentary – that are themselves sites of oligarchic power. Roberto Gargarella argues that attempts by Latin American countries in the middle of the twentieth century to hitch socialist or social-democratic rights to an essentially oligarchic system of governance (as, for example, with the 1938 Constitution of Bolivia and 1949 Constitution of Argentina) did not produce the desired outcomes (2010). This points to the importance of how a society arranges recruitment into these powerful official positions.

Without discounting permissive powers, Directive Principles and socioeconomic rights, together with certain policy prohibitions, it is therefore also crucial to be aware of these limitations, and to consider a second approach, one that seeks to limit oligarchic power directly through anti-oligarchic design of systems of representation, policy-making, and accountability.

3 Constitutional Defences against Oligarchic Power

In this section we first consider how familiar constitutional design choices in representative democracies can speak directly to limiting oligarchic power. We then consider a number of proposals specifically for tackling oligarchic power: direct democracy; sortition and Citizens' Assemblies; plebeian assemblies and participatory budgeting; and associative democracy.

3.1 The Relevance of Basic Constitutional Design Choices

Familiar constitutional design choices – such as whether a state is presidential or parliamentary, majoritarian or proportional in its electoral system, bicameral or unicameral in its legislature, federal or unitary – can all matter to limiting oligarchic power. Consider the Norwegian and Swedish constitutions, which are parliamentary, proportional, unicameral, and unitary. This combination is 'centripetal' (Gerring, Thacker, and Moreno 2005). Proportional electoral systems and parliamentarism make policy-making inclusive rather than exclusive, while the combination of unicameralism and unitary governance reduces the number of veto-players and makes policy implementation more coherent. These centripetal constitutions restrain abuses of power – they protect fundamental rights, establish accountability mechanisms, and prevent incumbent governments from easily changing the basic rules of democracy – but they do not place constitutional obstacles in the way of popularly supported majorities seeking to pursue anti-oligarchic policies (Arter 2006).

Centripetalism is harder to apply to large, diverse societies, where federalism and bicameralism may be necessary to represent regional differences. But in this kind of case, certain powers might be better exercised at the federal level to counter oligarchic power. For example, the mode of federalism adopted in India includes residual powers at the Union level, broad 'concurrent powers' in relation to which Union legislation prevails over State legislation, and provisions for State powers to be temporarily exercised by the Union. This reflects a desire to use the power of the Union government to overcome local oligarchies and pursue coherent policies of development and social justice (Austin 1966). A further complication, of course, is that reducing veto players through unitary governance could also make it easier for oligarchs to dominate the polity if they can capture the centre. There are no very simple or general prescriptions here other than to consider in context how basic constitutional design choices for a representative democracy have implications for oligarchic power.

3.2 Constitutionalising Campaign Finance and Anti-Corruption Measures

We turn now to measures aimed specifically at limiting oligarchic power. One obvious focus is the regulation of money in politics. The constitution, for example, could mandate the public funding of political parties, require limits on campaign spending and contributions to parties and campaigns, and require transparency for political donations. These are well-tested measures that, to greater or lesser extents, and with greater or lesser degrees of effectiveness, already exist around the world (Falguera, Jones, and Ohman 2014). Constitutional measures could also address the 'revolving door' between business and politics. For example, the constitution could specify that elected representatives and senior civil servants are prohibited from any paid directorship or consultancy while in, or for a substantial period (at least one full electoral cycle) after, office. Similarly, those in high office might be required to declare all their personal wealth and interests on entering and on leaving office, with independent audits to require them to justify any unexplained gains.

Many of these measures could be embodied in ordinary legislation rather than being constitutionalised. But insofar as constitutional laws are harder to repeal or amend (are 'entrenched') they will be less vulnerable to changes in government. A constitution is also the place in which a polity can make a clear, public declaration of how free speech protections relate to things like campaign spending and donations. In the USA, the Supreme Court has interpreted the First Amendment right to freedom of speech so as to rule out numerous legislative restrictions on campaign spending. In so doing, the Court downplays or denies what John Rawls calls 'the fair value of the political liberties,' that the value of political liberties, such as to vote and stand for office, should not be dependent on economic advantage (Rawls 1993). However, if limits on campaign spending and the like are mandated in the constitution itself, with an explicit statement that free speech rights may not be understood as undercutting these limits, then this will help protect such laws from judicial challenge.

3.3 Direct Democracy

Another possible response to oligarchic power is direct democracy. The idea is to endow the public with rights to initiate legislative proposals independently of elected representatives or to challenge the laws these representatives have made, with the final decision depending on a direct vote in a referendum. In the USA, many state constitutions have direct democracy provisions of this kind. These were mostly put in place in the early twentieth century as a response to the perceived oligarchic dependency of elected state legislatures (Smith and Lubinski 2002).

Direct democracy provisions, however, are often ineffective, even counterproductive, as anti-oligarchic measures. Oligarchs can mobilise their wealth to fund referendum initiatives and/or to block referendum proposals they dislike. Turnout in referendums is typically lower than for legislative elections, and this creates an opportunity for a well-resourced campaign to mobilise a relatively small minority of voters decisively to support or oppose a specific proposal (Smith 2009, 329). Moreover, turnout is highest among wealthier voters (Smith 2009, 332–33). One study of direct democracy at the state level in the USA concluded that while business corporations are not that effective in initiating legislative proposals they wanted, they are effective in using their resources to block legislation proposed in this way (Gerber 1999). As with elections to legislatures, it would be possible to some extent to limit the power of the wealthy and business corporations in direct democracy through tighter regulatory frameworks that limit spending on petition or voting campaigns. These frameworks can be constitutionally required. Absent these measures, however, those looking to direct democracy as a solution to oligarchic power will be disappointed.

3.4 Sortition and Citizens' Assemblies

Another response to concerns about the potential oligarchic dependency of elected representatives is to change the way of choosing representatives: choose them by lot, a process known as *sortition* (Dowlen 2008, Goodwin 2013 [1992]). In contemporary discussions, sortition is often connected with the model of the Citizens' Assembly (CA). Pioneered for consideration of electoral reform in British Colombia and Ontario, CAs have recently been used in Ireland to bring about liberalising reforms to the country's constitution (Lang 2007, Smith 2009, Farrell 2014). CAs are set up to be broadly statistically representative of the population along dimensions such as race, gender, and region, with participants being selected at random within the selected demographic categories. They are tasked with considering a question and move through stages of education on an issue, hearing evidence and testimony, and deliberating a recommendation. They are professionally facilitated.

Could CAs or similar sortition-based initiatives help limit oligarchic power? Some popular campaigns have presented CAs in particular as an anti-oligarchic device. There is a strong element of this in Extinction Rebellion's call for CAs on climate policy (Extinction Rebellion 2021). Most ambitiously, the philosopher Alexander Guerrero has proposed completely replacing elected legislatures with sortition-based assemblies (2014). He argues that while economic elites have ability and incentive to shape the preferences of elected representatives, the wider public has much less capacity for this. So, to overcome this elite bias inherent in elective democracy, all legislation should be made through sortition-based assemblies. Hélène Landemore has also recently argued for a substantial shift away from elected representation to sortition-based assemblies, pointing to the failure of elected representation to generate assemblies with the demographic and epistemic diversity necessary for quality deliberation (Landemore 2021, 42–43).

We consider that CAs do have some potential as tools in the anti-oligarchic toolkit, but we need to acknowledge their limitations and also be clear about the kind of institutional context in which they will have the potential to function as an anti-oligarchic device. To begin with, it seems implausible to us that CAs or similar sortition-based assemblies should altogether replace elected legislatures. The lack of election in this model raises questions about mandate and accountability. CAs decide in isolation, after intense deliberation supported by expert advice. Unless their decisions are tied to other stages in a decision-making process, which require decisions to be ratified by or responsible to the general public, there is a risk CAs may cause alienation. Public participation, in a system based solely on CAs, would be reduced to waiting for your number to come up to attend a CA – something that might happen only once in a lifetime (if that). There would be no need, if elections, manifestos, and campaigns were removed, for the public to take an ongoing interest in politics.

On the other hand, if CAs function in the way they typically do at the moment, as consultative bodies for elected politicians, then they might not perform an effective anti-oligarchic role. In most cases to date, CAs have been established at the initiative of elected representatives, to consider issues chosen by elected representatives, with recommendations usually being referred back to these representatives. In this consultative model, CAs cannot be used to raise issues or make legislative proposals independently of elected representatives and, consequently, probably cannot be a significant corrective to whatever oligarchic power is being exercised over elected representatives.

Sortition and CAs can fit into a political system in other ways, however. One possibility is to have a sortition-selected second chamber acting as a house of revision and review, with potential veto and agenda-setting powers, alongside a primary chamber elected in the usual way. In the UK context, Anthony Barnett and Peter Carty (2008) have suggested that a proportion of seats in a reformed House of Lords should be chosen by sortition: the so-called 'Athenian Option.' In the USA, Kevin O'Leary has proposed a People's House, consisting of 43,500 delegates – 100 from each of the existing congressional districts. Members of the People's House would keep their full-time jobs and would receive a 'modest per diem' for the 'two or three times a month' that the People's House sits online (O'Leary 2006). This People's House would not replace the existing Congress, but would sit alongside it, as a virtual third chamber. It would have powers to both veto and initiate legislative proposals. Another option is to amend the initiative power in direct democracy so that instead of citizens having the power to initiate a referendum, they have the power to initiate a CA on a topic of concern. This CA could itself have the power to put proposals to the elected legislature or, perhaps, to put them to a referendum (White 2020).

None of these possibilities is without its possible drawbacks, but they do show that sortition can be integrated into the political system in ways that enable non-rich citizens to put new issues on the agenda or even to block policies that have the support of the elected branch(es) of the legislature.

Of course, even in this case, sortition-based assemblies will only counter oligarchic power if they are themselves relatively insulated from oligarchic pressures. There need to be clear anti-corruption rules regulating these institutions (e.g., in terms of producing initial educational materials for participants and evidence gathering for CAs, and preventing conflicts of interest and 'revolving door' contracts for representatives).

3.5 Plebian Assemblies

CAs typically draw members from the whole citizen (or resident) population. But if the objective is specifically to press back against oligarchic power, one option is to create representative institutions whose members are specifically drawn from, or more weighted towards, commoners/

plebians. Historically, the civic republican 'mixed constitution' integrated this idea. For example, in the Roman republic the power of the Senate, exclusive to the patrician class, was balanced by that of the tribunes, elected by the plebs. As Sitaraman puts it, this current of constitutional thinking, traceable back to Aristotle's *Politics*, envisages 'class warfare' constitutions with formal representation of elites and commoners/plebs in distinct institutions that balance one another (Aristotle 1984, Sitaraman 2016b, 2017).

One proposal that moves somewhat in this direction is to reserve a proportion of seats in the elected legislature for 'non-elite' candidates (Hamilton 2013). This could work similarly to measures used to promote gender balance in Parliaments. Women's quotas, gender-balanced lists (in proportionally elected Parliaments) and all-women shortlists (in first-past-the-post elections) are now a relatively common form of institutional design (Dahlerup, Hilal, Kalandadze, and Kandawasvika-Nhundu 2014). Similarly, we could consider commoner quotas, class-balanced lists or all-plebian shortlists. Arguably India, which reserves a quota of seats for 'Scheduled Castes and Tribes' and 'Other Backward Classes,' currently approaches this technique.

Another proposal, explicitly echoing the Roman Republic, is for a national Tribunate, suggested by John McCormick for the USA (McCormick 2011). McCormick envisages the Tribunate as a permanent institution sitting alongside the US Presidency, the two houses of Congress and the Supreme Court. The Tribunate would have fifty-one members, selected by lot for a non-renewable term of one year. It would expressly exclude citizens in the top 10% of the wealth distribution and those holding (or who recently held) elected office. Sortition would be weighted so that Native American and African American citizens, who continue to be underrepresented in elected bodies, would have a better-than-equal chance of inclusion (McCormick 2011, 183). The Tribunes would have five powers, each of which, like a bee's sting, could be used only once during their year in office: to veto one Act of Congress, cancel one Executive Order, overturn one Supreme Court decision, call one national referendum, and impeach one federal official (McCormick 2011, 184). The powers of the Tribunate are therefore corrective and protective, designed to enable commoners to protect their interests against elites. Unlike O'Leary's proposal, McCormick's does not vastly expand the scale of representation. The Tribunes would be a handful in a population of hundreds of millions. There will need also to be safeguards against the pressures of lobbyists.

As with McCormick, Camila Vergara proposes a specifically plebeian institution as an addition to the existing US political system (Vergara 2019). The core institution in Vergara's proposal is the local assembly, a face-to-face assembly of around 500 people, scheduled to meet three times a year. All of those not in positions of political leadership – 'those who have the ability to formally exert power *over* others and unduly influence the creation of law and policy – for example, public officials and their staff, lobbyists, judges, military commanders, and religious leaders' will be members of a local assembly (Vergara 2019, 244). Each assembly has an agenda-setting council, chosen by lot from volunteers. The assemblies will operate on a tiered structure, such that proposals supported in one local assembly are then voted upon by those around them, going forward for adoption or for wider consideration if it gains enough support in other assemblies. Across the nation, the network of assemblies will have the power to veto policies, and by doing so to eject from office the elected officials who supported the policy; and the power to overturn judicial decisions, and thereby to remove the judges responsible for these decisions (Vergara 2019, 269). One possible problem with Vergara's proposal is the way she proposes to make the cut between oligarch and plebeian, using a notion of political power as the criterion rather than an economic ceiling. Once we move beyond the relatively easy case of elected officials, it is perhaps too contestable to try to make the cut on the basis of who has political power. In addition, Vergara's model will require a high level of consistent public participation which might not be forthcoming.

Although not formally plebeian assemblies, there are also lessons to be learned from India's *gram sabhas* or village assemblies (Parthasarathy, Rao, and Palaniswamy 2019). Shaped in part by Gandhian political thought, the 1993, 73rd amendment to the Indian constitution mandated the setting up of an elected council in every rural village (with a reserved proportion of places for women and for members of disadvantaged castes) and a village assembly of which every village resident is a member. The village assemblies are constitutionally required to meet at least twice a year, though this requirement has been raised in some states (e.g., at time of writing to six times a year in Tamil Nadu). They have a role in decisions concerning use of public funds in the village, e.g., for poverty alleviation and public infrastructure. Over 800 million rural residents are members of these assemblies, making them the 'the largest deliberative institution in human history' (Parthasarathy, Rao, and Palaniswamy 2019, 623). Their inclusive membership means that they can potentially offer a way for commoners/plebeians, in our terminology, to act as a counterweight to local elites. Recent research on the assemblies (focusing on assemblies in Tamil Nadu) indicates that people do exert real influence over public spending through them, although women face much higher barriers to effective participation than men (Parthasarathy, Rao, and Palaniswamy 2019). Another limitation of the assemblies is that their remit is delimited in geographical and policy terms, possibly leaving some important areas of policy off the table.

The Indian village assemblies are similar to the participatory budgeting (PB) approach developed in Porto Alegre, Brazil. The essential idea is that instead of a city's elected representatives making all public budget decisions, a proportion of the capital budget is allocated according to a deliberative process that builds up from local assemblies (Smith 2009, chapter 2). Popular participation in the basal assemblies is encouraged by weighting representation in higher decision-making bodies according to turnout in the more local assemblies. The shift to PB in Porto Alegre resulted in infrastructure and service spending becoming more targeted at poorer neighbourhoods. There were also relatively high levels of participation by poorer citizens (Smith 2009). Constitutionalising a role for PB in public spending decisions might therefore be another way of pushing back oligarchic power. However, there are again limitations to this approach. The efficacy of PB in terms of securing participation by poorer citizens depends on specific details of institutional design and on the extent to which PB works in a context of strong civil society groups that encourage their participation (Fung 2011). In this respect, PB's potential connects with the associative democracy strategies discussed below. Also, PB operates in a limited policy space. PB can shape how public funds are spent, but crucial questions about the overall level of public funding, as well as many other policy issues, are not typically for determination (see Wainwright 2009, 42).

3.6 Associative Democracy

Strong, encompassing associations in civil society, with a commoner membership, can provide a crucial counterweight to the organised power of oligarchs. The decline of labour unions, for example, seems to have been an important source of policy direction in the USA since the 1970s and in turn a major factor behind rising inequality (Hacker and Pierson 2011). In addition, associative democrats argue that associational life is not a pre-political and fixed feature of society but something that can be (and, consistent with the liberal value of freedom of association, in some ways may be) shaped by state policy (Cohen and Rogers 1994, Andrias 2015). A key challenge, therefore, is how to use the constitution to encourage the kind of associations that will serve as a counterweight to oligarchy.

One important application concerns trade unions. There is evidence that unions can increase levels of political participation, particularly among low-income groups, though there is also evidence that in some countries this is no longer the case, perhaps because unions have declined among these groups (O'Neill and White 2018, 256–58). Unions can offer their members – and indeed the wider public – an alternative source of information on public issues to that of oligarchically owned media. They can offer funds for campaigns, making elected representatives less dependent on oligarchs. They can provide valuable civic education functions. In terms of policy impact, higher levels of unionisation are often associated with lower levels of income inequality, more 'redistribution,' and a more expansive welfare state (Pontusson 2013, Kerrissey 2015).

The level, distribution, and form of union representation depend, however, on the legal regime that regulates union formation and action (Bogg 2009, Andrias 2016, Ewing and Hendy 2017). If it is thought undesirable to have the constitution mandate a specific industrial relations system, then a constitution can still define some key parameters that more detailed legislation must respect, such as that workers have effective rights to form and join unions, to collective bargaining through their unions, and an effective right to strike.

Another important potential counterweight to oligarchy is the political party. In much of the foregoing discussion we have pictured elected representatives from parties as potentially vulnerable to undue influence by oligarchs. But their responsiveness to oligarchs might be limited, for example, by robust internal party democracy in policy-making and candidate selection. If so, then perhaps an anti-oligarchic constitution should prescribe, or at least allow governments to make ordinary legislation that prescribes, robust internal party democracy in these areas. Electoral systems are also important, however. Proportional systems, for example, arguably make it easier for new parties to emerge to contest oligarchic influence over established parties. Moreover, parties arguably work best to contest oligarchic influence when they have strong links to organised interests such as labour unions (see Bagg and Bhatia 2021, for further discussion).

4 Conclusion: The Need for a Pluralist Approach

We have explored how we can use a constitution to advance anti-oligarchic politics. We began, in Section 1, by distinguishing the ideas of oligarchic power and impact and by reviewing some of the mechanisms by which oligarchic power and impact can emerge even within a formally egalitarian political system. Section 2 examined ways in which a constitution could limit oligarchic impact by pre-selecting policies to serve public interests and mandating the state to pursue those policies – or, at least, not to pursue contrary policies. Section 3 presented a range of constitutional options for limiting directly oligarchic power.

If there is an overall lesson it is that any effort to use the constitution to limit oligarchic impact and power must be pluralistic. It is important to address oligarchic power directly as well as seeking to anticipate the potential impact of such power. In seeking to limit oligarchic power, moreover, there is likely no single constitutional measure that will suffice. We need to think in terms of a toolkit and how different tools work together. Instead of thinking of say, citizens' initiatives/referendums, Citizens' Assemblies or associative democracy in isolation, we should think about how these (and/or other measures) might work together in mutually supportive, reinforcing ways.

Acknowledgements

The authors would like to thank the following for their very helpful comments: Udit Bhatia; the editors of this volume; and all of the participants in the conference for which this chapter was originally produced.

Notes

1. Sitaraman writes in the US context, but his points have a wider relevance.
2. There is another possible approach: use a constitution to prevent the rise of oligarchy, e.g., by measures that block the accumulation of large fortunes and spread wealth widely. This is one strand in the 'Anti-Oligarchy Constitution' tradition that James Fishkin and William E. Forbath discuss, and of the 'middle-class constitution' ideal that Ganesh Sitaraman discusses, in the US context (Fishkin and Forbath 2014, Sitaraman 2016b, 2017). We do not consider this approach explicitly here. However, this approach will have substantial overlap with the first, impact-focused approach that we do discuss. Our discussion also assumes the democratic nation state as its context, but has relevance to the development of transnational political structures too, which are arguably needed to tackle some aspects of oligarchical power (such as reduced taxation of corporate profits due to tax competition between nations and tax avoidance through offshore tax havens).
3. One urgent issue needing more attention than we can give it here is that of tax havens: territorial jurisdictions which offer low rates of taxation and secrecy protections for external investors. At present, multinational corporations and the global very rich are able to use tax havens to avoid democratically determined taxation for the common good (Zucman 2016). Multinational corporations, for example, can use transactions between different national branches of the business so that company profits appear only where tax rates are negligible. Tackling tax havens requires international cooperation, but national constitutional provisions can perhaps play a role in preventing this kind of oligarchic tax evasion. At the very least, constitutional provisions can place limits on a government's power to turn its own jurisdiction into a tax haven. One can also imagine a constitutional provision that directs the government to give priority to preventing tax avoidance in making future trade agreements. The measures considered in the third section of this chapter might also help by diminishing the power of oligarchs to block national governments from seeking to combine with others to address it.

References

Anderson, Elizabeth. 2017. *Private Government: How Employers Rule Our Lives (and Why We Don't Talk about It*. Princeton, NJ: Princeton University Press.

Andrias, Kate. 2015. "Separations of Wealth: Inequality and the Erosion of Checks and Balances." *University of Pennsylvania Journal of Constitutional Law* 18: 419–504.

———. 2016. "Building Labor's Constitution." *Texas Law Review* 94: 1591–622.
Aristotle, trans. C. Lord. 1984. *The Politics*. Chicago, IL: University of Chicago.
Arter, David. 2006. *Democracy in Scandinavia*. Manchester: Manchester University Press.
Austin, Granville. 1966. *The Indian Constitution: Cornerstone of a Nation*. Oxford: Oxford University Press.
Bagg, Samuel, and Bhatia, Udit. 2021. "Intra-Party Democracy: A Functionalist Account." *Journal of Political Philosophy*. https://doi.org/10.1111/jopp.12270.
Barnett, Anthony, and Carty, Peter. 2008. *The Athenian Option: Radical Reform for the House of Lords*. Exeter: Imprint Academic.
Bennett, Michael. 2021. "The Capital Flight Quadrilemma: Democratic Trade-Offs and International Investment." *Ethics & Global Politics* 14 (4): 199–217.
Block, Fred. 1987. *Revising State Theory: Essays in Politics and Postindustrialism*. Philadelphia, PA: Temple University Press.
Bogg, Alan. 2009. *The Democratic Aspects of Trade Union Recognition*. Oxford: Hart.
Bulmer, W. Elliot. 2015. *A Constitution for the Common Good: Strengthening Scottish Democracy After the Independence Referendum*. Edinburgh: Luath Press.
Christiano, Thomas. 2010. "The Uneasy Relationship Between Democracy and Capital." *Social Philosophy and Policy* 27 (1): 195–217.
Cohen, Joshua. 2009. "Money, Politics, Democratic Equality." In Joshua Cohen, *Philosophy, Politics, Democracy: Selected Essays*, 268–301. Cambridge, MA: Harvard University Press.
Cohen, Joshua, and Rogers, Joel. 1994. *Associations and Democracy*. London: Verso.
Dahlerup, Drude, Hilal, Zeina, Kalandadze, Nana, Kandawasvika-Nhundu, Rumbidzai. 2014. *Atlas of Gender Electoral Quotas*. Stockholm: International Institute for Democracy and Electoral Assistance.
Dowlen, Oliver. 2008. *The Political Potential of Sortition: A Study of the Random Selection of Citizens for Public Office*. Exeter: Imprint Academic.
Ewing, Keith, and Hendy, John. 2017. "New Perspectives on Collective Labour Law: Trade Union Recognition and Collective Bargaining." *Industrial Law Journal* 46 (1): 23–51.
Extinction Rebellion. 2021. 'Citizens' Assembly'. https://extinctionrebellion.uk/go-beyond-politics/citizens-assembly/. Accessed 2 February 2021.
Falguera, Elin, Jones, Samuel, and Ohman, Magnus. 2014. *Funding of Political Parties and Election Campaigns: A Handbook on Political Finance*. Stockholm: International Institute for Democracy and Electoral Assistance.
Farrell, David. 2014. "The 2013 Irish Constitutional Convention: A Bold Step or a Damp Squib?" In., *75 Years of the Constitution of Ireland: An Irish-Italian Dialogue*, edited by Giuseppe Franco Ferrari and John O'Dowd, 292–305. Dublin: Clarus.
Fishkin, James, and Forbath, William E. 2014. "The Anti-Oligarchy Constitution." *Boston University Law Review* 94: 669–96.
Fung, Archon. 2011. "Reinventing Democracy in Latin America." *Perspectives on Politics* 9 (4): 857–71.
Gargarella, Roberto. 2010. *The Legal Foundations of Inequality: Constitutionalism in the Americas*. Cambridge: Cambridge University Press.

Gavai, B. R. 2021. "Directive Principles and the Courts." *India Legal.* https://www.indialegallive.com/commentary/directive-principles-state-policy-relevance-contemporary-constitutional-jurisprudence/.

Gerber, Elizabeth R. 1999. *The Populist Paradox: Interest Group Influence and the Promise of Direct Legislation.* Princeton, NJ: Princeton University Press.

Gerring, John, Thacker, Strom C., and Moreno, Carola. 2005. "Centripetal Democratic Governance: A Theory and Global Inquiry." *American Political Science Review* 99 (4): 567–81.

Goodwin, Barbara. 2013 [1992]. *Justice by Lottery*, second edition. Exeter: Imprint Academic.

Guerrero, Alexander A. 2014. "Against Elections: The Lottocratic Alternative." *Philosophy and Public Affairs* 42 (2): 135–78.

Hacker, Jacob S., and Pierson, Paul. 2011. *Winner-Take-All Politics: How Washington Made the Rich Richer – and Turned its Back on the Middle Class.* New York, NY: Simon and Schuster.

Hamilton, Lawrence. 2013. *Freedom is Power: Liberty Through Political Representation.* Cambridge: Cambridge University Press.

Kaldor, Mary, and Selchow, Sabine. 2013. "The 'Bubbling Up' of Subterranean Politics in Europe." *Journal of Civil Society* 9 (1): 78–99.

Keogh, Dermot, and McCarthy, Andrew. 2007. *The Making of the Irish Constitution 1937: Bunreacht na hÉireann.* Cork: Mercier Press.

Kerrissey, Jasmine. 2015. "Collective Labor Rights and Income Inequality." *American Sociological Review* 80 (3): 626–653.

Khaitan, Tarunabh. 2018. "Directive Principles and the Expressive Accommodation of Ideological Dissenters." *International Journal of Constitutional Law* 16 (2): 389–420.

Klug, Heinz. 2010. *The Constitution of South Africa: A Contextual Analysis.* London: Bloomsbury Publishing.

Landemore, Hélène. 2021. *Open Democracy: Reinventing Popular Rule for the Twenty-First Century.* Princeton, NJ: Princeton University Press.

Lang, Amy. 2007. "But Is It for Real? The British Columbia Citizens' Assembly as a Model of State-Sponsored Citizen Empowerment." *Politics and Society* 35: 35–69.

Lessig, Lawrence. 2015. *Republic, Lost, Version 2.0: How Money Corrupts Congress – and a Plan to Stop It.* New York, NY: Twelve Books.

Lindblom, Charles. 1977. *Politics and Markets: The World's Political Economic Systems.* New Haven, CT: Yale University Press.

Manin, Bernard. 1997. *Principles of Representative Government.* Cambridge: Cambridge University Press.

McCormick, John. 2011. *Machiavellian Democracy.* Cambridge: Cambridge University Press.

Miliband, Ralph. 1969. *The State in Capitalist Society.* New York, NY: Basic Books.

Newham Democracy Commission. 2020. *Newham Democracy and Civic Participation Commission: Final Report.* London: Newham. https://www.newhamdemocracycommission.org/wp-content/uploads/Democracy-Commission-Report.pdf

O'Leary, Kevin. 2006. *Saving Democracy: A Plan for Real Representation in America.* Stanford, CA: Stanford University Press.

O'Neill, Martin, and White, Stuart. 2018. "Trade Unions and Political Equality." In *Philosophical Foundations of Labour*, edited by Hugh Collins, Gillian Lester and Virginia Mantouvalou, 252–68. Oxford: Oxford University Press.
Pettit, Philip. 1997. *Republicanism: A Theory of Freedom and Government*. Oxford: Oxford University Press.
———. 2012. *On the People's Terms: A Republican Theory of Democracy*. Cambridge: Cambridge University Press.
Parthasarathy, Ramya, Rao, Vijayendra, and Palaniswamy, Nethra. 2019. "Deliberative Democracy in an Unequal World: A *Text-as-Data* Study of South India's Village Assemblies." *American Political Science Review* 113 (3): 623–40.
Pontusson, Jonas. 2005. *Inequality and Prosperity: Social Europe vs Liberal America*. Ithaca, NY: Cornell University Press.
———. 2013. "Unionisation, Inequality and Redistribution." *British Journal of Industrial Relations* 51 (4): 797–825.
Rawls, John. 1993. "The Law of Peoples." *Critical Inquiry* 20 (1): 36–68.
Rousseau, Jean-Jacques, translated by Christopher Betts. 1994 [1762]. *The Social Contract*. Oxford: Oxford University Press.
Roznai, Yaniv. 2021. "The Basic Structure Doctrine Arrives in Kenya." *Verfassungsblog: On Matters Constitutional*. https://verfassungsblog.de/the-basic-structure-doctrine-arrives-in-kenya/
Sitaraman, Ganesh. 2016a. "The Puzzling Absence of Economic Power in Constitutional Theory." *Cornell Law Review* 101: 1445–532.
———. 2016b. "Economic Structure and Constitutional Structure: An Intellectual History." *Texas Law Review* 94: 1301–328.
———. 2017. *The Crisis of the Middle-Class Constitution: Why Economic Inequality Threatens Our Republic*. New York, NY: Alfred A. Knopf.
Smith, Daniel, and Lubinski, Joseph. 2002. "Direct Democracy During the Progressive Era: A Crack in the Populist Veneer?" *Journal of Policy History* 14 (4): 349–83.
Smith, Graham. 2009. *Democratic Innovations*. Cambridge: Cambridge University Press.
Vergara, Camila. 2019. *Systemic Corruption: Constitutional Ideas for an Anti-Oligarchic Republic*. Princeton, NJ: Princeton University Press.
Wainwright, Hilary. 2009. *Reclaim the State: Experiments in Popular Democracy*, Revised Edition. Calcutta: Seagull.
Weber, Max. 1948. "Bureaucracy." In *From Max Weber: Essays in Sociology*, edited by H.H. Gerth and C.W. Mills, 197–246. London: Routledge and Kegan Paul.
White, Stuart. 2020. "Citizens' Assemblies and Republican Democracy." In *Radical Republicanism: Recovering the Tradition's Popular Heritage*, edited by Bruno Leipold, Karma Nabulsi, and Stuart White, 81–99. Oxford: Oxford University Press.
Winters, Jeffrey E. 2011. *Oligarchy*. Cambridge: Cambridge University Press.
Young, Alison. 2017. *Democratic Dialogue and the Constitution*. Oxford: Oxford University Press.
Zucman, Gabriel. 2016. *The Hidden Wealth of Nations: The Scourge of Tax Havens*. Chicago, IL: University of Chicago Press.

15 Automation, Desert, and the Case for Capital Grants

Huub Brouwer

But what of the future? ... There would be a limited number of extremely wealthy property owners; the proportion of the working population required to man the extremely profitable automated industries would be small; wage rates would thus be depressed; there would have to be a large expansion of the production of the labor-intensive goods and services which were in demand by the few multi-multi-multi-millionaires; we would be back in a super-world of an immiserized proletariat and of butlers, footmen, kitchen maids, and other hangers-on. Let us call this the Brave New Capitalists' paradise. It is to me a hideous outlook. What could we do about it?

(Meade 1964, 33)

It is not difficult to recognise, in the world around us, elements of James Meade's dystopian Brave New Capitalist paradise. Billionaires such as Virgin founder Richard Branson, Tesla founder and CEO Elon Musk, and Amazon founder Jeff Bezos are so wealthy that they can pay for pleasure trips to space. When Bezos was interviewed after returning to earth on July 20, 2021, he thanked 'every Amazon employee and customer, because you guys paid for all this' (Spocchia 2021). Both Jeff Bezos and Elon Musk are on the list of the ten richest men in the world (Forbes 2022). Together, these ten men hold more wealth than the bottom 3.1 billion people (Oxfam 2022, 10). Wealth inequality in the United States has now reached levels only seen before in the Gilded Age (Zucman 2016): The richest 1% of the population holds 31% of the wealth (Federal Reserve 2022). Although debates about wealth inequality often focus on the United States, there is significant wealth inequality in many other countries, including many European welfare states. In the Netherlands, for instance, it is estimated that the richest 1% hold 33% of total wealth (Toussaint et al. 2020).

Over the past five decades, political theorists have debated many solutions to the problem of growing wealth inequality. In these debates, two prominent proposals include a basic income and a capital grant, a grant that every citizen gets when they become an adult. In this chapter, I examine the choice between basic income and a capital grant, assuming

DOI: 10.4324/9781003173632-18

that a second aspect of Meade's dystopian vision of a Brave New Capitalist paradise will materialise: 'the proportion of the working population required to man the extremely profitable automated industries would be small.' More specifically, I assume that automation will lead to technological unemployment, because machines carry out similar work at much lower costs than humans. This assumption fits with recent predictions about the employment effects of automation. Economist Carl Frey and computer scientist Michael Osborne predict that 47% of jobs in the United States are at a high risk of being automated within the next two decades (Frey and Osborne 2017). Middle-skilled jobs are at a (much) greater risk of being automated than higher-skilled jobs (Acemoglu and Autor 2011; Eichhorst and Portela Souza 2018; Cowen 2013; Hodgson 2016). Since middle-skilled jobs are frequently also lower paid jobs, rising technological unemployment is likely to exacerbate existing wealth inequality. In this chapter, I will engage with Meade's question: 'What could we do about it?'

It is interesting that many of the billionaires who stand to gain from automation advocate a universal basic income (UBI) to assist those who stand to lose. Elon Musk, for instance, said that:

> there is a pretty good chance we end up with a universal basic income, or something like that, due to automation. Yeah, I am not sure what else one would do. [...] People have time to do other things. Complex things. More interesting things.
>
> (Clifford 2016)

Jeff Bezos, Richard Branson, and Meta CEO Mark Zuckerberg have all indicated that they are sympathetic to a UBI, as way to counteract the negative effects of automation on the labour market (Clifford 2017). But is the implementation of a basic income really a good solution if technological unemployment were to rise? My main claim in this chapter is that it is not, and that rising technological unemployment strengthens the case for a capital grant. In showing how the political interventions of billionaires are not the most beneficial ones for our society, this chapter provides an illustration of the soundness of worries about the political interventions of the rich. What their perspectives and life experiences make them propose, is not necessarily in the best interest of society.

My argument proceeds in five steps. I start by introducing in greater detail the assumption that automation will lead to technological unemployment in Section 1. In Section 2, I explain the notion of desert and introduce a conception of it that can be used to evaluate both a basic income and a capital grant. In Section 3, I defend the claim that if technological unemployment rises significantly, both a universal and conditional basic income (UBI) would be unstable, because of the desert problem: the working will be unwilling to contribute to funding the basic incomes of those who do not work, because some of them may not deserve it. In Section 4, I defend the claim that a capital grant funded through an inheritance tax, and supplemented with a generous system of contribution benefits, can avoid the desert problem. The upshot of this paper is that if automation does indeed lead to a rise technological unemployment, then this strengthens the case for capital grants. Although my argument focuses on technological unemployment, it could well be that its validity extends to unemployment caused by other factors.

1 The Automation Threat

Predictions of the employment effects of automation vary enormously. Economist Carl Frey and computer scientist Michael Osborne made newspaper headlines when they predicted, in 2013, that about 47% of jobs in the United States are at a high risk of being automated within the next two decades (Frey and Osborne 2017). Their study is often cited in support of the claim that automation will lead to significant structural unemployment. However, Frey and Osborne's prediction was regarded as too dramatic by other economists. OECD economist Glenda Quintini, for instance, said that '[i]t was like saying that all the volcanoes in the world are going to explode next year and we'll all die' (Segal 2018). Together with her colleague Ljubica Nedelkoska, she estimates that, for the OECD countries, about 14% of jobs are at a high risk of being automated within the next two decades (Nedelkoska and Quintini 2018). There are some points of agreement among economists, though: they agree that middle-skilled jobs are at a much higher risk of being automated than higher skilled jobs (Acemoglu and Autor 2011; Eichhorst and Portela Souza 2018; Cowen 2013; Hodgson 2016). They also agree that automation will lead to the disappearance of certain jobs and cause temporary technological unemployment because of skills mismatches in the labour market (for an overview, see Autor, Mindell, and Reynolds 2020).

The main point of disagreement among economists is on the question whether automation will also lead to structural technological unemployment, unemployment following technological change that lasts for many years. The end of work has, after all, been predicted many times – and each time, these predictions were proven wrong. In the early nineteenth century, for instance, a group of weavers in England that called itself 'the Luddites' started to break into factories to smash mechanised looms, fearing that these would take their jobs.[1] Although the invention of mechanised looms did create temporary technological unemployment, it did not lead to structural technological unemployment. Increased demand for machines was matched by increased demand for labour, because new goods and services were invented, and existing goods and services became available to a larger share of the population.

Most individuals in the United States today are in jobs that did not exist yet in 1940 (Autor, Mindell, and Reynolds 2020, 10–11). Perhaps fears about the employment effects of automation are simply failures of our imagination. In *A World Without Work* (2020), Daniel Susskind argues that our imagination is, in fact, not failing us. This time really is different. He points out that economists who deny that automation will lead to structural technological unemployment are committed to the 'superiority assumption,' according to which 'humans are the best placed to perform whatever tasks are in demand as our economies grow and change' (131).

The superiority assumption, however, may no longer be warranted. Automation proceeds through task encroachment, such as email replacing letter writing and electronic calendar apps replacing paper calendars. Eventually, these changes will mean that the work that was previously carried out by, for instance, one secretary working fulltime for one person, can now be carried out by one secretary working parttime for five people – reducing the total demand for secretaries. With the rise of artificial intelligence, the number of tasks that can be automated is enormous. One can see this effect particularly starkly, Susskind argues, in the social media industry, with highly valuable companies like Facebook, Google, Instagram, Twitter, and YouTube employing very few people – but having billions of users who spend significant amounts of time on their platforms (119). Now we might object that there will always be demand for labour, because automation will simply drive wages down, and hence make labour more attractive again as a production factor. But that is, Susskind points out, not what happened with horses in the nineteenth century: 'No matter how cheap horses became, and how strong the incentive for entrepreneurs to take advantage of equine bargains, there was very little left for them to do that a machine could not do more efficiently' (121). The same, he argues, will eventually happen to many human beings for many tasks.

Even if Susskind is right that automation will lead to rising technological unemployment, this does not necessarily mean that automation is a threat. Rather than working fulltime, as most of the American working-age population does today, people could share jobs and work fewer hours. In 1930, John Maynard Keynes famously predicted a 'new disease' of which 'some readers may not yet have heard the name': 'technological unemployment' (1963 [1930], 364). According to Keynes, this new disease would only involve a 'temporary phase of maladjustment' (364). He predicted that 100 years later, all healthy, able-bodied people would only work 15 hours a week, a situation he called 'economic bliss' (373). Keynes added that:

> The pace at which we can reach our destination of economic bliss will be governed by four things—our power to control population,

our determination to avoid wars and civil dissensions, our willingness to entrust to science the direction of those matters which are properly the concern of science, and the rate of accumulation as fixed by the margin between our production and our consumption; of which the last will easily look after itself, given the first three.

(373)

Keynes seemed to assume that if everyone were to work less, there would still be work for everyone, but simply less of it (for a detailed discussion of his predictions, see Skidelsky and Skidelsky 2012, chapter 2). People could enjoy leisure during the time they previously spent working. Even though having so much leisure may initially appear to be a frightening prospect ('must we not expect a general "nervous breakdown"?' Keynes asks, 1963, 366), people would eventually get used to having more leisure and learn to 'live wisely and agreeably and well' (367).

There are, it seems to me, two reasons why job sharing is less of a good solution to the problem of rising technological unemployment than Keynes thought. First, although it may be desirable if all healthy, able-bodied people were to earn their own income by sharing jobs, this would not be economically rational for individual firms. For firms, it is cheaper to hire one person to work for 40 hours, instead of hiring four persons to work for ten hours, because they can avoid the costs of training three additional employees and the costs of coordinating work between the four people carrying out the shared job. Second, and more importantly, middle-skilled jobs are at a much higher risk of being automated than higher-skilled jobs – which would make job sharing a less feasible solution for these jobs, because there would be fewer jobs to be shared.

This brings us back to Meade's question: 'What could we do about it?' I will from here on simply assume that Susskind is right and that over the next few decades, technological development will result in some structural technological unemployment, but I will remain agnostic as to the share of the working-age population that would become structurally unemployed following automation. If it is, indeed, the case that a proportion of the population will be unemployed following advances in technology, how to respond to this? I will go on to evaluate three possible responses – a UBI, a CBI, and a capital grant – from the perspective of desert. The notion of desert is particularly relevant here, because a basic income is typically objected to on the grounds that paying everyone a basic income would require making transfers to the undeserving. In the next section, I will introduce a social contribution-based theory of desert and explain how it is able to resist some of the important challenges that have been raised against desert as a principle of distributive justice.

2 Desert

As those who defend desert tend to stress, Aristotle wrote that 'all people agree that what is just in distribution must be in accord with some sense of desert' (*Nicomachean Ethics* 1131a). Since then, many philosophers – including Gottfried Wilhelm Leibniz (1697), John Stuart Mill (1998 [1863]), and Henry Sidgwick (1981 [1874]) – have written approvingly about desert as a principle of distributive justice. In the contemporary philosophical literature on distributive justice, the notion of desert has gotten out of favour. Desert has often been criticised for being too harsh: it allows for justifying the high incomes of the privileged[2] and refusing assistance to the poor[3] (Herzog 2017, 103; Anderson 1999, 288–289). Moreover, philosophers have argued that people cannot be held responsible in a way that is required to deserve income (Rawls 1999, 88–89, 273–277), and that it is hard, if not impossible, to establish what people deserve (Arneson 1997). Many desert-less theories of distributive justice have been proposed, such as Rawlsian egalitarianism (1971, 1999), relational egalitarianism (Anderson 1999), and prioritarianism (Parfit 1991). These theories are often defended precisely on the grounds that they are not sensitive to desert (see Rawls 1999, 88–89, 273–277; Anderson 1999, 288–289).[4] In 1971 already, coinciding with the publication of Rawls's theory, John Kleinig observed that 'desert has, by and large, been consigned to the philosophical scrap heap' (1970, 71). Given that all these criticisms of desert have been known for decades and that there are many alternatives available to desert-based theories of justice, it is worth asking: Would it not be better to leave desert on the scrap heap, rather than use it to think about solutions to growing wealth inequality?

I think not, because desert plays a central role in people's intuitions about distributive justice. Samuel Scheffler (1992) was right, in my view, to argue that Rawls's liberal egalitarian theory of distributive justice is politically vulnerable, because it does not assign intrinsic importance to desert. Since most people are, as Shelly Kagan has put it, 'friends of desert' (2012, 3), it is unlikely that desert-less theories will be able to gather enough public support to effectuate change in our distributive practices. This is not just philosophical armchair theorising: a host of empirical studies claim to show that desert does indeed play a central role in people's intuitions about distributive justice (for overviews, see Konow and Schwettmann 2016; Miller 1992). I think that many of the objections to desert as a principle of distributive justice can be resisted, if desert is to play a limited role alongside other principles, including need, equality, and freedom. On this account, desert provides a *prima facie* reason to tax income and wealth that is undeserved and resist transfers to the undeserving – but these desert reasons can be overridden by other principles (Shor 1987, chapter 4 takes a similar approach when it comes to desert based on effort). To demonstrate this, I will go on to sketch a social contribution-based theory of desert that will be the basis for my evaluation of a basic income and a capital grant as a solution to the problem of automation.

Although there is much disagreement among those who write about desert, there are three uncontroversial received wisdoms about the notion.[5] These received wisdoms originate in Joel Feinberg's influential work on desert (1970). He argued that desert claims are three-place relations, uniting a desert subject, desert object, and desert basis. An example of a desert claim is 'Alexander deserves to be praised because he dared to open the box with very smelly, fermented fish.' There is a great deal of discussion among desert theorists about what permissible subjects, objects, and bases of desert claims are – and when these stand in an appropriate relation with each other. It would, for example, be excessive to claim that Alexander deserves to be a millionaire because he dared to open the box with smelly, fermented fish; praise is enough.

For the purposes of this chapter, I will assume that the appropriate desert subject is 'people,' the appropriate desert object 'money,' and the appropriate desert base 'social contribution.' This desert-based view is grounded in an ideal of reciprocity: people deserve to be rewarded in proportion to the contributions they make to society (see Arneson 1997, 339–340). The exact implications of the view will, of course, depend on the definition of social contribution. There is great deal of discussion among desert-theorists about how social contribution should be defined and measured (see Miller 1996; Mulligan 2018; Hsieh 2000; Dekker 2009; Sheffrin 2013). For the purposes of this chapter, I'll assume that David Miller is correct that we should accept: 'the obvious conclusion, over fairly large aggregates of people at least, that the money they are willing to put up to acquire goods and services provides a reasonable estimate of the value of these goods and services, and so a reasonable estimate of the contribution of the providers' (1996, 287).[6]

There are two further received wisdoms that regulate the relation between desert subject, object, and base: the aboutness principle and the responsibility requirement. The aboutness principle states that people can only deserve on the basis of their own acts or characteristics – not those of others (Feinberg 1970, 72–73; Olsaretti 2004, 4; Feldman 2016, 42). The aboutness principle is helpful in distinguishing desert claims from claims made by other principles in the language of desert. Consider the following claim: Alexander deserves a high salary because paying him this salary will aid in maximising utility. Although this claim uses the verb 'to deserve,' it is not a desert claim. The fact that paying Alex the salary will aid in maximising utility is, after all, not an act or characteristic of Alex. The responsibility requirement, finally, states that people can only deserve on the basis of things they can be held responsible for (Olsaretti 2006). Responsibility plays an important role in Rawls's critique of desert. He argued that 'there seems to be no way to discount' for the effects of 'good fortune' on people's performance on plausible bases for desert (1971, 103; for this interpretation, see Moriarty 2005, 207).[7] Doing so, however, is necessary if desert is to be a principle of justice: it would be unfair if people would be better off than others on the basis of factors they cannot be held responsible for.

There are many accounts of responsibility that could be adopted by defenders of desert. I will, for the purposes of this chapter, assume an account that is in line with luck egalitarianism. On this account 'inequalities in the advantages that people enjoy are acceptable if they derive from the choices that people have voluntarily made, but... inequalities deriving from unchosen features of people's circumstances are unjust. Unchosen circumstances are taken to include social factors like the class and wealth of the family into which one is born. They are also deemed to include natural factors like one's native abilities and intelligence' (Scheffler 2003, 5). I will also assume, against Rawls, that it is possible to make a distinction between 'voluntary choices' and 'unchosen circumstances.' The details on how to make this separation are not relevant to my argument (however, see Moriarty 2005 for a possible account).

I have sketched the outlines of the notion of desert that is at stake in this paper. It is important to note before continuing, though, that there are some accounts of desert for which my argument will not hold. Serena Olsaretti is right when she writes that the literature on desert consists of a 'fairly eclectic collection of contributions by desert theorists whose views differ widely' (2004, 6). Some defenders of desert, for instance, argue that people can, in fact, deserve on the basis of brute luck factors, such as their native intelligence (see, among others, Feldman 1995, 68–69; Mulligan 2018, 85–88, 170–175; Narveson 1995). It is impossible to do justice to all these contributions within the confines of this chapter. I will now go on to evaluate the first proposal for dealing with the distributive effects of growing technological unemployment: the implementation of a UBI.

3 Basic Income

A UBI is an 'an income paid by a government, at a uniform level and at regular intervals, to each adult member of society' (van Parijs 2000, 2). It is 'basic,' not because it would be enough to satisfy basic needs, but because 'it is something on which a person can safely count, a material foundation on which a life can firmly rest' (2000, 2). A great deal of discussion in the literature on UBI focuses on the question how high a UBI would have to be. Philippe van Parijs suggests that we should start with an amount that is somewhat below subsistence level and increase it to (at least) subsistence level over time, when people get a chance to experience the advantages of a UBI. A basic income at subsistence level in the United States would amount to approximately $1.000 per month. The poverty guideline for a person living alone in the United States was $12.880 last year, according to the United States Department of Health & Human Services (ASPE 2021). The UBI can, of course, be combined with other social assistance and security programs – but it is often defended on the grounds that it would render a significant share of such programs obsolete, simplifying the tax and transfer system and improving its efficiency.

UBI proposals are usually considered in connection to a world with work for (nearly) everyone. But different considerations apply when a UBI is to be implemented in a world with structural technological unemployment. A UBI at subsistence level would not be high enough if it is supposed to do what Elon Musk wants it to do: to allow those who become structurally unemployed to 'have time to do other things, more interesting things.' Having the time to do other things requires not having to worry about whether one will still be able to pay rent and the utility bill. To accommodate this concern, let's suppose that we were to, instead, implement a UBI of $2500. This amount is higher than any UBI proposal I am aware of. A major objection to UBI that has received significant attention in the literature is its perceived unfairness. A UBI that is (far) above subsistence level would allow its recipients to drop out of the labour force and spend their days surfing and watching TV – without contributing anything to funding the UBI. The people voluntarily dropping out of the labour force would, in a way, be free riding on the labour of others. This free riding objection is straightforwardly described in terms of desert. Those who voluntarily drop out of the labour force do not deserve to receive a UBI, because they do not make a social contribution by engaging in paid labour.

Some defenders of a UBI dig their heels in and argue that the fact that some might drop out of the labour force altogether is not a fundamental objection to UBI. The purpose of a UBI is precisely to give people real freedom, which includes the freedom not to work. As van Parijs and Robert van der Veen put it: 'The content of work, its organisation, and the human relations associated with it could and should be so altered that extrinsic rewards, whether material or not, would be less and less necessary to prompt a sufficient supply of labour. Work, to use Marx's phrase, could and should become "life's prime want"' (2006, 5). At the same time, some defenders of UBI, such as Joseph Carens (1981) and van Parijs (1991) himself, have argued that real freedom for all is compatible with the active promotion of a strong work ethos in a society. The promotion of such a work ethic would mean that those who voluntarily choose not to work face very strong disapproval from others.

In a world with structural technological unemployment, the promotion of a work ethic can no longer alleviate the worry that some people would free-ride on the labour of others – because there is no work for everyone. This means that the concern about the perceived unfairness of a UBI is alleviated somewhat: there is a portion of the working-age population that cannot contribute to funding it, because there are no jobs for them (for a defence of UBI in a world with structural technological unemployment, see Danaher 2019). It may, of course, still be the case that some people drop out of the labour force even though there are jobs for them, but if it is widely recognised that there is no work for everyone these will no longer be glaringly obvious cases of undeserved income. However, the desert objection to a UBI will pop up again in a slightly different form. As Daniel Susskind puts it:

> [i]n a world with less work, few societies will be able to allow those without a job to fill all their time with idleness, play, or unpaid work as they alone see fit … any society that allows that is likely to fall apart. Today, solidarity comes from a sense that everyone contributes to the collective pot through the paid work that they do and the taxes that they pay. Maintaining that solidarity in the future will require those without paid work to spend at least some of their time contributing to the pot in other, non-economic ways.
> (2020, 232–233)

The thought is this: even if people cannot contribute to society by engaging in paid work, they should still, if they are capable, contribute in other ways in order to be deserving of income. Susskind proposes to solve the issue by introducing a CBI. CBI is a basic income, the receipt of which is conditional upon making a meaningful contribution to society. He argues that what qualifies as a meaningful contribution is to be determined democratically. Although the outcome of such a democratic process cannot be predicted, the definition of 'meaningful contribution' is likely to include activities such as caring for children, the infirm, and the elderly – but it may also include 'reading, writing, composing beautiful music'; engaging in 'politics' and supporting 'local government'; and performing 'educational' activities (233). Susskind recognises that there are people who are physically and/or mentally incapable of making a social contribution. They would be exempt from the contribution requirement.

Although I think that Susskind is right to expect that there will be a significant contribution problem if a UBI were implemented in a world with less work, I am unconvinced by his proposal to implement a CBI instead. Part of the attraction of a UBI is that it would significantly reduce the administrative burden that comes with the redistribution of income and wealth. This advantage would be lost if the government had to evaluate for all adult citizens whether they were eligible for receiving the CBI. More importantly, I worry that even a CBI will be perceived as unfair on the grounds of desert. Desert requires that one's reward is in proportion to one's contribution. As John Christman puts it: 'it must be the case that the factors upon which the desert claim is based [the desert basis] are the determining ground of the magnitude of the benefit or harm deserved' (1994, 89). Such proportionality would be lost in the system Susskind proposes: some people will be making significant social contributions by spending most of their waking hours on, say, caring for the elderly and infirm – whereas others will only make the most minimal contribution, just to qualify for the CBI. All of them, however, will be paid the same amount.

It might seem as if there is a straightforward way out of the proportionality problem: introduce a minimal effort requirement, according to which anyone who makes a social contribution for a minimal number of hours per week would receive the CBI. Let's assume, for purely illustrative purposes, that the requirement would be set at 20 hours per week. That requirement would ensure CBI recipients make a social contribution for a significant amount of time. Although this would alleviate the proportionality problem somewhat, it will certainly not resolve it. Some people will contribute more because they work harder than others while they are working; and some people will work more than the minimal number of hours, whereas others do not. Really addressing the proportionality problem would require making the CBI proportional to the size of the contribution recipients make. However, it then seizes being a *basic* income. The CBI would be transformed into a contribution benefit: a benefit one receives in proportion to the contribution one makes to society. I will go on to defend capital grants supplemented by a system of contribution benefits in the next section.

4 Capital Grants and Contribution Benefits

A capital grant is a generous grant that every adult citizen receives early on in life, for instance when reaching the age of adulthood (White 2003). The purpose of a capital grant is to provide citizens with a solid material foundation that enables them to participate in and contribute to society. To aid in the realisation of that aim, many defenders of capital grants impose restrictions on what the grant can be spent on. Thad Williamson (2014), for instance, advocates for a capital grant that consists for 70% of capital that can only be spent on emergency relief, housing or stock holdings. In a similar vein, Stuart White advocates a capital grant that consists for 60% of a 'Participation Account' – which can be spent on 'education, training, setting up a new business, and, perhaps, leave from paid employment to undertake parental duties' and for 40% of a 'Life Account' – which citizens can draw on to supplement their income when they deem it necessary (2002, 14; he goes on to consider the possibility of adding a third account, for housing).

An important question in the literature on capital grants is how high capital grants would have to be. Thad Williamson (2014) advocates a capital grant of $50,000. Bruce Ackerman and Anne Alstott (1999) argue that citizens should receive a capital grant of $80,000 when they become adults. Piketty (2020, chapter 17) has recently advocated a capital grant of 60% of the average level of wealth in a country, which for the United States would amount $120,000. These amounts are clearly not high enough for recipients to meet their basic needs when they become technologically unemployed for an extended period of time; let alone, to cite Elon Musk one final time, to have the time to 'have time to do other things, more interesting things.' Hence, in a world without work for everyone, a capital grant would, as I will go on to argue, need to be supplemented by a generous contribution benefit scheme, which is to replace the unemployment benefit scheme.

Especially White's (2003) version of the capital grant proposal, funded through a tax on inheritance, fits well with the desert-based view that I assume in this chapter. Although the Life Account in White's proposal would allow citizens to withdraw temporarily from the labour market, it would be insufficient to allow them to permanently withdraw from it – alleviating the objection that a capital grant would involve making transfers to the undeserving. Also, White proposes to fund the capital grant scheme by taxing inheritance through a recipient-based system. His proposition is that everyone would have a life inheritance quota: a low amount they can freely inherit, with exemptions for transfers to charities and to spouses, after which the inheritances they receive are taxed at a 100% rate – or, at least, highly progressively (White 2003, 185–186; Piketty 2020, chapter 17 advocates a similar proposal). There is a strong desert-based case to be made for taxing inheritance in this way. First, inheritances are not rewards for the social contributions of the people who receive them, and therefore they would violate the requirement that the factors upon which the desert claim is based are the determining ground of the magnitude of the benefit. Moreover, receiving an inheritance is a clear case of good fortune for which recipients cannot be held responsible, violating the requirement that people can only deserve on the basis of things they can be held responsible for. Hence, allowing people to inherit would be to allow for transfers to the undeserving – just as in the case of a UBI.

Now, if a share of the population is going to be structurally unemployed due to automation, then a capital grant would have to be supplemented by a generous system of contribution benefits, which is to replace the unemployment benefit scheme. Such a replacement is necessary, because the unemployment benefit schemes in many countries are aimed at providing temporary assistance while encouraging people to quickly find a new job. In the United States, for instance, the maximum weekly benefit amount varies from $235 in Mississippi to $855 in Massachusetts; and the maximum number of weeks during which people can receive unemployment benefits varies from 12 weeks in Florida to 30 weeks in Massachusetts (FileUnemployment.org 2022). In the Netherlands, the maximum amount of unemployment benefits is 75%

of the previously earned salary during the first two months of unemployment, and 70% of the previously earned salary after that. The period people can collect unemployment benefits for is, at most, two years, and varies depending on how long they were employed (UWV 2022). In both the United States and the Netherlands, the unemployment benefit system requires benefit recipients to apply for jobs each week and submit proof of those applications. If people do not actively apply for jobs, they lose their unemployment benefits.

The requirement to actively apply for jobs straightforwardly follows from a desert-based perspective on unemployment assistance: people only deserve to get unemployment benefits if they actively try to regain paid employment and, in that way, make a paid contribution to society again soon. In a world without work for everyone, however, quickly regaining paid employment would be impossible for (some of) the technologically unemployed, which would make the requirement to apply for jobs demeaning and the maximum period during which unemployment benefits can be received viscerally unjust. The implicit message to recipients of the unemployment benefits is well-described by Elizabeth Anderson in her critique of responsibility-sensitive egalitarianism: 'Unfortunately, other people don't value what little you have to offer in the system of production. Your talents are too meagre to command much market value. Because of the misfortune that you were born so poorly endowed with talents, we productive ones will make it up to you: we'll let you share in the bounty of what we have produced with our vastly superior and highly valued abilities' (1999, 305).

The fundamental problem with the current system of unemployment benefits is that, especially in a society with structural technological unemployment, it fails to recognise adequately that people can make a valuable contribution to society in other ways than through paid employment. Hence, I think the unemployment benefit system in many countries would have to undergo a radical transformation. For starters, the application requirement and the maximum period during which benefits can be collected would have to be dropped. And, more importantly, the benefits people receive should be made proportional to the social contribution they make. That way, the system would ensure that those who receive a benefit would feel that their previously unpaid contributions are recognised and valued – instead of ignored. A system of contribution benefits would, of course, be faced with several important challenges. There would need to be agreement on what counts as a valuable contribution, on how to compare various types of contributions (for instance, care work and painting), on what the minimum benefit amount would be, and so on. Although these challenges are substantial, I believe that we should have the courage to face them to build an inclusive society grounded in the value of reciprocity, recognising a plurality of ways in which people can make a valuable contribution.

5 Conclusion

In this chapter, I examined the choice between a basic income and a capital grant from the perspective of automation. Automation can lead to technological unemployment if machines carry out similar work at much lower costs than humans. It is curious fact in debates about the employment effects of automation that several billionaires who stand to gain from automation, advocate the implementation of a basic income to assist those who stand to lose. I have defended two main claims in this chapter. First, I argued that both a UBI and a CBI do not provide a good solution to the problem of technological unemployment because they clash with widely shared desert-intuitions. Second, I defended the claim that these desert intuitions strengthen the case for a capital grant, supplemented with a generous system of contribution benefits. In showing how the political interventions of billionaires are not the most beneficial ones for our society, this chapter provided an illustration of the soundness of worries about the political interventions of the rich. What their perspectives and life experiences make them propose, is not necessarily in the best interest of society.

Acknowledgements

I would like to thank all the participants at the 2021 online Wealth and Power workshop and the 2022 Future of Work conference in Rotterdam for their contributions to this chapter. I am particularly grateful to Richard Arneson, Tom Parr, and Kate Vredenburgh who provided me with written comments. I would also like to thank Michael Bennett, Rutger Claassen, and Sam Langelaan for their editorial suggestions. I thank the Dutch Research Council (NWO) for funding under grant no. 360-20-390.

Notes

1 It is important to stress that although this the luddites are sometimes described solely as people who opposed technological change, the concerns that motivated the luddites were broader, including opposition to a new price system in the wool industry (National Archives n.d.).
2 The ratio between the pay of a chief executive and the average worker in the United States was 20-to-1 in 1965. In 2020, this ratio had grown to 351-to-1 (Mishel and Kandra 2021). In that year, CEOs at the top 350 firms in the United States were paid $24.2 million on average (Mishel and Kandra 2021). Economist Gregory N. Mankiw (2010, 2013) defends high CEO compensation packages by invoking the notion of desert. He argues that CEOs deserve to be paid handsomely because they make a substantial contribution to firms, which, in turn, contribute to the economy: 'My own reading of the evidence is that most of the very wealthy get that way by making substantial economic contributions, not by gaming the system or taking advantage of some market failure or the political process' (2013, 30). An important piece of evidence Mankiw cites, is a study by Kaplan

(2013) that shows that CEO pay is closely correlated with the performance of their firms on the stock market and that CEO turnover is much higher at firms with poor stock market performance.
3 In 1992, Bill Clinton campaigned on the slogan to 'end welfare as we know it' (Edelman 1997). He wanted to reduce chronic dependency on welfare by healthy, able-bodied Americans by requiring all welfare recipients to be working again after two years: 'two years and you are off' (Edelman 1997). The reason why this worked as a campaign slogan is that many Americans thought that part of the chronic welfare recipients are *undeserving*: They are, at least to a degree, responsible for being badly off and not contributing to society through paid employment. Hence, they should be encouraged to take responsibility and contribute. As Richard Arneson observed at the time: 'The new consensus [between conservatives and liberals] proclaims that our policies should be designed to reward the deserving and punish the undeserving' (1997, 328). This sentiment survived well into the next century. Former House Budget chairman Paul Ryan, for instance, said in a 2014 television interview that 'we have got this tailspin of culture, in our inner cities in particular, of men not working and just generations of men not even thinking about working or learning the value and the culture of work, and so there is a real culture problem here that has to be dealt with' (Volsky2014).
4 Parfit has argued against desert in other work (i.e., not his defence of prioritarianism), primarily on the grounds that he believes that no one deserves to suffer. See his *Reasons and Persons* (1987 [1984], 323–326) and *On What Matters* (2013 [2011], 258–272).
5 The only philosopher who, to the best of my knowledge, challenges these received wisdoms is Fred Feldman. He argues that desert claims are not necessarily three-place relations (2016, chapter 2) and that desert claims are not always subject to a responsibility requirement (1995). Although I am sympathetic to both of Feldman's challenges, they are not relevant to my argument here.
6 Contribution, according to Miller, should, in market settings, be measured by market prices. In non-market settings – such as in the case of public goods provision – contribution must, in part, by determined by a prior account of justice in the production of public goods. I will return to this issue in my critique of Susskind's conditional basic income proposal in Section 3 of this chapter. Note that even if a supplier's overall contribution could be identified, individuals can only be rewarded in accordance with desert if that overall contribution is, in turn, disentangled into the contributions of each individual involved in the production process. For those interested in the details of Miller's account, see his 'Two Cheers for Meritocracy' (1996; reprinted in his 2001, chapter 9).
7 The sentence quoted is absent from the revised edition of *A Theory of Justice* (it would have had to appear on 1999, 274). Still, Rawls does go on to write in the revised edition that '[t]he idea of rewarding desert is impracticable' (274).

References

Acemoglu, Daron, and David Autor. 2011. "Tasks and Technologies: Implications for Employment and Earning." In *Handbook of Labor Economics* (vol. 4), edited by Orley Ashenfelter and David Cards, 1143–1171. Amsterdam: Elsevier.
Ackerman, Bruce, and Anne Alstott. 1999. *The Stakeholder Society*. New Haven, CT: Yale University Press.

Anderson, Elizabeth. 1999. "What Is the Point of Equality?" *Ethics* 109(2): 287–337.
Arneson, Richard J. 1997. "Egalitarianism and the Undeserving Poor." *The Journal of Political Philosophy* 5(4): 327–350.
Autor, David, David Mindell, and Elisabeth Reynolds. 2020. "The Work of the Future: Building Better Jobs in an Age of Intelligent Machines." Retrieved on 15 April 2022 from <https://workofthefuture.mit.edu/wp-content/uploads/2020/11/2020-Final-Report2.pdf>.
ASPE. 2021. "2021 Poverty Guidelines." ASPE: Office of the Assistant Secretary for Planning and Evaluation. Retrieved on 04 May 2022 from <https://aspe.hhs.gov/topics/poverty-economic-mobility/poverty-guidelines/prior-hhs-poverty-guidelines-federal-register-references/2021-poverty-guidelines>.
Bureau of Economic Analysis. 2022. "GDP and Personal Income Mapping." Retrieved on 04 May 2022 from <https://apps.bea.gov/national/pdf/SNTables.pdf>.
Carens, Joseph H. 1981. *Equality, Moral Incentives, and the Market: An Essay in Utopian Politico-Economic Theory*. Chicago, IL: The University of Chicago Press.
Christman, John. 1994. *The Myth of Property: Towards an Egalitarian Theory of Ownership*. New York, NY: Oxford University Press.
Clifford, Catherine. 2016. "Elon Musk: Robots Will Take Your Jobs, Government Will Have to Pay Your Wage." CNBC. Retrieved on 04 May 2022 from <https://www.cnbc.com/2016/11/04/elon-musk-robots-will-take-your-jobs-government-will-have-to-pay-your-wage.html>.
———. 2017. "What Billionaires and Business Titans Say About Cash Handouts in 2017." CNBC. Retrieved on 04 May 2022 from <https://www.cnbc.com/2017/12/27/what-billionaires-say-about-universal-basic-income-in-2017.html>.
Cowen, Tyler. 2013. *Average is Over: Powering America Beyond the Age of Great Stagnation*. New York, NY: Dutton.
Danaher, John. 2019. "In Defense of the Post-Work Future: Withdrawal and the Ludic Life." In *The Future of Work, Technology, and Basic Income*, edited by Michael Cholbi and Michael Weber, 99–116. New York, NY: Routledge.
Dekker, Teun. 2009. "Desert, Democracy, Consumer Surplus." *Politics, Philosophy, Economics* 9(3): 315–338.
Edelman, Peter. 1997. "The Worst Thing Bill Clinton Has Done." *The Atlantic*. Retrieved on 15 May 2022 from <https://www.theatlantic.com/magazine/archive/1997/03/the-worst-thing-bill-clinton-has-done/376797/>.
Eichhorst, Werner, and André Portela Souza. 2018. "The Future of Work: Good Jobs for All." *International Panel on Social Progress Report*.
Federal Reserve. 2022. "DFA: Distributional Financial Accounts." Retrieved on 10 May 2022 from <https://www.federalreserve.gov/releases/z1/dataviz/dfa/distribute/chart/#range:2006.4,2021.4;quarter:129;series:Net%20worth;demographic:networth;population:all;units:levels>.
Feinberg, Joel. 1970. "Justice and Personal Desert." In *Rights and Reason: Essays in Honor of Carl Wellman*, edited by Marilyn Friedman, Larry May, Kate Parsons, and Jennifer Stiff, 221–250. New York, NY: Springer.
Feldman, Fred. 1995. "Desert: Reconsideration of Some Received Wisdom." *Mind* 104 (413): 63–77.

———. 2016. *Distributive Justice: Getting What We Deserve From Our Country.* New York, NY: Oxford University Press.
Fileunemployment.org. 2022. "Unemployment Benefits Comparison by State." Retrieved on 15 May 2022 from <https://fileunemployment.org/unemployment-benefits-comparison-by-state>.
Forbes. 2022. "Forbes World's Billionaires List: The Richest in 2022." Retrieved on 5 May 2022, from <https://www.forbes.com/billionaires/>.
Frey, Carl Benedikt, and Michael A. Osborne. 2017. "The Future of Employment: How Susceptible Are Jobs to Computerisation?" *Technological Forecasting and Social Change* 114(C): 254–280.
Gilens, Martin. 2009. "Preference Gaps and Inequality in Representation." *Political Science & Politics* 42(2): 335–341.
Herzog, Lisa. 2017. "Can Incomes in Financial Markets Be Deserved? A Justice-Based Critique." In *Just Financial Markets? Finance in a Just Society*, edited by Lisa Herzog, 103–121. Oxford: Oxford University Press.
Hodgson, Geoffrey. 2016. "The Future of Work in the Twenty First Century." *Journal of Economic Issues* 50(1): 197–216.
Hsieh, Nien-He. 2000. "Moral Desert, Fairness, and Legitimate Expectations in the Market." *Journal of Political Philosophy* 8(1): 91–114.
Kagan, Shelly. 2012. *The Geometry of Desert*. New York, NY: Oxford University Press.
Keynes, John Maynard. 1963. "Economic Possibilities for Our Grandchildren." In *Essays in Persuasion*, 358–373. London: W. W. Norton & Company.
Kleinig, John. 1970. "The Concept of Desert." *American Philosophical Quarterly* 8(1): 71–78.
Konow, James and Lars Schwettmann. 2016. "The Economics of Justice." In *Handbook of Social Justice Theory and Research*, 83–106. New York, NY: Springer.
Leibniz, G.W. 1697. *The Ultimate Origin of Things*, edited and translated by Jonathan Bennett, in the version by Jonathan Bennett presented at www.earlymoderntexts.com.
Meade, James. 1964. *Efficiency, Equality, and the Ownership of Property*. London: George Allen & Unwin.
Mankiw, N. Gregory. 2010. "Spreading the Wealth Around: Reflections Inspired by Joe the Plumber." *Eastern Economic Journal* 36: 285–298.
———. 2013. "Defending the One Percent." *Journal of Economic Perspectives* 27(3): 21–34.
Moriarty, Jeffrey. 2005. "The Epistemological Argument Against Desert." *Utilitas* 17(2): 205–221.
Mill, John Stuart. 1998. *Utilitarianism*, edited by Roger Crisp. Oxford: Oxford University Press.
Miller, David. 1992. "Distributive Justice: What the People Think." *Ethics* 102(3): 555–593.
———. 1996. "Two Cheers for Meritocracy." *Journal of Political Philosophy* 4(4): 277–301.
Mishel, Lawrence and Jori Kandra. 2021. "CEO Pay Has Skyrocketed 1,322% Since 1978." *Economic Policy Institute*. Retrieved on 15 May 2022 from <https://www.epi.org/publication/ceo-pay-in-2020/>.

Mulligan, Thomas. 2018. *Justice and the Meritocratic State*. New York, NY: Routledge.

Narveson, Jan. 1995. "Deserving Profits." In *Profits and Morality*, edited by Robin Cowan and Mario J. Rizzo, 48–87. Chicago, IL: University of Chicago Press.

National Archives. n.d. "Who Were the Luddites and What Did They Want?" Retrieved on 4 July 2022 from <https://www.nationalarchives.gov.uk/education/politics/g3/>.

Nedelkoska, Ljubica, and Glenda Quintini. 2018. "Automation, Skill Use and Training." *OECD Social, Employment and Migration Working Papers No. 202*.

Olsaretti, Serena. 2004. *Liberty, Desert, and the Market*. Cambridge: Cambridge University Press.

———. 2006. "Desert, Justice, and Luck." In *The Oxford Handbook of Political Theory*, edited by John Dryzek, Bonnie Honig, and Anne Philips, 436–449. Oxford: Oxford University Press.

O'Neill, Martin. 2009. "Liberty, Equality and Property-Owning Democracy." *Journal of Social Philosophy* 40(3): 379–396.

———. 2017. "Survey Article: Philosophy and Public Policy after Piketty." *The Journal of Political Philosophy* 25(3): 343–375.

Oxfam. 2022. "Inequality Kills: The Unparalleled Action Needed to Combat Unprecedented Inequality in the Wake of COVID-19." Retrieved on 15 May 2022 from <https://oxfamilibrary.openrepository.com/bitstream/handle/10546/621341/bp-inequality-kills-170122-en.pdf>.

Parfit, Derek. 1987. *Reasons and Persons*. Oxford: Oxford University Press.

———. 1991. "Equality or Priority." The Lindley Lecture: University of Kansas. Retrieved on 14 May 2022 from <https://www.stafforini.com/docs/Parfit%20-%20Equality%20or%20priority.pdf>.

———. 2013. *On What Matters. Volume 1*. Oxford: Oxford University Press.

Parijs, Philippe van. 1991. "Why Surfers Should be Fed: The Liberal Case for an Unconditional Basic Income." *Philosophy and Public Affairs* 20(2): 101–131.

———. 2000. "A Basic Income for All." *Boston Review* 25(5): 4–8.

Parijs, Philippe van, and Robert van der Veen. 2006. "A Capitalist Road to Communism." *Basic Incomes Studies* 1(1): 1–23.

Piketty, Thomas. 2020. *Capital and Ideology*. Cambridge, MA: Harvard University Press.

Pojman, Louis P., and Owen McLeod. 1999. *What Do We Deserve? A Reader on Justice and Desert*. New York, NY: Oxford University Press.

Rawls, John. 1971. *A Theory of Justice*. Cambridge, MA: Harvard University Press.

———. 1999. *A Theory of Justice*. Revised edition. Cambridge, MA Harvard University Press.

Scheffler, Samuel. 1992. "Responsibility, Reactive Attitudes, and Liberalism in Philosophy and Politics." *Philosophy & Public Affairs* 21(4): 299–323.

———. 2003. "What is Egalitarianism?" *Philosophy & Public Affairs* 31(1): 5–39.

Segal, Michael. 2018. "How Automation is Changing Work." *Nature* 563: S132–S135.

Sheffrin, Steven. 2013. *Tax Fairness and Folk Justice*. New York, NY: Cambridge University Press.

Sher, George. 1987. *Desert*. Princeton, NJ: Princeton University Press.

Sidgwick, Henry. 1981. *The Methods of Ethics*. Cambridge: Hackett Publishing.

Skidelsky, Robert, and Edward Skidelsky. 2012. *How Much is Enough? Money and the Good Life.* New York, NY: Other Press.

Spocchia, Gino. 2021. "Jeff Bezos Criticised by Amazon Workers and Customers After Thanking Them for Funding Space Launch." *Independent.* Retrieved on 5 May 2022 from <https://www.independent.co.uk/news/world/americas/amazon-workers-slam-jeff-bezos-b1887944.html>.

Susskind, Daniel. 2020. *A World Without Work: Technology, Automation, and How We Should Respond.* London: Allen Lane.

Toussaint, Simon, Bas van Bavel, Wiemer Salverda, and Coen Teulings. 2020. "Nederlandse vermogens schever verdeeld dan gedacht." *Economisch Statistische Berichten 105*(4789): 438–441.

UWV. 2022. "Werkloos." Retrieved on 15 May 2022 from <https://www.uwv.nl/particulieren/werkloos/ik-word-werkloos/index.aspx>.

Volsky, Igor. 2014. "Paul Ryan Blames Poverty On Lazy 'Inner City' Men." *Think Progress.* Retrieved on 15 May 2022 from <https://thinkprogress.org/paul-ryan-blames-poverty-on-lazy-inner-city-men-6448050b3059/>.

White, Stuart. 2003. *The Civic Minimum: On the Rights and Obligations of Economic Citizenship.* Oxford: Oxford University Press.

Williamson, Thad. 2014. "Realizing Property-Owning Democracy: A 20-Year Strategy to Create and Egalitarian Distribution of Assets in the United States." In *Property-Owning Democracy: Rawls and Beyond*, edited by Martin O'Neill and Thad Williamson, 225–248. Oxford: Wiley Blackwell.

Zucman, Gabriel. 2016. "Wealth Inequality." *The Poverty and Inequality Report.* The Stanford Center on Poverty and Inequality. Retrieved on 5 May 2022 from <https://inequality.stanford.edu/sites/default/files/Pathways-SOTU-2016-Wealth-Inequality-3.pdf>.

16 The Power of Private Creditors and the Need for Reform of the International Financial Architecture

Anahí Wiedenbrüg and Patricio López Turconi

The COVID-19 pandemic shed light on the many injustices that characterise the current global order, crudely exposing and reproducing asymmetries between and within countries in terms of wealth, power, and well-being. When the virus originated in late 2019, all states were arguably put in the same position: they had to take appropriate measures against a substantial public health threat, relying on the limited information and recommendations provided by specialised agencies such as the World Health Organisation. However, this 'starting position' was fraught with economic and power asymmetries that conditioned states' abilities to prevent the spread of the disease, provide appropriate healthcare and contain the socioeconomic crisis that followed.

Among the myriad of worrisome economic indicators, one of the most troubling ones was skyrocketing, unsustainable sovereign debt. Before the pandemic, a fourth wave of debt accumulation had already begun. Starting in 2010, this fourth wave of global debt accumulation was underway, with the largest, fastest, and most broad-based increase in global debt in five decades, spearheaded by developing countries. Driven by private debt which rose to 123% of GDP (World Bank 2021, 12), total debt in developing countries reached 176% of GDP in 2019, being just below 60% in 1970s, and roughly under 100% at the turn of the century (World Bank 2021, 14).

The pandemic has made the fourth wave of debt accumulation more dangerous. The sheer magnitude and speed of the debt build-up heightens the risk that not all of it will be used for productive purposes, since many LMICs still fall short in the strength of institutions that create distance between borrowing decisions and political pressures (World Bank 2021, 17). Moreover, amid the economic disruption caused by the pandemic, historically low global interest rates may conceal solvency problems that will surface in the next episode of financial stress (World Bank 2021, 14). The urgency of action is even more important, given that the inadequacies in the International Financial Architecture (IFA)[1] to deal with debt vulnerabilities in Low- and Middle-Income Countries (LMIC) precede – and will most probably also exceed – the current COVID-19 induced global crisis.

DOI: 10.4324/9781003173632-19

Without limiting the discussion to the pandemic, but clearly motivated by the increased urgency current debt vulnerabilities create, this chapter conceptualises the power that private creditors have when dealing with LMIC and the implications this has for the question of institutional design and IFA reform.

Our underlying premise is that the relation between private creditors and LMIC as debtor countries should reflect a certain equality in starting positions. We model this premise after the well-recognised legal principle of 'equality of arms,' which requires that each party be afforded a reasonable opportunity to present their case under conditions that do not place them at a disadvantage vis-à-vis their opponent.[2] This principle, which can be applied to all adjudicative processes, responds to the assumption that the unequal distribution of resources can affect the outcome of legal controversies in several ways, both in and out of court. This is held to be inconsistent with the ultimate goal of any adjudicative process, which is to provide just results (Wertheimer 1988, 304).

'Equality of arms,' or the idea that each party should have reasonable opportunity to present their case, can be easily translated to sovereign debt controversies. We hold that, in debt matters, both creditors and debtors must be afforded a fair opportunity to influence the conditions of lending, restructuring and reform of the IFA. This would imply that, when debtors and creditors interact, the background conditions should be such as to ensure that the starting positions are roughly equal. Complete equalisation will, of course, be impossible, as a range of determinants may shape the starting positions of the respective parties, which are in themselves already very different types of actors. Determinants include, for example, the negotiating skills or the mastery over the subject matter in the negotiation. Nonetheless, we maintain that if the background conditions are such that they are systematically tilted in favour of one of the parties, then the starting positions will be unjustifiably unequal, and the background conditions can be said to be unfair. In short, the starting positions of debtors and creditors should be such that no party has a substantial disadvantage at the time of lending and restructuring, or when deciding the most suitable policy options to reform the IFA.

By conceptualising the power of private creditors, this chapter thus contributes to the intellectual efforts required to reform the current IFA, which reproduces inequality in the global order. Most literature on IFA reform focus on making creditor-debtor relationships – in the moment of lending, restructuring and when influencing the structures against the backdrop of which these unfold – more efficient, rather than also making them more equitable. Putting a certain equality in the starting positions at the centre stage of this chapter is thus a major contribution to the literature. At the same time, this chapter is not trying to refine what is meant by equality in starting positions in this particular context, or what makes the lack thereof problematic. Other chapters in this volume are better positioned to answer these questions (see Arneson 2022). Rather, the main purpose of this chapter is more applied. We want to understand what follows for IFA reform and institutional design when we start from a fairly uncontroversial normative premise. This chapter thus complements some of the more theoretical chapters in this edited volume. It also broadens the scope from the volume, bringing an international dimension and widening the focus beyond Europe and North America. Finally, while it focuses on the realm of credit and sovereign debt, it engages in the very exercise other chapters in this volume call for, namely contributing to a new theory of power that better describes the lived reality of power under today's highly financialised form of capitalism (see Parvin 2022; Shoikhedbrod 2022).

The chapter proceeds as follows: Section 1 briefly reviews existing conceptualisations of power in the International Political Economy (IPE). Section 2 applies this power typology to the relation between private creditors and LMIC as sovereign debtors. Section 3 draws out the prescriptive implications for IFA reform of the diagnosis of the prior section, criticising some of the reform options proposed and discussing possible policy reforms at the multilateral level that could level the playing field between institutional private creditors and LMIC as sovereign debtors.

1 Preliminary Definitions: Relational and Structural Power

Since Susan Strange's canonical contribution to the debate of power in 'States and Markets' (1988), power in the IPE has been thought of being of one of two types: relational or structural.

Based on the work of realist writers (Dahl 1957), relational power is defined as the ability of actor A to get actor B to do something that B would otherwise not do (Strange 1988). It is exercised by one actor in a direct, one-to-one relation to another and is therefore targeted and intentional. Relational power, moreover, is sourced from the uneven distribution of ideational and material resources among actors.

Structural power, by contrast, is the ability (of actor A) to control or influence the structures that define the environment within which the interactions of actor A and actor B take place. It 'confers the power to shape frameworks within which states relate to each other, relate to people, or relate to corporate enterprises' (Strange 1988, 25). Robert Alford and Roger Friedland, building on the analysis of Steven Lukes, define it as the power which 'refers to the characteristics of different institutional settings which shape the decision-making agenda in ways which serve the interests of particular groups' (Wright 2001, 143). If actor A has structural power, intentional measures in the concrete interaction between actor A and actor B are no longer necessary, to get actor B to do something that B would otherwise not do. It is sourced not from their possession of resources, but from their capacity to control the structures that define the environment within which their interactions take place.

While no targeted and intentional measure is necessary for actor A to get actor B to do something that B would otherwise not have done, targeted and intentional actions are necessary – at some point in time X – to attain and maintain structural power. To attain or maintain structural power, an actor or group of actors with a similar set of particular interests will have had to engage in intentional actions to shape the structures in a manner that reproduce their particular interests. To that extent, structural power is not self-perpetuating. An actor can also simultaneously have relational power and structural power over an agent. It might be the case, for instance, that an agent holds structural power over another, yet decides to exert relational power in a targeted and intentional way.

According to Strange, the distinction between relational and structural power is much more useful in comprehending power-relations in the IPE than the distinction between economic and political power. The problem with this latter distinction is that it is very difficult to draw a clear distinction between economic and political power. In the IPE in particular, political power requires the power to purchase, to command production and/or to mobilise capital. Similarly, to have economic power requires the legal and physical security that can only be supplied by political authority (Strange 1988, 25).

2 Power in the IPE: The Relational and Structural Power of Private Creditors

Having briefly outlined this established typology of power in the IPE, let us now turn to the question of the power of private creditors. There is much talk about a country's creditor base becoming more and more diverse. First, there are retail creditors. Expressed non-technically, one can think of retail creditors as the common man or woman on the street who own bonds, but who are not professional or qualified investors themselves. Second, there are real money investors. Real money investors can be thought of as the 'blue-whales' of the financial sector. They are large, robust, cash-rich institutions that tend to be regulated and act as custodians of their clients' capital. As specialised investors, clients entrust their capital for them to invest as they see fit. In principle, as custodians of their clients' money, real money investors should be more concerned with the medium- and long-term return of their investments. Third, there are hedge funds. Hedge funds are smaller, more aggressive investors than real money investors. One can think of them as the sharks of the financial sector, as they attempt to make up in risk, what they lack in size. Hedge funds are not exposed to the same degree of regulatory oversight as real money investors. US-based hedge funds, for instance, are not obliged by law to register with the US Securities and Exchange Commission or with self-regulatory bodies in the investment business, though, some may choose to register their hedge funds anyway. In this chapter, we focus on real money investors and hedge funds. We will refer to them as institutional investors.

Against the backdrop of this diversity in private creditors, it would be an oversimplification to talk about private creditors as a homogenous group of investors. Notwithstanding, one thing that institutional investors do have in common is that their *raison d'être* is to invest money in a profitable manner. Everything they do is targeted towards that aim. This is different for debtor states. For states, having access to financing and investing in profitable ways is a means to a much more complex set of ends – their own *raison d'être* – related to the protection of their citizens' rights and promotion of well-being. It is in this context that the asymmetries in power between private institutional creditors and debtor states need to be apprehended.

We will now analyse private creditors relational and structural power by looking at three junctures, namely their power when lending, their power during a restructuring and their power in promoting or inhibiting different reforms in the IFA for sovereign debt restructuring. So far, scholars who have written about the power of creditors over debtors, have done so from a disciplinary perspective of IPE. What this entails, is that these analyses have focused on identifying power as a specific variable that could explain a given outcome (Brooks and Lombardi 2016; Roos 2019). By focusing on identifying and characterising instances in which private creditors hold relational and structural power over LMIC as sovereign debtors and focusing on three distinct moments (their power when lending, their power during a restructuring and their power in promoting or inhibiting different reforms in the IFA for sovereign debt restructuring) we offer a richer, multifaceted understanding of the different sources of relational and structural power private creditors' power over LMIC as sovereign debtors.

2.1 Relational Power of Institutional Private Creditors

Let us begin our analysis of institutional private creditor power by focusing on their relational power. Institutional private creditors source their relational power from three main sources: greater knowledge, greater financial resources, and better connections.

First, in the moment of *lending*, knowledge about financial markets is paramount. Institutional private creditors are experts in financial markets, in making risk judgments. Also states have expertise in this regard. After all, states are complex, collective agents and some of the officials who act in the name of the state – particularly those sitting in the finance ministry – have the specific role of ensuring that the state has the financial means it requires to pursue their ultimate ends. In practice, however, the expertise of the debtor state in the realm of finance varies greatly. As Buchheit and Gulati argue, 'sometimes the politicians in the borrowing country will be supported by a cadre of competent second-level bureaucrats. Sometimes a well-disposed bilateral or multilateral donor will assist the government in hiring outside experts to design and implement debt management policies. Often, however, there will be a disturbing asymmetry in the financial sophistication of the lender pushing an "innovative financial product" and the government official being pushed' (2010, 9). The greater knowledge of institutional private investors about financial markets and risk judgments may not only translate into a better assessment of a debtor state's capacity to pay (and hence a reduction in the losses suffered with potential defaults) but also in the potential exploitation of that knowledge to set higher risk premia. The setting of interest rates is more of an art than it is a science, and the greater the knowledge discrepancies between debtors and creditors in the moment of lending, the greater the potential that institutional private investors can exploit that knowledge differential in their favour.

Second, during *restructurings* all three sources of relational power are clearly visible, namely greater knowledge, financial resources, and connections. Debt restructurings are an incredibly specific area of expertise, which combines technical knowledge in finance, law, and international relations. Thus, while investors may have experienced professionals whose main area of expertise are sovereign debt restructurings and who conduct these negotiations on a regular basis as their day job, the same may not necessarily be said about the debtor state's officials, even those in the finance ministry. The basic insight is simple: knowledge is power and the greater the asymmetry in knowledge between creditors and debtors – both general knowledge about the workings of financial markets and specific knowledge in the field of expertise of debt restructuring – the greater will the asymmetry between both parties be during the negotiation.

Another potential asymmetry affecting restructuring negotiations between sovereign debtors and creditors resides in their respective contacts, networks, and channels of influence. First, creditors may have contacts within the debtor state, which they may use to de-stabilise the base of political support for the negotiating team at home. They could, for instance, de-stabilise the negotiating team by enhancing political frictions within governing coalitions. They may also have direct channels of access to powerful players in the international arena, such as the Treasury of the United States, or the International Monetary Fund (IMF). Here, the systemic importance of some of the financial institutions is of crucial importance. Some of the financial institutions that are creditors or custodians of states debt also provide important services to hegemonic states, such as the placing of their own bonds. Creditors' aim when lobbying these decision-makers is that these decision-makers, in turn, increase pressure on the debtor's state negotiating team.

Third, creditors relational power is also recognisable in their influence over *reforms of the IFA*. In the early 2000s, former Deputy Managing Director of the IMF, Anne Krueger, proposed the establishment of a Sovereign Debt Restructuring Mechanism (SDRM), a legal mechanism designed to approve payment standstills for states experiencing severe debt vulnerabilities and to facilitate debt restructurings in case they became needed (see Part III). Private creditors did not like the SDRM, not least because it would enhance the bargaining position of sovereign debtors during restructurings and ensure a more equitable burden sharing of the risk of sovereign default from the sovereign debtors and the IMF to banks and bondholders (Brooks and Lombardi 2016). The response was unequivocal and illustrative of private creditors relational power: According to the former director of the IMF's legal department, 'A number of leading financial industry associations joined forces to lobby against the SDRM proposal' (Hagan 2005, 391). Among these associations were the Institute of International Finance, the Emerging Market Traders Association, the International Primary Market Association, the Bond Market Association, the Securities Industry Association, the International Securities Market Association and the Emerging Market Creditors Association (Brooks and Lombardi 2016). The most promising avenue to stop the establishment of a SDRM was to present an alternative, more market friendly solution, namely Collective Action Clauses (CACs). Interviews conducted by Gelpern and Gulati 'confirm[ed] that industry representatives tried more than once to trade their acceptance of CACs for the official sector's commitment to "drop" SDRM' (2004, 10).

2.2 Structural Power of Institutional Private Creditors

In debt matters, institutional private creditors source their structural power from their rule making authority and their influence over the common sense.[3] The idea of 'common sense' makes reference to creditors' capacity to manipulate public knowledge and the beliefs of individuals to ensure that their position is always perceived as the correct and most sensible solution.

When it comes to *lending*, structural power is mainly exercised through the control of the rules and standard practices on sovereign borrowing. The international debt architecture is often referred to as a 'non-system' due to this very absence. In this non-system, rulemaking consists in influencing the market practice and regulatory policy, for instance, by developing a set of standard contractual terms in sovereign bonds and promoting their widespread acceptance. Once these clauses are accepted as the norm, sovereigns will have incentives to issue bonds containing them due to the value that creditors afford to bonds whose terms and conditions favour their interests. At that point, no concrete action from creditors will be necessary to get states to abide by their rules in future debt issues.

The so-called 'ICMA Clauses' strikingly illustrate this point. The International Capital Market Association (ICMA) is a trade association for private creditors and other capital market constituencies that seeks to unify industry representation through, precisely, its market practice and regulatory policy activities. Some ICMA members include BlackRock, Goldman Sachs, and JP Morgan, to name a few. ICMA has worked as an instrument for institutional private creditors to exercise their rulemaking authority through the production of standardised clauses. In particular, in 2014, ICMA developed new standard CACs for sovereign issuers, which were rapidly endorsed by the IMF. To this date, and just a few years later, ICMA model clauses have been adopted by approximately 50% of the outstanding foreign law-governed sovereign bonds (Chung and Papaioannou 2020). The fast and wide acceptance of the new ICMA standards reveals how creditors, operating in a trade group, can be effective in shaping the rules of the game and influencing the operation of the market for sovereign bonded debt documentation.

CACs are also a reflection of creditor power at the time of *restructuring*, since they are intended to operate during restructuring negotiations and were ultimately designed to work as a practical solution to the issue of blocking minorities (ICMA 2015). In addition, structural power may also be exercised through creditor's influence over the common sense. Creditor's conventional and long-held narrative around fiscal profligacy, the principle of *pacta sunt servanda*,[4] and the sanctity of contracts has been instrumental in demonising distressed debtors, thus weakening the sovereign's bargaining position by subverting its legitimacy in the eyes of the public (Stiglitz and Rashid 2020).

Finally, institutional creditors have also used their structural power to stall any *IFA reform proposal* that would depart from the current contractual framework to sovereign debt lending and restructuring. To reiterate, private creditors source their structural power from their rule-making authority. The emergence of CACs is a perspicuous example of how this authority can be exerted to control the legal institutions in which debtor-creditor interactions take place: fearing that anything like an international bankruptcy court would trump the value of their contracts and their relational power over distressed debtors, private creditors almost uniformly rejected the SDRM proposal (Gelpern and Gulati 2004, 13). Creditors argued that the existing contractual-based and market approach worked reasonably well, and already protected sovereigns in default (Setser 2010, 322). As a 'best alternative' to the SDRM, private creditors pushed the more widespread use of CACs in sovereign bonds, and eventually got the IMF to drop the SDRM to endorse contractual CACs as a 'standard market practice' (IMF 2003a, para. 14).

3 The Need for Reform of the International Financial Architecture: Policy Evaluations

The different ways in which creditors exert their power in modern sovereign debt markets call for wide-ranging reforms of the IFA that will favour greater equality in starting positions. The absence of a multilateral framework for debt treatments in the IFA has long been recognised as a serious gap in the IFA. Starting from as early as the 1970s, several proposals for reform were put forward by academics and international organisations, going from amendments to the policies and practices of the IMF to the idea of establishing new, independent international institutions for handling sovereign debt restructuring and cross-border investment disputes.[5] However, more often than not, the political momentum for materialising these reforms was impeded as a consequence of the pressure exerted by creditors and creditor-led states (Brooks and Lombardi 2016).

In this section, we will not be explaining why and how creditors have managed to stall previous initiatives for reform. Rather, we will evaluate which arrangements are better suited for minimising power asymmetries between creditors and debtors, both at the moment of lending and restructuring. First, we briefly summarise two popular types of reform proposals, i.e., statutory approaches and contractual approaches, detailing how they mostly fail to comprehensively address private creditors' power. We will then focus on multilateral, quasi-legal solutions to debt lending and restructuring, highlighting the different ways in which a regime of this sort can help advance equal power or influence of all actors involved.

3.1 Statutory or Conventional Approaches

A first category of reform schemes includes all proposals for the establishment of statutory or treaty based mechanisms to deal with sovereign debt matters at the international or regional levels. These kinds of initiatives are a form of hard legalisation, as they seek to create rules that are binding on both creditors and sovereigns, and that can be legally enforced either by the same mechanism or some other institution that is charged with that task.

Establishing a framework based on a treaty or convention that will provide for orderly and efficient debt restructurings has some apparent institutional benefits. The main benefit is the legally binding character of any agreements reached within such mechanism. This would arguably favour all parties involved, as it reduces collective action problems and facilitates enforcement before local courts.[6] A clear set of rules that is inherent to any hard law arrangement can maximise uniformity and predictability in debt restructuring, which is something is undoubtedly missing in the current non-system.

However, these hard law arrangements are objectionable from the point of view of equality in starting positions, insofar as any conventional agreement entails a loss of domestic and Westphalian sovereignty. Following Krasner (1999), domestic sovereignty refers to the formal organisation of political authority within the state and the ability of public authorities to exercise effective control within the borders of their own polity. This includes the authority over the state's economic system. Westphalian sovereignty refers to the exclusion of external actors, whether *de facto* or *de jure*, from the territory of a state. Agreements that recognise external authority structures – such an international bankruptcy court with the authority to issue enforceable sentences – would undermine the exercise of Westphalian sovereignty. This is especially true when it comes to proposals for the establishment of anything like an international bankruptcy court, which would necessarily require states to waive their jurisdictional immunities. Any State that wanted to become a party to such mechanism would be required to resign their principal source of authority and independence in international relations, which allows them to not only retain public power over their citizens and territory, but also exclude other states and international organisations from interfering in their internal affairs (Koskenniemi 2005, 240). Sovereigns would have to sign away to their sole right of decision and restrict their behaviour for all present and future debt matters that may fall under the purview of such a mechanism.

Even if loss of sovereignty is intrinsic to all international treaty-making and may benefit states in some instances, sovereigns would need to forfeit a great deal to make any international bankruptcy court work. A simple comparison of the degree and nature of sacrifices that each party would need to make clearly illustrates how hard law arrangements would lead to deeply unequal starting positions. In effect, any conventional approach would require an extremely broad waiver of state power that has no correlation on the part of non-state actors who, at the very least, would only be asked to renounce to their claims before domestic courts on a case-by-case basis. Losing the ultimate power to decide over financial and economic policy issues is a serious curtailment for states who, in a world plagued with economic and power asymmetries, are charged with the protection of the most vulnerable. In effect, history has shown that – in the context of restructuring – states may be forced to adopt fiscal consolidation measures that require disinvestment in public services, which are essential for the fulfilment of core economic, social, and cultural rights.

Many approaches of this sort have been proposed, but we will focus on examining the IMF's proposal for a statutory SDRM. We consider this case to be of great analytical importance for being a proposal that generated a serious public debate on the need for a formal sovereign bankruptcy regime (Setser 2010).

The SDRM was the first IMF proposal for the establishment of a formal sovereign bankruptcy process. A project led by Anne Krueger, the SDRM sought to create an improved sovereign debt restructuring process that would facilitate the orderly, predictable, and rapid restructuring of unsustainable sovereign debt, while protecting asset values and creditors' rights. To reduce the risks to debtor's sovereignty, the SDRM was designed as a voluntary mechanism that could only be invoked or activated by states (Krueger 2002, 4; IMF 2002a, 7–8). The mechanism was thought to act as a forum in which sovereigns and a qualified majority of creditors could reach an agreement that would then be made legally binding on all dissenting creditors subject to the restructuring. The SDRM proposal also envisaged the establishment of a Sovereign Debt Dispute Resolution Forum, an 'efficient and impartial' organ of the Fund that would have exclusive jurisdiction over the conduct of the SDRM process and disputes arising from that process (IMF 2002a, 8). Recognising that contractual frameworks cannot provide a comprehensive and durable solution to collective action problems, Krueger argued that the most effective legal basis for the SDRM would have been a treaty framework through an amendment of the IMF's Articles of Agreement (2002, 31–34).

Despite providing advantages to sovereign borrowers, we claim that this mechanism would not have solved the underlying power asymmetries at the time of restructuring for different reasons that become apparent when closely studying the institution design of the SDRM.

Before all else, the SDRM was a treaty-based solution, which would have resulted in a substantive loss of power on the part of sovereigns. The celebration of a new treaty or the amendment of the IMF's Articles would have required states to, once again, renounce their domestic and Westphalian sovereignty over debt matters in favour of a mechanism coordinated by the IMF. Even more, sovereigns would have subjected themselves to the legally binding decisions of a quasi-judicial body, which would have had broad and exclusive jurisdiction over disputes relating

The Power of Private Creditors and the Need for Reform of the IFA

to the SDRM process. While explaining this mechanism, Krueger herself understood that this proposal asked for countries 'to cede or share their sovereignty over decisions that are important to their citizens to international forums' (IMF 2002b). The nature of the power that sovereigns would have had to concede is not comparable to any burdens that the SDRM could have imposed on creditor power. This stems from the fact that, as Krueger acknowledged, states would have been delegating their full control over economic and financial matters to an international organisation.

In the end, this was one of the very reasons why the SDRM never materialised. According to the IMF, despite having received considerable support within the Executive Board, the proposal failed to command the majority needed to amend the Fund's Articles 'due to the members' reluctance to surrender the degree of sovereignty required to establish such a framework' (IMF 2013). Creditors also rejected the proposal, fearing it would diminish their relational and structural power over sovereign debtors (Brooks and Lombardi 2016).

In addition to the issue of sovereignty, the SDRM's design would not have addressed the relational power differentials in a given restructuring. Rather, it would have enhanced the ability of creditors and creditor-led states to get sovereign debtors to do something that they would otherwise not do. Indeed, despite being described as a 'voluntary' mechanism that could only be invoked by sovereigns, the Fund was supposed to use its powers to make all actors turn to the SDRM in cases of debt crises. This is not mere speculation but, on the contrary, was quite explicitly explained by the Fund's authorities. For instance, in her 2002 proposal, Krueger clarified that 'the IMF would rely on its existing financial powers to create the incentives for the relevant parties to use the mechanism appropriately' (2002, 24). As Sean Hagan, former Director of the IMF's Legal Department, plainly put forth in his proposal:

> Of course, the IMF would still exercise considerable influence over the process through the exercise of its traditional financial powers. Perhaps most important, in circumstances in which it discontinues financing because of a determination that the member's debt is unsustainable, this would probably leave a country with little choice but to initiate the SDRM.
>
> (2005, 228–229)

Additionally, some SDRM proposals even granted considerable power to the IMF's Board of Governors – where a members' wealth, represented in its quota, is a key determinant of its voting power – over the functioning and authority of the SDRM's Dispute Resolution Forum (DRF). For instance, it was suggested that the Board of Governors should be able to overrule rules and regulations adopted by the Forum by a decision of a qualified majority of the total voting power (IMF 2003b, para. 72). Proponents of this feature acknowledged that it 'would place some limit on the DRF's authority in the rule-making area,' merely claiming that it would nonetheless 'not compromise in any way its independence' (IMF 2003b, para. 72). Pursuant to this proposal, sovereign debtors would have then subjected themselves to the broad and exclusive jurisdictional powers of a dispute resolution mechanism that was in theory independent of the Fund, but whose procedure would have still been ultimately controlled by creditor-led or wealthy states as represented in the IMF's Board of Governors.

3.2 Contractual Approaches

The statutory sovereign bankruptcy process envisaged by the IMF never materialised due to both the lack of the required membership support and the opposition of private creditors, who almost uniformly rejected the proposal. As a 'best alternative' to the SDRM, private creditors pushed for a different instance of hard legalisation: the more widespread use of CACs in sovereign bonds to address creditor coordination problems at the time of restructuring. CACs were ultimately endorsed by the IMF after the SDRM proposal was dropped (IMF 2003a).

Being an initiative driven by private creditor groups, it is not surprising that CACs cannot comprehensively solve the unequal distribution of power between creditors and debtors. Before anything else, since they are designed to achieve effective restructurings, CACs are not tailored to reducing asymmetries or any other type of power imbalances at the time of lending. CACs are also not designed to prevent over-lending on the part of creditors, as recent evidence shows that inclusion of both enhanced CACs and regular CACs did not lead to increased moral hazard concerns but is rather associated with lower borrowing costs for the sovereign (Chung and Papaioannou 2020).

But CACs may also further exacerbate creditors' ability to shape the outcome of a restructuring, as these contractual instruments still leave much room for creditors to exert their relational power. First, CACs only regulate the requisite majorities for modifying key characteristics of bonds in the restructuring process, such as the due date of payment, the principal amount or the governing law. But CACs do not contain any rules on the validity of the terms of the restructuring agreement and, as such, cannot prevent a qualified majority of creditors from using their sources of power to pressure for inequitable agreements, solutions that do not provide for a sustainable debt profile, or agreements that do not take into account public policy or human rights considerations. Furthermore, even if CACs have helped to minimise holdout behaviour, they still have not prevented a qualified majority of creditors from using disruptive litigation (or the threat thereof) in the context of a debt workout to exert pressure on sovereigns, as an expression of their relational power (see Mander 2020; do Rosario and Millan 2021).

Perhaps the most salient flaw of CACs is that they are, in essence, reforms at the contractual level. As such, they cannot be considered durable solutions to the unequal distribution of power in debt restructurings. This is because, being contracts, any improvements to the distribution of bargaining power between creditors and debtors in a certain bond can be reversed in the next bond indenture agreement.

The recent Argentine experience is a striking example of the risk of normative retrogression.[7] During the debt workouts, Argentina offered to issue exchange bonds using the standard 2014 ICMA CACs, included in most bonds being restructured and broadly adopted by the market. However, at some point in the negotiations, holders of the eight series of bonds issued in 2005 – that included pre-2014 CACs – demanded that the new bonds be issued without the 2014 ICMA CACs to prevent a loss of their relational power (see Ad Hoc Argentine Bondholder Group et al. 2020; Dell'Oca 2020). Indeed, the main difference between both types of clauses is that the 2014 ICMA CACs minimise the hold out risk and enhance the Sovereign's ability to restructure when supported by a meaningful majority. The Argentine government ultimately refused to make such amendments, as 'the contractual forms developed by the International Capital Market Association (ICMA), which were adopted by Argentina in 2016, (…) enjoy[ed] widespread support' (Ministry of Economy of Argentina 2020).

For these reasons, CACs cannot be considered the optimal mechanism to attain equality in starting positions in debt matters. In order to undercut power inequalities, contractual developments should be complemented with durable solutions at the multilateral level. The next subsection discusses quasi-legal, multilateral frameworks for sovereign debt restructuring that can help level the playing field for creditors and debtors

3.3 Quasi-Legal or Soft Law Approaches

The last category of reform schemes includes all proposals for the establishment of a multilateral soft law regime to promote responsible borrowing and to provide for orderly and efficient debt restructurings. For the purposes of this chapter, we use the term soft law to refer to any document, instrument, procedure or set of rules that is not legally binding to the actors involved (Boyle, 2019). These initiatives usually propose the creation of an independent regulatory body or institution with the mission of, first, producing soft law norms for sovereign lending and restructuring and, second, mediating the sovereign restructuring process without the authority to adopt binding or enforceable decisions (Herman 2016; Guzmán and Stiglitz 2018).

From a standpoint of equality in starting positions which seeks to eliminate or reduce relational and structural power asymmetries, we consider soft law to be a superior institutional alternative when compared to any statutory or conventional approach insofar as it eliminates the issue of sovereignty. In effect, unlike the SDRM, a multilateral debt authority under a soft law regime would not have the authority to make legally binding decisions in the process of a restructuring. This means that the ultimate right to decide over economic and financial matters would remain within the sovereign, who would be free to reach an agreement with debtors only under the assistance of a mediating entity. Relational and structural power asymmetries in the moment of lending, restructuring and seeking or inhibiting reform would be reduced because LMICs would benefit from the assistance of the mediating entity (something they lack with contractual approaches), while not having to renounce to the ultimate power to decide over financial and economic policy issues (like the hard law approach would require).

Opting for a soft law would offer additional advantages. First, it would be easier to gather the political consensus that is necessary for a structural reform of the IFA to take place, as a proposal of this type would simply not require states to once again delegate the power over their financial affairs to international organisations. This is valuable in itself, as it is precisely the reason why the SDRM proposal ultimately stalled. Similarly, a soft law mechanism would allow including non-state actors – such as creditors or business participants – in the formulation, adoption, and implementation process with equal standing and power of decision, something that has been normally harder to achieve in the treaty-making context (Webb 2019). This broad participation would, in turn, probably help legitimise the mechanism's authority and contribute to its better functioning as, in the end, the value of soft law governance depends on inducing compliance on the basis of accommodation and widespread social acceptance, rather than hierarchical legal values.

Our purpose here is not to propose a specific institutional design for this soft law mechanism, but rather to show how its inherent flexibility can help tackle the sources of creditors' relational and structural power, both at the time of lending and restructuring. For this reason, we will highlight some core features that any soft law mechanism should have to equal the distribution of power between all parties involved in debt workouts.

To reduce power asymmetries at the time of lending, any such mechanism's mandate should include:

- *Providing technical assistance to states to allow for responsible sovereign lending.* Increasing the amount of knowledge with which states come to make a decision on indebtedness is particularly relevant to counteract the exercise of relational power at the time of lending, particularly in cases of sovereigns who may lack the necessary technical and human resources due to budgetary constraints. Accordingly, one of the essential features of the mechanism should be to provide technical and legal advice to assist sovereigns on a case-by-case basis. For instance, the mechanism could produce its own independent assessment about the state's debt stocks and borrowing capacity, at the request of the sovereign, allowing that state to make informed credit decisions.

- *Producing credit ratings.* Credit rating agencies have a direct impact on sovereign lending and borrowing and are one of the ways in which private creditors exercise their structural power. Certain UN mandate holders have underscored that the 'big three' credit rating agencies – Standard & Poor's, Moody's and Fitch Ratings – control over 92% of the global market and suffer from conflict of interests, biased decision-making, oligopoly, and wrong business model (United Nations Human Rights Council 2021). A soft law mechanism could respond to this concentration of power by producing its own credit ratings to provide objective expert-based ratings of the creditworthiness of sovereigns to promote global public goods (UNCTAD 2020).
- *Developing soft law instruments on sovereign lending.* As mentioned, private creditors source their structural power from their rule-making authority. A striking example of this is creditors' insistence in opting for CACs instead of a statutory SDRM. An independent soft law mechanism could level the playing field by producing international soft law instruments on sovereign lending that are free from creditor or debtor interference. For instance, the mechanism could constantly revise existing CACs and develop new standard clauses or guidelines on how to interpret contractual instruments. These improved clauses could be incorporated in future bonds, while the envisaged guidelines could be used by domestic courts in their interpretation and application of CACs. This would ultimately contribute to the normative development and predictability in the use of contractual instruments at the time of lending.

Similarly, to advance equality in starting positions at the time of restructuring, the soft law mechanism could be charged with:

- *Producing information.* Information asymmetries are a constant issue in sovereign debt restructurings and are one of the sources of private creditors' relational power. A soft law mechanism could minimise these power imbalances by acting as an information and data hub, in at least two respects.

First, by establishing a sovereign debt database or registry containing, *inter alia*, past exchange offers, debt restructuring agreements and other forms of state practice to guide sovereigns in the restructuring process. This international registry of debt could be aimed at generating a standard reference of global debt data. It would work as a screening mechanism to reduce information asymmetries between parties involved in sovereign debt restructuring and reduce the costs of monitoring. For creditors, this registry would help shape *ex ante* incentives as it would allow lenders to properly assess the risks they are incurring, recoveries in case of default, and the adequate risk spreads of the particular loan or bond issue. Based on this registry, an early warning system could be developed which identifies situations in which debt might not be sustainable unless restructured.

Second, by producing a Debt Sustainability Analysis (DSA) at the request of the sovereign. In a given restructuring, creditors may exert their relational power at the time of restructuring by questioning or manipulating the state's own macroeconomic assumptions, and what the state understands – conceptually – by 'debt sustainability.' A soft law mechanism could minimise this exertion of power by facilitating a DSA with an impartial assessment of the debtor's situation, governed by public interest and taking into account economic, social, and human rights considerations. This DSA would provide an international standard against which creditors and other interested parties can assess sovereign debt workouts. DSAs could also examine the nature and origin of the debt determining, for instance, if the debt is to be considered odious. As soft-law instruments, DSAs would not be enforceable. However, they would be a legitimate guide for all stakeholders, and could even be used by sovereign to counter the pressure exerted by private creditors.

- *Acting as a neutral forum for sovereign debt negotiations.* A neutral multilateral framework must work as mechanism to invite all relevant parties to one forum. Any soft law framework should have the capacity to mediate between parties, at the request of any of the actors involved, ensuring that the principles of sustainability, equitable treatment and good faith are respected throughout the negotiations. Additionally, the mechanism could facilitate the participation of civil society organisations when possible, in order to boost transparency and contribute to the legitimacy of the whole process (for an elaboration of this proposal, see Herman 2016; Guzmán and Stiglitz 2018)
- *Contributing to the legal and institutional framework that governs sovereign debt restructuring.* As a way to weaken private creditors' structural influence over the domestic legal frameworks for debt restructuring, the soft law mechanism could also be charged

with drafting model legislation. Model laws could complement the existing contractual framework by incorporating the 2015 United Nations Principles on sovereign debt restructuring or some anti-vulture funds[8] norms. Each state would have the choice of adopting the model law in its domestic legislation.

Model laws could achieve greater uniformity in how debt restructurings are carried out at the municipal levels, reducing uncertainty for both creditors and debtors. Indeed, many states may be interested in enacting model laws in order to persuade parties to choose their domestic law to govern new debt issuances. Sovereigns will also want their debt to be governed by a law that minimises the holdout problem and adheres to the principles of good faith, impartiality and equality of treatment, to name a few. Even if were not adopted by a large number of countries, a model law would provide incremental steps towards developing uniform and consistent norms for sovereign debt restructuring. Like most soft-law instruments, model legislation on debt restructuring would serve as a guide for domestic legislation and for judges.[9]

A small parallel with the politics of human rights may be illustrate how this process would unfold. Initially, Western countries would oppose to the notion of economic, social, and cultural rights (ESCR), arguing that their recognition in international law would imply the turn to a centralised, planned economy, and the destruction of free enterprise. This was especially the case for the United States, which has historically argued that any international covenant imposing state obligations to respect, protect, and fulfil ESCR would be equal to 'back-door communism' or the promotion of 'state socialism, if not communism, throughout the world' (Porsdam 2009, 108). However, few states currently consider this type of rights to be equivalent to a socialist model, partly due to the paradigm shift produced by the high degree of ratification of the International Covenant on Economic, Social and Cultural Rights, the multiple soft-law developments by the ESCR Committee, and the fact that many states have incorporated these treaties into their domestic legislation. Despite initial opposition from the West, and ongoing opposition from the United States, the normative development shepherded by the United Nations successfully modified the old institutional order, influenced by the Cold War diplomatic rivalry, and characterised by mounting opposition to the recognition of ESCR as basic human rights.

We are convinced that this is what a multilateral, soft law approach to debt issues can do to contribute to the legal and institutional framework on sovereign debt management. If a multilateral mechanism is charged with the production of, *inter alia*, soft-law guidelines, standard CACs, and model laws that are later adopted by the states, then it will naturally have the potential to progressively modify the constitutive rules behind the current IFA, that have been promoted by creditor-led states and internalised by the international community.

4 Conclusion

In this chapter, we thought to conceptualise the power that private creditors have when dealing with LMICs as sovereign debtors and to outline the implications that this power has for the question IFA reform. We argued that private institutional creditors hold relational and structural power at the moment of lending, restructuring and in promoting or inhibiting IFA reform. The implications for the institutional design, we argued, is that neither a binding statutory approach, nor an exclusively contractual approach will adequately limit the power of private creditors over LMICs as sovereign debtors. What is needed is a non-binding, soft-law regime that promotes responsible borrowing and provides orderly and efficient debt restructurings. While a soft-law approach does not require problematic concessions of sovereignty, it does have the capacity to tackle the different sources of creditors' relational and structural power, both at the moment of lending and during restructurings.

Notes

1. The IFA can be loosely defined as the 'collective governance arrangements at the international level for safeguarding the effective functioning of the global monetary and financial systems' (Elson 2010, 17).
2. Even though 'equality of arms' has its origins in criminal law, legal scholarship has sought to extend the application of this principle to civil proceedings (Wertheimer 1988).
3. This is complementary to the idea that private creditors source their structural power from their capacity 'to withhold the short-term credit lines' on which all economic actors in the borrowing countries depend (Roos 2019, 5). Rather than reducing the source of creditors structural power exclusively to this straightforward capacity, we argue that structural power can take different forms in different moments (in the moment of lending, restructuring, and when pushing for or inhibiting reform).
4. '*Pacta sunt servanda*' is the Latin formula for the legal principle that 'agreements should be kept' or 'treaties shall be complied with'.
5. At the United Nations level, a group of experts proposed the establishment of an independent, international bankruptcy court for dealing with debt-related disputes. Similar proposals have been put forth within the framework of the European Union (see United Nations General Assembly 2009; Gianviti et al. 2010).
6. This would, however, depend on the relationship between international and municipal law in a given state.
7. Jerome Roos' ground-breaking book *Why not Default* (2019), discuses three cases in depth, namely Mexico during Latin America's debt crises (1982–1989), Argentina's default and restructuring at the turn of the century (1999–2005)

and Greece's debt debacle at the heart of the European Union (2010–2015). While space constraints make it impossible for us to dive into any of these examples in greater length, we agree with Roos that 'hard times of fiscal distress' (2019, 4) merit study, precisely because they lay bare the power dynamics 'that, during normal times, are quietly at work beneath the surface' (2019, 4). The recent Argentine restructuring with its private creditors (2019–2020) would merit a more detailed study.

8 'Vulture funds' are investment funds whose business model is to acquire, either by purchase, assignment or some other form of transaction, defaulted or distressed debts, and sometimes actual court judgements, with the aim of achieving a high return (United Nations Human Rights Council 2010, 5).

9 UNCITRAL Model Law on International Commercial Arbitration is a striking example of how a model-law approach can boost international legal reform. Legislation based on the UNCITRAL Model Law has been adopted in 84 States, in a total of 117 jurisdictions.

References

Ad Hoc Argentine Bondholder Group, Exchange Bondholder Group, and Argentina Creditor Committee. 2020. Joint Debt Restructuring Proposal of Ad Hoc Argentine Bondholder Group, Exchange Bondholder Group, and Argentina Creditor Committee. July 20, 2020. Retrieved on 27 May 2022 from <https://static1.squarespace.com/static/5eb2e6606e11e67a7b983448/t/5f184f53b665812c47c593ea/1595428692287/Argentina_Joint_Restructuring_Term_072020.pdf>.

Arneson, Richard. 2022. "Two Liberal Egalitarian Perspectives on Wealth and Power." In *Wealth and Power: Philosophical Perspectives*, edited by Michael Bennett, Huub Brouwer, and Rutger Claassen. London: Routledge.

Boyle, Alan. 2019. "The Choice of a Treaty: Hard Law versus Soft Law." In *The Oxford Handbook of United Nations Treaties*, edited by Simon Chesterman, David M. Malone, and Santiago Villalpando, 101–118. Oxford: Oxford University Press.

Brooks, Skylar and Domenico Lombardi. 2016. "Private Creditor Power and the Politics off Sovereign Debt Governance." In *Too Little, Too Late: The Quest to Resolve Sovereign Debt Crises*, edited by Martin Guzmán, José Antonio Ocampo, and Joseph E. Stiglitz, 56–74. New York, NY: Columbia University Press.

Buchheit, Lee C. and Mitu Gulati. 2010. "Responsible Sovereign Lending and Borrowing." *Law and Contemporary Problems* 73(4): 63–92.

Chung, Kay and Michael G. Papaioannou. 2020. "Do Enhanced Collective Action Clauses Affect Sovereign Borrowing Costs?". *IMF Working Paper WP/20/162*. Retrieved on 27 May 2022 from <https://www.imf.org/en/Publications/WP/Issues/2020/08/07/Do-Enhanced-Collective-Action-Clauses-Affect-Sovereign-Borrowing-Costs-48960>.

Dahl, Robert A. 1957. "The Concept of Power." *Behavioral Science* 2(3): 201–215.

Dell'Oca, Marcia. 2020. "Mark Sobel: 'It Would Set a Damaging Precedent For Other Countries if Argentina Were to Accept the Indenture Requested by Creditors'." *La Política Online*, June 22, 2020. Retrieved on 27 May 2022 from <https://www.lapoliticaonline.com/nota/127462-mark-sobel-it-would-be-a-harmful-precedent-for-other-countries-if-argentina-agreed-to-the-indenture-the-creditors-claimed/>.

do Rosario, Jorgelina and Carolina Millan. 2021. "Kicillof, Bondholders' Old Foe, Plays Default Hardball." *Buenos Aires Times*, March 30, 2021. Retrieved on 27 May 2022 from <https://www.batimes.com.ar/news/economy/kicillof-bondholders-old-foe-plays-default-hardball.phtml>.

Elson, Anthony. 2010. "The Current Financial Crisis and Reform of the Global Financial Architecture." *The International Spectator* 45(1): 17–36.

Gelpern, Anna and Mitu Gulati. 2004. "How CACs Became Boilerplate, or, The Politics of Contract Change." *Initiative for Policy Dialogue Working Paper Series*. Retrieved on 27 May 2022 from <https://doi.org/10.7916/D8FX7H98>.

Gianviti, Francois, Anne O. Krueger, Jean Pisani-Ferry, André Sapir and Jürgen von Hagen. 2010. *A European Mechanism for Sovereign Debt Crisis Resolution: A Proposal*. Brussels: Bruegel.

Guzmán, Martín and Joseph E. Stiglitz. 2018. "A Soft Law Mechanism for Sovereign Debt Restructuring Based on the UN Principles." In *Sovereign Debt and Human Rights*, edited by Ilias Bantekas and Cephas Lumina, 446–457. Oxford: Oxford University Press.

Hagan, Sean. 2005. "Designing a Legal Framework to Restructure Sovereign Debt." In *Current developments in Monetary and Financial Law*, edited by the IMF, 228–229.Washington, DC: IMF.

Herman, Barry. 2016. "Toward a Multilateral Framework for Recovery from Sovereign Insolvency." In *Too Little, Too Late: The Quest to Resolve Sovereign Debt Crises*, edited by Martin Guzmán, José Antonio Ocampo, and Joseph E. Stiglitz, 206–222. New York, NY: Columbia University Press.

International Capital Market Association (ICMA). 2015. "ICMA Publishes New York Governing Law Model Collective Action, *Pari Passu* and Creditor Engagement Clauses to Facilitate Future Sovereign Debt restructuring." May 11. Press Release. Retrieved on 27 May 2022 from <https://www.icmagroup.org/assets/documents/Media/Press-releases-2015/11-May-2015-CACs-pari-passu-and-creditor-engagement-clause-press-release—final-version.pdf >.

International Monetary Fund (IMF). 2002a. "The Design of the Sovereign Debt Restructuring Mechanism – Further Considerations." *IMF*, November 27. Retrieved on 27 May 2022 from <https://www.imf.org/en/Publications/Policy-Papers/Issues/2016/12/31/The-Design-of-the-Sovereign-Debt-Restructuring-Mechanism-Further-Considerations-PP471>.

———. 2002b. "Sovereign Debt Restructuring and Dispute Resolution – Speech by Anne Krueger, First Deputy Managing Director." *IMF*, June 6. Retrieved on 27 May 2022 from <https://www.imf.org/en/News/Articles/2015/09/28/04/53/sp060602>.

———. 2003a. "Communiqué of the International Monetary and Financial Committee of the Board of Governors of the International Monetary Fund". *IMF*, April 12. Retrieved on 27 May 2022 from <https://www.imf.org/en/News/Articles/2015/09/14/01/49/pr0350>.

———. 2003b. "Proposed Features of a Sovereign Debt Restructuring Mechanism". *IMF*, February 12. Retrieved on 27 May 2022 from <https://www.imf.org/external/np/pdr/sdrm/2003/021203.htm>.

———. 2013. "Sovereign Debt Restructuring—Recent Developments and Implications for the Fund's Legal And Policy Framework." Retrieved on 27 May 2022 from <https://www.imf.org/external/np/pp/eng/2013/042613.pdf>.

Koskenniemi, Martti. 2005. *From Apology to Utopia*. Cambridge: Cambridge University Press.
Krasner, Stephen D. 1999. "Globalization and Sovereignty." In *States and Sovereignty in the Global Economy*, edited by David A. Smith, Dorothy J. Solinger, and Steven C. Topik, 34–52. New York, NY: Routledge.
Krueger, Anne O. 2002. *A New Approach to Sovereign Debt Restructuring*. Washington, DC: IMF.
Mander, Benedict. 2020. "Creditors to Argentina's Provinces Fight to Avoid Painful Restructurings." *Financial Times*, December 9. Retrieved on 27 May 2022 from <https://www.ft.com/content/1c102b0c-2fa8-40b8-b81a-f36dba725a8a>.
Ministry of Economy of Argentina. 2020. "Republic of Argentina's Press Release on the Process to Restore the Sustainability of Public Debt Issued in Foreign Currency." *Ministry of Economy*, July 25. Retrieved on 27 May 2022 from <https://www.economia.gob.ar/en/republic-of-argentinas-press-release-on-the-process-to-restore-the-sustainability-of-public-debt-issued-in-foreign-currency/>.
Parvin, Phil. 2022. "Hidden in Plain Sight: How Lobby Organisations Undermine Democracy." In *Wealth and Power: Philosophical Perspectives*, edited by Michael Bennett, Huub Brouwer, and Rutger Claassen. London: Routledge.
Porsdam, Helle. 2009. *From Civil to Human Rights. Dialogues on Law and Humanities in the United States and Europe*. Northampton: Edward Elgar Publishing.
Roos, Jerome. 2019. *Why Not Default? The Political Economy of Sovereign Debt*. Princeton, NJ: Princeton University Press.
Setser, Brad W. 2010. "The Political Economy of the SDRM." In *Overcoming Developing Country Debt Crises*, edited by Barry Herman, José A. Ocampo and Shari Spiegel, 317–346. Oxford: Oxford University Press.
Shoikhedbrod, Igor. 2022. "Private Wealth and Political Domination: A Marxian Approach." In *Wealth and Power: Philosophical Perspectives*, edited by Michael Bennett, Huub Brouwer, and Rutger Claassen. London: Routledge.
Stiglitz, Joseph E. and Hamid Rashid. 2020. "Averting Catastrophic Debt Crises in Developing Countries Extraordinary challenges call for extraordinary measures." CEPR Policy Insight No. 104. Retrieved on 27 May 2022 from <https://cepr.org/active/publications/policy_insights/viewpi.php?pino=104>.
Strange, Susan. 1988. *States and Markets*. London: A&C Black.
United Nations Conference on Trade and Development (UNCTAD). 2020. *Trade and Development Report 2020*. New York, NY: United Nations.
United Nations General Assembly. 2009. "Recommendations of the Commission of Experts of the President of the General Assembly on Reforms of the International Monetary and Financial System" A/63/838, ¶ 48. April 29.
United Nations Human Rights Council. 2010. "Report of the Independent Expert on the Effects of Foreign Debt and Other Related International Financial Obligations of States on the Full Enjoyment of all Human Rights, Particularly Economic, Social and Cultural Rights." Cephas Lumina. A/HRC/14/21. April 29.
——. 2021. "Report of the Independent Expert on the Effects of Foreign Debt and Other Related International Financial Obligations of States on the Full Enjoyment of All Human Rights, Particularly Economic, Social and Cultural Rights." Yuefen Li. A/HRC/46/29. February 17.

Webb, Philippa. 2019. "The Participation of Nonstate Actors in the Multilateral Treatymaking Process." In *The Oxford Handbook of United Nations Treaties*, edited by Simon Chesterman, David M. Malone and Santiago Villalpando, 633–648. Oxford: Oxford University Press.

Wertheimer, Alan. 1988. "The Equalization of Legal Resources." *Philosophy and Public Affairs* 17(4): 303–322.

World Bank. 2021. *Global Economic Prospects, January 2021*. Washington, DC: World Bank Group.

Wright, Erik O. 2001. "Class and Politics." In *The Oxford Companion to Politics of the World*, edited by Joel Krieger, 142–159. Oxford: Oxford University Press.

Index

Note: Page references in italics denote figures, in bold tables and with "n" endnotes.

Ackerman, Bruce 305
Adler, Paul 98
Alford, Robert 316
Allen, Gordon 159
Alstott, Anne 305
Amazon 169, 171, 176, 191
American Legislative Exchange Council (ALEC) 190, 204n13
anarchism 104–120; defined 107; and property rights 107–108
anarchists 104; arguments for redistribution 105; on duty to obey 107; opposition of enforcement of laws 106; on property rights 107–108; on stateless society 107; in states 110–112
Anderson, Elizabeth 307
anti-corruption measures 283–284
Apple 166, 171, 176
aristocratic republicanism 30
Aristotle 287, 300
Arneson, Richard 309n3
Arrow, Kenneth J. 70
assessment: Corporate Social Assessment 159; undemocratic practices 191–192
associative democracy 289–290
asymmetric information 74–75
automation 18; threat 297–299

Bagg, Samuel 39
Barnett, Anthony 286
Bartels, Larry 139
basic income 119–120, 302–305
Baumgartner, Frank R. 244
Belinfanti, Tamara 158
Benefit Corporation 149
Benkler, Yochai 221n4
Biale, Enrico 267n5

big tech companies: competition law 167–170; competition law as counter-power 178–181; and corporate power 170–178; Modern Bigness 174–179; political power of 168–169
Black, Duncan 67, 70
Black Act of 1723 99n2
Blackstone, William 154
Blaufarb, Rafe 3
Bond Market Association 320
borders 119–120
Branson, Richard 295, 296
Brennan, Geoffrey 80
Buchanan, James M. 70, 71, 77, 80
Buchheit, Lee C. 319
Bulmer, Elliot 76
'business confidence' 277–278
business ethics: and democratic theory 187; 'market failures approach' (MFA) to 195

campaign contributions 72–73
campaign finance 2, 4–5, 17–18, 50, 239, 252, 259–263; constitutionalising 283–284; and parties 263–266; regulations 264–265; schemes 264–266
campaigns: and hard money 260; as 'information environments' 255; motivational 256; use of private money in 259–260
capital grants 18; and contribution benefits 305–307
capital investment 131, 218; and unions 130
capitalism 90, 119–120; corporate state 122n15; crony 13, 17, 79–80, 240; defined 79; free market 122n15

Carens, Joseph 303
Carnegie, Andrew 197
Carty, Peter 286
Casassas, David 30
Chari, Raj 229
charities 232–233
Chartier, Gary 121n11
Chicago-school economics 168–169, 182n3
'Chicago School-rationalists' 168
Christiano, Thomas 193, 195, 200, 260
Christman, John 304
Ciepley, David 6
Citizens' Assemblies 285–286
Citizens United v. FEC 260
civic norms 35, 37
civic virtue 31–32, 37–38, 40, 43n12
civil rights movement 53, 245–246
co-determination 132–133
Cohen, Joshua 262
collaborative power 134–135, 136
Collective Action Clauses (CACs) 320–327
collective bargaining 127, 130, 132–133, 137
common property regimes in natural resources 216–218
competition law: debate over aims of 167–170; legal vocabulary and counter-power 178–181
complete markets 136–137
conflictual power 135, 136
Congleton, Roger 78
constitutional defences: against oligarchic impact 278–282; against oligarchic power 282–290
constitutional design 282–283
constitutional-institutional correctives 27–30
constitutionalism 18, 30, 33, 38
constitutions: and oligarchic power 275–278; against oligarchy 274–291
constructive equality of power 136
contestatory citizenry 37
contestatory culture 37, 38
contractual approaches, and IFA 326–327
contribution benefits, and capital grants 305–307
conventional approaches, and IFA 322–326
Cordelli, Chiara 203n4

Corneo, Giacomo 159
corporate governance: purpose-driven 157–159; worker participation in 127–142
corporate power 6, 145, 147, 152, 157; across economic and other domains 170–174
corporate purpose: general incorporation regime 145, 146–148; politicisation or de-politicisation 149–153; politicising 145–161; properly politicising 155–157; social purpose regime 145, 148–149; special charter regime 145, 153–155
Corporate Social Assessment 159
corporate social responsibility (CSR) 2, 16, 188–191; and democracy 192–196
corporate state capitalism 122n15
corporations 15; general incorporation regime 145, 146–148; purpose/power regimes 145; regimes comparison 160; social purpose regime 145, 148–149; special charter regime 145, 153–155; and state wealth 146
corruption 30–31, 145–146, 157, 260–263; avoidance of 156; business and governments relations 15; and corporate privileges 155–156; and inequality 34; of political equality 5; *quid pro quo* 261; and structural character 32
COVID-19 pandemic 25, 27, 166, 175, 240–241, 314
credit rating agencies 329
crony capitalism 13, 17, 79–80, 240; norms of 248
Crouch, Colin 4
culture: contestatory 37, 38; political 35

Dahl, Robert A. 128, 237
decentralised decision-making 133
deliberation: democratic 192, 198, 233, 237; political 38; public 262–263; sustained 60
democracy 139, 151; associative 289–290; and corporate social responsibility 192–196; direct 284; Marx on 96; vs. monarchy 96; philanthropy and 197–199; property-owning 5, 11, 159; in workplace 6

Index 339

democratic: -conforming market 98; decision-making 48–49; equality 135; forbearance 186–202; institutions and wealth 17–19; norms 193; political equality 25; spirit 41; state and disaggregated power 231–236
democratically managed cooperatives 97–98
Demsetz, Harold 217
dependence corruption 261–262
de-politicisation 149–153
desert 300–302
De Wispelaere, Jurgen 30, 40
dictatorship 36, 61
direct democracy 284
doctrine of balance 32
Downs, Anthony 67, 70
Du Bois, W.E.B. 37
Dutch East India Company 153
Dworkin, Ronald 65n2, 93, 262

economic democracy 10, 11, 12
economic inequality 25, 27–28
economic power 186–202
Edmundson, William 5
efficiency, and markets 128–133
egalitarianism 13, 19, 50–51
egalitarian liberals 240
elected representatives 276–277
electoral campaigns 252–266
elite accountability 40
English East India Company 153
equal basic liberties 53–55
equality: democratic 135; democratic political 25; within markets 128–133; political 34–42; social 56–57, 61, 64, 107
equality of opportunity 13, 54–55, 134–136
equality of power: competitive *vs.* constructive 136; decentralised decision-making 133; equality of opportunity 134; in markets 133–138; *see also* power
equal opportunity for political influence (EOPI) 47, 55–64; Kolodny's interpretation of 59; and Rawls 59
Estlund, David 69
European Commission 170
European Union (EU): Charter 170; competition law debate 169; Transparency Register 232
exploitation 201, 319

Facebook (Meta) 166, 171, 176, 191, 298
fair equality of opportunity 135
fair value 5, 59, 92, 284
Feinberg, Joel 301
Feldman, Fred 309n5
finance: campaign (*see* campaign finance); technical knowledge in 319
free citizen 13, 26, 41–42
free markets 15, 17, 122n15, 128–129, 168
French Revolution 3
Frey, Carl 296, 297
Friedland, Roger 316
Friedman, Milton 189, 203n6
Fuchs, Doris 172–173

Gelpern, Anna 320
general incorporation regime 145, 146–148
generality 157
Germany: and co-determination 132; and unions 130
Gilens, Martin 4, 139
global financial crisis (2008) 25
global justice 61, 63–64
Goodin, Robert 256–257
Google 171, 176, 191, 298
Gourevitch, Alex 211
Gramitto, Sergio 158
group ownership 215
Guerrero, Alex 285
Gulati, Mitu 319, 320

Habermas, Jürgen 93, 95
Hagan, Sean 325
Hamilton, Lawrence 39
Hardin, Gareth 216–217
Harrington, James 12, 30–34, 211, 213
Hasen, Richard L. 263
Hayek, F.A. 78
Heath, Joseph 195, 200
Hegel, Georg Wilhelm Friedrich 89
Hertel-Fernandez, Alex 193
Hilt, Eric 156
Honneth, Axel 95
Hsieh, Nien-hê 188, 202n3
Huemer, Michael 108
Human Rights Act 1998 (UK) 280
Hume, David 33

'ICMA Clauses' 321
income inequality 133, 290
independence: and basic non-domination 211–214; in the commons 206–221
'independent expenditure committees' 260
Industrial Revolution 213
inequality: constitutional-institutional solutions to 30–34; and corruption 34; economic 27–28; political problem of 27; U-shaped pattern in 3–4; wealth (*see* wealth inequality)
inheritance 297, 306
innovation 171, 175; and conglomerates 166; and corporation tax 247; democratic 233, 237; and unions 130
Instagram 298
Institute for Economic Affairs, UK 246
Institute of International Finance 320
institutional private creditors: relational power of 318–320; structural power of 320–322
institutions: contestatory 39; democratic 17–19; just 54; and norms 37–38; Roman 35
insulation: strategy, and wealth inequality 50; transgressions of the private/public divide 9–10, *10*
intellectual property rights 109
interest groups 74–75
International Capital Market Association (ICMA) 321, 327
International Covenant on Economic, Social and Cultural Rights 331
International Financial Architecture (IFA) 314–316; contractual approaches 326–327; defined 332n1; policy evaluations 322–332; quasi-legal/soft law approaches 327–332; reform of 322–332; statutory/conventional approaches 322–326
International Monetary Fund (IMF) 235, 320, 324; Articles of Agreement 324; Board of Governors 325–326
International Political Economy (IPE): policy evaluations 322–332; relational power of private creditors 317–322; structural power of private creditors 317–322
International Primary Market Association 320

International Securities Market Association 320
involuntary unemployment 279

Jech, Alexander 40–41
Johnson, Charles 122n15
Judge Brandeis 168–169
justice: distributive 5; global 61, 63–64; Rawls on 54; values 54
'justice failures' 200–201
just institutions 54

Kagan, Shelly 300
Kaldor, Mary 274
Katz, Bruce 41
Keynes, John Maynard 298–299
Kleinig, John 300
knowledge commons 219–221
Kogelmann, Brian 157
Kolodny, Niko 56–57, 59
Krasner, Stephen D. 323
Krueger, Anne 320, 324–325

Landemore, Helene 236
large-scale philanthropy 197
law enforcement 106
Lechterman, Theodore M. 203n5, 203n10
legislative favours 72–73
Leibniz, Gottfried Wilhelm 300
Leipold, Bruno 94
Levillain, Kevin 149–150, 152, 155
liberal egalitarianism: overview 47–48; and power 47–64; and wealth 47–64; *see also* egalitarianism
liberalism: defined 7; egalitarian incarnation of 13; and political economy 13; public/private distinction 6–7
liberal socialism 5
libertarianism/libertarians 67, 76, 238, 240–243
lobbying 81n8, 231, 236–238; Baumgartner on 244; critiques 238–242; libertarians on 240; problem with 238–242
localism 13, 41
Lohmann, Susanne 74
Low- and Middle-Income Countries (LMIC) 314–316
Lukes, Steven 316

Machiavelli, Niccolò 28–30, 32, 34–37, 43n12
Madison, James

Maier, Pauline 153
Mair, Peter 4
Manin, Bernard 234
Mankiw, Gregory N. 308n2
market-based strategies: market failure regulation 11; redistribution strategies 11; and transgressions of the private/public divide *10*, 11
market capitalism 240
market failure regulation 11
'market failures approach' (MFA) 195
market power 166–167, 181n2
markets: complete 136–137; defined 128; and efficiency 128–133; equality of power in 133–138; equality within 128–133; free 15, 17, 128–129; perfectly competitive 136–137
market shares 170
market socialism 202n2
Marx, Karl 3, 14, 85–86, 90–96, 303; on democratically managed cooperatives 97; on private wealth 87; and rational right 88–89
Mayer, Colin 149
McConnell, Mitch 186, 189
McCormick, John 5, 12, 26–29, 287
Meade, James 11, 295–296, 299
Miliband, Ralph 92
Mill, John Stuart 300
Miller, David 301, 309n6
Modern Bigness 16, 167, 176; big techs' corporate power as 174–178
modern republicanism 30–34
monarchy *vs.* democracy 96
monetary systems 121n4
money: 'gatekeeping' 260–261; hard 260; as 'influence on public opinion' 260–261
monopsony 129
Morgenstern, Oskar 70
Muldoon, James 36
Munger, Michael C. 79–80
Musk, Elon 295–296, 303, 306

natural resources 216–218
natural rights: and enforced property rights 109–110; and intellectual property rights 109; and property rights 107–108
Nedelkoska, Ljubica 297
neo-Brandeisians 168–169, 179
Netting, R.M. 218
networked horizontalism 42

new localism 41
Nixon, Richard 256
nondemocratic power 187
non-domination: basic 207–211; full 207–211
'No-Party Democracy' 257
norm(s): civic 35; democratic 34–35; importance of 34–35; and institutions 37–38; and Roman institutions 35; and structural barriers to reform 242–248
Nowak, Jeremy 41

oligarchical democracy 27–30
oligarchic power: and anti-corruption measures 283–284; associative democracy 289–290; basic constitutional design 282–283; and campaign finance 283–284; Citizens' Assemblies 285–286; constitutional defences against 282–290; direct democracy 284; and impact as constitutional problems 275–278; plebian assemblies 286–289; sortition 285–286
oligarchs: 'business confidence' 277–278; shaping popular preferences 277; shaping preferences of elected representatives 276–277; shaping preferences of other state officials 277
oligarchy 39; and constitutionalism 18; constitutions against 274–291; and democracy 5
Olson, Mancur 70, 75, 241
O'Neill, Martin 5
On the Jewish Question (Marx) 87
Osborne, Michael 296, 297
Ostrom, Elinor 216, 217–218
Ottonelli, Valeria 267n5
ownership, and basic non-domination 211–214

Page, Benjamin 4
parliamentarism 256
participation: in collective decision-making 134; in economic life 134
Parvin, Phil 39, 157
Pateman, Carole 138, 140
perfectly competitive markets 136–137
Pettit, Phillip 5, 12, 26–27, 29–30, 94, 207–209

Pevnick, Ryan 261, 267n3
philanthropy 188–191; defined 188; and democracy 197–199; large-scale 197
Philosophy of Right (Hegel) 89
Piketty, Thomas 3, 306
Pisto, Katherina 99n4
plebeian power 33
plebian assemblies 286–289
political action committees (PACs) 260, 267n11
'political CSR' 194
political culture 35
political domination: faces of 90–96; and private wealth 85–99
political economy: constitutional 76; critique of 90; and liberalism 13
political equality 34–42; achieving 69; defined 68–70; and interest groups 74; and worker participation 138–141
political inequality 67; defined 68; eliminating 75–79; and public choice theory 68–70; and rent seeking 67; sources of 72–75
political participation: and democracy 275; and unions 289; and worker participation 128, 140–141
political parties 253–254; campaign finance 259–263; and campaign finance 263–266; parties and electoral campaigns 254–259; role in electoral campaigns 252–266
political power 1–3, 7, 234, 237, 252–253; arbitrary 26, 33; of big companies 168–169; citizens' 27; *vs.* economic power 317; impact of wealth on 52, 104; and responsiveness of politicians 139
Politics (Aristotle) 287
post-democracy 4
Poulantzas, Nicos 92
power: collaborative 134–135, 136; conflictual 135, 136; corporate 6; democratic state as a site of disaggregated 231–236; discursive dimension of 172, 173–174; in the economic sphere 14–17; in economy 8–9; instrumental dimension of 172; instrumental dimension of big techs' 173; in the IPE 317–322; liberal egalitarian perspectives on 47–64; political 7; problem of 49–50; relational 316–322;

relational egalitarianism implications for 57–58; structural 316–322; structural dimension 172, 173; and wealth 2; welfarist egalitarians perspective on 50–52; and workplace 15
prioritarianism 50–51, 300
private creditors: institutional 318–322; relational power of 317–322; structural power of 317–322
private power 86–89
private wealth: inequality in 28; Marx on 87; and political domination 85–99; *see also* wealth
privatisation 86, 151, 198, 281
profits 79–80
'profit-with-purpose' corporations 149
property: consolidation of 34; distribution of 32; 'indeterminate' forms of 87; individual 206, 216; and power 3; private 87; productive 90; regimes 216–218; and rights 106–110; rules of 2; social 97
property-owning democracy 5, 11, 93, 159, 202n2
property rights 193–194; and anarchism 107–108; enforcement 109; and natural rights 107–108; and redistribution 117–118
public choice theory 13, 76; characterisation of 71; defined 67, 70; development of 68; and political inequality 68–70; and rational choice theory 70–71; and rent seeking 71–72
Puck, Wolfgang 27

quasi-legal/soft law approaches 327–332
quid pro quo corruption 261
Quintini, Glenda 297

racist norms 245
rational choice theory 70–71
rationalists 168, 182n3
rational right 88–89
Rawls, John 5, 11, 13, 64, 92–93, 301–302, 309n7; egalitarianism 300; and EOPI 59; equal basic liberties 53–55; on justice 54; just institutions 54; 'property owning democracy' 202n2; on relational egalitarianism 53–56; social justice 53

'realistic utopia' 55
real profits 79–80
redistribution 104–120, 121n9;
    anarchist arguments for 105;
    instrumental case for 112–115;
    non-instrumental case for 115–117;
    and property rights 117–118;
    strategies 11
reforms: of IFA 322–332; structural
    barriers to 242–248
regulations: campaign finance
    264–265; market failure 11
Reich, Rob 197
relational egalitarianism 47, 53, 300;
    implications for wealth and power
    problem 57–58; Kolodny on 56–57;
    Rawls on 53–56
relational egalitarians 47–48; vs.
    welfarist egalitarians 61–64
relational power: of institutional
    private creditors 318–320;
    preliminary definition 316–317;
    of private creditors 317–322
rent seeking 67; and economic
    inefficiency 72; and political
    inequality 67, 75–79; proposals
    for eliminating 76–79; and public
    choice theory 71–72
representative democracy 234
republicanism: aristocratic 30;
    modern 30–34; socialist 27, 36
responsibility-sensitive egalitarianism
    307
rights: -based anarchists 14; civil 53;
    natural 107–110; natural property
    107–109; property (see property
    rights); rational 88–89
Riker, William H. 70
Roberts, William Clare 94
Rogers, Melvin 40
Roman institutions 35
Roos, Jerome 332n7
Rousseau, Jean-Jacques 31, 35–36
Russell Sage Foundation 197

Salman, Yara Al 41
Scheffler, Samuel 56, 300
Schweickart, David 98
Securities Industry Association 320
Segrestin, Blanche 149–150, 152, 155
Selchow, Sabine 274
sharing in common 214–216
Sidgwick, Henry 300
Singer, Abraham 200–201

Sitaraman, Ganesh 274, 287, 291n1
Skinner, Quentin 94
Smith, Adam 99n1, 137
social equality 56–57, 61, 64, 107
socialism 5, 202n2, 213, 331
socialist republicanism 27, 36
social norms, and values 245
social purpose regime 145, 148–149
social science 3–4
social status 48, 60, 69–70, 188,
    207–208
social theory 93
société à mission 149
sortition and citizens' assemblies
    285–286
sovereign debt restructuring 330–331
Sovereign Debt Restructuring
    Mechanism (SDRM) 320, 322,
    324, 325
sovereign lending 329
special charter regime 145, 153–155
Special Purpose Company 149
stateless society 107
statutory approaches, and IFA
    322–326
Stout, Lynn 158
Strange, Susan 316–317
Streeck, Wolfgang 4
Strine, Leo 149
structural power 172: of institutional
    private creditors 320–322;
    preliminary definition 316–317;
    of private creditors 317–322
structural unemployment 297
Super PACs 267n11
Susskind, Daniel 298, 299, 304–305,
    309n6

taxation 11, 116, 291n2, 291n3
technological unemployment 18,
    296–299, 302–304, 308
Thomas, Alan 5
Thompson, Dennis 259, 261
TikTok 177
Tocqueville, Alexis de 13, 26,
    40–41
Trump, Donald 1, 25, 27
Tullock, Gordon 70, 71
Turner, Stephen 198
Twitter 298

Uber 239
undemocratic power 187
undemocratic practices 191–192

Index

undemocratic private power: in ideal theory 199–202; in real world 199–202
unemployment: benefit scheme 306–307; compensation 62; involuntary 279; structural 297; technological 18, 296–299, 302–304, 308
unions 140; and capital investment 130; effects of 131; and Germany 130; and inequality of income 130; and innovation 130; and United States 130
United Kingdom (UK): Human Rights Act 1998 280; influence of lobby groups in 229, 232–233, 246; labour unions 239; Lobbying Act (2014) 243; monetary policy 235; political parties' expenditures 260; Special Purpose Company 149
United Nations 235
United States of America: Benefit Corporation 149; Chamber of Commerce 230; creation of business corporations 153; economic inequality in 25; Securities and Exchange Commission 318; and unions 130, 247
universal basic income (UBI) 296, 302–304

van der Veen, Robert 303
van Parijs, Philippe 302–303
Vergara, Camila 33, 39, 287–288
Villarreal-Diaz, Mario 79–80
Visa 191
visitorial power, and corporations 154
voluntarist sharing 215
von Neumann, John 70
'vulture funds' 333n8

Waldron, Jeremy 150, 151
Walmart 1, 19n1, 191
Walzer, Michael 95
wealth: and democratic institutions 17–19; liberal egalitarian perspectives on 47–64; and politics 2; and power 2; private 7–8; problem of 49–50; relational egalitarianism implications for 57–58; in the state 7–8; welfarist egalitarians perspective on 50–52
wealth inequality 4, 25, 49; and democratic say 58; and elimination strategy 50; and insulation strategy 50
wealth-power nexus: conceptual framework 6–12; contemporary political philosophy 5–6; contemporary social science 3–4; historical background 2–3
welfarist egalitarianism 47–48; perspective on power 50–52; perspective on wealth 50–52; vs. relational egalitarianism on wealth and power 61–64
Westphalian sovereignty 323
White, Jonathan 253
White, Stuart 76, 305–306
Widerquist, Karl 121n9
Wikipedia 219–220, 221n4
Williamson, Thad 5, 305
Winter, Jaap 149
worker cooperatives 131–132
worker participation 15; and co-determination 132–133; and collective bargaining 130; in corporate governance 127–142; importance of 128; and inequality of power 129, 137–138; and political equality 138–141; and political participation 140–141
workplace: democracy in 6; and power 15
World Bank 235
World Health Organisation 314
Wright, Erik Olin 97–98

Ypi, Lea 253

Zack, Naomi 121n4
Zuckerberg, Mark 296